Learn Unity 3D Programming with UnityScript

Unity's JavaScript for Beginners

Janine Suvak

Apress®

Learn Unity 3D Programming with UnityScript: Unity's JavaScript for Beginners

ISBN-13 (pbk): 978-1-4302-6586-3

ISBN-13 (electronic): 978-1-4302-6587-0

Publisher: Heinz Weinheimer
Lead Editor: Louise Corrigan
Technical Reviewer: Graham McAllister
Editorial Board: Steve Anglin, Mark Beckner, Ewan Buckingham, Gary Cornell, Louise Corrigan, Jim DeWolf, Jonathan Gennick, Jonathan Hassell, Robert Hutchinson, Michelle Lowman, James Markham, Matthew Moodie, Jeff Olson, Jeffrey Pepper, Douglas Pundick, Ben Renow-Clarke, Dominic Shakeshaft, Gwenan Spearing, Matt Wade, Steve Weiss
Coordinating Editor: Christine Ricketts
Copy Editor: James Fraleigh
Compositor: SPi Global
Indexer: SPi Global
Artist: SPi Global
Cover Designer: Anna Ishchenko

Distributed to the book trade worldwide by Springer Science+Business Media New York, 233 Spring Street, 6th Floor, New York, NY 10013. Phone 1-800-SPRINGER, fax (201) 348-4505, e-mail orders-ny@springer-sbm.com, or visit www.springeronline.com. Apress Media, LLC is a California LLC and the sole member (owner) is Springer Science + Business Media Finance Inc (SSBM Finance Inc). SSBM Finance Inc is a Delaware corporation.

For information on translations, please e-mail rights@apress.com, or visit www.apress.com.

Apress and friends of ED books may be purchased in bulk for academic, corporate, or promotional use. eBook versions and licenses are also available for most titles. For more information, reference our Special Bulk Sales–eBook Licensing web page at www.apress.com/bulk-sales.

Any source code or other supplementary material referenced by the author in this text is available to readers at www.apress.com. For detailed information about how to locate your book's source code, go to www.apress.com/source-code/.

For Rob, Paige, Justin, and Taylor: for enriching my life and making every day worthwhile.

Contents at a Glance

Contents

About the Author

Janine Suvak was born and raised in the San Francisco Bay Area and studied electrical engineering at CalTech before going on to serve in the U.S. military. There she worked with avionics systems before switching to medical school, only to return to the military as a flight surgeon. Her interest in programming began in junior high with the Apple II, and she applied this interest throughout her military career to various projects, from the early transition of maintenance parts tracking from paper to computers, to writing personnel tracking database systems and proprietary electronic medical records programs before such products were commercially available.

After leaving military service, Janine turned her favorite pastime of programming into a full-time freelance career, initially developing iOS applications before delving into Android development. Her recent endeavors resulted in winning entries for two of five categories in the Samsung Hope for the Children competition for educational games development, which are to be released later this year. She is particularly interested in 3D games and augmented reality.

About the Technical Reviewer

Graham McAllister was first involved in the games industry when he was 15 years old, drawing loading screens in Deluxe Paint for 16-bit games on the Amiga.

He originally enrolled in university to study electronic engineering; however, this only lasted two weeks when he realized that he didn't think in terms of hardware at all. Transferring to a degree in software engineering, he immediately felt at home, going on to earn a PhD in computer graphics.

After a brief period as a software engineer in telecoms, he returned to academia as a lecturer in music technology at Queens University Belfast. In early 2006 he went on a three-month secondment to a little-known company in Copenhagen developing an exciting new games engine. It was called Unity. Graham wrote the first FPS tutorials, which many people would use to learn the essentials of making games in Unity.

Realizing that making games isn't just about the technology, but also the human aspects, he moved to the University of Sussex where he was a senior lecturer in Human-Computer Interaction.

Leaving academia behind in January 2012, Graham founded Player Research, a user research and playtesting studio based in Brighton, UK. Player Research works with video game studios at all stages of game development, from concept through release, providing evidence to support design decisions and deliver the best possible player experience. Their clients include Sony, NaturalMotion Games, Mind Candy, Jagex, Ninja Theory, Madfinger Games, Hutch Games, and Channel4, among many others.

Graham also writes the column on user research for EDGE, www.edge-online.com/author/gmcallister.

Acknowledgments

I would like to thank the entire Apress team involved in the production of this book. Special thanks to Louise Corrigan and Christine Ricketts for their support and encouragement, James Fraleigh, and especially technical reviewer Graham McAllister for his thorough review and helpful suggestions.

Introduction

If you have the desire to create video games but have no experience with programming or game development, this is the book for you. Unity is a powerful game development ecosystem for creating 2D and 3D games. With its basic but still powerful free version, Unity has blasted away the barriers to learning game development. While the Unity editor is visual and intuitive in nature, you will have to learn to script in order to complete your game. Not to fear—all you need is a computer, an Internet connection, and motivation. This book is written for the complete beginner in both game development and programming.

Scripting, *programming*, and *coding* are synonymous terms that all refer to the process of writing computer code to direct some portion of the game behavior. While it may seem a little daunting, as with any other endeavor you simply start at the beginning and learn one thing at a time. You can't make a game without writing some code, but creating the code is only a part of the game development process. You'll have just as much fun learning to find and use characters, animations, special effects, and other assets as you will writing code for directing their interaction within your game.

Unity Technologies, the maker of Unity3D, provides excellent support documentation that most often includes working sample code. When I was a beginner developer, whether in mobile apps or video games, I found that almost all of the documentation was just about as clear and useful as if it were written in hieroglyphics—pretty much incomprehensible. I was stuck in a hole where I needed documentation on how to use the documentation!

The purpose of this book is to bridge this initial gap—to give you a foundation in programming within the context of using Unity to make a simple game, while connecting what you are learning to the relevant information found in the documentation, and even to using some of the sample code. This book is meant as a launching pad: by the time you are through working on its examples, you should be able to confidently build on your newfound knowledge and skills with the many resources introduced to you throughout this book.

With that in mind, read the chapters in order. After an introduction to the basics of programming concepts and to the Unity editor in the first few chapters, the subsequent projects will begin building upon each other from one chapter to the next. To get the most out of this book, follow along and complete the projects step by step from scratch. The best way to learn and (just as important) retain what you are learning is by doing. Besides, it's fun and definitely more satisfying to do it yourself.

The game development industry is in constant motion, and with over half of all game developers using Unity, from individuals to large studios, you can bet that Unity Technologies is constantly pushing the envelope to provide better tools and game engine performance. In particular, during the time this book was written, several radical changes were made affecting animations, particle systems, and better assets for rapid prototyping. Any changes affecting the instructions in this book from Unity or elsewhere will be noted in the Errata section of the book's Apress web page, www.apress.com/9781430265863.

Sometimes it is helpful to have the finished project as a reference. You will be able to find the source code and finished projects for the examples in this book under the Source Code/Downloads tab of its Apress web page.

The best way to learn how to make games is by making games, so turn the page to get started!

Getting Started with Unity

This is a great time to learn to develop games. Unity has emerged as one of the most popular game engines for game developers, and Unity Technologies continues to make dramatic changes to make Unity more accessible to indie developers. There are now more platforms to which Unity games can be ported (meaning it can be used on many devices), the Asset Store is available for centralized game resources, and Unity provides outstanding support that has expanded to include professional assessment and feedback for your game. There is even an entire new (at the time of writing) division that collaborates with developers and publishes games. Making games is an amazing experience and provides even more bragging rights than a high score or near-impossible headshot. Welcome to the fun!

By "games" the folks behind Unity also recognize the expanding field of "serious games"— simulations and other immersive, interactive experiences developed using Unity3D for a rising number of different industries and uses. From NASA's Mars exploration and CliniSpace's virtual medical training environments to CrossPlatform DeSign's animated crime scene reconstructions and virtual industrial trainers, serious games are appearing in new venues at a rapid rate. If serious game development is the direction in which you want to go, I believe that Unity is the best tool for it and this book is the best place to get started.

This book assumes you have a computer and that you are familiar enough with using an Internet browser to download files—and that is all. If you have an interest in game development but no prior experience in Unity, programming, or digital art/content creation, you are in the right place. If you have some background in one or the other, you'll find this book helpful for introducing you to Unity, programming, or Unity scripting.

You may have a game idea or want to help others bring theirs to life. The best games are those that provide the best user experience. The user experience comes from both the look and the feel of the game, which is another way of saying the graphics and the code. The graphics, or artwork, is vitally important for the obvious reason: this is what the user sees. It sets the mood and engages the user. The code is what is under the hood and is equally as important. The best graphics in the world cannot make up for a game that is slow, responds unexpectedly, doesn't flow as the game advances, or simply crashes. Unity is a powerful, popular tool for game developers because it allows you to control and smoothly integrate both of these important aspects to create an enjoyable experience.

A common approach in beginners' books is to walk the reader through creating a simple game, introducing and explaining its particular features along the way, and then to refer the reader to "the documentation." Quite often the documentation reads like ancient hieroglyphics and is about as useful. As a beginner, I often found myself frustrated by this, and I wasn't sure how to proceed beyond the context of the example game.

This book is intended to launch you into the world of game development. I would like you to learn how to use Unity while getting a solid foundation in scripting, particularly a familiarity with the pattern of programming. I'll show you how to read the documentation and how it fits into this pattern so you can confidently use it to continue to build your skills and expand your knowledge for making bigger and better games after you complete this book.

The book's companion web site is www.learn-unityscript.com, where you can ask questions and share your games—be sure and let me know about them! You can also reach me at janine@learn-unityscript.com. You can find the source code for this book under the Source Code/Downloads tab on its page at www.apress.com.

What Is UnityScript?

UnityScript is a .NET-based dialect of JavaScript, so the syntax is similar to the popular web dialect of JavaScript. You will see it referred to as "UnityScript," "JavaScript," "Java Script," and "Javascript" on the Unity web site and in the editor, but it is not same as JavaScript for web sites. For practical purposes, this means (1) code snippets of JavaScript found on Internet searches may not work if they weren't written specifically for Unity, and (2) there is no speed or performance difference among C#, UnityScript, and Boo, all of which are supported by Unity.

Prerequisites

No programming, game development, or graphic art experience is required. Diving into game development is not for the faint of heart, but it is definitely fun and personally rewarding. You must enjoy learning—this is a rapidly advancing field, so there is always something new to learn, but this also means that it gets better and better over time, with more cool features for your games and improved tools with which to build them. I think developing games is as much fun as playing them, so I find the process is more like "leveling up" my skills.

Of course you must have a computer, as well as an Internet connection. At the time of this writing the current version of Unity is 4.3, and the system requirements for your computer are listed in Figure 1-1.

System requirements for Unity development

- Windows XP SP2 or later; Windows 7 SP1; Mac OS X "Snow Leopard" 10.6 or later. Note that Unity was not tested on server versions of Windows and OS X.

- Graphics card with DirectX 9 level (shader model 2.0) capabilities. Any card made since 2004 should work.

- Using Occlusion Culling requires GPU with Occlusion Query support (some Intel GPUs do not support that).

Figure 1-1. Unity System requirements

Meet Unity

First things first: The Unity web site is http://unity3D.com (see Figure 1-2).

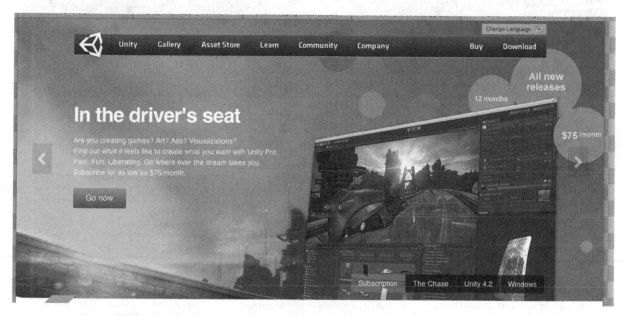

Figure 1-2. Unity web site home page

You could spend days perusing the web site; the gallery of game demos and previews is especially fun. Don't get lost in it yet, though—you have games of your own to create!

On the Unity home page you'll see the Asset Store in the top navigation bar. The Asset Store is just that—a store full of assets for everything you might need for your game, including animation, audio, and scripts, plus one of my favorite things: sales and daily discounts! It also has a number of free assets, some of which you will use later in this book as you learn more about how the Unity editor and the Asset Store are designed to interact with each other to facilitate your workflow. The more you work with Unity, the more you will appreciate how Unity is focused on helping you build great games—fast.

On the same navigation bar you'll also see "Community." The Unity community is made up of the hundreds of thousands of people like you who love games so much they want to make them. This is a great place to meet and get help from like-minded people, and before you know it you'll be helping others along as well. When you click into this area, you'll see that there is a forum, sections for answers and feedback, and much more (see Figure 1-3).

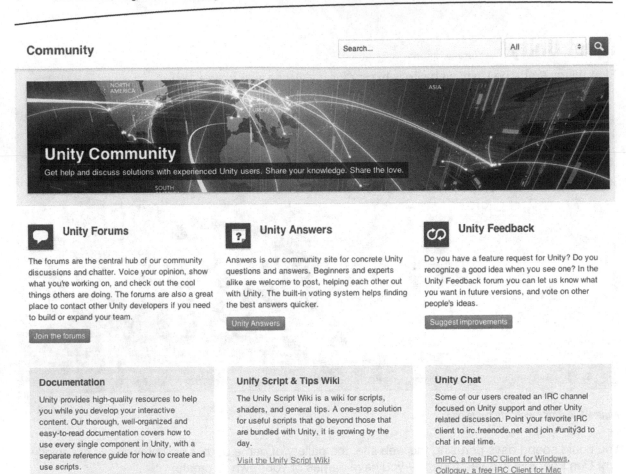

Figure 1-3. Unity Community

In addition to video tutorials, the "Learn" section is where you will find the documentation: the Unity User Manual, the Component Reference, and the Scripting Reference (see Figure 1-4).

Learn with Unity

There are many ways to learn Unity. In these pages you'll find everything you need to become a Unity developer. So why not start learning and join the community today? In Tutorials you'll find video and article based content, our Documentation are a complete written manual and scripting reference, and if you'd like some time with our experts, sign up for a live Q&A session and ask your questions directly.

Tutorials

Video and text tutorials in an array of topics & levels. Start learning

Documentation

Explore Unity's Component reference and browse the Scripting API. Read more

Live training

Want to dive into a live classroom and ask questions as you learn? Take a class

Community

Our forums and Answers offer a wealth of solutions to problems. More

Figure 1-4. Additional learning resources for Unity

It is impossible to memorize the vast capabilities of a powerful development tool like Unity, and the folks at Unity are constantly improving it and adding new features and capabilities. As you follow the examples in this book, you will become familiar with these resources and comfortable with consulting them throughout the game development process.

Go ahead and select Documentation in the blue top submenu of the Learn tab (see Figure 1-5).

Figure 1-5. Accessing the Learn section of the Unity web site

Now click the "View User Manual" button, which you'll see on the page that has loaded (Figure 1-6).

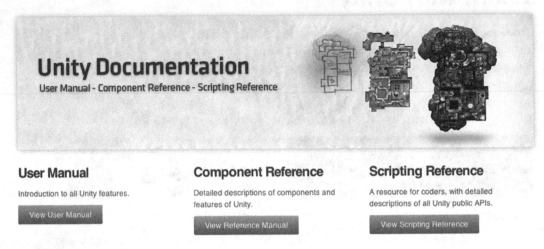

Unity Documentation
User Manual - Component Reference - Scripting Reference

User Manual

Introduction to all Unity features.

View User Manual

Component Reference

Detailed descriptions of components and features of Unity.

View Reference Manual

Scripting Reference

A resource for coders, with detailed descriptions of all Unity public APIs.

View Scripting Reference

Figure 1-6. Unity Documentation resources

Under the welcome, scroll down to User Guide ➤ Unity Basics, and click Unity Hotkeys (see Figure 1-7).

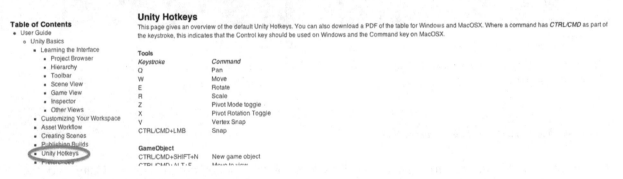

Table of Contents
- User Guide
  - Unity Basics
    - Learning the Interface
      - Project Browser
      - Hierarchy
      - Toolbar
      - Scene View
      - Game View
      - Inspector
      - Other Views
    - Customizing Your Workspace
    - Asset Workflow
    - Creating Scenes
    - Publishing Builds
    - Unity Hotkeys
    - Preferences

Unity Hotkeys

This page gives an overview of the default Unity Hotkeys. You can also download a PDF of the table for Windows and MacOSX. Where a command has *CTRL/CMD* as part of the keystroke, this indicates that the Control key should be used on Windows and the Command key on MacOSX.

Tools

Keystroke	Command
Q	Pan
W	Move
E	Rotate
R	Scale
Z	Pivot Mode toggle
X	Pivot Rotation Toggle
V	Vertex Snap
CTRL/CMD+LMB	Snap

GameObject

CTRL/CMD+SHIFT+N	New game object
CTRL/CMD+ALT+F	Move to view

Figure 1-7. Unity Hotkeys topic in the User Manual

Here you can download a PDF of common Unity keyboard shortcuts for PC or Mac. You'll find this quite helpful to have handy as you become familiar with the Unity editor. You can see what it looks like in Figure 1-8.

Figure 1-8. Unity Hotkeys printable quick reference

Tip   When using hotkeys as they are mentioned in this book, the + symbol means to hold the first key down before pressing the second. For the Mac, ⌘+X means hold the ⌘ key down, then press the X key. For the PC, Ctrl+X means hold the Control key down, then press the X key.

Setting Up the Development Environment

Now it's time to set up your development environment so it's ready to make some games. Go back to the main Unity home page and select Download on the right side of the top menu bar (see Figure 1-9).

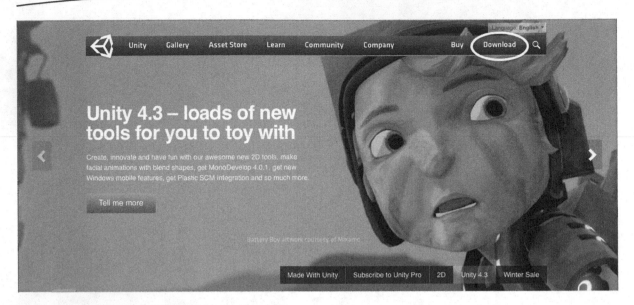

Figure 1-9. The Download tab on the Unity site home page

Click the big blue button that says "Download Unity 4.3" (Figure 1-10). It will take a few minutes to download.

The free version of Unity for OS X. Includes publishing support for iOS, Android, Windows Store, Windows Phone, BlackBerry, desktop and Web, and a 30 day trial of Unity Pro (with Pro publishing for iOS, Android, Windows Store, Windows Phone and BlackBerry).

Download Unity 4.3

Looking for an older version?

System Requirements
License Comparison
Release Notes

Developing on Windows?

Figure 1-10. Download the latest version of Unity

> **Note** The version of Unity that is shown on the site may be later if you bought this book after they have updated the software. If you have any questions, head on over to the companion web site for this book at www.learn-unityscript.com.

Double-click on unity-4.3 in your operating system's Downloads folder (or wherever you chose to save it) to open it. Now double-click on the Unity icon in the Unity Installer window that opened up (Figure 1-11).

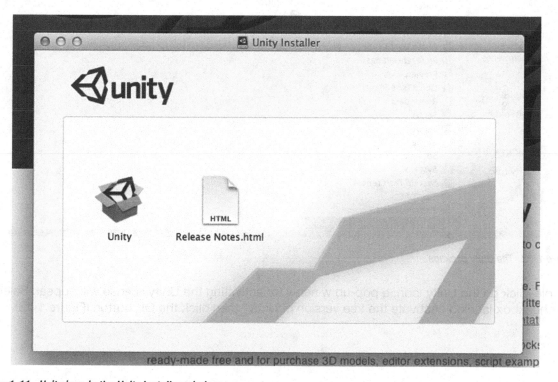

Figure 1-11. Unity icon in the Unity Installer window

Click Continue in the Install Unity pop-up window, and select Continue to proceed past the welcome to the Unity License terms. Choose Agree in the pop-up menu (after carefully reading all the terms and conditions, of course).

Unless you have a strong preference otherwise, let Unity use the default destination for installation. Click Install; for now let the wizard perform a standard installation without customizing or changing the install location. Depending on your computer's security settings, you may have to enter a password to allow the installation. Then click Install Software. It will take a few minutes for the actual installation.

You'll get a message in the Install Unity window confirming a successful installation. You can close this window by clicking the Close button. Now you can also close the Unity Installer window.

At this point a Finder window will open, displaying Unity within the Applications folder. You can drag both the Unity and MonoDevelop icons to the Dock for easy access (Figure 1-12).

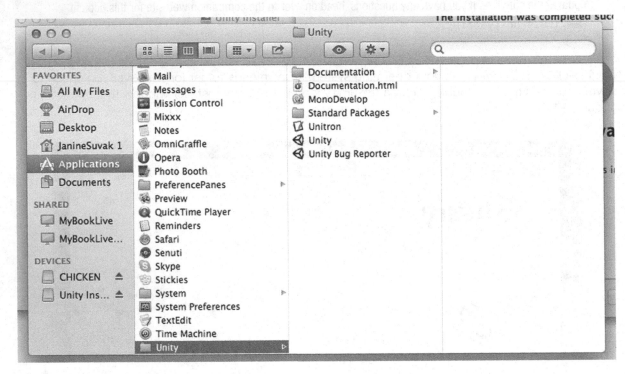

Figure 1-12. The Unity package

Double-click on the Unity icon; a pop-up window for activating the Unity license will appear. Select the checkbox labeled "Activate the free version of Unity" then click the OK button (Figure 1-13).

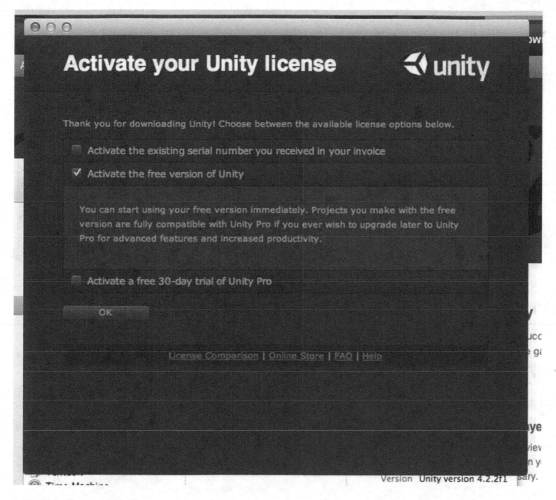

Figure 1-13. Unity license activation

The next step is to create your Unity account (Figure 1-14). You'll also use this for the Unity Asset Store and community forums. I recommend getting the monthly newsletter for staying on top of what's new with Unity.

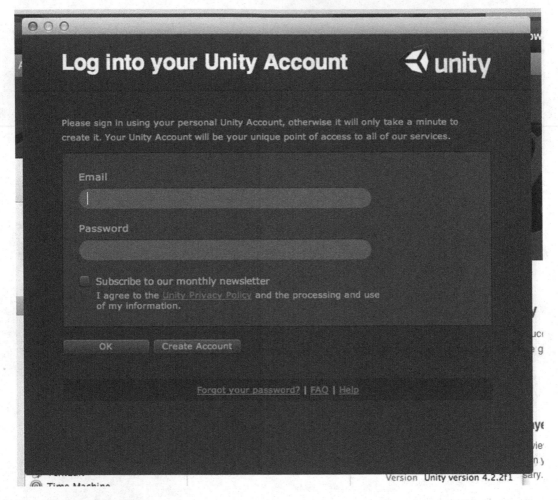

Figure 1-14. Create a Unity account

After you have created your account, a friendly thank-you appears. Click the big blue "Start using Unity" button (Figure 1-15).

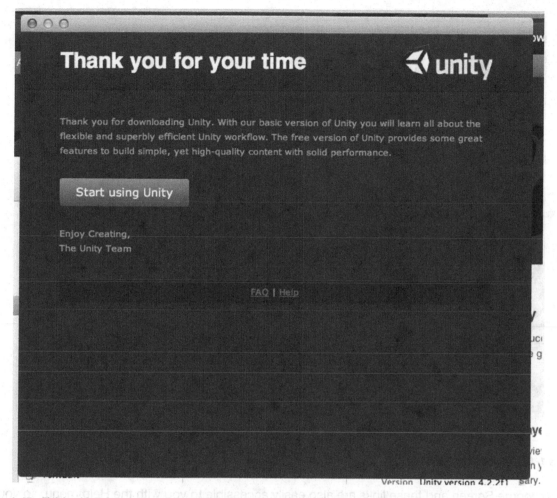

Figure 1-15. Finish with Unity package download and account creation

The "Welcome To Unity" screen will appear on top of the Unity editor interface screen (Figure 1-16). The welcome screen contains links to the various topics on the Unity3D web site that you just went over. This window will appear every time you start the editor unless you uncheck the Show at Startup box found in the bottom right corner.

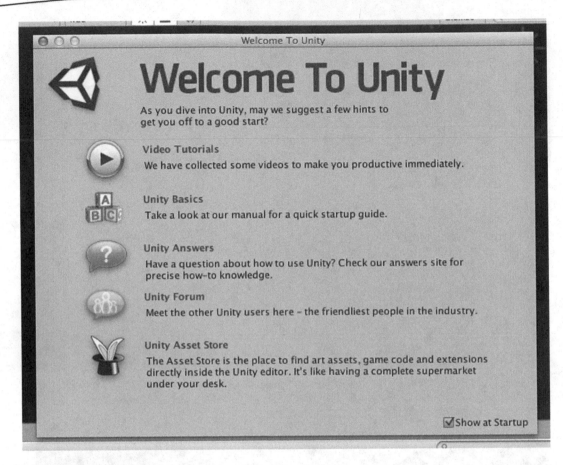

Figure 1-16. Unity welcome window

The Welcome Screen and these links are also easily accessible to you with the Help menu, so you can uncheck Show at Startup to skip this window (Figure 1-17), then close it to see the Unity editor (Figure 1-18).

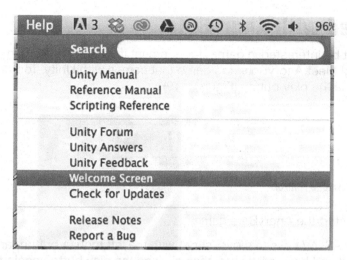

Figure 1-17. *Unity welcome window accessible from the Unity editor Help menu*

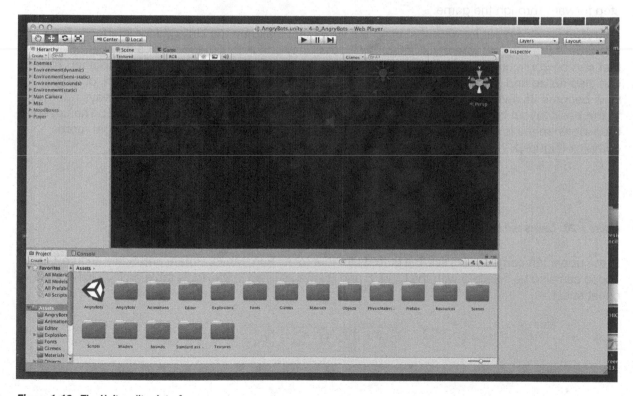

Figure 1-18. *The Unity editor interface*

Getting Started with AngryBots

You probably wouldn't be interested in game development if you didn't like games, so you can guess the best part—playing! Meet AngryBots, the demo that comes with Unity. Top and center of the Unity editor you will see the play button (Figure 1-19).

Figure 1-19. Unity editor Playmode controls

Hit the play button to start the AngryBots game.

Use the arrow keys or ASDW keys to move, shoot with the left mouse button, and use the mouse to look around. Go ahead and have a little fun, then click on the play button again to quit the game. The pause button is to the right of the play button, and the button to its right is used in testing to step forward through the game.

AngryBots is also great for demonstrating the views that make up the Unity editor interface. The interface is the window where you interact with the Unity editor. It is made up of a number of views that can be configured by using the Layout drop-down menu in the upper right of the toolbar. You can also resize and drag the various views around by their tabs to customize the layout, or have a view become its own window by dragging it out of the editor window area. You can always return to the basic layout by choosing Revert Factory Settings in the Layout drop-down menu. The Layers drop-down menu is useful for hiding and showing different content when your games get more complex (Figure 1-20).

Figure 1-20. Layers and Layout drop-down menu controls

In the upper left corner, you'll see the buttons for four tools: Pan, Move, Rotate and Scale (Figure 1-21). These can also be selected with the Q, W, E and R keys as listed in the Tools table on the Unity Hotkeys cheat sheet.

Figure 1-21. Pan, Move, Rotate, and Scale tool selectors

To the immediate right of these tools are a couple of toggles that also have corresponding hotkeys you'll find on the hotkey list you downloaded earlier: Z for the Pivot Mode toggle that switches between local space and world space, and X for the Pivot Rotation toggle that switches between center or pivot-point rotation (Figure 1-22). You'll learn more about these technical details later; this is just an introduction to what you see on the editor.

Figure 1-22. Pivot Mode and Pivot Rotation toggle switches

You can also use hotkeys from the Window table to change the focus to the various views that I will go over next.

Game View (⌘+2)

You've already used the Game view to play AngryBots (Figure 1-23). You will use the Game view frequently because game development is an iterative process. This means that you will constantly repeat the steps of building your game one piece at a time, testing that piece by playing it in the Game view, making adjustments, then testing again until you are satisfied it is working the way you want it to before adding the next piece. You will make changes to settings while playing in order to fine-tune your gameplay, but be aware that any changes you make to game objects in gameplaying mode won't be saved. To help you avoid the frustration of losing changes you meant to keep, press ⌘+, (comma key) to open the Unity Preferences menu (Figure 1-24).

Figure 1-23. AngryBots seen in Game view

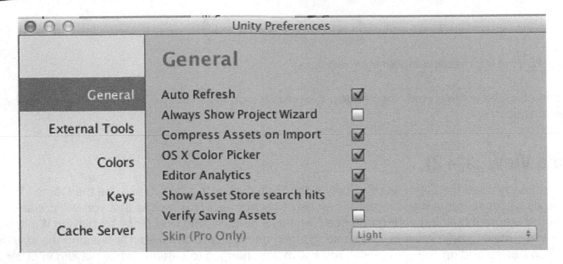

Figure 1-24. Unity Preferences menu

Check OS X Color Picker, then select Colors on the left. Double-click in the Playmode tint display to open the color picker, select a color, then close the color picker window and the Unity Preferences window (Figure 1-25).

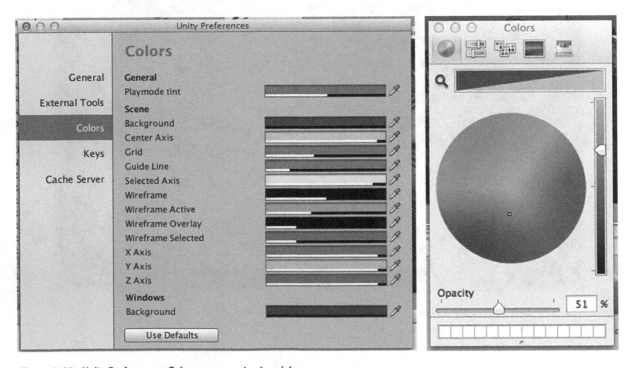

Figure 1-25. Unity Preferences: Colors menu and color picker

Close the Colors and Unity Preferences windows, click Play, and see the editor change color as a reminder that you are in active Play mode. Along the top of the Game view you'll find the control bar (Figure 1-26). If you'd like AngryBots to fill the window while you are playing, select Maximize on Play (Shift + spacebar) from the top of the Game view before clicking the Play button.

Figure 1-26. Game view control bar

The Aspect drop-down menu on the left allows you to test gameplay using the screen proportions for the device or platform you are targeting (Figure 1-27).

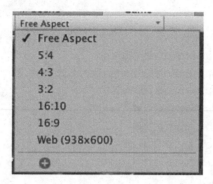

Figure 1-27. Game view Aspect drop-down menu

Selecting Stats activates a display of performance statistics (Figure 1-28).

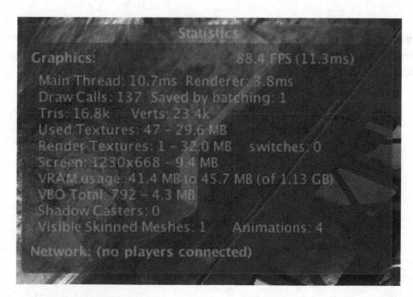

Figure 1-28. Game statistics display in Game view

Last, the Gizmos button allows visual identification of gizmos which will be discussed in the section covering Scene view.

Hierarchy View (⌘+4)

The Hierarchy view contains a list of every object present in the displayed scene, in alphabetical order. Objects can be grouped as "parent" objects that may have corresponding "child" objects. If you expand any of the items in Figure 1-29 as you are exploring the editor interface, you'll find an indented alphabetical list of child objects nested under the parent object. You will learn all about parent–child relationships of game objects in upcoming chapters.

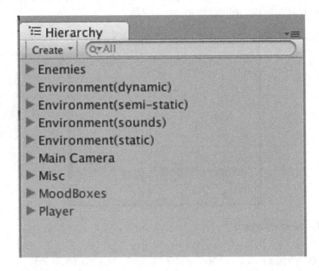

Figure 1-29. Hierarchy view

There is often more than one way to perform any particular action in the Unity editor. The Create button in the Hierarchy view works the same as the top-menu GameObject ➤ Create (Empty or Other) selection for generating a number of things for your game (Figure 1-30).

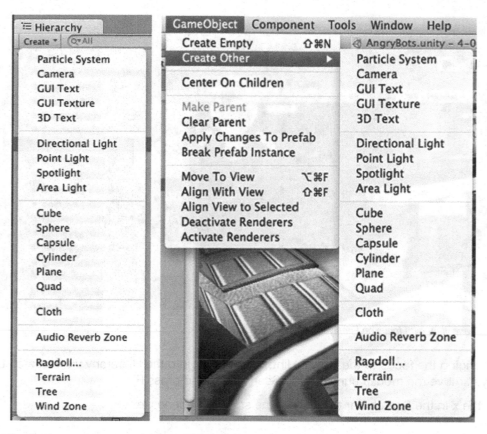

Figure 1-30. Alternate ways to create a new game object

Type **EnemySpider** into the Hierarchy view search field. As you would expect, a list of EnemySpider game objects appears in the view. Click on any of the EnemySpider objects in the list, then place your mouse cursor over the Scene view and press the F key. F moves the focus of the Scene view to the object you selected in the Hierarchy view. Notice the Scene view also grayed out everything except the objects in your Hierarchy view search results (Figure 1-31).

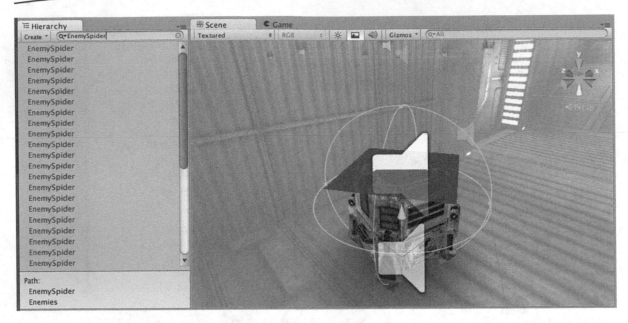

Figure 1-31. Scene view with focus on EnemySpider

Now try changing the focus to the Player. Hint: Type **Player** into the Hierarchy view Search bar, select Player, move the mouse cursor to the Scene view, and press F.

Last, click the x in the Search bar to return to the standard Scene view.

Scene View (⌘+1)

In the early days games were created completely from code. A great deal of the power of Unity to create beautiful games much faster lies in using intuitive tools such as the Scene view, where you can visually build your game from the environment on up to positioning game objects (Figure 1-32).

Figure 1-32. The Scene view

You can navigate the Scene view a number of ways. Select the hand tool (Q) and click-drag with the mouse. Orbit around your point of interest by pressing the Alt key while click-dragging, or zoom by pressing Ctrl and click-dragging. Have a little fun in first-person Flythrough mode by holding the right mouse button and using the A, S, D, W, Q, and E keys for navigation.

Select the Player game object in AngryBots by clicking on it. Display the Translate (W), Scale (E) and Rotate (R) gizmos with their respective buttons located to the immediate right of the hand tool. Notice the x, y, and z axes in each are color-coded with red, green, and blue. You can manipulate the position of the game object with the mouse by click-dragging the gizmo or with the Inspector by typing in precise values. The scene camera's viewing angle can be adjusted in the same way with the Scene Gizmo (Figure 1-33).

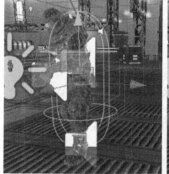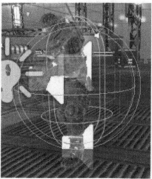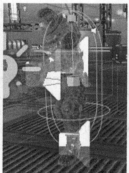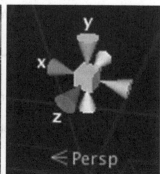

Figure 1-33. Scene view Translate, Rotate, Scale and Camera gizmos

You can view the scene in a variety of modes and preview audio by using the Scene view control bar (Figure 1-34).

Figure 1-34. Scene view control bar

Inspector (⌘+3)

The Inspector panel contains the settings for every game object, asset, and editor preference. It is context sensitive, meaning that it changes depending upon what you have selected in the Unity editor. You may have noticed the contents of the Inspector changing between selections. Notice the different settings of EnemySpider compared to Player (Figure 1-35).

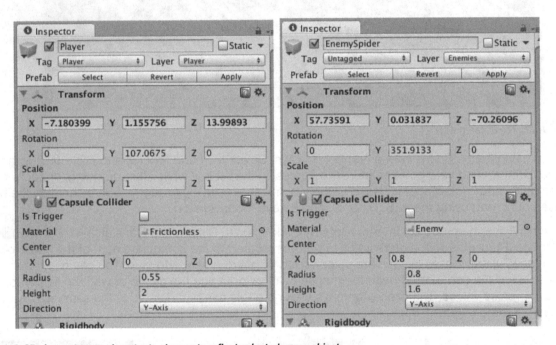

Figure 1-35. Inspector panel contents change to reflect selected game object

Project Panel (⌘+5)

All of the assets that make up your game are stored in the Project Panel (Figure 1-36). You can create new assets or import them from other sources such as the Asset Store. Do not use your operating system for moving files within your Unity project. Unity keeps track of where these are stored in its internal project file library, and how you move or edit them with the Project panel.

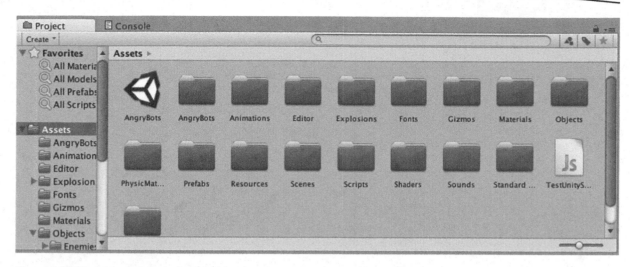

Figure 1-36. Project panel displaying AngryBots assets

Console (SHIFT+⌘+C)

The console (Figure 1-37) displays output from your game during the development process such as messages, warnings, and errors.

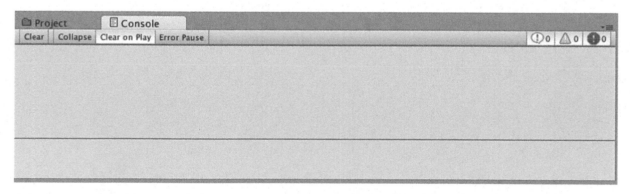

Figure 1-37. The Console

Summary

In this chapter, you got a general idea of the resources available on the Unity web site, and you will get more familiar with these as you use them in upcoming projects. You downloaded the Unity editor, had some fun killing angry robots, and took a tour of the views that make up the Unity editor itself. You are all set up and ready to go!

Chapter 2

Game Programming 101

Now that you know your way around the Unity editor, you are ready for an introduction to the scripting editor MonoDevelop. These are your two primary tools for game development. The Unity editor is where you build your game visually, assembling the layout of your scene by placing the game objects within it. MonoDevelop is the scripting editor where you write your code. The code tells the game objects how to behave, such as responding to player input or to each other. Your code script is incorporated into your game when you attach it to a game object. In this chapter you will learn how to create a script, write some simple code, then attach the script to a game object.

You installed MonoDevelop along with Unity in Chapter 1. You may have seen it in the Applications ➤ Unity folder (Figure 2-1), but you can also get to MonoDevelop directly from the Unity editor. It is the default choice under External Script Editor in Unity Preferences ➤ External Tools (Figure 2-2).

	Documentation	▶
	Documentation.html	
	MonoDevelop.app	
	Standard Packages	▶
	Unitron.app	
	Unity Bug Reporter.app	
MonoDevelop.app | Unity.app | |

Figure 2-1. *MonoDevelop.app icon and Finder menu of downloaded Unity package*

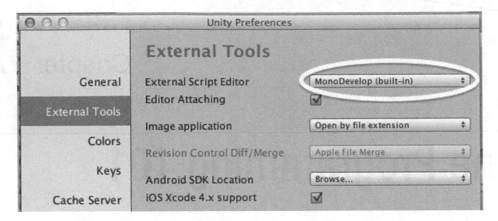

Figure 2-2. Unity Preferences menu

With the AngryBots project still open, in your Project Panel open the Assets ➤ Scripts ➤ Animation folder and click the PlayerAnimation icon (Figure 2-3).

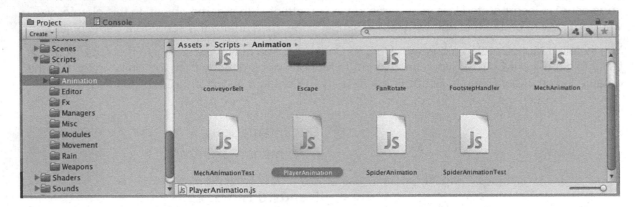

Figure 2-3. PlayerAnimation script icon in Project panel

In the Inspector panel you will see additional information about the PlayerAnimation script's contents (Figure 2-4). You can open this script in MonoDevelop by double-clicking it or by selecting the Open… button (Figure 2-5).

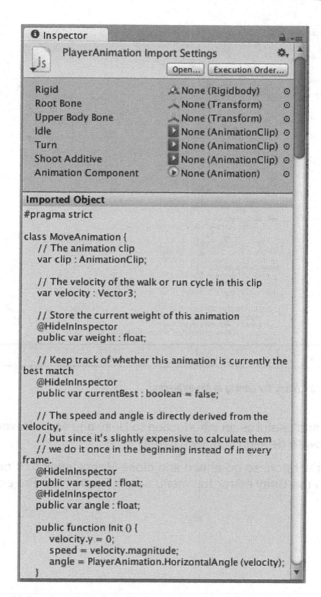

Figure 2-4. *PlayerAnimation script icon in Inspector panel*

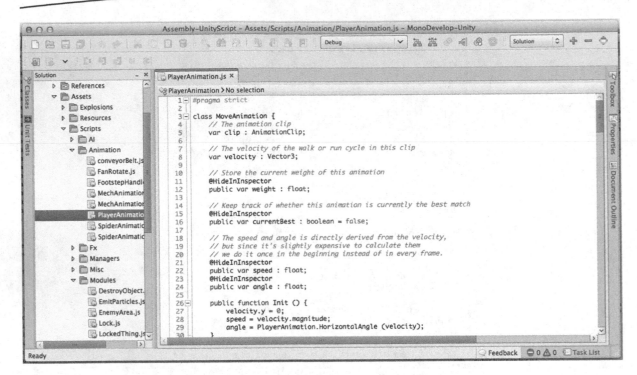

Figure 2-5. PlayerAnimation script ready for editing in MonoDevelop

AngryBots is fun to play and useful as an introduction to Unity and MonoDevelop, but now it's time to get started learning how to develop your own game.

You will be starting from scratch, so go ahead and close MonoDevelop. If prompted, do not save any changes. From the Unity editor top menu select File ➤ New Project to open the Project Wizard (Figure 2-6).

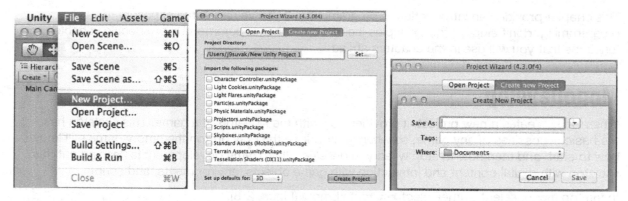

Figure 2-6. Unity ➤ File ➤ New Project menu and Project Wizard

Don't save any changes to AngryBots if prompted. Give your new project a name and click Create Project. Unity presents a default location and project name for you. The Set… button opens up a Create New Project window you can use as an alternative means to name and relocate your new project if you find this format more convenient. Give your project a descriptive name if you like; you can rename it later. You can see individual asset packages found in the Standard Packages folder that was downloaded with Unity, but don't select any this time. Make sure the Create new Project tab is selected, leave the setup default as 3D, and create your new project.

The new project appears as depicted in Figure 2-7.

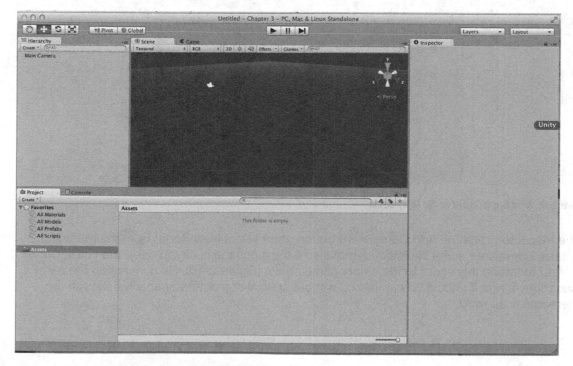

Figure 2-7. Appearance of the new project in the Unity editor interface

This chapter provides an introduction to programming. If you've had some exposure to programming, don't skip it—the examples include a number of common Unity-specific variables and functions that you will use in the chapters ahead.

MonoDevelop

When Unity creates a new project, it provides you with the skeleton of a game. This skeleton has the basic necessities of any game, so when you click on the Play button the empty game still knows how to start, and then how to stop when you deselect Play. Game development is fleshing out this skeleton with digital content and interaction with game objects, environments, and scripts.

In the top menu, select GameObject ➤ Create Empty (Figure 2-8).

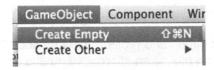

Figure 2-8. Unity top menu GameObject ➤ Create Empty

You will see the new GameObject listed in the Hierarchy view, its transform gizmo in the Scene view, and further details in the Inspector (Figure 2-9).

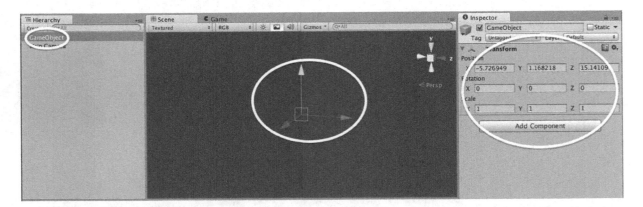

Figure 2-9. New GameObject in the Unity editor

In the Inspector, click the Add Component button, then select New Script from the menu that appears. Name your script HelloWorld, make sure the language is Java Script, then click Create and Add to attach this script to the empty game object (Figure 2-10). By convention the name is descriptive, and it should be capitalized without special characters or spaces, though the underscore is allowed.

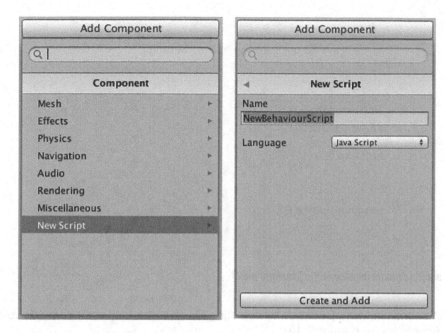

Figure 2-10. Add Component pop-up windows). for adding a new script

The script is now listed in the Inspector as a component of the GameObject, and you will see an icon for the script has appeared in the Assets folder (Figure 2-11).

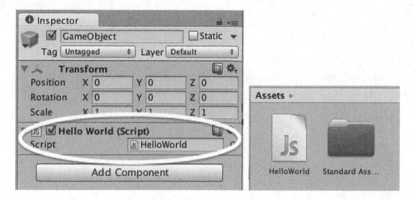

Figure 2-11. New script in the Inspector panel as a component and the Project panel Assets as an icon

Click once on this icon to select it and see the contents of the script in the Inspector (Figure 2-12).

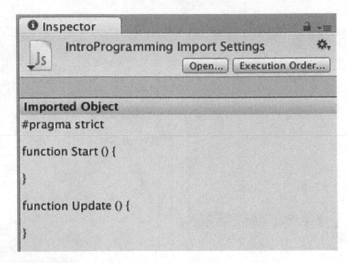

Figure 2-12. New script contents as seen in the Inspector panel

You can open the script in MonoBehavior by selecting Open in the Inspector or by double-clicking the icon in the Assets folder (Figure 2-13).

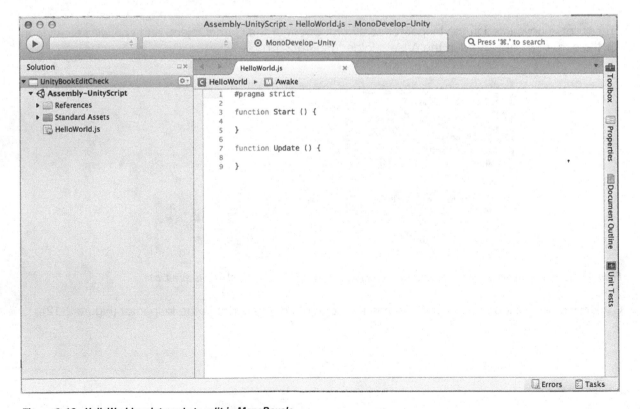

Figure 2-13. HelloWorld script ready to edit in MonoDevelo

Like Unity, MonoDevelop also has some keyboard shortcuts that you can find at MonoDevelop ➤ Unity Preferences ➤ KeyBindings (Figure 2-13).

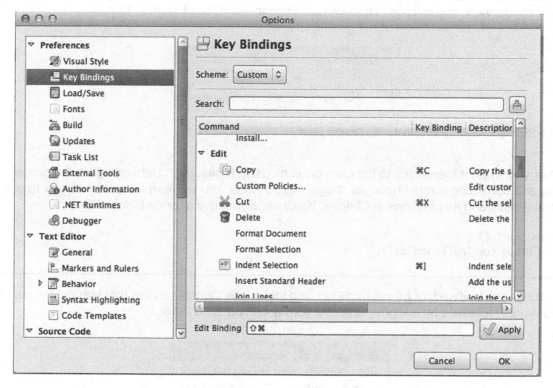

Figure 2-14. MonoDevelop ➤ Unity Preferences ➤ Key Bindings menu of keyboard shortcuts

When you create a new script, Unity automatically includes a few items. #pragma strict will be at the beginning of all of your scripts. It tells the compiler that variables must have type declarations, which you will learn more about later in this chapter. It also creates the empty Start() and Update() functions. For now, go ahead and delete the Update() function, including the open and close braces:

```
function Update () {

}
```

Since this new script is attached to the game object, the Start() function will be called once when the game object enters a scene. In the sample project here, the game object is already present in the scene, so its Start() function is called as soon as game play is started. Type your first line of code between the braces of the Start() function to see this in action.

```
function Start () {
    print("Hello World!");
}
```

Press ⌘+S to save, then return to the Unity editor. In the Project panel, select the Console tab. This is where you will see the output appear as a result of the code you just wrote. In the Game view, make sure Maximize on Play is deselected so it won't obscure the Console. Now go and click Play. In the Console view, you will see "Hello World!" appear—yay! (See Figure 2-15.)

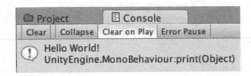

Figure 2-15. "Hello World!" print output in the Console panel

Another way to print messages to the Console is by using Debug.Log. "Debugging" is the process of finding and correcting errors known as "bugs" in your code. You will learn more about how to use the Debug class and its functions in Chapter 10. Change your line of code to look like this:

```
function Start () {
        Debug.Log("Hello World!");
}
```

Save, run in the Unity editor by clicking Play, and look in the Console to see that you get the same "Hello World!" followed by a slightly different commentary (Figure 2-16).

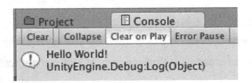

Figure 2-16. Hello World! Debug.Log output in the Console panel.

Game development is a constant learning process. The folks at Unity are continually adding new capabilities and new platforms to which you can port your games. Even the most seasoned developer must keep up with the latest changes and additions, most commonly by referring to the provided documentation. Each new game project likely has something you may not be familiar with or that you may want to double-check for changes. Just as you will learn UnityScript best by creating the examples from this book in Unity and MonoDevelop yourself, you will get used to referring to the documentation most quickly by using it.

Stop the game and go back to the script in MonoDevelop. (⌘+Tab is a nice shortcut for when you are working between two windows.) Click anywhere on the word Debug, then press ⌘+' to open the Debug.Log scripting reference in your web browser (Figure 2-17).

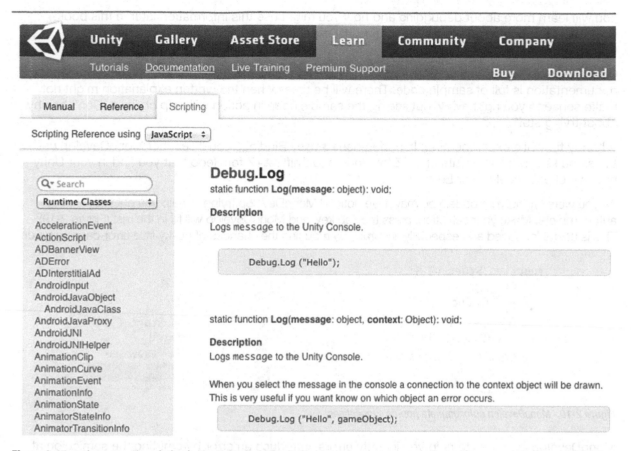

Figure 2-17. *Debug.Log description in the Unity Scripting Reference*

You'll see in the description that Debug.Log logs a message to the Unity Console, followed by an example line of code similar to yours.

There is a second description with sample code for providing you with more information in case of an error. Alter your line of code by adding the gameObject reference: Debug.Log("HelloWorld!", gameObject); press ⌘+S to save, and click Play in the Unity editor. Now the "Hello World!" message appears along with some additional information provided by the Debug.Log function (Figure 2-18).

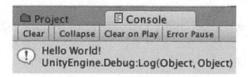

Figure 2-18. *Debug.Log output in console with Object context*

You will learn more about debugging and how you might use this information later in this book. For now, it's enough that you have successfully experimented with sample code from the documentation.

Game development is an interactive process, including the classic method of trial and error. The documentation is full of sample code. There will be times when the written explanation might not make sense to you right away, but seeing the sample code in action will help clarify it. Don't be shy about trying stuff!

A handy tip while experimenting: In Preferences ➤ Key Bindings you'll see that MonoDevelop uses the same keyboard shortcuts of ⌘+Z for Undo and Shift+⌘+Z for Redo that you find in your Unity hotkeys cheat sheet under Edit.

As you were typing your code, you may have noticed MonoDevelop trying to help you out with autocomplete. Make your selection, press the Tab key, and MonoDevelop will fill in the rest (Figure 2-19). This is useful for speed and especially accuracy by reducing the chances of pesky little error-causing typos.

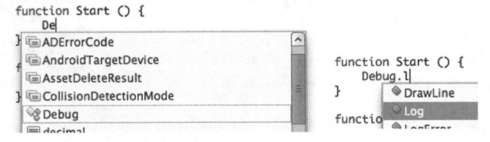

Figure 2-19. MonoDevelop autocomplete pop-up suggestions

MonoDevelop also tries to help you identify errors. Introduce an error by omitting the semicolon at the end of the line and save. In the Unity editor, you will see a warning displayed in the console, with a helpful suggestion from Unity for fixing the error (Figure 2-20).

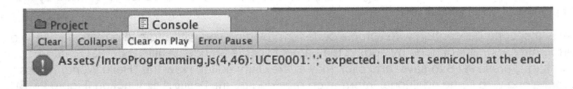

Figure 2-20. Error warning in Console panel

If you click Play anyway, Unity will insist that you fix the error (Figure 2-21).

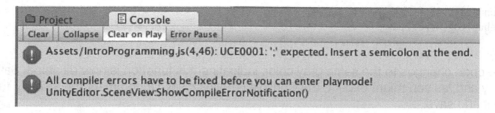

Figure 2-21. Additional error warning in Console panel after Play attempt with error present

Big red warnings are ugly, so go ahead and fix the code, then save.

Variables and Functions

A computer only does what you tell it to do. It uses variables to hold data, and follows the instructions for manipulating or processing the data you give it in the form of functions.

Change your code to look like this:

```
#pragma strict

// declare the variable myVar of type integer and give it a value of 8.
var myVar : int = 8;

function Start () {
        Debug.Log(myVar);
}
```

First, take a closer look at the second line. Adding the double forward slash // at the beginning of a line makes it a comment, indicated in MonoDevelop by a gray-colored font. Comments are used for notes to yourself or other developers, such as describing the purpose of the subsequent block of code. Code that seems perfectly clear when you are working on it may not be to someone else, or it may become a lot fuzzier to you when you review it days, weeks, or much later. Do yourself and your teammates a favor by building a good habit of commenting on your code as you go.

> **Note** Commenting out code is useful during debugging. You can disable it by commenting instead of deleting it, then easily re-enable it as needed.

For multiple lines put /* at the beginning and */ at the end of the comments or code. Try this by commenting out the Start() function.

```
#pragma strict

// declare the variable myVar of type integer and give it a value of 8.
var myVar : int = 8;
```

```
/* function Start () {
        Debug.Log(myVar);
} */
```

Notice the code changes to the same gray color, indicating this function is now disabled. Save and run in Unity and, as you might expect, the Console remains clear. Uncomment the Start() function to enable it and save.

A **variable** is used for storing and retrieving data. This is how your game program remembers the things it needs for managing gameplay.

Take a look at this line of code:

```
var myVar : int = 8;
```

Breaking it down into parts:

```
(1)     (2) (3)   (4)     (5)   (6)  (7)
var   myVar :    int      =    8   ;
```

1. Declare a variable with the var statement.

2. The variable name. Variable names should be descriptive, which helps to make your code more readable. You can use any alphanumeric character and the underscore, but no other punctuation marks or special characters. Another good practice for making your code readable is to follow standard programming conventions. The standard convention for naming variables is that if the first character of the variable name is a letter, it is not capitalized.

3. Colon separating the variable name from the data type.

4. The data type of the variable, in this case int for integer.

5. The assignment operator, used to assign a value to the variable you just declared and named. You do not have to assign a value to an integer when you declare it.

6. The value being assigned to the variable, in this case an integer. Integers are whole numbers, including negative numbers (indicated by a minus sign in front). Commas and spaces are not allowed—while 24, 0, and –3 are valid integers, 2,500 is not, but 2500 is.

7. A semicolon indicating the end of the statement. All statements must end with a semicolon.

In the Start() function, the Debug.Log message printed to the Console is the value of myVar. Save and play to confirm.

While variables hold data, functions do something. The instructions for whatever process the function carries out is contained within the braces. Take a look at the components of the Start() function:

```
    (1)      (2) (3) (4)
function Start ()  {
                (5)
        Debug.Log(MyVar);
(6)
}
```

1. Declare the function with the reserved word function.

2. Name the function. Function names begin with capital letters.

3. Arguments for handling information passed to the function. The parentheses are required, so if no arguments are needed they remain empty.

4. Open brace indicating the beginning of the function's contents.

5. The instructions for the function to follow in the form of statements—in this example, the Debug.Log statement.

6. Close brace indicating the end of the function. Since it is the end of a function rather than a statement, no semicolon is used.

Notice that MonoDevelop indented the Debug statement. Indentation is used to make your code more readable. This way, you can easily identify separate blocks of code. MonoDevelop will do this automatically for you, but at times you will find you need to reorganize your code for legibility. In MonoDevelop Preferences ➤ Key Bindings ➤ Edit you'll find the keyboard shortcuts ⌘+] to indent or ⌘+[to unindent that will shift any size block of code that you highlight. Give it a try with your Debug statement, then with the entire Start function. Easy, right?

For a quick review of arithmetic operators (Table 2-1), replace your Debug line of code in the Start function with the following lines:

```
        print(6+2);
        print(6-2);
        print(6*2);
        print(6/2);
        print(6%2);
```

Table 2-1. Definitions of Arithmetic Operators

Arithmetic Operators	Meaning
+	addition
-	subtraction
*	multiplication
/	division
%	modulus

Save and play. The output in the console will look like Figure 2-22:

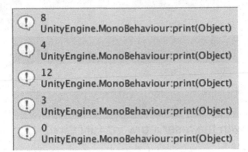

Figure 2-22. Results output from arithmetic operators

You probably recognize the first four operators. The modulus operator is another handy one that gives you the remainder, in this case the remainder of 6 divided by 2. Try changing the 6 to a 5, save, and play. This time the last line of output is 1, the remainder of 5 divided by 2.

Like most programming languages, UnityScript follows the standard order of operations where multiplication and division are given precedence over addition and subtraction.

Alter your Start function to the following:

```
print(6+2*4);
```

Reading from left to right, the sum of 6 and 2 is 8, which multiplied by 4 is 32. Save and play, and you'll see that Unity multiplied 2 by 4 first to get 8, then added 6 for an output of 14.

You can change the order of evaluation by using parentheses. Operations inside parentheses are given higher precedence. Change the same line of code as follows:

```
print((6+2)*4);
```

Now when you save and play, your output is 32 because Unity performed the addition operation inside the parentheses first.

These same arithmetic operators can be used on numerical values held by variables. Replace the same line of code with this statement:

```
print(myVar + myVar);
```

With the previously assigned value of 8 for myVar, now you will get 16 as the result.

So far you have been working with integers, but you can also declare a variable as a **float** data type to handle decimal digits. Variables can contain all sorts of data types, including **string**, **boolean**, and more complex data types. In fact, you used a string in your very first line of code:

```
print("Hello World!");
```

The string is the characters contained within the double quotes. **Concatenation** is the term for putting together individual strings into a single string. While I could have said that you can "add" strings together, it is important for you to learn the proper terminology as it is introduced, which will come in handy for performing a forum search on Unity Answers when you need help, or for sounding really smart at cocktail parties. Edit your code to the following:

```
#pragma strict

// declare the variable myVar of type integer and give it a value of 8.
var myVar : int = 8;
var myString1 : String = "Hello ";
var myString2 : String = "World!";
var myNewString: String;

 function Start () {
        myNewString = String.Concat(myString1, myString2);
        Debug.Log(myNewString);
}
```

Save, play, and your output should be "Hello World!" The most common mistake here is to forget about including spaces where you need them.

`String.Concat` resembles `Debug.Log` in that they both contain a **dot operator**. The dot operator is a form of coding syntax, where the dot separates words of code. `Concat` is an element of `String`, just as `Log` is an element of `Debug`. You can use the now-familiar ⌘+' on `String` and `Debug` to see more of their elements in the Unity Scripting Reference.

The `Start` function has worked well for demonstrating these basic concepts, but now you are ready to write your own functions. A **function** accepts information, called **arguments**, and performs some kind of action with the information, then optionally returns a result.

Delete the string variable declarations and edit the `Start` function as follows:

```
var myVar : int = 8;

 function Start () {
        myVar = AddFive(myVar);
        Debug.Log(myVar);
}
```

The statement `myVar = AddFive(myVar);` calls the function named `AddFive()` that you will create next, and sends it the integer stored in `myVar`.

After the close brace of the `Start()` function, write the new function called in `Start` named `AddFive`:

```
function AddFive (numberFromStartFunction : int) {
        var newVar : int;
        newVar = numberFromStartFunction + 5;
        return newVar;
}
```

Unlike the Start() function, AddFive() needs to receive information in order to process it by adding five. Within the parentheses is the parameter numberFromStartFunction that is declared as an integer data type. This means that when this function is called, it must be sent an integer. You already declared myVar as an integer, so you are correctly sending the AddFive() function an integer data type in your AddFive(myVar) function call. numberFromStartFunction works like a variable within the AddFive() function to hold the integer received from the caller.

The first statement of the AddFive() function is the following:

```
var newVar : int;
```

Here you are declaring a new variable named newVar of type integer. You may recall from the breakdown of a function described previously that you do not have to assign a value to a variable when you declare it.

newVar is declared within the AddFive() function so it can only be used within this function. This is an example of a **local variable**, since its scope is limited to the function in which it is declared. myVar is an example of a **global variable;** with a much broader scope, it can be utilized by any function in this script.

The second statement in this function, newVar = numberFromStartFunction + 5;, is the actual processing of your instructions, where 5 is added to the integer received in the parameter numberFromStartFunction. The result of this calculation is then stored in the local variable newVar.

Last, return newVar; returns the value assigned to newVar where it is assigned to myVar.

This process is depicted in Fig 2-23. Run (save and play) the script and, sure enough, Unity gives you a result of 13. Yay!

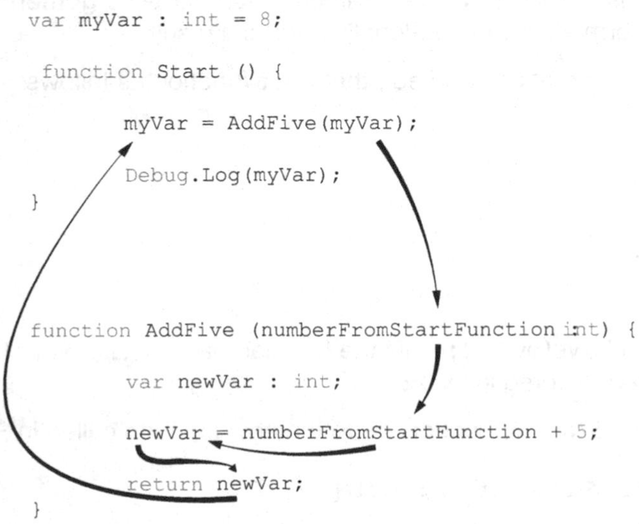

Figure 2-23. Flow of data between two functions

Math is necessary to game development, but for those of you who don't get a special thrill from solving math problems for fun, I have great news: Unity provides tons of built-in math functions for you. After all, doing routine calculations super-fast is what computers do best, and the purpose here is to facilitate your overall game development.

Mathf is one of the collections of handy math variables and functions provided by Unity. In MonoDevelop, update your code to look like this:

```
#pragma strict

 function Start () {
        Debug.Log(Mathf.PI);
}
```

Click on `Mathf.PI`, then press ⌘+' to open up its Unity Scripting Reference (Figure 2-24):

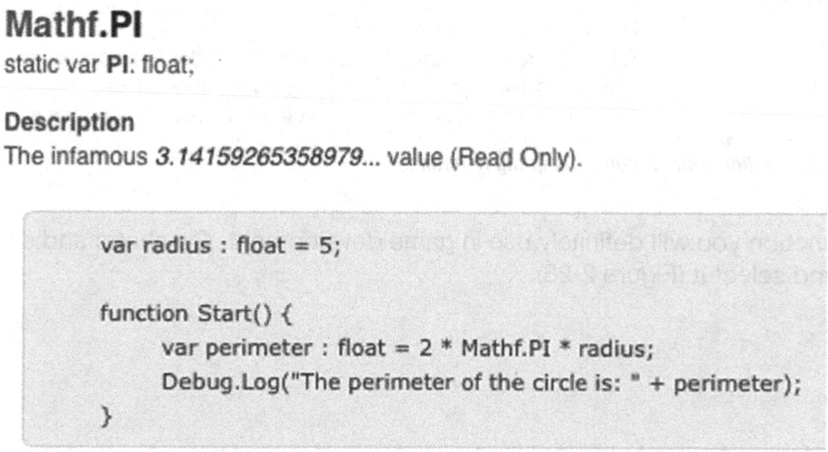

Mathf.PI

static var **PI**: float;

Description
The infamous *3.14159265358979...* value (Read Only).

```
var radius : float = 5;

function Start() {
        var perimeter : float = 2 * Mathf.PI * radius;
        Debug.Log("The perimeter of the circle is: " + perimeter);
}
```

Figure 2-24. `Mathf.PI` description from the Unity Scripting Reference

Here you find that `Mathf.PI` is a static variable of data type float. The value of pi is constant, and a variable that is **static** means that it won't let your code change the value that `Mathf.PI` is holding. Remember that when you create a function, the argument type has to match the data type it is accepting. The reference helpfully informs you that it is a float data type, and provides short sample code for how you might use it.

Run your script and you'll find that you don't get nearly as many decimal places displayed in the console as is shown in the reference. That's okay—it's unlikely that you'll need more precision than this in common game usage.

Click on the blue "Mathf" in the title of the Scripting Reference to get the complete list of the `Mathf` variables and functions (Figure 2-25).

Mathf

Description

A collection of common math functions.

Static Variables

Deg2Rad	Degrees-to-radians conversion constant (Read Only).
Epsilon	A tiny floating point value (Read Only).
Infinity	A representation of positive infinity (Read Only).
NegativeInfinity	A representation of negative infinity (Read Only).
PI	The infamous 3.14159265358979... value (Read Only).
Rad2Deg	Radians-to-degrees conversion constant (Read Only).

Static Functions

Abs	Returns the absolute value of f.
Acos	Returns the arc-cosine of f - the angle in radians whose cosine is f.
Approximately	Compares two floating point values if they are similar.
Asin	Returns the arc-sine of f - the angle in radians whose sine is f.

Figure 2-25. Mathf *description from the Unity Scripting Reference*

Rounding is a function you will definitely use in game development. Go ahead and scroll down to the Round function and select it (Figure 2-26).

Mathf.Round

static function **Round**(f: float): float;

Description

Returns f rounded to the nearest integer.

If the number ends in .5 so it is halfway between two integers, one of which is even and the other odd, the even number is returned.

```
// Prints 10
Debug.Log(Mathf.Round(10.0));
// Prints 10
Debug.Log(Mathf.Round(10.2));
// Prints 11
Debug.Log(Mathf.Round(10.7));
// Prints 10
Debug.Log(Mathf.Round(10.5));
// Prints 12
Debug.Log(Mathf.Round(11.5));
// Prints -10
```

Figure 2-26. Mathf.Round *description from the Unity Scripting Reference*

Here you find that `Mathf.Round` is a static function that accepts a float data type as an argument, followed by some examples. Go ahead and copy-paste some of these examples to MonoDevelop and give them a try.

Notice the last comment in the description tells you that the `Mathf.Round` function doesn't round everything that ends in .5 up, but rather up or down, whichever way yields an even number. In the fourth example given, you'll see that 10.5 is rounded down to 10 rather than up to 11 like you would expect. When you look anything up in the Scripting Reference, take the time to read the entire description—it may save you some aggravation later over behavior that Unity tried to tell you about.

Great job! You've made it through the basics of variables and functions. You are getting comfortable with referring to the Unity Scripting Reference and using the built-in functions that Unity provides. Don't worry if the concepts seem a little fuzzy; you are going to get a lot of practice from here on out. Keep working the examples and with practice you'll soon get the hang of it.

Conditionals

In addition to mathematical calculations, your scripts will also use logic functions to define the rules of your game, such as how many hits before an enemy is destroyed, a character's behavior based on accumulated power and abilities, and of course the conditions that must be met for the big win.

Boolean Logic and Conditionals

A boolean type variable only has two possible values: `true` and `false`.

In MonoDevelop, edit your script to the following:

```
var skyIsClear : boolean = true;

 function Start () {
        Debug.Log(skyIsClear);
}
```

Run your script and the console displays `true`. Boolean variables are often used to monitor or "flag" a state or condition. For example, I might say, "If the sky is clear then I will go out and play." I need to test to see if the sun is up, then make a decision based on that condition.

Update the code in the `Start()` function to:

```
if (skyIsClear == true) {
        Debug.Log("I will go out and play");
}
```

This code is fairly readable. The condition you wish to test goes in parentheses after the keyword `if`. If the condition is met, then the statement block within the braces is executed. Notice that the comparison operator for "is equal to" is ==, as opposed to the assignment operator = that you use for setting the values of variables. Go ahead and run the script. Yay—I get to go outside and play!

Wait—what if the sky is clear but it's nighttime? I shouldn't go outside to play in the dark. Under your first variable declaration, add a second:

```
var sunIsUp: boolean = true;
```

Now I want to say, "If the sky is clear and the sun is up, then I will go out and play." Edit your conditional if statement to the following:

```
if (skyIsClear == true && sunIsUp == true) {
```

&& is the logic operator AND. Now both conditions must be met for the code inside the statement block to execute.

The logic operator OR is represented as | |, by pressing Shift+\ twice on a Mac. OR means exactly what it sounds like: if one condition or the other is met, but not necessarily both, then the statement block executes.

If you want different blocks of code to execute under certain conditions, you can use more than one if statement:

```
function Start () {
        if (sunIsUp) {
                Debug.Log("I will get out of bed");
        }
        if (skyIsClear) {
                Debug.Log("I do not need an umbrella");
        }
}
```

Since both variables are set to true, when you run your script you see both statements appear in the console.

In this example, if the sun is not up and the sky is not clear then nothing happens. When you want an alternative block of code to execute if none of the previous conditions are met, you can use else:

```
function Start () {
        if (sunIsUp) {
                Debug.Log("I will get out of bed");
        }
        if (skyIsClear) {
                Debug.Log("I do not need an umbrella");
        }
        else {
                Debug.Log("I am staying in bed");
        }
}
```

Your variables are still set to true, so running your script doesn't do anything different, but you can see there are many ways you can test a variety of conditions to direct your gameplay.

The if statement can compare numerical values as well. Other comparison operators (Table 2-2) you can use include <, >, <=, >=, and !=. ! represents "not," so != is the comparison operator "is not equal to."

Table 2-2. Definitions of Comparison Operators

Comparison Operators	Meaning
==	Equal to
!=	Not equal to
<	Less than
>	Greater than
<=	Less than or equal to
>=	Greater than or equal to

The switch-case conditional works in place of a chain of if-else statements for when you need to compare a variable against different values.

Edit your script to the following:

```
#pragma strict
    var diceRoll : float;

function Start () {
    diceRoll = Random.Range(1, 6);

    switch (diceRoll) {
        case 1:
            print ("You rolled a 1!");
        break;
        case 2:
            print ("You rolled a 2!");
        break;
        case 3:
            print ("You rolled a 3!");
        break;
        case 4:
            print ("You rolled a 4!");
        break;
        case 5:
            print ("You rolled a 5!");
        break;
        case 6:
            print ("You rolled a 6!");
        break;
```

```
        default:
                print ("It's your turn - roll!");
        break;
    }
}
```

Here is a case where you are declaring a variable but not assigning a value right away. Instead, when the Start() function is called, the diceRoll variable is assigned a randomly generated number between 1 and 6.

Random number generation is another common function in games for determining things such as the location of new game objects appearing in the scene or the number of enemies in the next attack wave. From the line of code diceRoll = Random.Range(1, 6); you can probably guess what is going on, but go ahead and ⌘+' on Random.Range for the Scripting Reference (Figure 2-27):

Random.Range

static function **Range**(**min**: float, **max**: float): float;

Description

Returns a random float number between and min [inclusive] and max [inclusive] (Read Only).

```
// Instantiates prefab somewhere between -10.0 and 10.0 on the x-z plane
var prefab : GameObject;
function Start () {
        var position: Vector3 = Vector3(Random.Range(-10.0, 10.0), 0, Random.Range(-10.0, 10.0));
        Instantiate(prefab, position, Quaternion.identity);
}
```

static function **Range**(**min**: int, **max**: int): int;

Description

Returns a random integer number between min [inclusive] and max [exclusive] (Read Only).

If max equals min, min will be returned. The returned value will never be max unless min equals max.

```
// Loads a random level from the level list

Application.LoadLevel(Random.Range(0, Application.levelCount));
```

Figure 2-27. Random.Range description from the Unity Scripting Reference

Just as you suspected, when the Start() function is called, diceRoll is assigned a randomly generated number based on the two arguments in the parentheses, min and max. Notice these parameters are "inclusive," or you would have to use different arguments to generate the numbers 1 through 6.

Next, the switch statement takes the value assigned to diceRoll and compares it against the constant values of each case, in this example 1 through 6. When a matching case value is found, the statement block that follows is executed.

The break statement ends the execution of the switch statement. After the final case, you'll see a default statement that works similarly to the else statement—it is executed if none of the case values match the argument originally passed to the switch statement.

Loops

Loops are useful for repeating lines of code. You might be checking the state of a group of game objects, or creating new ones where you need to use identical lines of code for each item in the group.

The for Loop

To demonstrate a for loop, in MonoDevelop edit your code to the following:

```
#pragma strict

        var targets : int = 4;

function Start () {
        for(var i: int = 0; i < targets; i++)
        {
                Debug.Log("This is target #" + i);
        }
}
```

Breaking down the for loop into parts:

```
        (1)        (2)      (3)      (4)      (5) (6)
for(var i: int = 0; i < targets; i++)
    (7)
    {
                        (8)
        Debug.Log(" This is target #" + i);
(9)
  }
```

1. The keyword for.

2. Declaring the index variable as an integer and assigning an initial value of 0. Computers start counting at 0 instead of 1, which can take a little getting used to and is often mistaken as a bug when forgotten.

3. A semicolon separating the first and second components of the for statement.

4. The conditional statement. As long as the condition is met, the loop statement block will be executed. If the condition is not met, the loop is terminated and program execution jumps to the statement that follows the loop, in this case the closing braces of the Start() function.

5. A semicolon separates the second and third components of the for statement.

6. The increment of the loop. This could be written as i = i + 1, or even i += 1, but the increment operator ++ means to add 1 and is a nice shorthand notation. Here 1 is added to the index variable before it is evaluated by the conditional statement in the next iteration of the for loop. Similarly, the index variable can also be decremented using the decrement operator -- (or -=).

7. Open brace for the body of the for loop.

8. The statement block that contains the code to be executed on each iteration of the for loop.

9. Close brace for the body of the for loop. Like a function, the for loop ends with the close brace rather than a semicolon.

Run your script, and you'll see that you have four target statements reflecting the counting-from-zero effect (Figure 2-28).

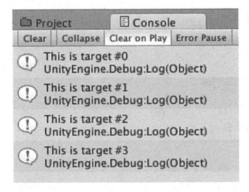

Figure 2-28. For loop output to the Console panel

The while Loop

The while loop gives you more flexibility because it will loop any number of times as long as the conditional results with true.

Change your code to the following:

```
#pragma strict

var numberOfTires : int = 0;
```

```
function Start () {
        while(numberOfTires < 4)
        {
                Debug.Log("I replaced an old tire on my car!");
                numberOfTires++;
        }
}
```

Breaking it down shows the following parts:

```
   (1)            (2)
while(numberOfTires < 4)
        (3)
        {
                        (4)
                Debug.Log("I replaced an old tire on my car!");
                numberOfTires++;
        (5)
        }
```

1. The while keyword.

2. The conditional statement.

3. Open braces for the body of the while loop.

4. The statement block that contains the code to be executed on each iteration of the while loop.

5. The close braces for the body of the while loop. Just as with the for loop, the while loop ends with the close braces rather than a semicolon.

One of the biggest differences here, and a common cause of problems, is that if your conditional expression never evaluates to false, the while loop continues to run. This is what is known as an **infinite loop**—something you do not want your game trapped in!

Run the script and you will see that you have put four new tires on your car. You could rewrite these simple examples using either a for loop or a while loop interchangeably. You will get a feel for the subtle difference between them when choosing to use one or the other as you continue to apply them in real game development scenarios.

As a rule of thumb, for loops are more commonly used in more precisely defined situations, such as when the number of loops to be executed is predetermined or if the same variable is used for the initial value, the conditional statement, and as the increment.

The do-while Loop

Just like the for loop, if the conditional for a while loop never resolves to true, then the statement block is never executed. There will be times when you want your statement block run at least once before the conditional is tested. The do-while loop expands on the while loop to give you this ability.

Edit your code as follows:

```
#pragma strict

function Start () {
        var someCondition : boolean = false;
        do
        {
                Debug.Log("Print something anyway");
        }
        while(someCondition == true);
}
```

Here the first thing you do is set the variable someCondition to false. After the keyword do, the body of the do statement is executed once before it gets to the while statement, where it finally has a condition to test. Based on your variable declaration, the conditional will resolve to false and the program exits the loop. Run your script, and the "Print something anyway" line appears once in the console as you expected.

The difference between a for loop and a while loop may not seem obvious, but you will get practice using these in upcoming demonstrations. You will get a much better feel for loops and when to use the various types in the context of game development.

Coordinate Geometry and Vectors

Okay, time for a little huddle. This book is written with the beginner in mind. Not the beginner who happens to have an advanced degree in mathematics, but the average person who happens to have an interest in game development . . . though of course I think that makes you much cooler than the average person. If you happen to have that degree in mathematics, then you will appreciate the elegant genius that it takes to make such a complex development tool like Unity so user-friendly.

You don't have to understand combustion-engine theory to drive a car, solid-state circuit design to use a computer, or anything about electric motors to use a drill. Most importantly, you don't have to be a math whiz to learn to develop games. You'll definitely pick up more than you might think as you go, and it won't even hurt. I promise.

The creators of Unity intend for it to be intuitive, meaning easy to use and understand, and they have been incredibly successful. "Intuitive" also means having a feeling or instinct for how something works, which you will quickly learn by doing. Experimenting to see what happens in your game is how you develop this intuition. Even when I wasn't just fooling around on purpose, I can't tell you how many times the difference between what I thought I told Unity to do and how it interpreted my scripts gave me unexpected results. But my computer never blew sparks or melted down, and often that botched result was as funny as a movie blooper. Learning game development really *is* entertaining—have fun with it!

Most games, especially 3D games, are all about movement. Vectors and Transforms are respectively some of the most commonly used structs (see hereafter) and classes that you will use. They describe where your game objects are and how they move. This section is a brief review of the basics of coordinate geometry and vector mathematics, along with the associated Unity variables and functions, that you can always refer back to when needed. As you work your way through this section, don't get hung up on the math. While I remember fondly my time at CalTech having to hand-jam vector calculations, you won't have to—Unity will handle this for you. For now your focus should be on learning the vocabulary and visualizing vectors and their functions in 3D space rather than the math itself.

Unity uses the Cartesian coordinate system for describing points in space using an x axis and y axis that are perpendicular to each other (Fig 2-29). The **origin** is the point where they intersect, defined where both the values of x and y are zero or (0, 0). Every unique point in 2D space can be described by its x and y value using the syntax (x, y).

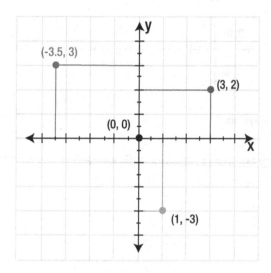

Figure 2-29. The Cartesian Coordinate system

The variables that you've used up to this point—int, float, boolean, and string—are classified as **value** data types because they contain a specific value such as 8, hello, or false. A more complex version of a value type variable is known as a **structure**, or **struct**. A struct is a variable containing an aggregate of values.

Vector2 is a struct that contains the x and y values to describe positions and vectors in two-dimensional space. (x, y) gives you the location of a point in 2D space. To describe a line or vector you would normally need to know the coordinates for the points at both ends of the line, but in Unity vectors are expressed as lines relative to the origin (0, 0), so (x, y) is enough information to describe the vector as well (Fig 2-30).

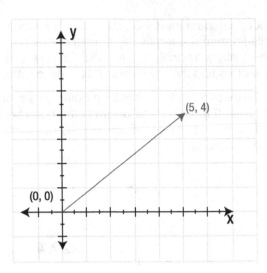

Figure 2-30. The Cartesian Coordinate system

Search for Vector2 in the Unity Scripting Reference (Figure 2-31).

Vector2

Description

Representation of 2D vectors and points.

This structure is used in some places to represent 2D positions and vectors (e.g. texture coordinates in a Mesh or texture offsets in Material). In the majority of other cases a Vector3 is used.

Figure 2-31. Vector2 description in the Unity Scripting Reference

In MonoDevelop, update your code to look like this:

```
#pragma strict

var myVector : Vector2 = Vector2(2, 3);
function Start () {
        Debug.Log(myVector);
}
```

Click Play to test and you'll see the (x, y) coordinates of (2, 3) that you assigned to myVector displayed in the Console panel (Figure 2-32).

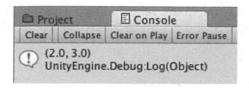

Figure 2-32. Vector2 coordinate (x, y) values displayed in the Console panel

Unity provides some commonly used static variables in the Scripting Reference (Figure 2-33).

Static Variables

kEpsilon	*Undocumented*.
one	Shorthand for writing Vector2(1, 1).
right	Shorthand for writing Vector2(1, 0).
up	Shorthand for writing Vector2(0, 1).
zero	Shorthand for writing Vector2(0, 0).

Figure 2-33. Vector2 static variables described in the Unity Scripting Reference

Replace myVector with Vector2.up in the Debug.Log statement to confirm that you get (0, 1) as the output in the Console. If you are wondering why there isn't a .down or .left, you just use -.up and -.right for their opposites.

The length of a vector is called its **magnitude**. You may or may not remember using the Pythagorean Theorem in geometry class to find the distance between two points, but Unity steps in here for you with Vector2.magnitude when you need to determine the distance between game objects. Click on "magnitude" to take a quick look at the description of Vector2.magnitude (Figure 2-34).

Vector2.magnitude

var **magnitude**: float;

Description

Returns the length of this vector (Read Only).

The length of the vector is square root of (x*x+y*y).

If you only need to compare magnitudes of some vectors, you can compare squared magnitudes of them using sqrMagnitude (computing squared magnitudes is faster).

See Also: sqrMagnitude.

Figure 2-34. Vector2.magnitude description from the Unity Scripting Reference

Unity is doing the calculations in terms of the vector's x and y coordinates, but you can see it is following the same formula with a, b, and c from geometry class (Fig 2-35):

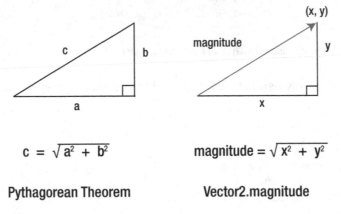

$$c = \sqrt{a^2 + b^2}$$

$$magnitude = \sqrt{x^2 + y^2}$$

Pythagorean Theorem   Vector2.magnitude

Figure 2-35. *Vector2 magnitude derived using the Pythagorean Theorem*

As an example, find c when a = 3 and b = 4. First, a^2 = 9 and b^2 = 16. Add them together to get 25, then take the square root of 25 to find the length c = 5. Now let Unity do the same calculation for the Vector2 (3, 4). Edit your script to the following:

```
#pragma strict

function Start () {
        var myVector : Vector2 = Vector2(3, 4);
        Debug.Log(myVector.magnitude);
}
```

Play to test and the Console displays the magnitude of 5.

Look again at the Vector2.magnitude description. Unity is giving you a tip: when you want to compare the magnitude of two vectors, you can also use sqrMagnitude. Either way you can determine if the magnitude of one vector is larger or smaller than the other, but using sqrMagnitude will work faster. Whether in the scripting references or the Unity Forums, you will often see comments regarding speed. Games take a lot of computational power, so the faster or more efficiently any individual computation can be accomplished, the smoother your game will function.

At the bottom of the Vector2 scripting reference, you'll also find some handy mathematical and comparison operators you can use (Figure 2-36).

Operators

operator -	Subtracts one vector from another.
operator !=	Returns true if vectors different.
operator *	Multiplies a vector by a number.
operator /	Divides a vector by a number.
operator +	Adds two vectors.
operator ==	Returns true if the vectors are equal.
Vector2	Converts a Vector3 to a Vector2.
Vector3	Converts a Vector2 to a Vector3.

Figure 2-36. *Vector2 operators described in the Unity Scripting Reference*

Three-dimensional space is handled much the same way, but with the value representing the third dimension added to the mix. The z axis is perpendicular to the x axis and y axis. In Unity, they are oriented such that x is laid out horizontally left and right across your computer monitor, y is vertically up and down on your monitor, and z is depth, or "into" and "out of" your monitor. Put another way, the xz plane is the "floor" and y is altitude. The origin is (0, 0, 0), representing the values of x, y, and z. In Unity this is also referred to as **world zero**—the center of your game world. Just as you saw in 2D space, a vector in 3D space is also expressed relative to the origin (Fig 2-37):

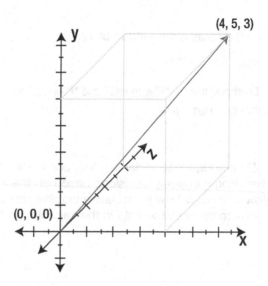

Figure 2-37. A vector in 3D space

Vector3 is a struct that holds the values for x, y, and z. Look up Vector3 in the Unity Scripting Reference, and you will find that it closely resembles Vector2 with handy, commonly used static variables, the x, y, and z component and vector magnitude values, and many of the same functions and operators.

To compare, take a look at Vector3.magnitude in the Unity Scripting Reference (Figure 2-38):

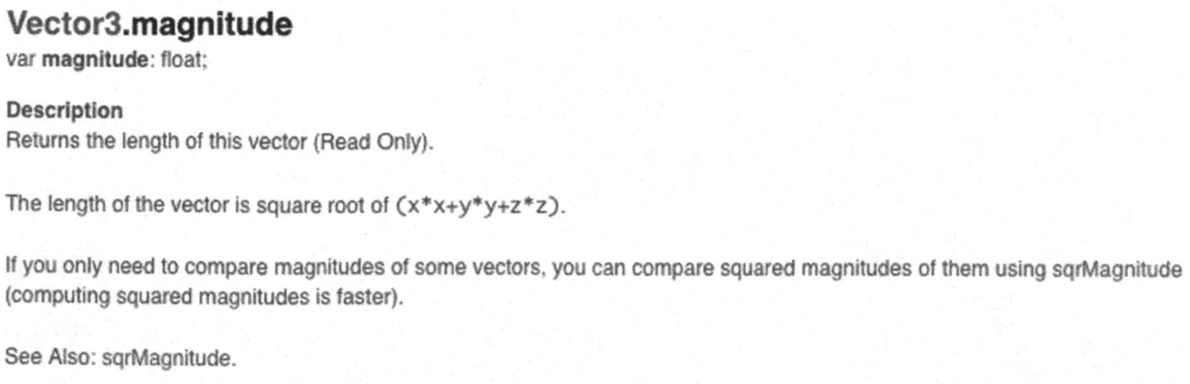

Vector3.magnitude
var **magnitude**: float;

Description
Returns the length of this vector (Read Only).

The length of the vector is square root of (x*x+y*y+z*z).

If you only need to compare magnitudes of some vectors, you can compare squared magnitudes of them using sqrMagnitude (computing squared magnitudes is faster).

See Also: sqrMagnitude.

Figure 2-38. Vector3.magnitude description in the Unity Scripting Reference

Now the calculation takes the z component value into account. Update your code to find the magnitude of a three-dimensional vector like so:

```
#pragma strict

function Start () {
        var myVector : Vector3 = Vector3(3, 4, 12);
        Debug.Log(myVector.magnitude);
}
```

Play-test, and the Console should display a magnitude of 13.

> **Note**   "Play," "Run," "Test," "Enter play mode," "Play to test," and "Playtest" are all interchangeable terms for playing the scene in the Unity editor Game view.

Whether you are using 2D or 3D vectors, these variables, functions, and operators comprise a good portion of the basic tools for handling gameplay decisions based on the locations and directions of your various game objects. Now you know how to declare variables including structs like Vector2 and Vector3, how to call functions to process the data in the variable, and where to find the built-in Unity functions.

Summary

You now know how to use the Unity scripting editor MonoDevelop, and have been introduced to basic programming terms and concepts—good job! While this chapter gives you a necessary foundation by serving as both an introduction and a reference, from here on out you will get to see the result of your scripts on game objects within the Unity editor. And by results I mean you are on your way to more action, explosions, and sound effects—woo!

Chapter 3

Making a Simple Scene

So far you've set up your game development environment, and now have a familiarity with programming basics, your scripting tool MonoDevelop, and the Unity Scripting Reference. This chapter's focus is on your primary game development tool, Unity, and how to create and manage the fundamental parts that make up a rudimentary game scene.

A game is made up of scenes, a scene is made up of game objects, a game object is made up of components, and components have properties that are governed by their internal functions, as you can see in Figure 3-1. In this chapter you will get a hands-on introduction to putting these together in a scene using the Unity editor interface, along with an introduction to the Standard Assets packages Unity provides for your convenience.

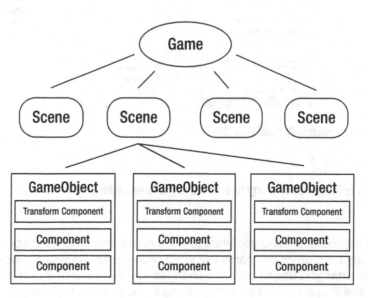

Figure 3-1. Elements of a game in Unity

New Project, New Scene

Time to get to it. As you did in Chapter 2, create a new project using the Unity editor top menu to select File ➤ New Project. The Project Wizard window will open. Name your project, make sure the Create new Project tab is selected, leave the setup default as 3D, and create your new project. As before, your new project with an empty scene will appear in the Unity editor. In that fast and simple process, Unity set up a ready-to-play skeleton game for you.

If you are curious, you can take a peek at the contents of the basic files necessary for a game in Finder or Explorer (Figure 3-2). **Assets** are items you create or import into your project such as models, animations, scripts, and audio clips; these are automatically put into the Assets folder. Unity accepts a wide variety of file types, then converts them to a compatible version internally. At the same time, Unity generates additional data called **metadata**, placed in the Library folder that, among other things, helps it know where to find these converted assets and how they relate to one another as you use them in your game. Unity automatically organizes these folders and files in a particular fashion, so if you move these folders or files around the Unity editor won't be able to find them.

Figure 3-2. New project files automatically created by Unity

> **Note**   Always use the Project view to organize assets in the Assets folder.

Back in the Unity editor, the first thing you want to do is name and save your scene. Unity handles saving a little differently than other programs like word processors. As you are working on your game scene, Save Scene is what you use to save the changes you've made to it. While you might think from its name that Save Project would save everything in the project, including the scene you are working on, it actually saves everything in the project *except* for the current scene, such as assets or overall project settings. As with anything involving a computer, it is a good habit to save your work frequently.

Visually, a **scene** is the 2D or 3D space displayed in the Scene view of the Unity editor that contains the content of the game in the form of game objects. While one scene could constitute an entire game, typically unique scenes are used for each of the levels and menus that make up the whole game.

The dimensional space of the scene is defined using the Cartesian coordinate system. To see this, in the Unity editor top menu select GameObject ➤ Create Other ➤ Cube (Figure 3-3).

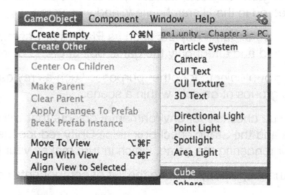

Figure 3-3. Unity top menu GameObject ➤ Create Other ➤ Cube

The new game object appears in the Hierarchy view as "Cube," a cube with its gizmo appears in the Scene view, and its components appear in the Inspector view. In the Inspector view, you'll see in the Transform component that the position of the game object is described in terms of its coordinates (x, y, z). By default, Unity places the new game object at the origin of (0, 0, 0), or world zero. (Figure 3-4).

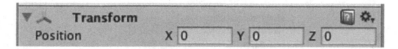

Figure 3-4. Cube game object position displayed in the Inspector panel

The Game Object

While game objects are best thought of as containers for components, for your convenience Unity provides primitive game object shapes like Cube ready made with some basic components you will see listed in the Inspector (Figure 3-5).

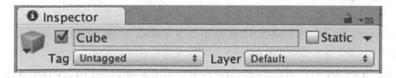

Figure 3-5. Cube game object header displayed in the Inspector panel

Starting with the header in the Inspector panel, as you can see in Figure 3-5, the first checkbox indicates the game object is active in the scene. If you deselect it, you will notice the cube disappears from the Scene view but not the Hierarchy view. It hasn't been deleted from your project; deselecting it allows you to move it out of the way while you are working on something else. Leave this box checked.

Next, the default name of the game object is Cube. If you change the name in the Inspector panel, you will see the change reflected in the Hierarchy view, and vice versa.

Tags are used to identify groups of game objects such as Players or Enemies. This enables you to write scripts that can easily find and affect only the game object group of interest.

Layers is a different way to group objects for other purposes such as ray casting, lighting, and rendering limited to specific groups of objects within a scene.

The Static checkbox should be checked for environmental objects that will not be moving around in your scene. Using Layers and the Static checkbox helps Unity reduce the overall amount of calculations it must make for rendering the game, which in turn makes your game run more smoothly.

The rest of the contents in the Inspector panel are the list of components comprising the Cube game object.

Components

The true power of the Unity game engine is in its components. Components govern the look, behavior, and interaction of the game objects. Unity provides you with bunches of ready-made components from which to build your game objects. Take a look at the Component top menu and the contents of the drop-downs in it (Figure 3-6).

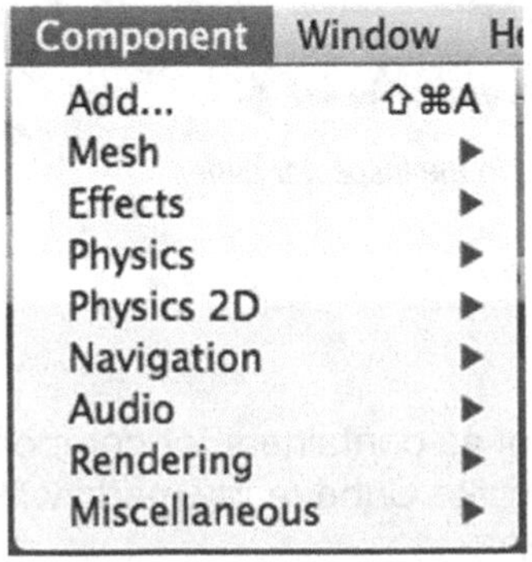

Figure 3-6. Unity Component top menu

You can add components to game objects through this menu, or as you did with your script in Chapter 2 by using the Add Component button in the Inspector panel.

Most important is the Transform component, the one component that every game object must have. The position, rotation, and scale properties of Transform define the game object's existence in the scene in terms of location, orientation relative to the scene, and size. Even an Empty game object must have a Transform component.

The Inspector panel doesn't just display a list of the components attached to a game object; it is also an interface for configuring the component properties. You can type in new values to change any of the default settings for the trio of Transform properties. Alternatively, you can visually manipulate the game object gizmo in the Scene view by clicking and dragging the gizmo handles, and see these changes reflected in the Inspector. Go ahead and give it a try. Remember, you can use the W, E, and R keys to quickly alternate between the Transform properties.

In the upper right corner, the little blue book with the question mark is a link to Unity's Component Reference. The gear icon gives you a means to quickly reset to the component's default values, along with other editing functions (Figure 3-7). When you are done test-driving the Cube transform gizmo, reset the Transform properties.

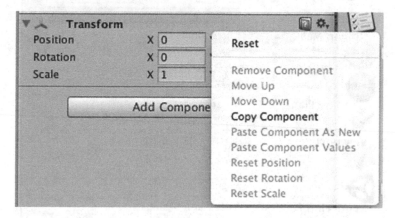

Figure 3-7. Component gear icon drop-down menu

Unity expedites the game development process by providing out of the box many of the components that game developers most commonly use. Scripts are components, too—they also affect the look, behavior, or interaction of game objects. Scripts are essentially custom components that you create for the unique requirements of your game.

The Main Camera

The new scene wasn't created completely empty; it comes prepopulated with one game object, the Main Camera game object. Like any game object, you can move it, apply scripts to it, and do anything else that applies to game objects in general. The Main Camera is the viewport through which the player sees the scene. It's not much of a game if you can't see it, so it makes sense that this is always included in a new scene. Select the Main Camera in the Scene view or Hierarchy view to display its contents in the Inspector (Figure 3-8).

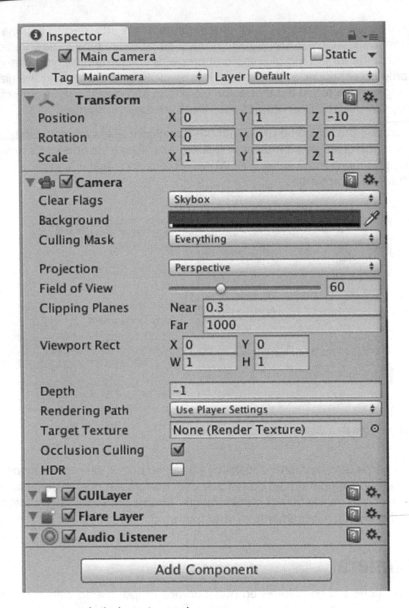

Figure 3-8. Main Camera components in the Inspector panel

Transform

As always, the mandatory Transform component comes first.

Tip   A good habit to develop is to list the components in a consistent order to make them easier to find.

While any new game object you create will be automatically placed at the origin, the Main Camera's Transform placement it such that these new objects appear in its field of view, as helpfully displayed for you in the Camera Preview located in the lower right corner of the Scene view (Figure 3-9). Enter Play mode and you'll find the Game view was accurately represented, then exit Play mode.

Figure 3-9. Camera Preview showing the Cube game object

Camera

The Main Camera is a game object that contains a camera component. For simplicity it's easier to just call it "camera." The actual camera component has a number of properties, briefly described next.

Clear Flags

Clear Flags is used to set the background. The background is whatever is left over after all of the game elements have been drawn. The default is Skybox, but as yet there is no Skybox asset set in this project. Let's take care of that now.

In the Unity top menu select Assets ➤ Import Package ➤ Skyboxes. The Import window will have every skybox option from the Standard Assets checked already. Leave them checked, click Import, and you'll see them appear in the Project view. You might just see a Standard Assets folder appear. Go ahead and expand the Standard Assets/Skyboxes/Textures folders until you see the selection of skybox textures (Figure 3-10). Take a moment to check them out and decide which one you want to apply to the scene.

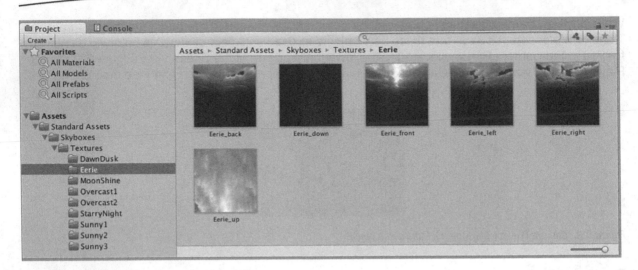

Figure 3-10. Skyboxes displayed in the Project view

Again in the Unity top menu select Edit ➤ Render Settings. The Inspector now displays the rendering properties that apply to this scene. Each scene's rendering property settings are unique to the scene. You can set the skybox material you chose by clicking the little target icon to the right of the Skybox Material property in the Inspector to get a pop-up window of the skybox materials, or you can drag the material from the Skybox folder in the Property view and drop it directly into the Skybox Material property in the Inspector (Figure 3-11). The property field will turn blue when you have the material dragged into the correct position.

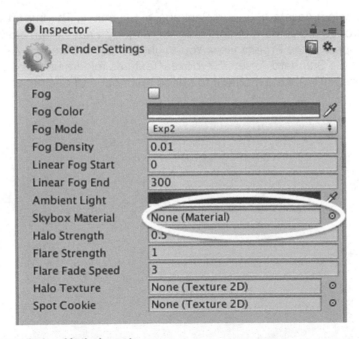

Figure 3-11. Render Settings displayed in the Inspector

Pan around the Scene view to check out your new skybox background, and notice that it also appeared in the Camera Preview. Any part of the screen not occupied with game elements will now be filled in with the skybox.

You can have more than one camera in a scene. In the Inspector panel, the Depth only drop-down setting for Clear Flags is used in this scenario, where the different cameras could be used for a heads-up display (HUD)or mini-map. Each of these different cameras' views are layered on top of each other as seen by the player. Clear Flags for additional cameras are set to Depth only, while the Main Camera's Clear Flags setting usually remains as Skybox and has the lowest depth setting to make it the scene's final background.

The Don't Clear drop-down setting means the previous frame is not cleared before the next one is drawn, resulting in a smear-looking effect. This isn't often used.

Background

With Solid Color selected as your Clear Flags property, you can then use the Background property to select a color that indicates screen areas remaining after the game elements have been drawn.

Culling Mask

Culling Mask designates which layers from your scene will be rendered by the camera. Layers are used to group objects. You may only want a certain layer of objects to be rendered by one camera while other layers are rendered by another. As an example, Unity recommends as a good practice to keep your User Interface (UI) in a separate layer (Figure 3-12).

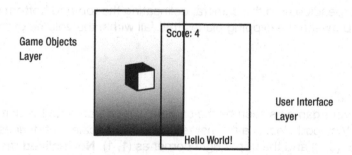

Figure 3-12. Keeping the Game Objects layer and User Interface layer separate

Projection

The Projection property toggles between Perspective and Orthographic views of the camera. The camera will render everything inside a special shape called a **frustum** (see Figure 3-13).

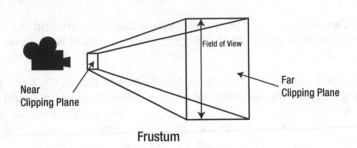

Figure 3-13. *The frustum shown with the near clipping pane and far clipping pane*

When the near clipping plane is smaller than the far clipping plane in Perspective mode, the rendered scene gives a sense of diminishing perspective or a foreshortening effect, where objects and even parts of objects appear smaller the farther away they are. This is the more common projection used in 3D games. In Orthographic mode, the near and far clipping planes are the same size, causing objects to be viewed in parallel by the camera. This mode is more common for 2D games, or 2D layers of a game like the UI. In the Unity editor you can see the outline of the frustum in the Scene view when the Main Camera is selected.

Field of View

The vertical viewing angle of the camera, measured along the local y axis in degrees.

Clipping Planes

Clipping Planes are perpendicular to the camera, delineating the top and bottom of the pyramid-like frustum. Only objects between the clipping planes that fall within the volume of the frustum will be rendered.

Viewport Rect

Ultimately the view of your game as seen by the camera is rendered onto the screen, which is two-dimensional. The Viewport Rect is a normalized coordinate scale that defines the lower left corner of the screen as (0, 0) and the upper right corner as (1, 1). **Normalized** means that no matter what the actual screen size is, say on a monitor or a handheld device, (0, 0) is still the lower left of the screen and (1, 1) is the upper right. It is used to designate the relative location on the screen where the camera view is to be drawn.

Depth

As discussed previously in Clear Flags, when using multiple cameras Depth is where you designate each camera's layer level, with the lowest value being the bottom, and so its view is rendered first.

Component Reference

The remaining camera component properties are far more advanced use than the scope of this book. For a highly detailed description of any of these properties, click on the blue book/question mark to open the Component Reference for Camera in your web browser.

> **Tip**   You should always review the documentation to familiarize yourself with new components.

Seriously, take the time to review the documentation. You'll find that much like the useful sample code snippets in the Scripting Reference, Unity provides you with super-handy practical hints for using components (Figure 3-14).

Hints
- Cameras can be instantiated, parented, and scripted just like any other GameObject.
- To increase the sense of speed in a racing game, use a high **Field of View**.
- Cameras can be used in physics simulation if you add a **Rigidbody** Component.
- There is no limit to the number of Cameras you can have in your scenes.
- Orthographic cameras are great for making 3D user interfaces.
- If you are experiencing depth artifacts (surfaces close to each other flickering), try setting **Near Plane** to as large as possible.
- Cameras cannot render to the Game Screen and a Render Texture at the same time, only one or the other.
- Pro license holders have the option of rendering a Camera's view to a texture, called Render-to-Texture, for even more unique effects.
- Unity comes with pre-installed Camera scripts, found in **Components->Camera Control**. Experiment with them to get a taste of what's possible.

Figure 3-14. Hints for Camera found in Unity's Component Reference

GUILayer

The GUILayer attached to the Main Camera allows rendering of GUIText and GUITextures, which are 2D objects commonly used as parts of the UI. The checkbox is used for enabling or disabling the GUILayer.

Flare Layer

Lens flares are an optical effect from the glass lenses in a real camera. This effect is simulated with FlareLayer component and will be demonstrated later in this chapter.

Audio Listener

Sound is also important to the user experience. Unity gives you a selection between 2D and 3D sound. An audio source is a game object containing the sound clip you assign and acts as a speaker for it. You might place any number of audio sources throughout your scene. 2D sound plays at a constant volume throughout the game and is more appropriate for ambient background sound effects or music. 3D sounds are location dependent in the scene; they get louder when approached and fainter the farther away they are. This variation in volume to produce the 3D effect is handled automatically by Unity, so there are no properties in the Audio Listener to adjust.

The Audio Listener gathers the sound from the various audio sources to deliver to the player through their device speakers. Only one Audio Listener is needed for each scene. Unity attaches it to the Main Camera so any new scene will be audio capable, but you could move it to another game object, typically the player, depending on your game needs.

Light

At this point you have a new scene with a skybox background and a Cube game object. If you enter Play mode, the cube remains dark. No matter how much light might be present in the skybox texture, it is just a texture, or image of a sky, and does not project light onto the game objects in the scene. For this you need a Light game object. Examples include:

1. *Directional light*: Acts like sunlight to illuminate every game object in the scene, though it does not come from a single point source.

2. *Spot light*: Cone-shaped area of light from a single point that acts like a spotlight or flashlight.

3. *Point light*: Acts like a light bulb, shining in all directions from a central point.

4. *Area light*: Used for baking into lightmaps and is beyond the scope of this book.

Using either the Create button in Hierarchy view or Game Object ➤ Create Other from the top menu, add a directional light to the scene. If you select Main Camera, you'll see in the Camera Preview that the cube has brightened considerably. Reselect the Directional light and take a look at the properties in the Inspector.

The first property is Type. Even though you created a directional light, you can change it to another type of light using this drop-down menu. Notice the Inspector remains context sensitive and the properties change depending on the type selected, but the name "Directional light" in the Hierarchy view does not reflect any changes made here.

Common Light Properties

I want to mention again the importance of hands-on experimenting with Unity. The following description of light properties is not meant to come across as a droning lecture—these properties are better seen and experienced rather than passively read about. Though I'm not including step-by-step instructions for each one, I highly encourage you to test each one in Unity so you can see what it does both in the Scene view and in Play mode. Remember, you can always use the Light component's gear icon to reset the properties.

Color

Clicking in the box opens a pop-up color picker for selecting light of any color. If you click on the dropper icon, you'll see the color in the box changes to reflect the color of whatever the mouse cursor happens to be hovering over—for example, using the mouse cursor to grab a sample color from an image displayed in another window on your computer screen.

Intensity

This is the brightness of the light, with 8 being the brightest and 0 essentially unlit. Though the value won't change if you change the light Type, when you create a new light the default for a Directional is 0.5 and the default for Point and Spot lights is 1.

Cookie

A cookie acts like a mask or screen in front of the light, giving it a shadowed pattern. In the Unity editor, use the gear icon of the Transform component to select Reset. Now set the light Transform position to (0, 0, −2) and Type to Spot. From the top menu select Assets ➤ Import Package ➤ Light Cookies. The Import Packages window will open with a list of cookies available in Unity's Standard Assets. Click Import, then check the Assets folder in the Project panel to find the Light Cookies folder has joined the Skyboxes folder in the Standard Assets folder (Figure 3-15).

Figure 3-15. Contents of the Light Cookies package in Unity's Standard Assets

Drag any one of these into the Cookie property in the Inspector panel to see how the light pattern shows up on the Cube game object.

To clear the Cookie property, click the target icon to the right of the property field for the Select Texture pop-up (Figure 3-16). Here you'll find all the textures from all of the packages that you've imported so far. At the top of the list, select None, see the change reflected in the Cookie property, and close the pop-up.

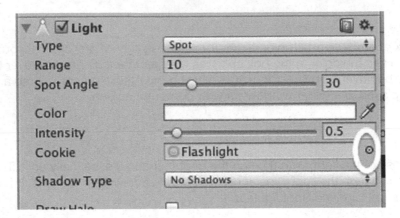

Figure 3-16. Target icon for opening the Select Texture pop-up window

If you happen to have Photoshop skills, you can find instructions for making your own Cookies in the Unity Manual under Frequently Asked Questions ➤ Graphics Questions ➤ How do I make a Spot Light Cookie?

Shadow Type (Pro Only)

When you are ready to kick your game up a notch, you will definitely want to take a look at the many additional effects available in Unity Pro. Along with new features, improved developer tools, and more target platforms, Unity has also recently revamped its pricing structure to make the Pro version much more accessible to the indie developer. You can find more information about this on the Unity web site by selecting Buy in the top menu.

Draw Halo

The "halo" of the Draw Halo property gives an effect of particles in the air around the light when checked.

Flare

Set the light Transform position to (0, 2, 3) and Type to Point. From the top menu select Assets ➤ Import Package ➤ Light Flares. The Import Packages window will open with a list of light flares available in Unity's Standard Assets. Click Import, then check the Assets folder in the Project panel to find the Light Flares folder has joined the Light Cookies and Skyboxes folders in the Standard Assets folder. Drag the Sun asset into the Flare property window and see its effect in the Scene view or the Game view (Figure 3-17).

Figure 3-17. Game views showing Light with and without Sun light flare effect

Render Mode

This designates the importance of the light. Calculating lights and shadows can take up a lot of computational power at runtime. Things that take a lot of computational power are referred to as "expensive" when they affect the quality and performance of the game. Rating the relative importance of a light assists Unity in optimizing the performance of the game, a topic covered later in this book.

Culling Mask

This works the same as the Culling Mask property in the Camera component, where you can identify which layers you want affected by the light.

Lightmapping

Realtime Only means the light is used for dynamically lighting the scene at runtime. Baked Only refers to lightmapping, which is beyond the scope of this book. Auto allows for both.

Other Properties

There are also a few properties that are specific to the type of light you choose. These properties will appear in the context-sensitive Inspector depending upon your selection.

Range

For Point and Spot lights, Range refers to the effective distance of the light emitted from the source. Game objects outside of the range will not be illuminated. With the light selected, the range is represented visually in the Scene view with a yellow sphere.

Spot Angle

For Spot light. Measured in degrees, the Spot Angle determines the width of the cone of light coming from a Spot light.

The Cube

It's time to take a closer look at the Cube game object. Select it to display its components in the Inspector (Figure 3-18).

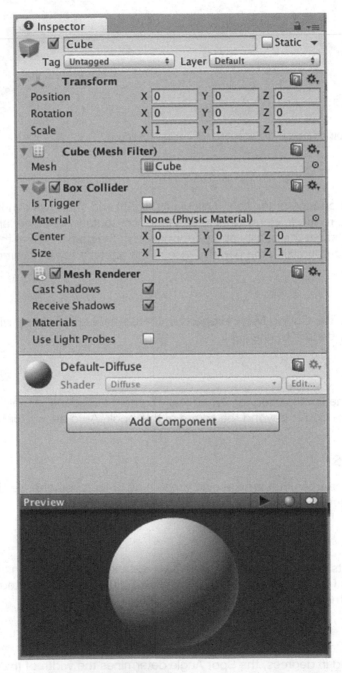

Figure 3-18. Cube game object components in the Inspector

Transform

By now you are familiar with the Transform component, its Position, Rotation, and Scale properties, and their respective hotkeys and gizmos. One thing you may have noticed about the gizmos is that Unity color-coded them to be easily remembered, where (x, y, z) = (r, g, b) for red, green, and blue.

One comment about scaling game objects: for performance purposes it is best if the model is scaled appropriately for your game prior to its import into Unity.

Mesh Filter

Before talking about the Mesh Filter property, first a little discussion about what a mesh is. All 3D game object shapes are fundamentally made up of interconnected triangles called **polygons**. Each polygon is defined by its three sides (or **edges),** and the points where these edges meet, called **vertices** or **verts**. The **mesh** is the collection of polygons making up the 3D geometry of a game object. To see the polygons that make up the Cube game object, in the Scene view control bar select Wireframe (Figure 3-19).

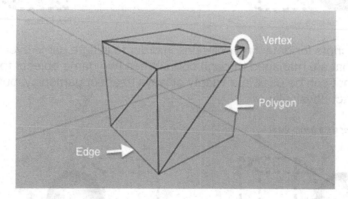

Figure 3-19. Scene view wireframe of Cube game object

The mesh asset named in the Mesh Filter's Mesh property holds the vertex coordinates and other data describing the model geometry mathematically. The more polygons, the more data your computer has to process. This means that polygon count can have an impact on game performance. The Mesh Filter passes this mesh data to the Mesh Renderer for the model to be rendered, making it visible as a light gray object just as you see the cube now.

Box Collider

The Box Collider uses similar Cube mesh data for purposes other than rendering the model to the screen. While the Mesh Filter and Mesh Renderer make the game object visible, a **collider** is an invisible component used to detect contact with other game objects that have collider or Rigidbody components. When these two game objects collide, the Collider component passes information about the game objects to the game engine.

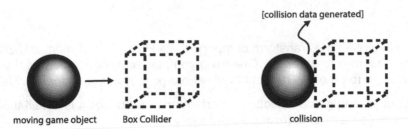

Colliders use the game object model's volume to detect whether or not an impact with another game object has occurred. At least one of the involved game objects must have also have a Rigidbody component attached for them to react physically with each other in the game world space.

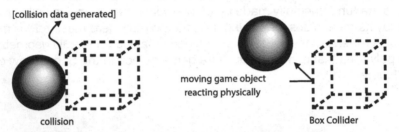

Triggers are used in scripts for detecting collisions in order to initiate game events other than physical interactions that are managed through code. When two game objects touch, data about the objects is generated that can be used in a variety of ways to affect gameplay, but the game objects do not appear to interact physically.

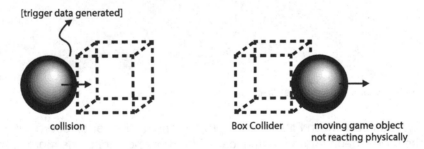

When used as a collider in physical interactions where at least one game object also has a Rigidbody component attached, the Physic Material attached to the Material property affects the way the physics engine determines the collision behavior. For example, a Physic Material might give the game object more or less "bounciness."

A collider does not have to match the shape of the game object it is attached to. Simple collider shapes can also be put together and used for a more complex 3D model. The Center and Size properties are used to position and scale this collider relative to the game object model. You will learn more about colliders, triggers, Physic Materials, and the physics engine in Chapter 6.

Mesh Renderer

The Mesh Renderer assembles the geometry data passed from the Mesh Filter that determines the shape of the model and puts it together with the material, textures, lights, and shadows to render the model to the screen. The properties are for Unity Pro users and are beyond the scope of this book.

Material

Materials set the appearance of the model, such as the difference between a dull or shiny reflective quality, by combining **shader** scripts and **texture** images. See Figure 3-20 for examples from the dozens of shaders that Unity provides.

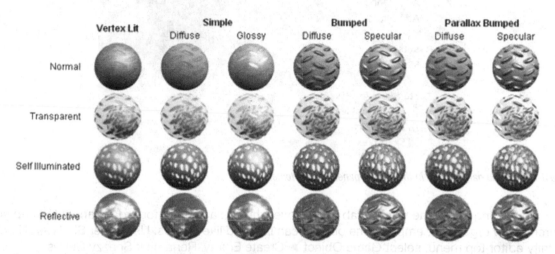

Figure 3-20. Examples of some of the available shaders as shown in the Unity User Manual

Time to make the cube a little snazzier. In the Unity editor top menu, select Assets ➤ Import New Asset… to open a pop-up window. Browse your files for an image you like or use the pink rose image included in the downloadable resources for this book (you can find these resources at http://www.apress.com/9781430265863). Click Import and the image file will appear in the Project panel. Drag the image to the cube in the Scene view and several things happen. A material incorporating the new texture image is created and appears in the Materials folder in the Project view, while at the same time the new material is applied to the faces of the cube, as you can see in the Scene view. The image file originally imported into the Assets folder is still there in its original form.

Prefabs

Unity is all about efficient game development. Now that you have configured a snazzy cube, you can store it as a prefab to be used to quickly create more snazzy cubes for your game. Organization is key to efficiency, so first create a Prefabs folder to hold this and any future prefabs you create for this scene.

In the Project panel select Create ➤ Folder and name it Prefabs. In the Hierarchy view, first rename Cube to Pink Rose Cube by double-clicking slowly. Once renamed, drag it from the Hierarchy view and drop it into the Prefabs folder. Doing this creates a template for this game object, distinct from the original cube (Figure 3-21). In the Hierarchy view, go ahead and delete the game object by selecting it, then pressing ⌘+Backspace.

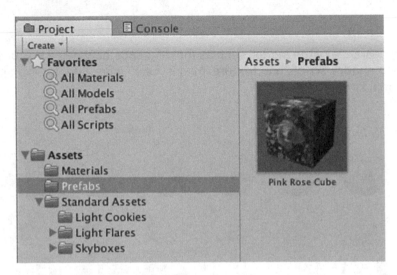

Figure 3-21. Prefab game object in the Project panel Prefabs folder

Before populating the scene with prefab cube clones, here is a nifty tip for organization: to keep your Hierarchy view organized, empty game objects can be used like folders. Use either Shift+⌘+N or, in the Unity editor top menu, select Game Object ➤ Create Empty. Rename it Snazzy Cubes.

From the Prefabs folder in the Project panel, drag a Pink Rose Cube and drop it into Snazzy Cubes in the Hierarchy view. The new prefab game object appears at origin in the Scene view. With this new game object selected, press ⌘+D (D for duplicate) or from the top menu use Edit ➤ Duplicate to create a new instance of the game object. A second Pink Rose Cube game object appears in the Hierarchy view, indented under Snazzy Cubes to indicate it is a child object of the Snazzy Cubes parent object (Figure 3-22).

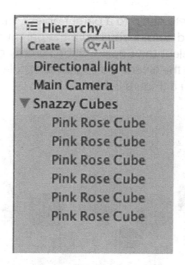

Figure 3-22. *Parent-child relationships displayed in the Hierarchy view*

The Scene view appears the same because this second game object was placed at the origin just like the first. Use the gizmo to reposition the objects. Repeat this until you have a half-dozen game objects distributed around your scene near one another where you can see them all at once (Figure 3-23).

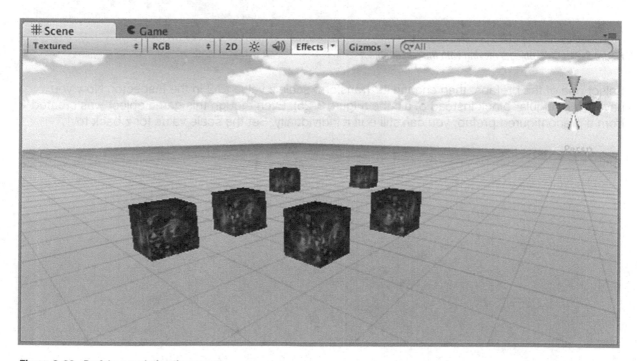

Figure 3-23. *Prefabs populating the scene*

When game objects have a child relationship to a parent object, their Transform position becomes relative to the parent instead of world zero. If you move the parent object, the child objects will maintain that relative positioning. Select the Snazzy Cubes empty game object in the Hierarchy view. Using its gizmo that now appears in the Scene view, grab a handle and move it around. As you can see, all of the cubes are moving with it (Figure 3-24).

Figure 3-24. Child objects moving with the parent object

Select one of the prefabs, then change its Transform scale z value to 2 in the Inspector. Now you have a rectangular block instead of a cube (Figure 3-25). Even though this game object was created from a preconfigured prefab, you can still edit it individually. Set the scale value for z back to 1.

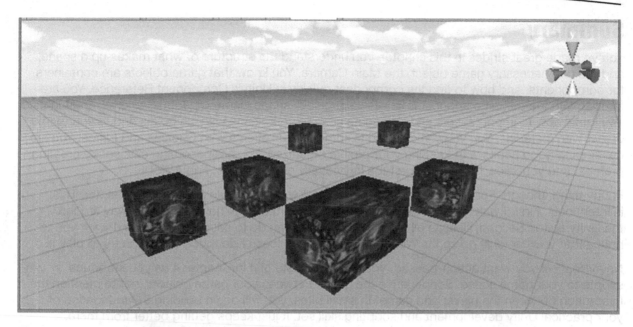

Figure 3-25. Prefab game object edited individually

Now select the prefab Pink Rose Cube game object in the Prefabs folder. In the inspector, change its Transform scale y value to 2. This time, all of the prefabs in your Scene view are tall rectangular blocks (Figure 3-26). If you make changes to the properties of your prefab template, the changes are reflected in all of the instances of the prefab.

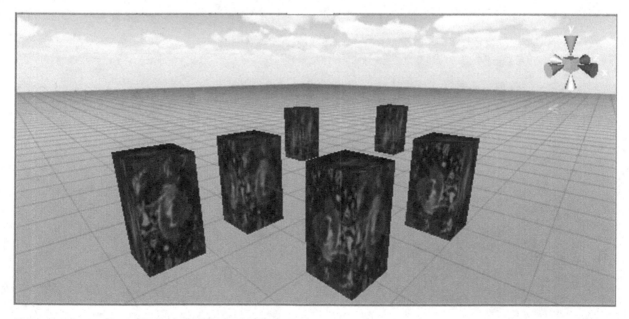

Figure 3-26. All prefabs affected by editing the prefab template

Summary

You've made great strides in this chapter. You understand the structure of what makes up a scene, and the one necessary game object, the Main Camera. You know that game objects are containers for components, and how to find the component quickly in Unity's Component Reference. You are familiar with the default components of Unity's primitive shape Game Objects, Cameras, and Lights. You know how to import assets and add some color to your scene with skyboxes and to your game object with materials. You've even dabbled in some special effects with Cookies and Flares. You are developing good habits with keeping your project organized. You are becoming efficient by creating prefabs, and you know how to edit prefabs individually or as a group. Fantastic!

Funny thing, though. For a book about scripting, there wasn't a single script in this chapter. This is intentional. First, I want you to have a chance to get comfortable navigating your way around the Unity editor. Second, despite all the nifty things you can do to set up your scene, I want you to notice that you can only go so far. Without scripts, it just doesn't do much when you try to play it.

Never fear—if you want action-packed, you will get a taste of it in Chapter 4 as you introduce scripts to your game scene. Scripts drive the action between your game objects, not to mention the interaction between the player and game. In small bites, you will begin building the foundation of your practical Unity development and scripting skill set. It just keeps getting better from there, as you add animation, real-life physics behavior, particle effects, and more.

Chapter 4

Using Scripts and the GameObject

Now that you have programming basics under your belt and a good grasp on the Unity editor and accompanying developer tools, it's time to introduce scripting to the game scene.

Scripts work hand-in-hand with the Unity game engine. Your scripts customize game object behaviors using the classes, functions, and variables of the Unity API. You've already seen when you create a new project, Unity creates a very basic, functional game that consists of one empty scene. Similarly, when you create a new script, Unity populates it with an empty Start() and Update() function.

The Unity game engine does a lot of work behind the scenes. It runs the Start() and Update() functions on every game object whether you attach a script or not. When you add code between the curly braces of the Start() or Update() functions like you did in Chapter 2, you are **overriding** the function.

The Unity game engine will still run the Start() and Update() functions at the appropriate time during game initiation and play. But where initially they were empty and did nothing, adding your code has redefined what occurs within the game when each of these functions is called.

It is important to understand a little of this behind-the-scenes action. You need to understand when the game engine is calling the various functions in order to decide which function is the right one to override so the game objects behave the way you want them to.

You'll start using some of the programming commands introduced in Chapter 2 to affect the game object's behavior either directly or with player interaction. You'll also start using classes and functions from the Unity API that are common to just about every game genre.

I strongly recommend that you take the time to type the sample code directly into the script yourself rather than cutting and pasting it. It does take a little longer, but that's the point. Typing it in yourself forces you to slow down and focus on each piece of the code, which in turn helps you remember and recall the concepts learned here.

Scripts as Behavior Components

Continuing on from our previous project, select Assets ➤ Import Package ➤ Scripts in the editor top menu (as shown in Figure 4-1).

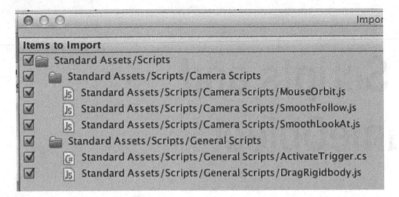

Figure 4-1. Scripts found in Unity's Standard Assets

Import all, and in your Project panel you'll see a new Scripts folder appears in the Standard Assets folder. Double-click the Scripts folder to open it, then select the Camera Scripts folder to reveal the contents. Here you'll find the three scripts: MouseOrbit, SmoothFollow and SmoothLookAt, as you can see in Figure 4-2.

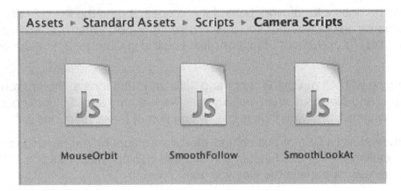

Figure 4-2. Standard Assets camera scripts

The MouseOrbit script is going to act as a behavior component for the Main Camera. The camera's viewpoint will be focused on a single game object and you will be able to control its movement around the game object with the mouse.

You can add the MouseOrbit script to the Main Camera a number of ways. You can drag it from the Project panel and drop it on Main Camera in the Hierarchy view, or you can drop it directly on the Main Camera game object in the Scene view. When you try the second option, you'll see a green circle with a white plus in it when you have dragged it close enough to the Main Camera game object.

A third way is to select the Main Camera in the Hierarchy view, then use the Add Component button that appears in the Inspector. You'll see a Component pop-up window that has already organized components by behavior, in this case those scripts involving camera behavior into a Camera-Control menu selection. Click it to see the script icons and select Mouse Orbit from the list (Figure 4-3).

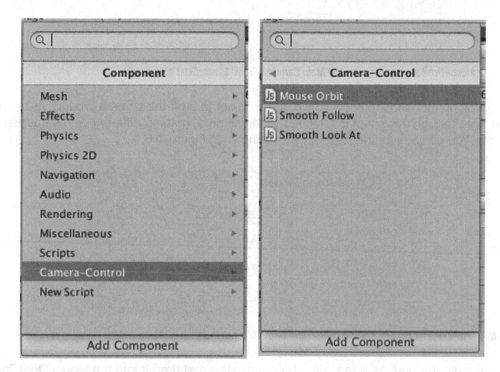

Figure 4-3. Using Add Component to attach the MouseOrbit script

If you're trying out each of these methods, remember you can remove the component through the same gear icon you used for resetting component property values (Figure 4-4).

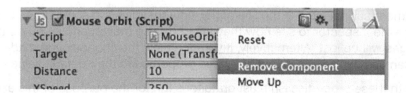

Figure 4-4. Removing a component from the gear drop-down menu in the Inspector

In Chapter 2 you learned that if you declare a variable as public, it will appear in the Inspector view as an editable property. In Figure 4-5 you see the properties in the MouseOrbit component compared to the public variables declared in the MouseOrbit script. You can compare for yourself by selecting the MouseOrbit script icon in the Project panel; the script will appear in the Inspector.

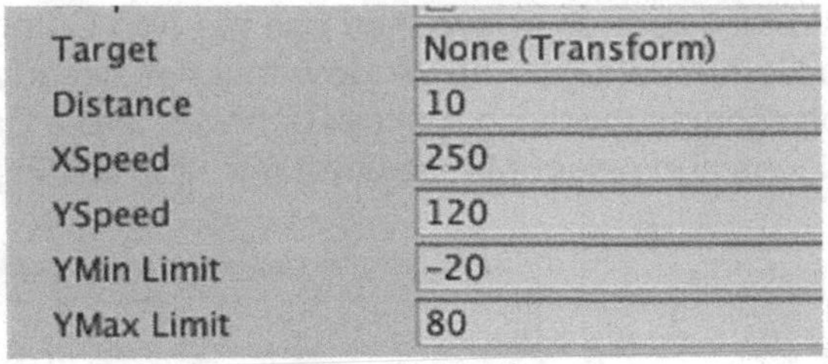

Target	None (Transform)	var target : Transform; var distance = 10.0;
Distance	10	
XSpeed	250	var xSpeed = 250.0; var ySpeed = 120.0;
YSpeed	120	
YMin Limit	-20	var yMinLimit = -20;
YMax Limit	80	var yMaxLimit = 80;

Figure 4-5. Left: MouseOrbit script component of Main Camera. Right: MouseOrbit script code

The MouseOrbit script needs to know which game object to orbit the camera around. Its default is "None," so even though this script is attached to the camera, nothing different would happen if you played it now. You can see the target property as shown in Figure 4-6.

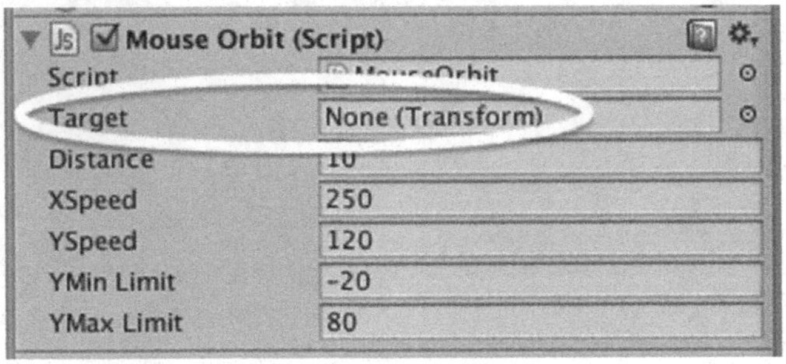

Figure 4-6. Target property of the MouseOrbit component of the Main Camera

Select one of the cube prefabs listed in the Hierarchy view and drop it into the MouseOrbit Target property in the Inspector. The cube's name should replace the word None.

Play (⌘+P), and see how the camera moves in conjunction with your mouse movement while staying focused on the cube you selected. Look around and check out the flare effect you have on your light—it's even remarkable with movement.

With the Main Camera still selected in the Hierarchy, now try adjusting some of these MouseOrbit script properties in the Inspector to see how they affect mouse movement. If you do this during Play mode, your changes will be lost. Alternatively, if you don't like the changes you made while out of Play mode, you can use the gear icon to reset these properties to their default values.

Playing around with these properties isn't just gratuitous fun for the purpose of this exercise; it is practice in developing your intuitive "feel" for gameplay. You know what games you like, you know how they feel, and you can tell if they just seem off. Play mode is how you test the user experience. If you think it's acting subpar or just strangely, you can bet your users will, too. Okay, playing around with the properties can be a little gratuitous, but that's the point. It's a game—it's supposed to be fun!

Select the MouseOrbit icon in the Assets folder of the Property panel to display the script in the Inspector (Figure 4-7).

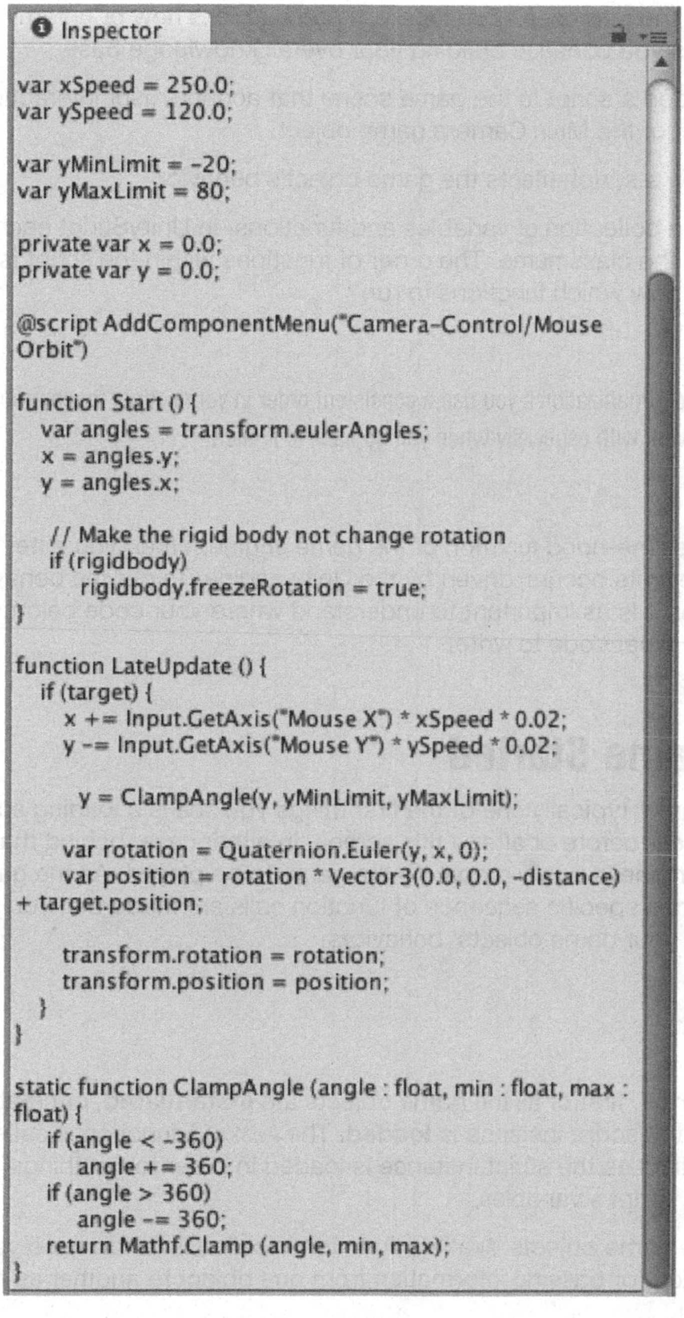

```
var xSpeed = 250.0;
var ySpeed = 120.0;

var yMinLimit = -20;
var yMaxLimit = 80;

private var x = 0.0;
private var y = 0.0;

@script AddComponentMenu("Camera-Control/Mouse
Orbit")

function Start () {
    var angles = transform.eulerAngles;
    x = angles.y;
    y = angles.x;

    // Make the rigid body not change rotation
    if (rigidbody)
        rigidbody.freezeRotation = true;
}

function LateUpdate () {
    if (target) {
        x += Input.GetAxis("Mouse X") * xSpeed * 0.02;
        y -= Input.GetAxis("Mouse Y") * ySpeed * 0.02;

        y = ClampAngle(y, yMinLimit, yMaxLimit);

        var rotation = Quaternion.Euler(y, x, 0);
        var position = rotation * Vector3(0.0, 0.0, -distance)
+ target.position;

        transform.rotation = rotation;
        transform.position = position;
    }
}

static function ClampAngle (angle : float, min : float, max :
float) {
    if (angle < -360)
        angle += 360;
    if (angle > 360)
        angle -= 360;
    return Mathf.Clamp (angle, min, max);
}
```

Figure 4-7. *MouseOrbit script in the Inspector*

You'll see variable declarations followed by a few functions, including the familiar Start() function. Within those functions are some not-so-familiar items like eulerAngles and Quaternions. These are beyond beginner-level topics, but not knowing what they are didn't stop you from using the script or customizing its properties to your satisfaction. I do suggest you do a read-through in the Scripting

Reference, and reread the reference each time you come across new or unfamiliar topics. You'll find they become clearer as you continue building your overall knowledge base.

Awesome—you've added a script to the game scene that accepts user interaction and provides user control over movement of the Main Camera game object.

Let's look closer at how a script affects the game object's behavior.

A **class** is very simply a collection of variables and functions. In UnityScript each script is a class, and the script name is the class name. The order of functions within the script isn't important, but then how does Unity know which functions to run?

> **Note**   For the sake of organization if you use a consistent order in your scripts for commonly-used functions, it is much easier to work with especially when you go back to it later.

This is part of the under-the-hood function of the game engine. When you enter Play mode, a specific sequence of events occurs, driven by the Unity engine. To get the behavior in your game that you are looking for, it is as important to understand where your code belongs in relation to these events as it is to know what code to write.

Getting the Game Started

When you launch a game, typically one of the first things you see is a loading screen. Depending on the game it might appear before or after a title screen. In either case, behind that loading screen and status bar the game engine is busily preparing the game to be played. As the game objects and their scripts are instantiated, a specific sequence of function calls are made that you can utilize within your scripts to control your game objects' behaviors.

Awake

When the game is started, first of all the game objects are **instantiated,** or created. After a game object is instantiated, the script instance is **loaded**. The Awake() function is called this one time during the script's lifetime as the script instance is loaded in order to get things set for gameplay such as initializing the script's variables.

The order in which the game objects' Awake() function is called is random, so you would not want to use the Awake() function for passing information from one object to another as the receiving object might not be ready yet.

Start

Start() is also called only once, when the script is **enabled**. This only takes place after Awake() has been called on every object in the scene.

Update

Once the script is enabled and the Start() function has been called, Update() is called every frame the game renders after that. This is the function where the game behavior is implemented. But what does this mean?

In simple terms, games are interactive animations. Animation, or movement within the game, works just like a video where the viewer sees a series of still images. Within each image, there is an incremental change in the position of the subject, such that when the frames are presented quickly in sequence, there is an illusion of movement (see Figure 4-8).

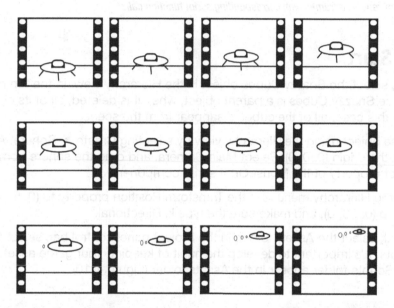

Figure 4-8. Frame-by-frame sequence of a UFO launching

To **render** a game means to draw it to the screen, frame by frame, at a rate fast enough to provide this same illusion of movement in the game. The Unity game engine calculates everything—where each game object is or has moved since the previous frame, each game's object based on the location and lighting, then after all the changes in the scene are implemented, how the scene appears from the Main Camera's viewpoint and finally renders this new frame to the screen.

Unlike videos, games have an additional element of interaction. Before rendering each frame, the Unity engine has to calculate the changes from the previous frame based on the behavior of the game objects as determined by each game object's components, including any scripts. Code scripted in the Update() function drives the ongoing action of the game, as you can see in Figure 4-9.

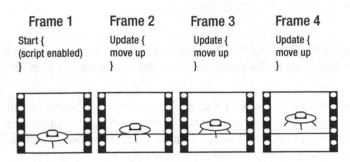

Figure 4-9. *Sequence of rendered frames with corresponding script function calls*

Scripting in Start

In the Unity editor, select the Snazzy Cubes object in the Hierarchy view. In the top menu, select Edit ➤ Delete. Since Snazzy Cubes is a parent object, when it is deleted, all of its child objects are deleted as well. In this case, all of the cubes disappear from the scene.

Create a new game object using the Hierarchy view by selecting Create ➤ Sphere. As expected, a sphere appears at the origin (0, 0, 0). Select Main Camera, and drag the sphere from the Hierarchy view into the Target property of the MouseOrbit script component.

Select the light in the Hierarchy menu. Set the Transform Position property to (0, 5, 0), and the Rotation property to (0, 30, 0), and make sure the type is Directional.

In the Project panel, select the Assets folder. In the Project panel control bar, select Create ➤ Folder, then name it Scripts. It's important to develop the habit of keeping your game assets organized. You will see your new Scripts folder appear in the Assets folder (Figure 4-10).

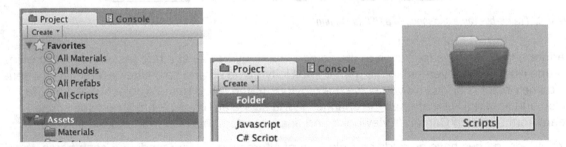

Figure 4-10. *Creating the Scripts folder in the Project panel*

With the new Scripts folder selected, select Create ➤ Javascript and name the new script SphereColor (Figure 4-11).

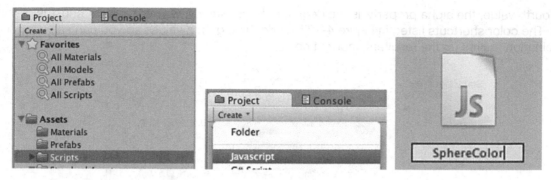

Figure 4-11. Creating the SphereColor script

Open the script in MonoDevelop using the Open button in the Inspector Panel and you will find it already has empty Start() and Update() functions. Add the following line of code to the Start() function:

```
gameObject.renderer.material.color = Color.red;
```

Save the script. In the editor, drag the script from the Project panel and drop it onto the Sphere in either the Hierarchy view or Scene view to attach it to the Sphere game object. Play to see the red sphere. The Start() function is called once, and the sphere material is set to red. Exit Play mode.

Breaking this line of code down shows the following:

```
     (1)        (2)        (3)    (4)      (5)  (6)
gameObject.renderer.material.color = Color.red;
```

1.   gameObject refers to the sphere, as this is the game object to which script is attached.

Using dot syntax, you drill down to

2.   the Mesh Renderer component,

3.   the attached default material, and

4.   the color property of the material.

Then you assign a value to the color property using

5.   the Color class,

which has a few shortcuts including

6.   red.

Color

You can ⌘+' on Color to see more about the class in the Scripting Reference, including other shortcut colors available to you. Colors are made up of four properties: red, green, blue, and alpha. Each of the three color properties is a float value between 0 and 1, where 0 is no color and 1 is the full color. Colors are additive, so r, g, b values of 0, 0, 0 yield black, while 1, 1, 1 yields white.

The fourth value, the alpha property, is the degree of transparency, where 0 is clear and 1 is solid. The color shortcuts listed in Figure 4-12 include the r, g, b, a values so you can see what combination makes up the resultant shortcut color.

Static Variables

black	Solid black. RGBA is (0, 0, 0, 1).
blue	Solid blue. RGBA is (0, 0, 1, 1).
clear	Completely transparent. RGBA is (0, 0, 0, 0).
cyan	Cyan. RGBA is (0, 1, 1, 1).
gray	Gray. RGBA is (0.5, 0.5, 0.5, 1).
green	Solid green. RGBA is (0, 1, 0, 1).
grey	English spelling for gray. RGBA is the same (0.5, 0.5, 0.5, 1).
magenta	Magenta. RGBA is (1, 0, 1, 1).
red	Solid red. RGBA is (1, 0, 0, 1).
white	Solid white. RGBA is (1, 1, 1, 1).
yellow	Yellow. RGBA is (1, 0.92, 0.016, 1), but the color is nice to look at!

Figure 4-12. Shortcut colors provided in the Color class

For any color other than the shortcuts, you'll have to set the r, g, b, a values directly. Edit the script to the following:

```
#pragma strict

// Declare the variables to contain the color values.
private var red : float;
private var green : float;
private var blue : float;
private var alpha : float;

function Start()
{
// On Start, set the color property values by calling a random-number generating function.
        red = RandomColorValue();
        green = RandomColorValue();
        blue = RandomColorValue();
        alpha = RandomColorValue();
        gameObject.renderer.material.color = Color(red, green, blue, alpha);

// Print the random color values to the Console.
        print(gameObject.renderer.material.color);
}

// Generate a random value between 0.000 and 1.000.
function RandomColorValue() {
        var randomValue : float;
        randomValue = Random.Range(0.000, 1.000);
        return randomValue;
}
```

Save the script, and back in the editor enter Play mode to see the sphere with a random color upon the start of the game. Notice the r, g, b, a color values also print to the Console. Exit Play mode.

You used Random.Range in Chapter 2, where you learned that the two parameters it accepts are the minimum and maximum of the range you want the random number selected from. ⌘+' Random.Range to open the Scripting Reference and refresh your memory if necessary.

Frame Rates

Now you've got code setting up the sphere's material color in Start(). Start() only gets called once, so any further changes to the color needs to take place in Update(). Update() is called every frame, and the rate at which the game engine renders frames is called frames per second or **FPS**. Too slow of a frame rate and the illusion of movement is lost, A higher frame rate means a smoother, more responsive game experience.

The frame rate of a game in play is constantly changing because it depends upon the number of computations each frame requires. A single frame can require thousands of calculations, but here the numbers are kept simple for the sake of illustration. The clunkier (less optimized) your code, the longer the processing time per frame (Figure 4-13).

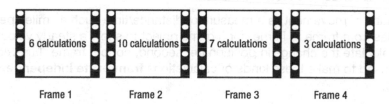

Frame 1   Frame 2   Frame 3   Frame 4

Figure 4-13. The number of computations can vary for each frame

In addition to the code requirements, computational power of the hardware in the main processor and graphics chips also puts a limit on frame rates. When you are comparison-shopping for computers and you see specifications like "2.9 GHz Intel Core i7," the 2.9 GHz (gigahertz) refers to the processing speed of the Intel chip's internal "clock."

In this simplified example, assume that the processor can complete one calculation with each cycle or "tick" of the clock. Processor A has a slower chip speed than Processor B. Given identical game conditions, Processor A will have a lower frame rate than Processor B (illustrated by Figure 4-14).

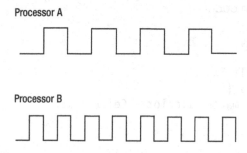

Figure 4-14. Illustration of differing internal clock speeds for two different processors

As faster processors are manufactured for new game consoles and devices, older devices will have relatively slower clock speeds. At some point the older chips just can't keep up with the complexity of newer games and game engines. The more efficient your code, the easier it is for older chips to handle your game, in turn making your game available to a broader market.

Using the most efficient functions and code structure to reduce computational requirements in order to increase frame rate is called **optimization**. While Chapter 12 focuses on game optimization, you will see tips throughout this book and the Unity documentation aimed at good practices in game development for better optimization.

Time.deltaTime

You know from videos and movies that you see smooth character movement based on a steady frame rate. If the frame rate for games varies from frame to frame, you will get choppy, uneven movement. You just learned that both hardware processing speeds and scripting computations affect frame rate. What to do?

Time.deltaTime comes to the rescue. "Delta" refers to the Greek letter delta (D), the symbol used in mathematics to indicate a change in values. In this case, it means specifically the change in time in seconds that it took to render the previous frame.

For example, velocity, or movement, is a measure of distance/time such as miles per hour. Since the frame rate varies from frame to frame, for a game object to show a steady velocity the game engine needs to calculate the change in position per second, not per frame. Time.deltaTime is the conversion factor used to make these kinds of calculations **frame-rate independent**, meaning based on real time.

Scripting in Update

Add the following variable declaration to the others in your script:

```
public var waitTime : float = 5f;
```

waitTime is a public variable holding a value representing the number of seconds to wait until the sphere color changes. Since it is a public variable, you can adjust it directly in the Inspector to override the script variable declaration assigning a value of 5 to change the time from the start of play until the sphere turns a random color.

Now add the Update() function code:

```
function Update()
{
        waitTime -= Time.deltaTime;
        if (waitTime < 0.0f) {
        gameObject.renderer.material.color = Color.blue;
        }
}
```

This new code breaking down as follows:

(1)   `waitTime -= Time.deltaTime;`

Every time the `Update()` function is called, the time since the previous frame rendering is subtracted from `waitTime`.

(2)   `if (waitTime < 0.0f) {`

Check to see if the `waitTime` has counted down to zero.

(3)   `gameObject.renderer.material.color = Color.blue;`

If the `waitTime` has elapsed, change the sphere material color to blue. If the `waitTime` has not elapsed, the code between the brackets is not executed and the current material color remains unchanged for this frame.

Save and play. Wait for it and . . . yes! After five seconds the sphere turns from a random color to blue. Since you declared `waitTime` as a public variable, you can find it in the Inspector as part of the script component. Any changes made here in the Inspector will override the initial scripted `waitTime` of 5.

User Input

That was a little more interesting, but entering and exiting Play mode is getting tedious. Add some player interaction so when the N key (for New color) is pressed, a random color is generated for the sphere's material. You don't know when the player might press the N key, so use the `Update()` function to check for this with every frame. Edit the `Update()` function to add the following lines of code at the end:

```
function Update()
{
        waitTime -= Time.deltaTime;
        if (waitTime < 0.0f) {
                gameObject.renderer.material.color = Color.blue;
        }

        if(Input.GetKey(KeyCode.N)) {
                red = RandomColorValue();
                green = RandomColorValue();
                blue = RandomColorValue();
                alpha = RandomColorValue();
                gameObject.renderer.material.color = Color(red, green, blue, alpha);
                waitTime = 5;
        }
}
```

Breaking down this new code:

```
(1)     if(Input.GetKey(KeyCode.N)) {
```

Check to see if the N key on the keyboard has been pressed. ⌘+' Input.GetKey to find it in the Scripting Reference (Figure 4-15). Here you learn GetKey is a boolean value that returns true if the designated key, in this case N, is pressed. The reference also gives you a handy link to key identifiers including modifier keys, function keys, and other special keys.

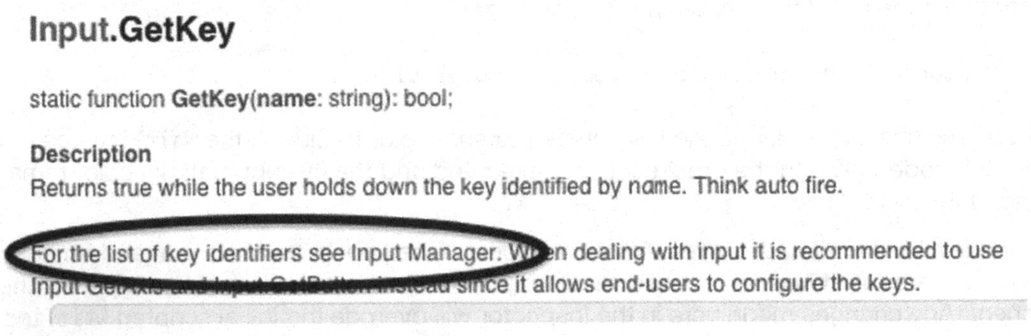

Input.GetKey

static function **GetKey**(**name**: string): bool;

Description
Returns true while the user holds down the key identified by name. Think auto fire.

For the list of key identifiers see Input Manager. When dealing with input it is recommended to use Input.GetAxis and Input.GetButton instead since it allows end-users to configure the keys.

Figure 4-15. Input.GetKey and key identifier link in the Unity Scripting Reference

```
(2)            red = RandomColorValue();
(3)            green = RandomColorValue();
(4)            blue = RandomColorValue();
(5)            alpha = RandomColorValue();
(6)            gameObject.renderer.material.color = Color(red, green, blue, alpha);
```

Identical lines of code from the Start() function for generating a new random material color.

```
(7)            waitTime = 5;
```

Reset the waitTime to 5. The sphere will still automatically change color to blue five seconds after the new color change occurs.

Save and play. Now you are using the mouse for camera control, and the keyboard to make changes to the game object's color—yay!

Cleaning Up Your Code

Look again at the description of lines 2 through 6. They are identical to lines of code from the Start() function. Scripts with big blocks of duplicate lines of code are "clunky," meaning less efficient. When you find yourself using identical lines of code, this is an indication that it's time to streamline your code by creating a single function containing the duplicated block of code, then using a simple function call in place of the code blocks.

Underneath the Update() function, add the NewColor() function:

```
function NewColor() {
            red = RandomColorValue();
            green = RandomColorValue();
            blue = RandomColorValue();
            alpha = RandomColorValue();
            gameObject.renderer.material.color = Color(red, green, blue, alpha);
            waitTime = 5;
}
```

Now instead of using this code block twice, you can replace it in the Start() and Update() functions with a call to NewColor():

```
function Start()
{
// On Start, set a random color for the sphere material.
        NewColor();

// Print the random color values to the Console.
        print(gameObject.renderer.material.color);
}

function Update()
{
        waitTime -= Time.deltaTime;
        if (waitTime < 0.0f) {
                gameObject.renderer.material.color = Color.blue;
        }

        if(Input.GetKey(KeyCode.N)) {
                NewColor();
        }
}
```

Your Start() function is cleaner and easier to read and so is your Update() function. If you find you would like to change the sphere color during some other process you add in the future, you can do it with the single line of code, NewColor();.

Cleaning up your code by rewriting portions of it is known as **refactoring**. Refactoring as a project progresses in order to keep the scripts clean and simple is an excellent habit to develop and ultimately makes life easier for you.

Say you also would like to give the user the option of changing the sphere color with the click of the mouse. Add the following function to your script underneath `NewColor()`:

```
function OnMouseDown() {
        NewColor();
}
```

Isn't that much nicer than duplicating six lines of code again? Save and play.

If you didn't read the `OnMouseDown()` scripting reference first, you might be surprised to find that clicking with the mouse just anywhere in the Game view doesn't cause a color change, you must click directly on the sphere.

⌘+' `OnMouseDown()` and you'll find in the Scripting Reference description that this function is only called when the mouse button is clicked while the mouse cursor is hovering over the GameObject collider.

Select the sphere in the Hierarchy or Scene view and you'll see that in the Inspector that just as when you used Unity's cube primitive game object, Unity created the sphere primitive game object with the necessary collider component required for it to work as advertised with the `OnMouseDown()` function.

Enabling and Disabling Components

In addition to manipulating the properties of components to engender the desired behavior, you can also enable and disable entire components. `OnMouseDown()` requires interaction with a collider component. You just proved that it works with a collider component, now test to see if it fails to work when the collider component is disabled.

An easy way to prove this is to simply uncheck the box in the Inspector panel for the sphere's Sphere Collider to disable it. This checkbox represents a boolean **flag**, where if the box is checked then the enabled flag is set to `true`, and if the box is unchecked then the enabled flag is set to `false`.

Go ahead and uncheck the box, then enter play mode to test. As expected, if you try clicking on the sphere with the mouse while the collider component is disabled, nothing happens. Exit Play mode and check the box to enable the collider component again. While this is an easy way to test the concept, enabling or disabling a component during gameplay takes place in a script.

Add a new variable declaration to the list after `#pragma strict`:

```
private var sphereCollider : Collider;
```

This variable declaration is a little different than the ones you've made before in that its type is Collider. The `sphereCollider` variable is necessary for accessing the enable property of the collider component from within the script. Unlike a float or int variable that holds a specific numerical value, `sphereCollider` is a **reference variable**. It holds a reference to the memory address where the data that defines the Collider is held, not the data itself.

In the Start() function, add the following line of code to the end of the function:

```
sphereCollider = GetComponent(Collider);
```

GetComponent(Collider) gets the reference to the sphere's collider component and assigns it to the sphereCollider variable. In later chapters you will use GetComponent() to access the components, including scripts, of other game objects.

⌘+' on GetComponent() and you will be presented with a short list of options (Figure 4-16). Select the first one: Component.GetComponent. Near the end of the reference you'll find one of Unity's tips on optimizing performance. In this case, Unity is helpfully recommending that when possible, use GetComponent with a type rather than a string. In our example we are using a type: our sphereCollider variable of type Collider, rather than a string variable holding the name or tag of a game object or component.

Your search for "*GetComponent*" resulted in 5 matches:

Component.GetComponent

Returns the component of Type type if the game object has one attached, null if it doesn't.

GameObject.GetComponent

Returns the component of Type type if the game object has one attached, null if it doesn't. You can access both builtin components or scripts with this function.

Component.GetComponentInChildren

Returns the component of Type type in the GameObject or any of its children using depth first search.

GameObject.GetComponentInChildren

Returns the component of Type type in the GameObject or any of its children using depth first search.

Object.Instantiate

Clones the object original and returns the clone.

Figure 4-16. Scripting Reference ⌘+Scripting Reference lider, rGetComponent

Now add this conditional statement to the end of the Update() function:

```
if(Input.GetKey(KeyCode.C)) {
        sphereCollider.enabled = !sphereCollider.enabled;
}
```

This conditional checks to see if the player has pressed the C key. If this is the case, then the collider enable flag, a boolean value, is switched to its opposite. Look at this line of code closely:

```
            (1)                      (2)
sphereCollider.enabled = !sphereCollider.enabled;
```

In Chapter 2 you learned that "!" represents the logical operator NOT.

1. The boolean value of sphereCollider.enabled is either true or false. Whichever value it is,

2. The NOT-value, or opposite value, is reassigned to the sphereCollider.enabled flag.

Using the ! operator to flip a boolean value is often referred to as **toggling** because it behaves like a physical toggle-switch that can only be flipped two ways, like a light switch between "on" and "off." In this example, the player pressing the C key works exactly like you checking or unchecking the box to enable and disable the component in the Inspector. In fact, pay attention to the checkbox in the Inspector panel during gameplay and you will see the box check and uncheck in response to your pressing the C button.

So far, the complete listing of the script is as follows:

```
#pragma strict

// Declare the variables to contain the color values.
private var red : float;
private var green : float;
private var blue : float;
private var alpha : float;
public var waitTime : float = 5f;
private var sphereCollider : Collider;

function Start()
{
// On Start, set a random color for the sphere material.
        NewColor();

// Print the random color values to the Console.
        print(gameObject.renderer.material.color);
// Assign the sphere's collider component to the sphereCollider variable.
        sphereCollider = GetComponent(Collider);
}

// Generate a random value between 0.000 and 1.000.
function RandomColorValue() {
        var randomValue : float;
        randomValue = Random.Range(0.000, 1.000);
        return randomValue;
}

function Update()
{
        waitTime -= Time.deltaTime;
        if (waitTime < 0.0f) {
                gameObject.renderer.material.color = Color.blue;
        }

        if(Input.GetKey(KeyCode.N)) {
                NewColor();
        }
```

```
        if(Input.GetKey(KeyCode.C)) {
                sphereCollider.enabled = !sphereCollider.enabled;
        }
}

function NewColor() {
        red = RandomColorValue();
        green = RandomColorValue();
        blue = RandomColorValue();
        alpha = RandomColorValue();
        gameObject.renderer.material.color = Color(red, green, blue, alpha);
        waitTime = 5;
}

function OnMouseDown() {
        NewColor();
}
```

Save the script and give it a try.

Destroying Game Objects

A more permanent option than enable/disable is using the Destroy() function to remove components or entire game objects. This can be accomplished a number of different ways.

One way might be with a timer similar to our countdown to turning the sphere blue. Using the double forward slash, comment out the line of code in the Update() function that changes the sphere color to blue in order to deactivate it.

```
//gameObject.renderer.material.color = Color.blue;
```

Immediately underneath it, and still within the curly braces of the conditional statement add:

```
Destroy(gameObject);
```

Save and play. Instead of turning blue after five seconds, the sphere disappears.

Back in the script, comment out the call to Destroy(). With both lines commented out, nothing will change at the five-second mark. Using the double forward slash to comment out code is a great shortcut to enable and disable short blocks of code for testing or debugging instead of having to retype or cut and paste lines of code.

You can let the player destroy the sphere by adding another GetKey() conditional to the Update() function as follows:

```
if(Input.GetKey(KeyCode.D)) {
        Destroy(gameObject);
}
```

Save the script and play. When you press the D key, the sphere is immediately destroyed. But wait, you say, I missed something. You cleverly used ⌘+' to skim the Destroy() function scripting reference and noticed that it can take an optional second float parameter that represents a built-in time delay.

Change the line Destroy(gameObject); to Destroy(gameObject, 2);. Save and play to demonstrate that there is now a two-second delay after you press the D key before the sphere is destroyed. Using this parameter instead of our previous code to create a time delay reduces the total number of lines of code needed to accomplish the same goal.

There is often more than one way to get the same result. Keep your eyes open and don't hesitate to refactor your code when you find a more effective solution.

Instantiation

So far you've gone through the complete lifecycle of a game object from the start of the game, determining its behavior during gameplay by writing code to modify, enable and disable game object components.

You learned to destroy the game object at runtime, but not to create one. Throughout these examples you used a sphere game object that was created and positioned in the scene prior to runtime.

Instantiate() is particularly useful for creating duplicates of game objects. What are game object duplicates? Prefabs! You know a prefab is a blueprint of a game object. Instantiation is the process of creating a copy of a game object from this blueprint, called an **instance**.

From the Hierarchy view, drag the Sphere into the Prefabs folder in the Project panel. You'll see a new Sphere prefab appear next to the Pink Rose Cube prefab. Delete the Sphere from the Scene view by selecting it in the Scene or Hierarchy view then selecting Edit ➤ Delete from the editor top menu. Again using the editor top menu, select GameObject ➤ Create Empty. The empty game object's Translate gizmo will appear in the Scene view.

In the Project panel, select the Scripts folder, then in the control bar select Create ➤ Javascript and name the new script CreateSpheres. Drag the script icon to the empty GameObject in the Hierarchy view to attach it. The CreateSpheres script should appear in the Inspector as a new component of the empty game object (Figure 4-17).

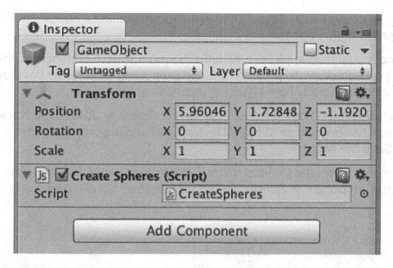

Figure 4-17. The CreateSpheres script shown as a component of the empty game object in the Inspector

Open the CreateSpheres script in MonoDevelop. Under `#pragma strict` declare a new variable for the new instance of the sphere prefab.

```
public var newSphere : GameObject;
```

In the `Update()` function, add the following lines of code:

```
if(Input.GetKey(KeyCode.Space)) {
        var instance : GameObject = Instantiate(newSphere);
}
```

Save the script and return to the editor. Now you can see the `newSphere` variable that Unity prettied up to label as "New Sphere." Select the Prefabs folder in the Project panel. Drag the Sphere prefab from the Project panel into GameObject's New Sphere property in the Inspector panel and drop it over None, so that it's showing in the New Sphere area (see Figure 4-18).

Figure 4-18. The New Sphere variable in the Inspector panel before and after assigning the Sphere prefab

Save the Scene by selecting File ➤ Save Scene in the top menu. Play, and when you hit the spacebar a new sphere prefab appears.

If you keep pressing the spacebar, you are instantiating more sphere prefabs, but they each appear at origin, overlapping each other. To keep the prefabs from piling up, use the `Destroy()` function to get rid of the newly instantiated sphere after two seconds.

In the Project panel, select the Scripts folder. Then select Create ➤ Javascript. Name the new script DestroySphere. Open DestroySphere in MonoDevelop and add `Destroy(gameObject, 2f);` to the `Start()` function. Save the script.

Return to the editor and select the Prefabs folder in the Project panel. Select Sphere, then in the Inspector select AddComponent ➤ Scripts and choose Destroy Sphere from the list of scripts (Figure 4-19).

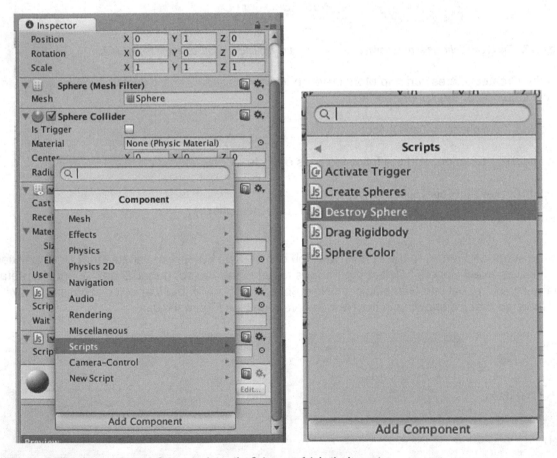

Figure 4-19. Adding the new Destroy Sphere script to the Sphere prefab in the Inspector

In the top menu select File ➤ Save Scene. Enter Play mode. When you press the spacebar, a sphere prefab with a randomly generated material color will appear, then, after a two-second delay, disappear. Perfect!

Summary

You've certainly come a long way in one chapter. Unity provided you with some common scripts in the Standard Assets package as a starting point. You understand the structure of gameplay and the life cycle of a game object from `Awake()` to `Destroy()`, and you got a little introduction to optimization and code refactoring. The game player has appeared and interacted with your game. You can create scripts and attach them to game objects, and you've picked up a few Unity classes and functions to use on your game objects. In short—you are scripting!

The next chapter is all about adding action to the game, starting with simple game object movements and continuing on to an introduction to Unity's Mecanim animation system. This is how you put the "action" into "action-packed"!

Chapter 5

Moving the GameObject

You have built a basic scene and populated it with GameObjects. You've added scripts to allow user interaction to add and destroy GameObjects, as well as change their appearance. Now it's time to add movement.

First you'll learn how to use the GameObject's Transform component to move the GameObject through a script. Then you'll get an introduction on how to use Unity's Mecanim system with more complex GameObject characters from the Asset Store. These come with built-in animations that you will learn to manipulate via your scripts.

The Unity game engine also provides for GameObject movement and interaction in response to forces like gravity or collisions with other GameObjects. These are controlled by Unity game engine physics and will be covered in Chapters 6 and 7.

Rotate

Since a sphere looks the same from any angle, it isn't the best shape to use for demonstrating rotational movement. Rather than delete it, let's just disable it for now. In the Prefabs subfolder found in the Assets folder of the Project panel, select the Sphere prefab. Near the top of the Inspector, uncheck the box to the left of the prefab name Sphere to disable it (Figure 5-1).

Figure 5-1. Disable the Sphere prefab in the Inspector

In the Hierarchy view, select Create ➤ Cube. Unity's primitive object cube will appear in the Scene view at (0, 0, 0).

In the Inspector view, select Add Component ➤ New Script, name it MoveCube, and make sure the Language property is JavaScript. Click the Create and Add button to see it appear as a component in the Inspector. In the Project panel, the script appears in the Assets root folder. To keep your project organized, move it to the Scripts folder.

Now open up MoveCube in MonoDevelop. To get the illusion of movement, you want Unity to render the cube in a slightly different position in each frame, which means that you want to use the `Update()` function. In the `Update()` function between the curly braces, add the following line of code: `transform.Rotate(Vector3.up);`. Save the script, click Play to test, and your cube is rotating—yay!

Let's break down this line of code in order to understand what is going on here:

```
   (1)      (2)    (3)   (4)
transform.Rotate(Vector3.up);
```

1. Transform is the one mandatory component for every game object; it holds its position, rotation, and scale information. In this line of code, you can use `transform` here with a small `t` and the compiler knows that this means the Transform component of the game object to which this script is attached. Affecting the Transform component of one game object from a script attached to a second game object is slightly more involved and will be covered beginning in Chapter 6, Accessing Other Game Objects.

2. `Rotate()` is a function of the Transform class. You can ⌘+' to read the Scripting Reference. It applies a rotation around the axis of its Vector3 parameter in Euler angles. **Euler angles** is an advanced mathematical term regarding the rotation in degrees around the game object's axes.

3. The Vector3 parameter defining the axis around which the rotation will take place.

4. `.up` is the Vector3 static variable shortcut for the vector (0, 1, 0).

Take a closer look at the cube's translate gizmo and remember that the y axis is "up" in Unity's world space. Play again to confirm visually that the cube rotation is occurring around the y axis. Take a look at the Inspector, and you can see the y value of the rotation property of the Transform component is changing in accordance with the changing rotation of the cube (Figure 5-2).

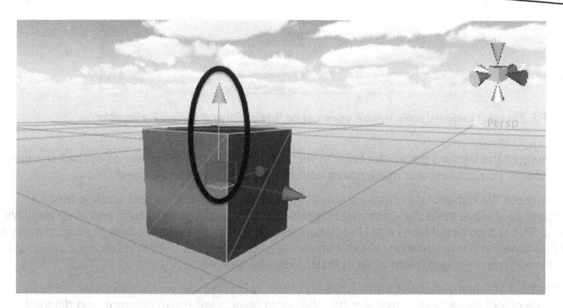

Figure 5-2. Vector3.up *is parallel to the positive y axis*

Vectors do have a direction, so while `Vector3.up` and `Vector3.down` both parallel the y axis, they point in opposite directions. Replace `Vector3.up` with `Vector3.down`. Save, play and notice that now the cube appears to be rotating in the opposite direction. This is because the rotation is now calculated around the downward-directed vector (0, **−1**, 0).

You aren't limited to Vector3 shortcuts, and in fact you could pass in a Vector3 variable of any value. Replace (`Vector3.down`) with the (x, y, z) values of (2, −5, 4), save, and play. Now you see the cube tumbling at an angle, as the rotation is calculated around this random vector. The cube also appears to be tumbling faster now that rotation calculations applied to all three axes are added together.

Editing Properties While Playtesting

Now that you can rotate the game object around an axis in any direction you like, it would be nice if you could control the speed as well. Even better is being able to test and tweak the speed from the Unity editor, rather than going back and forth to the script.

Back in MonoDevelop, under `#pragma strict`, declare the public float variable `rotationSpeed` and give it a starting value of 5:

```
public var rotationSpeed:float = 5;
```

Edit the `Update()` function to:

```
transform.Rotate(Vector3.up * rotationSpeed);
```

You are multiplying the default rotation calculations by a factor you control: the variable `rotationSpeed`. Save and return to the Unity editor. With the Cube game object selected in the Hierarchy, now you will see `rotationSpeed` appears as a property of the MoveCube script component, with the initial value of 5 (Figure 5-3).

Figure 5-3. The `rotationSpeed` *public variable appears as the Rotation Speed property in the Inspector*

You changed the Vector3 parameter back to `Vector3.up` just to make it easier to eyeball changes you make as you playtest and make adjustments to the `rotationSpeed` property.

Play, and see the cube rotate about the y axis again. While still in Play mode, change the `rotationSpeed` value (note the Cube must be selected). Try faster, slower, zero, and even negative values. This is a powerful feature of Unity where you can instantly see the effect of your changes as you fine-tune the game experience. Exit Play mode, and notice that the `rotationSpeed` value reverts to 5. Remember, changes made while in Play mode aren't saved.

In Chapter 4 you learned about frame rates and `Time.deltaTime`. As you make adjustments to the game object movement, remember that the game objects will move differently on different computers, based on the frame rates. The solution was to multiply by `Time.deltaTime` to make the motion frame-rate independent. Edit the `Update()` function to the following:

```
function Update () {
        transform.Rotate(Vector3.up * rotationSpeed * Time.deltaTime);
}
```

Add User Interaction

Save and play. The speed of the cube has changed with this additional factor, but you can readjust your `rotationSpeed` property to get back to the speed that you like. The difference now is that anyone who plays your game on a different machine will have the same experience you create on yours.

Add some user interaction via the keyboard much like you did in Chapter 4, this time for controlling the cube rotation. Edit the `Update()` function by adding a conditional that checks to see if the user is pressing the left arrow key.

```
function Update () {
        if(Input.GetKey(KeyCode.LeftArrow)) {
                transform.Rotate(Vector3.up * rotationSpeed * Time.deltaTime);
        }
}
```

Save and play. Now the cube rotates only when the left arrow is pressed. Similarly you can let the user rotate the cube in the opposite direction with the right arrow key, by using `-rotationSpeed`.

```
function Update () {
        if(Input.GetKey(KeyCode.LeftArrow)) {
                transform.Rotate(Vector3.up * rotationSpeed * Time.deltaTime);
        }
```

```
        if(Input.GetKey(KeyCode.RightArrow)) {
                transform.Rotate(Vector3.up * -rotationSpeed * Time.deltaTime);
        }
}
```
Save and play.

Translate

Translate() is another function of Transform, used for moving the GameObject. Like Rotate(), it also takes a Vector3 argument, but in this case the Vector3 describes the direction and distance of GameObject movement to take place. Add a public variable you can use as a multiplication factor to adjust the speed of the cube in the editor. Underneath the rotationSpeed variable declaration, add a travelSpeed variable.

```
public var travelSpeed:float = 5;
```

Let the player move the cube up and down with the up and down arrows by adding the following lines of code to the Update() function.

```
if(Input.GetKey(KeyCode.UpArrow)) {
transform.Translate(Vector3.up * Time.deltaTime * travelSpeed);
}
if(Input.GetKey(KeyCode.DownArrow)) {
transform.Translate(Vector3.down * Time.deltaTime * travelSpeed);
}
```

Save and play. This time, rather than using -travelSpeed for the down direction, you used Vector3.down. Either would have worked, just as -Vector3.up is also equivalent to Vector3.down. There is often more than one way to get the same result; it's largely personal preference. If you have a choice, opt for the most efficient code and if all else is the same, the more readable the better.

Transform.position

Whereas Translate() is a function that moves the transform, position is a variable holding the (x, y, z) values of the position of the transform. You can also move the GameObject to a specific location by simply assigning a new position. In this example, we'll use the O key to send the GameObject back to the origin (0, 0, 0).

First, add a new private variable declaration underneath the public variable declarations.

```
private var originPosition : Vector3 = new Vector3(0, 0, 0);
```

In the Update() function, add the following:

```
if(Input.GetKey(KeyCode.O)) {
transform.position = originPosition;
}
```

Save and play. Move the cube around with the arrow keys, then press O to return it to the center of the Game View. Notice that this resets the cube's position without having any effect on its rotation.

While effectively instantaneous, this movement is rather abrupt. If you'd like a slower, smoother return to origin for the cube, Unity has a great function just for this purpose called Lerp().

Smoothing It Out with Lerp

Unity's Lerp() function can smooth the cube's transition back to the origin. **Lerp** stands for Linear Interpolation, which is a mathematical way of approximating a smooth line or curve between two values. In this case we are using Lerp() for smoothing the movement of the cube from the position the player moved it to, back to the origin. If you take a moment to search "Lerp" in the Scripting Reference, you'll find Lerp() can be used to transition between two values representing just about anything including colors, materials, and quaternions (Figure 5-4).

Your search for "*Lerp*" resulted in 14 matches:

Color.Lerp
Interpolates between colors a and b by t.
Mathf.Lerp
Interpolates between a and b by t. t is clamped between 0 and 1.
Color32.Lerp
Interpolates between colors a and b by t.
Vector2.Lerp
Linearly interpolates between two vectors.
Vector3.Lerp
Linearly interpolates between two vectors.
Vector4.Lerp
Linearly interpolates between two vectors.
Material.Lerp
Interpolate properties between two materials.
Quaternion.Lerp
Interpolates between from and to by t and normalizes the result afterwards.
Mathf.LerpAngle
Same as Lerp but makes sure the values interpolate correctly when they wrap around 360 degrees.
Vector3.Slerp
Spherically interpolates between two vectors.
Mathf.InverseLerp
Calculates the Lerp parameter between of two values.
Mathf.MoveTowards
Moves a value current towards target.
Vector2.MoveTowards
Moves a point current towards target.
Vector4.MoveTowards
Moves a point current towards target.

Figure 5-4. Static functions using Lerp() in Unity

Specifically, you'll be using `Vector3.Lerp`. Select it in the Scripting Reference for a quick read-through.

`Vector3.Lerp` has three parameters: the `from` Vector3, the `to` Vector3, and a float value used in the actual linear interpolation calculations.

First, declare a `smoothing` public float variable after the other variable declarations that you can use to adjust the cube's movement from the Inspector:

```
public var smoothing : float;
```

Change your code in the `Update()` function for returning the cube to the origin as follows:

```
//move the cube back to the origin
if(Input.GetKey(KeyCode.0)) {
            transform.position = Vector3.Lerp(transform.position, originPosition, smoothing *
Time.deltaTime);
        }
```

Breaking down the key line of code, we see the following:

```
       (1)              (2)                (3)                (4)            (5)
transform.position = Vector3.Lerp(transform.position, originPosition, smoothing *

       (6)
Time.deltaTime);
```

1. Sets the GameObject's Transform position,

2. smoothed with the `Vector3.Lerp()` function,

3. from the GameObject's current position,

4. to the origin,

5. with a smoothing multiplier we can use for customization,

6. based on real time rather than varying frame rates.

Save and return to the Unity editor. With the Cube game object selected in the Hierarchy, in the Inspector change the Smoothing property to 3. Enter Play mode. Now when you press and hold the O key, the cube moves smoothly and in such a way that its movement becomes gradually slower the closer it gets to the origin, ultimately coasting to a stop.

Now you've animated your primitive game object with a variety of movements in a number of different ways. You've played games that effectively use simple motions like these for fun, interactive experiences, but this only scratches the surface of what Unity can do. The remainder of this chapter will give you an introduction to Mecanim, Unity's animation system, along with the wonderful variety of characters and animation packs that can be found in the Asset Store.

Mecanim

Mecanim is Unity's animation system. The Mecanim system has been integrated into the Unity editor, and is similarly designed to be a visual, intuitive tool for the game developer. While the character and its basic animation clips are created prior to importing to Unity, Mecanim is used to manage and blend these animations for a smoother, better game play experience.

Best of all, through the use of avatars, Mecanim allows you to take an animation from one character model and retarget it onto another, rather than having to create an entirely new animation sequence for the second character. This might sound simplistic, but it is yet another example of the folks at Unity making something very complex into something very easy to use while saving you hours and days of work.

After all, this is a book about learning Unity with a focus on scripting, and scripting is ultimately necessary to integrate the animated character with the gameplay code in order to play the game. You want to be efficient in your efforts, though—remember, the goal here is to complete an awesome game and publish it.

Development tools are constantly being upgraded to be more intuitive, more visual, and, most importantly, more efficient by taking away the burden of creating raw code for commonly used and oft-repeated functions. Mecanim provides a Visual Programming Tool you can use for complex animation interactions before scripting the gameplay code.

The creation and animation of 3D character models is done prior to integrating them into your Unity game project. While character creation is well beyond the scope of this book, you will learn the basics of taking a ready-made character and combining it with ready-made animation clips in preparation for using it in your game.

This section will give you an introduction to setting up a character and its animations using Mecanim along with accompanying scripting to provide for user input in order to control the character. To really understand the beauty of Mecanim, you are going to choose a character and configure its avatar and animation and then quickly apply this animation to a second character, using free content from the Asset Store. This ability to mix and match characters and animations gives you a huge library of options for your game prototypes while being mindful of containing costs as you learn.

I'm a Doctor, Not a . . . !

Before going further, I'd like to make a few general observations about working in the game development industry. There is often a friendly rivalry between the artists and the developers, usually defined as the creative types versus the logical types. I would encourage you—a beginning game developer—not to limit yourself to either of these categories.

While artists are in fact creative, the truly skilled artist must have an in-depth knowledge of his or her chosen medium, which is actually very technical in nature, as is learning and practicing the use of any tools or motor skills required to manipulate the art medium to take the creative concept from idea to reality.

Developers use various programming languages that are all based on pure mathematical functions and logic. It doesn't get much more technical than that. On the other hand, it takes great creativity to come up with a solution within the strict limitations of computer code to bring an app or game concept to life.

A great game is that beautiful combination of art and code coming together to produce an outstanding experience for the player. Always keep your mind open, including for those opportunities to learn more about whatever the heck it is those other team members do. The better you can understand how it all fits together, the better you can communicate with your 3D artist collaborators, and ultimately the better your final product will be.

Modeling, Rigging, and Skinning

Computer-generated animation is an entire industry in and of itself, with individuals who specialize in modeling, rigging, animation, and more. Each of these is needed just to create and animate a new character. Maya, 3ds Max, and Blender are used to create characters from scratch, and there are other character generator tools out there as well. That is beyond the scope of this book, but you will need to understand some of the terminology.

Modeling is the process of creating the three-dimensional shape of the game object, where this shape is made up of a number of triangles typically referred to as **polygons** (Figure 5-5). Recall that more complex models require more computational power.

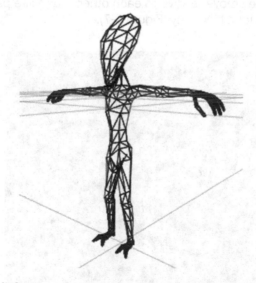

Figure 5-5. Alien character model wireframe

One of the most common descriptors for models in the Asset store is the number of "polys" or "tris" used in the model. Metaio, an augmented-reality SDK that supports Unity, says it best: "Whenever you design a 3-D model, keep in mind to use as few polygons as possible, but as many as necessary." The same goes for choosing ready-made models for your game.

While you will learn best practices like this for optimizing your game, you'll have to go to the documentation of your target platform for more specific limitations. For example, to put their recommendation into practical terms, Metaio also provides an excellent summary of performance versus polygon count on multiple platforms (and multiple devices) for developers (Figure 5-6).

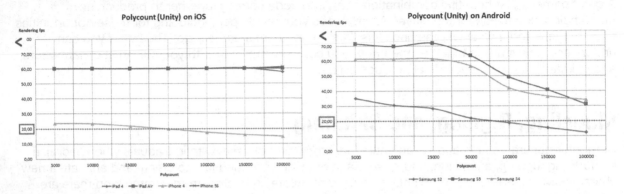

Figure 5-6. Performance vs. polygons for the Metaio augmented-reality SDK

If you are working with an artist who is creating a custom character, it is helpful for them to know if there are specific polygon count limitations.

Bones are used to control the movement of the character. They make up a **skeleton** or **joint hierarchy** that defines how they move relative to each other, much like parent-child game objects. **Rigging** is the creation of this joint hierarchy (Figure 5-7).

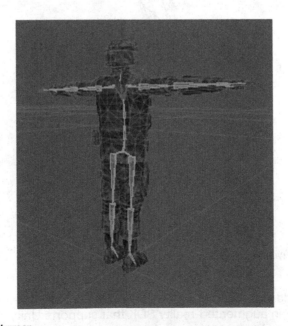

Figure 5-7. Rig depicted in bright green

Once the joint hierarchy is created, it must be connected to the character mesh in order for the mesh to move in response to a joint being animated. Connecting the mesh to the bones of the joint hierarchy is called **skinning** (Figure 5-8).

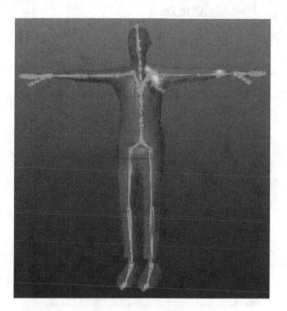

Figure 5-8. Illustration of Interactive Skin Bind from the Unity User Manual

If you are going to make your own character models, you can find helpful guidelines in the Unity User Manual.

The Asset Store

Fortunately for indie game developers there is the Unity Asset Store. The Asset Store is a fantastic resource for models, scripts, textures, audio, complete projects, and more. Don't let the name fool you—there are many free assets available for you that are great for learning and prototyping, not to mention that it's a great way to sample what the various artists and studios have to offer.

The Unity Asset Store works much like an app store, where the assets might be from an indie artist or developer, a studio, or even Unity Technologies itself. You can find simple bits and pieces all the way up to complete finished projects. The Unity editor is designed to integrate easily with the Asset Store. To access the Asset Store, in the editor top menu, select Window ➤ Asset Store (Figure 5-9).

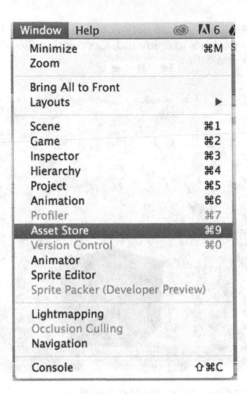

Figure 5-9. Accessing the Unity Asset Store through the editor menu

The Asset Store home page opens up in a separate window (Figure 5-10). It presents featured items in the first two rows on the left, and a menu of the store categories on the right. Just below the Categories menu is the 24 Hour Deal, where a different item is featured every day at a significant discount.

Figure 5-10. Unity Asset Store home page

In Categories, select 3D Models ➤ Characters ➤ Humanoids. On the top left are featured items from this subcategory, and underneath is the complete listing of available 3D humanoid models. At the top of this listing are sorting options; select PRICE. This organizes the assets by price from lowest to highest, putting the free assets at the top of the list (Figure 5-11).

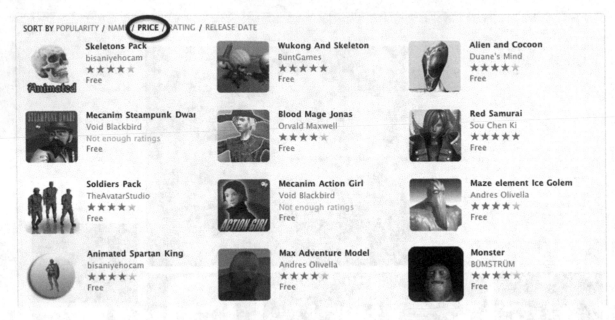

SORT BY POPULARITY / NAME / PRICE / RATING / RELEASE DATE

Skeletons Pack
bisaniyehocam
★★★★☆
Free

Wukong And Skeleton
BuntGames
★★★★★
Free

Alien and Cocoon
Duane's Mind
★★★★☆
Free

Mecanim Steampunk Dwai
Void Blackbird
Not enough ratings
Free

Blood Mage Jonas
Orvald Maxwell
★★★★☆
Free

Red Samurai
Sou Chen Ki
★★★★★
Free

Soldiers Pack
TheAvatarStudio
★★★★☆
Free

Mecanim Action Girl
Void Blackbird
Not enough ratings
Free

Maze element Ice Golem
Andres Olivella
★★★★☆
Free

Animated Spartan King
bisaniyehocam
★★★★☆
Free

Max Adventure Model
Andres Olivella
★★★★☆
Free

Monster
BÜMSTRÜM
★★★★☆
Free

Figure 5-11. 3D humanoid models available from the Unity Asset Store, sorted by price

Clicking on any of these takes you to the product page that has a brief description, a graphic, an optional area for more images of the character, and finally the detailed contents of the downloadable package. For comparison purposes, take a look at Alien and Cocoon, and Animated Spartan King (Figure 5-12).

Alien and Cocoon
Duane's Mind
★★★★☆
Free

Animated Spartan King
bisaniyehocam
★★★★☆
Free

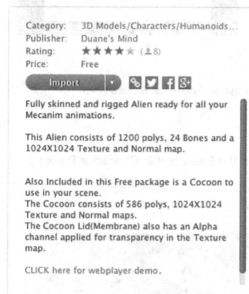

Alien and Cocoon

Category: 3D Models/Characters/Humanoids...
Publisher: Duane's Mind
Rating: ★★★★☆ (⬇8)
Price: Free

`Import` ▾ 🔗 🐦 f 8+

Fully skinned and rigged Alien ready for all your Mecanim animations.

This Alien consists of 1200 polys, 24 Bones and a 1024X1024 Texture and Normal map.

Also Included in this Free package is a Cocoon to use in your scene.
The Cocoon consists of 586 polys, 1024X1024 Texture and Normal maps.
The Cocoon Lid(Membrane) also has an Alpha channel applied for transparency in the Texture map.

CLICK here for webplayer demo.

Animated Spartan King

Category: 3D Models/Characters/Humanoids...
Publisher: bisaniyehocam
Rating: ★★★★☆ (⬇90)
Price: Free

`Download` ▾ 🔗 🐦 f 8+

This Spartan King model comes with 11 animations.

- 0-100 : Waiting(idle)
- 101-137 : Walking
- 138-160 : Running
- 161-183 : Charging
- 184-234 : Waiting for Battle
- 235-270 : Resist with the Shield
- 271-352 : Victory
- 353-429 : Salute
- 430-500 : Dying (Normal)
- 501-566 : Dying Hard (Spin)
- 567-602 : Swing Sword (Attack)

Textures are *.psd
Watch the video!

Figure 5-12. Comparing 3D models on the Unity Asset Store

The brief descriptions are provided by the publisher, and the content can vary. Poly counts are often mentioned as these can affect performance or possibly limit the devices that can support your game. Mecanim is relatively new and a significant upgrade from Unity's Legacy animation system, so you may see comments like that for the Alien specifying that it is in fact Mecanim compatible.

Animations might be provided separately, or part of one long animation where you need to know where in the single clip the individual animations reside. In the Spartan King description, the publisher gives you the specific frame ranges for each animation clip.

Best of all, both of these publishers provide a means by which you can actually see the animations prior to download. The Alien and Cocoon link takes you to a Unity web player where you interact as the player, moving the alien around a few simple levels, while the Spartan King link takes you to a YouTube video where you can watch the character perform each of the available animations (Figure 5-13).

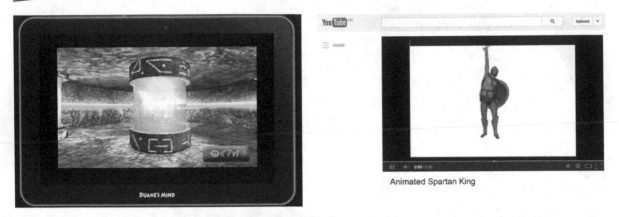

Animated Spartan King

Figure 5-13. Asset Store contributors present their animations in a variety of ways: web player vs. YouTube video

Import a Character Model

In the Asset Store window, scroll down just a bit until you find the free Zombie Character Pack by Mixamo, and select it to open the product page (Figure 5-14).

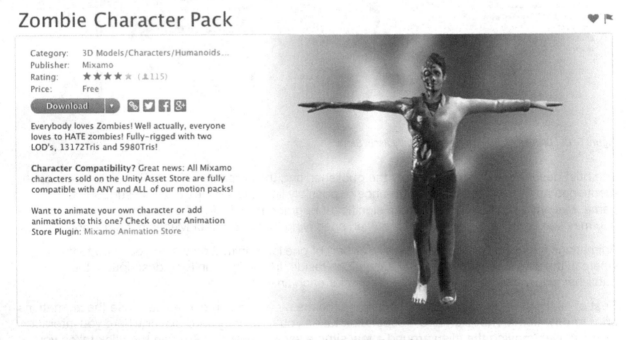

Figure 5-14. Zombie Character Pack icon and product description in the Unity Asset Store

Click the blue Download button. If you didn't already set up a Unity account, follow the instructions to set up one now. If you have, the Download button will change to "Please Wait" and then a number indicating the percent download completed. Finally, the Importing Package window will open with all of the package contents checked for import. Leave all of these checked and click Import in the bottom right corner of the window (Figure 5-15).

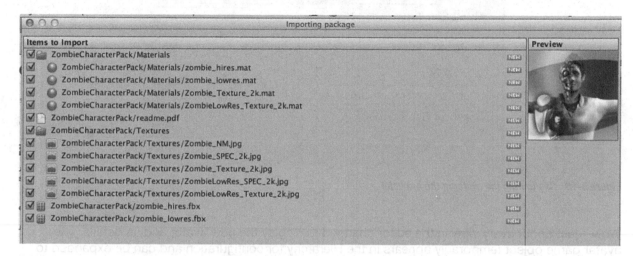

Figure 5-15. Import window with Zombie Character Pack contents

The ZombieCharacterPack folder now appears in the Assets folder in the Project panel.

Create and Configure the Avatar

In the Project panel, in the ZombieCharacterPack folder, select the zombie_lowres model. In the Inspector view, select the Rig tab. Change the Animation Type to Humanoid and leave the Avatar Definition as Create From This Model. Click Apply. Now the Configure... button is active, so select it. Select Save in the Dialog box that appears. Once configured, a small checkmark will appear to the left of the Configure... button (as shown in Figure 5-16).

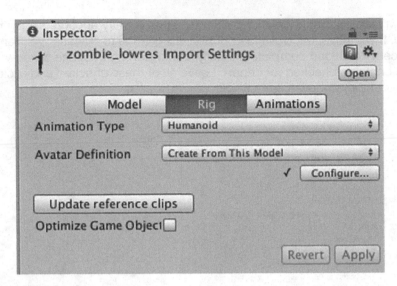

Figure 5-16. Configuring the avatar in the Inspector

Wow—just about every view in the editor changed to display the new avatar and its details. The avatar game object temporarily appears in the Hierarchy for configuration and can be expanded to display all of the child game objects that make it up. Its image appears in the Inspector (Figure 5-17). Underneath the avatar image is the list showing you which avatar bones were matched to which corresponding character bones. There is a way to manually assign any bones not matched properly, but in this case they are correct so go ahead and select the Done button in the bottom right of the Inspector to close this view, and the editor returns to its previous state. Your avatar is ready!

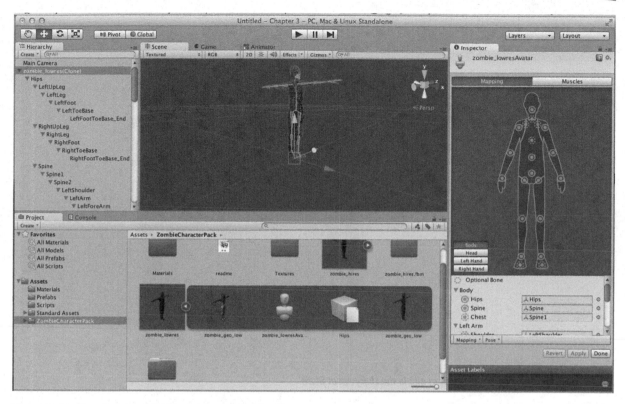

Figure 5-17. *The newly created avatar appears in the editor*

The avatar no longer appears in the Hierarchy because you haven't yet placed the zombie character into the game Scene. It was only there temporarily for the purpose of configuring the avatar.

Import the Animation

Often characters come with a number of ready-made animations, but it's simple to add other animation assets. Back in the Asset Store, search for "creature zombie running" (Figure 5-18), then download and import it the same way you did the Zombie Character Pack. In the Project panel, select the Assets root folder, then Create ➤ Folder and name it Animations. Keep your project organized by moving the newly imported alpha@zombie_running animation clip to the Animations folder.

Creature zombie running

Category: Animation/Bipedal
Publisher: Mixamo
Rating: ★ ★ ★ ★ ☆ (±41)
Your Rating: ☆ ☆ ☆ ☆ ☆
Price: Free

Import ▾   🔗 🐦 f ⑧

FREE – zombie run – loop

Version: 1.0 (Nov 13, 2012)   Size: 43.5 kB   Support E-mail   Support Website   Visit Publisher's Website

Figure 5-18. *Zombie running animation clip in the Unity Asset Store*

Select the animation clip in the Animations folder so its properties appear in the Inspector. At the top, check the Loop Time box. Unchecked, the zombie performs one cycle of a running stride with left and right legs. Looping the animation means the zombie will continue to run.

Create an Animator Controller

Now that you have a character and an animation, you need a controller to play it. The Animator Controller is the game object component used to connect the behavior of animation clips to the game object model.

First select the Assets folder, then select Create ➤ Folder and name it Animator Controllers, then double-click it to open it. Next select Create ➤ Animator Controller and name it zombieController01. Double-click zombieController01 to open it in the Animator view (Figure 5-19).

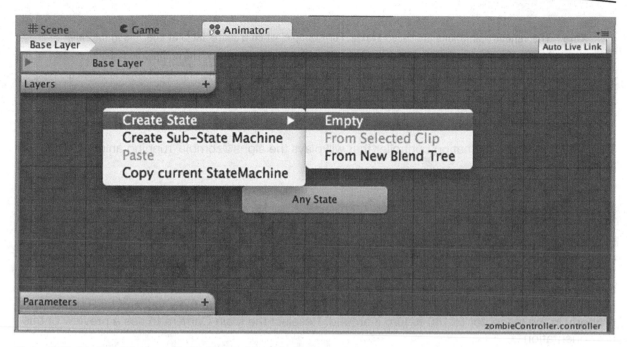

Figure 5-19. The Visual Programming Tool in the Animator window

With the mouse cursor in the Animator view, right-click the grid and in the context menu select Create State ➤ Empty.

A new box named New State appears in the Animator window. The orange color indicates the default state. Select this box, and in the Inspector change the name to Zombie Run. Then drag the alpha@zombie_running clip from the Animations folder into the Motion field (Figure 5-20).

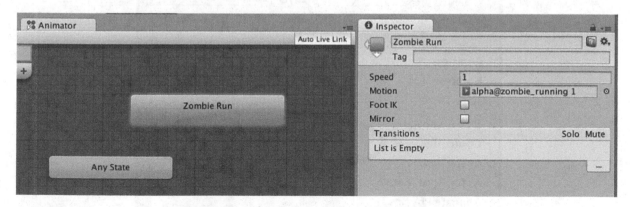

Figure 5-20. The Zombie Run animation clip's default animation state appears orange

> **Note**   The various animations are called **states**. For example, when a character is at Idle, it is in the "Idle state." Moving from one state to another is a **transition**, denoted by an arrow. The compilation of states and transitions that you design in the Animator window for your Animator Controller represent what is called a **state machine**.

That's it for a simple animation controller that will plays the alpha@zombie_running animation clip as its default.

Run Zombie Run

First set up the scene. In the Hierarchy view, select the Cube game object, then in the Inspector deactivate it by unchecking the box at the top by its name. Now drag the zombie_lowres model from the Project panel into the Hierarchy view to add it to the Scene. Select Main Camera and see how the preview looks. Reposition the camera to (0, 1, –3). The zombie character appears in the scene facing away from the camera, so select it in the Hierarchy and change the y value of its Rotation property in the Inspector to 180 to turn it around. Reselect the Main Camera to see a preview of this new orientation

Now take a look at the zombie character's Animator component in the inspector, and you'll notice that its Controller property is empty. Drag the zombieController01 from the Project panel and drop it into the Controller field (Figure 5-21). Save the scene. Play and now the zombie is running after you!

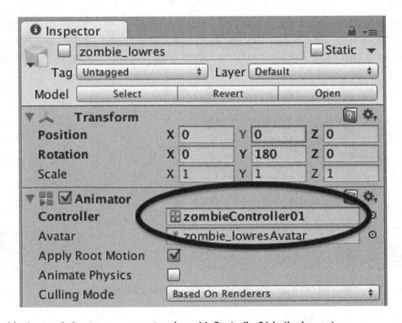

Figure 5-21. The zombie_lowres Animator component and zombieController01 in the Inspector

Run Like a Zombie

A fundamental concept in development is DRY or Don't Repeat Yourself. You've already seen an application of this in Chapter 4, when you refactor your script by taking a block of code that is repeated and making it into its own function. This concept is also behind the power and flexibility of Mecanim, only instead of not repeating blocks of code, the idea is to not have to repeat creating the same kind of animation for different but similarly rigged characters. The use of **avatars** makes this possible.

An avatar is a simplified humanoid bone structure that Mecanim understands how to animate. The bones of the avatar are matched with similar units in the character model, so moving the avatar in turn moves the character with the same motion as the underlying animation clip. A simple analogy is that moving the strings of a marionette puppet moves the puppet in a particular way, regardless of what character the puppet is. If you were to exchange one puppet with another, the second puppet would respond in the same way to the same movements of the strings (Figure 5-22). With Mecanim, you can similarly retarget different characters with the same animation clip. This is a tremendous streamlining of the animation workflow in Unity.

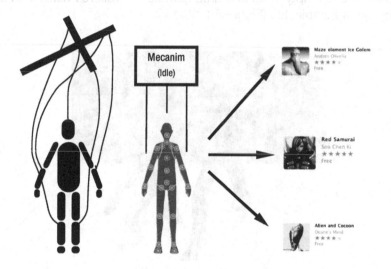

Figure 5-22. A marionette puppet compared to a standard avatar

Now you get to see the real efficiency from Mecanim. In the Asset Store, find the Maze element Ice Golem (Figure 5-23). Download and import it to your project. A folder named "player" will appear in your Asset folder. Drill down to the golem character and select it.

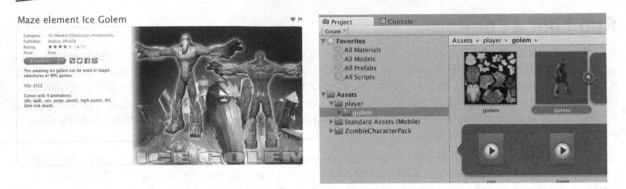

Figure 5-23. Golem character in the Asset Store and the Project panel

Follow the same steps in Create and configure an Avatar for this golem character. Once complete, drag the golem character with its new avatar into the Hierarchy view. In the Scene view, move the golem until it is standing beside the zombie. You'll see in the Inspector the golem's Animator component Controller field is empty. Drag and drop zombieController01 here, then click Play. Now the golem is running like a zombie, too (Figure 5-24)!

Figure 5-24. The zombie and golem characters running together

More Animations

Finally getting to see the characters move is definitely fun, and you've gotten a taste of how easy it is to transfer an animation clip to another character. We are going to add more animations to the zombie character, so go ahead and deactivate the golem for now. A character that only loops through one animation clip isn't that useful for a game, so where to find more animations for the zombie?

You can find more in the Asset Store, either as animation clips and packs or within complete projects like the Mecanim Demo produced by Unity Technologies. You're familiar with navigating your way around the Asset Store by now, so I'd like to introduce another source for animations that takes it a step further by giving you some editing capability.

Animation clips, like the character model, are typically prepared prior to import into Unity. Mixamo is the publisher of the zombie character we are using in this example. In addition to a nice catalog of Mecanim-compatible characters and animations, Mixamo also has nifty free tools, including one for applying animation to your character.

Using your Internet browser, go to www.mixamo.com. To sign up for a free account, simply provide your e-mail address and create a password. Once you are signed up, select ANIMATE (Figure 5-25) from the top menu to get to the catalog of ready-made animations (Figure 5-26).

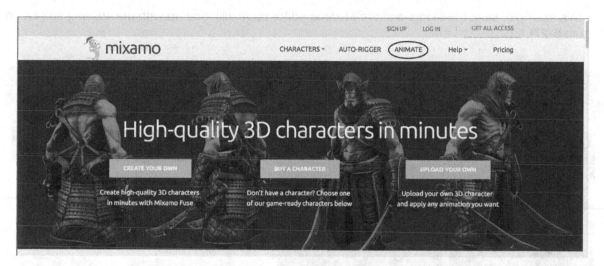

Figure 5-25. *ANIMATE top-menu selection on the Mixamo home page*

Figure 5-26. *Sampling of animations available from Mixamo*

Awesome, right? Who doesn't want their character to dance Gangnam Style? Go ahead, take some time to check out the animations. When shopping around for your game, just like in the Unity Asset Store be sure and check out the packs, too, as they are usually a pretty good deal.

In the upper right corner, select the orange UPLOAD 3D CHARACTER button. Select UPLOAD FILE. Choose the zombie_lowres.fbx character for upload. The zombie character is a free character made by Mixamo, so you should get the "Your character was successfully mapped!" message pretty quickly. Select APPLY ANIMATION, which brings you back to the animation catalog.

For this example, select Walking, and the Mixamo editor page will load up with the walking animation (Figure 5-27).

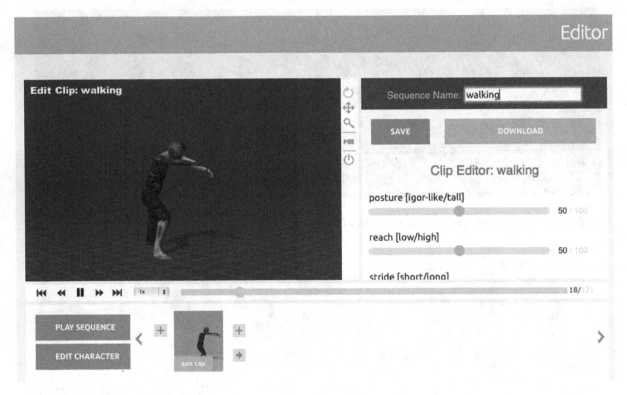

Figure 5-27. The Mixamo animation editor

Leave the Sequence Name as walking. In the lower left, select Edit Clip if it is not already selected. Experiment with the sliders to see how you can customize the animation (Figure 5-28).

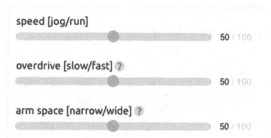

speed [jog/run]

50 / 100

overdrive [slow/fast] ?

50 / 100

arm space [narrow/wide] ?

50 / 100

Figure 5-28. *Simple sliders for editing the animation clip*

When you are finished experimenting, lower the arms with the reach slider to approximately the same angle as in the Zombie Run animation. This sets up for a smoother transition between the two animation clips. I prefer a zombie with a slower, shuffling step but configure the other parameters however you like. When you have adjusted it to your satisfaction, select Save, then Download.

A checkout pop-up window appears with the animation in your shopping cart for a total of $0. Select Checkout and a Download Tray pop-up window appears with your animated character. Select it, then near the bottom for Download Format select FBX for Unity, then the big orange Download button (Figure 5-29).

| Download Format: | FBX for Unity (.fbx)' | Remove Namespace: ☑ | DOWNLOAD |
| Key Frame Reduction: | Off | Framerate: 30 | CUSTOMIZE |

Figure 5-29. *Mixamo animated-character download settings*

You can add the downloaded animated character model to your Unity project by dragging and dropping it into the Project panel, or through the Unity editor top menu by selecting Assets ➤ Import New Asset. Drag and drop your newly created animated character model to the Assets ➤ Animations folder. Save the scene and save your project.

You'll need a few more animation clips for this project. First, repeat this process for creating the walking animation but name it walkingWithMotion. When you are done editing it, scroll down to underneath the sliders and change the In Place setting to Off (Figure 5-30). Save and download.

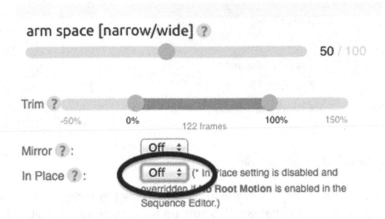

Figure 5-30. *In Place setting set to Off in the Mixamo animation editor*

In the same fashion, create, save, and download the Idle animation. In this case there is no In Place setting option because the animation is of the zombie character standing in one place anyway. As before, download these animations to your project's Assets ➤ Animations folder. Save your project.

Configure the Animations

You should now have Idle, walking, and walkingWithMotion animations for your zombie character in the Animations folder. Since they are combined with the zombie_lowres model, their labels appear as zombie_lowres@*animation name*. Each of these will have to be configured before you use them. In the Animations folder select zombie_lowres@walkingWithMotion.

In the Inspector, select the Rig tab (Figure 5-31). Just as you did with the zombie_running animation, change Animation Type to Humanoid and Avatar Definition to Create From This Model.

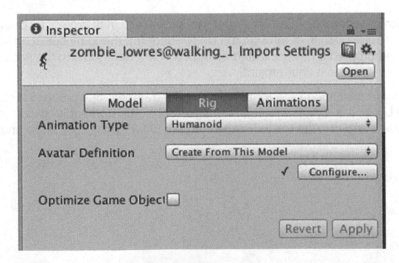

Figure 5-31. *Configure the animation Rig settings in the Inspector*

Root Motion

Whereas animation involves the movement of the character's head, body, and limbs relative to itself, Root Motion involves the movement of the character relative to game world coordinates. For example, you will see that the zombie walking animation without Root Motion gives you a character walking in place, whereas the walkingWithMotion animation with Root Motion gives you a character that has a forward movement in the game scene. Like the animation movements, whether or not an animation contains Root Motion is determined in the creation of the character and animation prior to import into Unity.

Select the Animations tab. Notice at the bottom there is a Preview where you can play the animation. Pay attention to the grid of the plane the zombie character is standing on and notice that the zombie is walking in place.

Scroll down in the Inspector until you see where you can check Loop Time and, immediately underneath it, Loop Pose. For Root Transform Rotation, check Bake Into Pose, then set Based Upon to Body Orientation. Next, for Root Transform Position (Y) check Bake Into Pose and, beneath it, set Based Upon (at Start) to Original. For Root Transform Position (XZ) leave Bake Into Pose unchecked. Finally, click Apply (Figure 5-32).

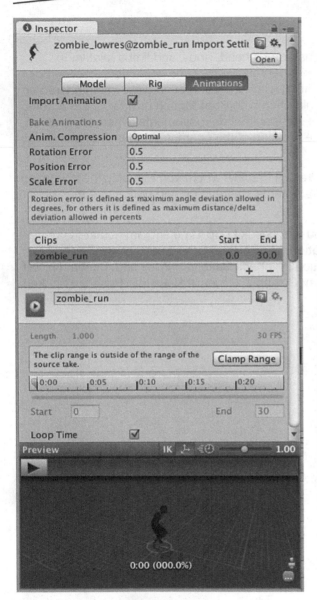
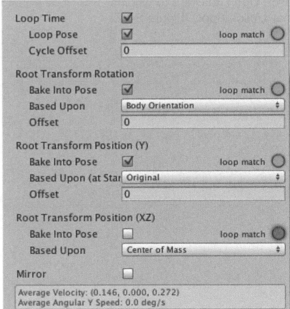

Figure 5-32. Configure the Animations settings in the Inspector

Breaking this down by settings, checking Loop Pose means the animation clip will repeat or **loop**. If unchecked the animation clip will play only once.

Root Transform Rotation describes how much the animation rotates the model during the animation clip. By checking Bake Into Pose, you are "baking" the original rotation coordinates into the character and preventing it from rotating during the animation clip. This is what you want to prevent it from **drifting** during the walking animation where you want the character only to move forward in a straight line.

Under Mirror you can see the average velocity from the Root Motion. Fractional velocities along axes other than the one you are interested in are an indicator of possible drifting. You can choose whether this animation clip should continue from the character's previous movement vector Based Upon either the model's body orientation or the original forward movement vector it has at the time this clip is played.

Offset allows you to further fine-tune the transform to account for any discrepancies that might be introduced by the animation clip.

Root Transform Position (Y) works similarly to Rotation. In this case, you would want to check Bake Into Pose for a walking animation to prevent upward or downward drift, but you would leave it unchecked for a Jump animation to allow up and down movement while jumping.

Root Transform Position (XZ) addresses movement along the xz plane, which is the same as the "floor." Recall that in Unity, the y axis represents up and down in the game world. By leaving Bake Into Pose unchecked, the character will move in the scene on the xz plane while performing the animation. Idle is an example of a common animation clip where you would want to check Bake Into Pose to prevent inadvertent movement.

The green circles are an indicator of how smoothly the animation will loop, based on how similar the transform properties of the model are in the first and last frames of the clip. The warning indicators change to yellow, then red as the transitions from the end of one loop to the beginning of the next diverge. The indicator for Root Transform Position (XZ) is red, as the zombie will move a step forward to a new position with each animation loop.

Now your animation is ready to test, but it's easier to see the walking Root Motion with some background for perspective rather than a flat color. Create a plane for your scene and set its transform to (0, 0, 0) and its scale to (30, 1, 30). In the top menu select Assets ➤ Import Package ➤ Terrain Assets and click Import. Find the Terrain Textures folder in this package and drag the Grass&Rock texture to the Plane in the Hierarchy view. The texture should appear on the plane in the Scene view. In the plane's Mesh Renderer component, set the x and y Tiling values to 5.

Find the zombieController01 in the Animators folder in the Project panel. Double-click it to open in the Animator window. Select the Zombie Run state. Rename it Walk in the Inspector, then drag the walkWithMotion animation clip from the Animations folder in the Project panel to the Motion field in the Inspector. Note that you do not want the entire zombie_lowres@walkWithMotion file, just the animation clip. Click the arrow on the zombie_lowres@walkWithMotion icon to expand it and locate the animation clip (Figure 5-33).

Figure 5-33. Animation clip icon within zombie_lowres@walkWithMotion

Play, and you'll see the zombie perform the walking animation while moving forward in the game world across the plane. Cool!

In professional-grade games, the animated movement of game objects is typically a combination of animation-based Root Motion, scripted motion, physics, and more. Precisely how these are applied depends on the game, but always the goal is to provide the best game experience—the most realistic or style-appropriate, consistent, responsive animation.

OnAnimatorMove

You can use scripts to provide motion for animation clips without Root Motion or to further customize Root Motion within an animation clip with OnAnimatorMove. For the finest control you would want to create and use animation curves that are available in Unity Pro, but the following example will give you a taste of controlling character movement directly with scripting.

For this example, from the Project panel create a new Animator Controller and call it ZombieMotionController. Drag the walking animation clip to the Animator window, where it should appear orange as the new default state. Select the zombie_lowres game object in the Hierarchy view, then change the Controller in its Animator component either by dragging the ZombieMotionController to the Controller field or using the circle select button to the right of the Controller field. Play to confirm the zombie is walking in place.

In the Project panel, create a new script with Create ➤ Javascript and name it ZombieMotionScript. Double-click to open it in MonoDevelop. Delete the empty Start() and Update() functions, then add the following code:

```
public var WalkX:float = 0;
public var WalkZ:float = 0;

function OnAnimatorMove()
{
        var animator : Animator = GetComponent(Animator);

        if (animator)
        {
                var newPosition:Vector3 = transform.position;

                newPosition.x += WalkX * Time.deltaTime;
                newPosition.z += WalkZ * Time.deltaTime;

                transform.position = newPosition;
        }
}
```

This breaks down as follows:

```
(1)      public var WalkX:float = 0;
         public var WalkZ:float = 0;
```

You are declaring public float variables for the x and z component of the zombie's transform position so you can adjust them in real time in the Game view.

```
(2)      function OnAnimatorMove()
```

As you know from reviewing the Scripting Reference (*cough cough* You DID review it, right?) the OnAnimatorMove() function is called every frame after the state machines. This occurs before OnAnimatorIK(), where IK stands for "Inverse Kinematics," another animation method available in Unity Pro.

```
(3)              var animator : Animator = GetComponent(Animator);
                     if (animator)
```

The animator variable is null if an Animator Component is not attached to the zombie game object, so in the following line it is used in the conditional if statement. If the game object has an animator, the following block of code will be executed, but if there is no animator, it is skipped.

```
(4)              var newPosition:Vector3 = transform.position;
```

Within the conditional, the newPosition Vector3 type variable is declared, then assigned the current transform position of the zombie game object.

```
(5)              newPosition.x += WalkX * Time.deltaTime;
                 newPosition.z += WalkZ * Time.deltaTime;
```

The transform's x and z coordinates are updated each frame by the WalkX and WalkZ factors and smoothed with the now familiar Time.deltaTime.

```
(6)              transform.position = newPosition;
```

Finally, the zombie game object's transform position is updated with the new x and z property values.

Save the script. In the Unity editor, drag the script from the Property panel to the zombie_lowres game object in the Hierarchy view to attach it. Two things happen in the Inspector when you do this. The ZombieMotionScript appears as a component, as you expect. Additionally, the Animator component's Apply Root Motion changed to Handled by Script when it detected the OnAnimationMove() function within the script (Figure 5-34). Save the scene and the project.

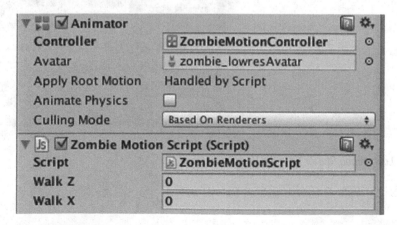

Figure 5-34. Newly attached ZombieMotionScript component, and Handled by Script update in the Animator component's Apply Root Motion property

With the zombie_lowres game object selected, play to test. The zombie is walking in place as before, because the WalkX and WalkZ values are initially set to 0 in the ZombieMotionController script. While still in Play mode, try adjusting the WalkX and WalkZ values in the Inspector. Fine-tune them until the zombie appears to walk across the plane without any drift. Remember to make note of your final values before exiting Play mode, since your changes will not be saved in the Inspector.

Transitions

So far you've only worked with the default animation state. State machines can be quite complex, incorporating any number of animation states that you might need for your character. Moving from one animation state to another is called a **transition**.

For this last Animation Controller you will need to download and import Unity's Mecanim Locomotion Starter Kit from the Asset Store (Figure 5-35). This package has a ready-made Mecanim rig and controller for you, but to understand how it works you will use a few of its animations to build a controller from scratch.

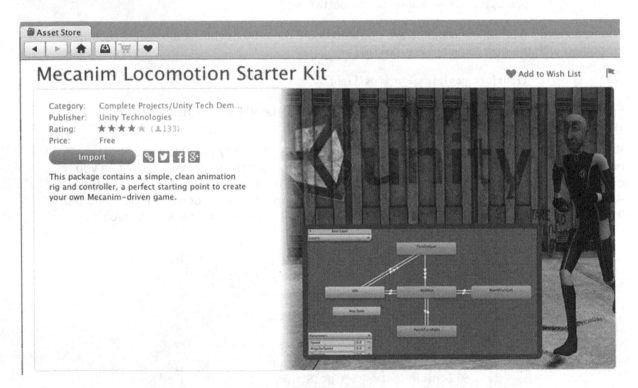

Figure 5-35. Mecanim Locomotion Starter Kit in the Unity Asset Store

Importing this package is performed exactly as you did with the Zombie Character Pack. In the Unity editor top menu, select Window ➤ Asset Store to open a separate window to the Unity Asset Store. In the search bar, type **Mecanim Locomotion Starter Kit** and click the blue Download button. The Importing Package window will open with all of the package contents checked for import. Leave all of these checked and click Import in the bottom right corner of the window, and the Locomotion Setup folder containing the Mecanim Locomotion Starter Kit will appear in the Project panel.

In the Project panel, select the Animators folder. Create a new Animator Controller named ZombieLocomotionController, then double-click to open it.

To find the Idle animation clip, in the Project panel search bar enter **Idle**. Select the DefaultAvatar@Idle_Neutral icon and confirm that it is the Setup/Locomotion/Animations/ DefaultAvatar@Idle_Neutral.fbx by looking at the breadcrumb trail that appears at the bottom (Figure 5-36).

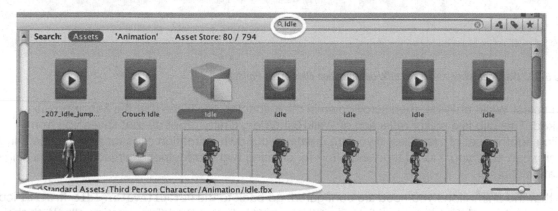

Figure 5-36. DefaultAvatar@Idle_Neutral icon selected in the Project panel

First, configure the animations: With the Idle icon still selected in the Project panel, in the Inspector select Rig. Animation Type should be Humanoid, then change Avatar Definition to Create From This Model and click Apply (Figure 5-37). A checkmark should appear next to the Configure... button. The Animation settings can be left as is. Now the animation clip is compatible with the zombie model animation avatar you created earlier in this chapter.

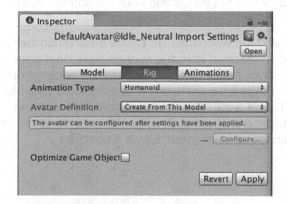

Figure 5-37. Animation.fbx Rig settings in the Inspector

Repeat these steps to configure two other animations you'll use in this example: DefaultAvatar@ WalkForward_NtrlFaceFwd.fbx, and DefaultAvatar@WalkForwardTurnRight_NtrlWide.fbx. For the second one, select Animations ➤ DefaultAvatar@WalkForwardTurnRight_NtrlWide to find both WalkRightWide and WalkLeftWide Clips in the Inspector (Figure 5-38).

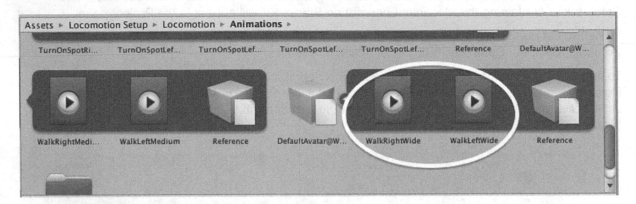

Figure 5-38. WalkRightWide and WalkLeftWide animation clips in the Project panel

If you select WalkLeftWide, then scroll down in the Inspector, you'll see that the Mirror box is checked. This clip is a mirror reflection of WalkRightWide, a nifty property that saves you from needing another set of .fbx files. If you are creating your own animation clips for a game, the mirror property can save you a lot of time and effort for creating two symmetrical animations from a single animation clip.

Now that the animations you need are configured, go back to the DefaultAvatar@Idle_Neutral icon in the Project panel. Expand it by clicking on the arrow to display the Idle animation clip. With the Idle animation clip selected in the Project panel, you can preview by playing it in the bottom of the Inspector. Drag the animation clip icon from the Project panel to the Animator window, then drop it. It should now be the orange default state for the controller.

In the same fashion, locate and expand the DefaultAvatar@WalkForward_NtrlFaceFwd animation to display the Walk animation clip. Drag and drop it into the Animator window. Since Idle is already the default animation state, the Walk state will appear as a gray box. You could change it to the default state by right-clicking and selecting Set As Default from the context menu that appears, but leave it as is for now.

You now have the Idle state and the Walk state. To create a transition between the two, right-click the Idle state and select Make Transition from the context menu that appears. Now if you move the mouse cursor around the window, it will drag a white arrow extending from the Idle state. Click the Walk state to set the transition. Click the white arrow and it should turn blue while displaying its properties in the Inspector (Figure 5-39). You set the conditions for changing from one animation state to another with the transition properties. The Atomic property is checked by default, which means the animation clip cannot be interrupted. Leave it checked.

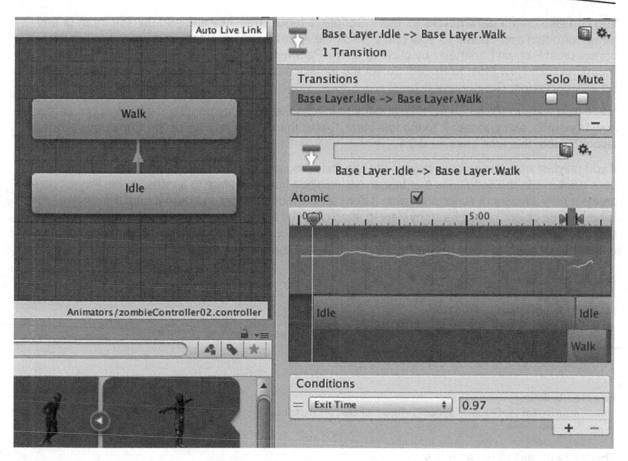

Figure 5-39. Transition properties in the Inspector

> **Tip**   You can drag the state boxes around to keep them organized, and pressing Alt while dragging in the
> Animator window moves the entire grid.

You have different conditions to choose from to trigger the transition. The default Exit Time property
of 0.92 means that the transition will trigger when the clip is 92% through. In the Hierarchy panel,
select the zombie_lowres game object, then in the Inspector change the Animator Controller to
ZombieLocomotionController either by dragging the controller from the project panel into the
property field in the Inspector or by clicking the circle select button to the right of the Controller
property and choosing ZombieLocomotionController from the pop-up menu.

Playtest, and you'll see that the zombie begins in the Idle state, then automatically transitions to the
Walk state based on the Exit Time condition. You can experiment with smoothing the transition in
the Inspector by dragging the blue start and end values of the graphic overlap between the Idle and
Walk clips. Exit Play mode and save the scene.

You can also create **parameters** for use in scripts to trigger transitions based on user input or any other condition appropriate to your game. Click the Animator window tab, and in the bottom left corner create a float parameter by clicking on the Parameters + symbol and selecting Float. Change the name from New Float to Speed. Select the transition arrow in the Inspector, change Exit Time to Speed, and select Greater and 0.1.

You'll also want to transition from Walk back to Idle. In the same fashion, right-click Walk, create a new transition, and connect it to the Idle state. Select the transition, and for the Conditions property select Speed, this time Less, and 0.1.

If you playtest now, the zombie stays in the Idle state. You will need to create a script that defines what user input meets the conditions that trigger the transition from one state to another. In the Project panel, create a new JavaScript script and name it ZombieLocomotion. Drag and drop it onto the zombie_ lowres game object in the Hierarchy view to attach it to the zombie character. The ZombieLocomotion script will appear as a new component in the Inspector. Double-click the ZombieLocomotion script icon in the Project panel to open it in MonoDevelop, then edit the code as follows:

```
#pragma strict

private var animator : Animator;

function Start () {
        animator = GetComponent(Animator);
}

function Update () {
        animator.SetFloat("Speed", Input.GetAxis("Vertical"));
}
```

This code breaks down as follows:

(1)   `private var animator : Animator;`

Declare an Animator type reference variable. If you did this in one line in the `Start()` function like you did previously in the `OnAnimatorMove()` function in the ZombieMotion script, the scope of the animator variable would be limited to the `Start()` function. By declaring it here, you make it available to any function within the ZombieLocomotion class.

(2)   `animator.SetFloat("Speed", Input.GetAxis("Vertical"));`

Here you are setting the Speed parameter you created based on the user input. Playtest and you'll find the zombie walks forward when the up arrow key or the W key is pressed.

Any State

Any State is a special state provided by Unity in the spirit of DRY, discussed earlier in the "Run Like a Zombie" section. It serves as a shorthand to allow you to transition from any of the animation states in your controller to some other particular state. A common usage of this would be Death, assuming your character could take a hit of some kind regardless of what animation state it is currently in. You set up this transition just like you would any other transition, the difference being that you do it directly from the Any State box to the Death box only once, not from each individual animation state.

The reverse is not true. You cannot transition from an animation state to the Any State because it does not represent a unique animation state, but rather all of the animation states, so the Unity engine would not know which precise animation state to which to transition. It is not configured to be used as a means to transition to a random animation state. As such, if you do try to create a transition to it, the arrow just won't stick.

User Input and the Input Manager

What's going on with this Input.GetAxis? One of the powerful features of Unity is that you can build one game, then deploy it to a wide variety of platforms. This presents a particular challenge for dealing with user input, which might come from the keyboard, mouse, joystick, gamepad, or the touch and accelerometer input of mobile devices.

Instead of having to hard-code every possibility into your scripts, Unity's Input Manager comes to the rescue. With the Input Manager, you can configure the various input devices, then access them all through a scripting interface as you did here with Input.GetAxis.

You get the default input axes shown in Table 5-1 when you create a project.

Table 5-1. Input Manager default settings

Input Axes	Input
Horizontal/Vertical	WASD and arrow keys
Fire1, Fire2, Fire3	Ctrl, Option/Alt, ⌘
Mouse X/Mouse Y	Mouse movement delta
Window Shake X/Window Shake Y	Window movement

In the Unity editor top menu, select Edit ➤ Project Settings ➤ Input to change these settings or add new virtual axes. Bear in mind that as part of a good game experience, your users will expect some standardization, where common inputs engender common actions. They expect the arrow keys and WASD keys will control movement. At the same time, the Input Manager also allows end users to configure the keyboard so they can adjust it to their personal preferences (Figure 5-40).

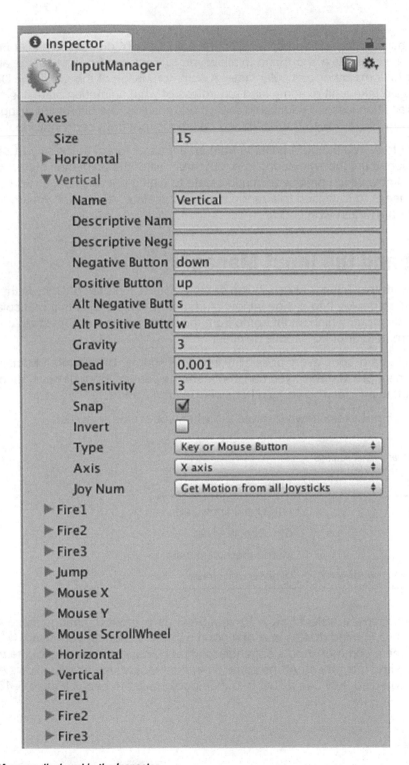

Figure 5-40. Input Manager displayed in the Inspector

> **Tip** Use Input.GetButton for action events like shooting a weapon or picking up an object. Use Input.GetAxis for movement.

For keyboard input and joystick input the neutral position equals 0, where each axis has a value between –1 and 1. A positive button gives a positive value. To see this in action, in the ZombieLocomotion script add the following lines of code to the Update() function:

```
var inputValue : float = Input.GetAxis("Vertical");
Debug.Log(inputValue);
```

Save the script. In the Unity editor Project panel, select the Console tab so you can watch the Debug.Log output. Enter Play mode. Notice that inputValue is 0. Press and hold the up arrow or W key and watch it change to 1. Since you set the transition condition to Greater than 0.1 in the Animator Controller, as soon as the inputValue exceeds 0.1, the transition from the Idle state to the Walk state is triggered. Release the key, see the inputValue drop to 0, and the transition back to the Idle state is triggered when it gets below 0.1.

Blend Trees

While transitions are used to switch from one animation state to another, a **blend tree** incorporates several animation clips together to **blend** the motion for a smoother resultant animation movement.

Blend trees are commonly used with walking and running animations. For best results the movement of the clips to be blended must be similar and take place at the same point in terms of normalized time. "Normalized time" means that the clips can be of different lengths, where the first frame has a normalized value of 0.0 and the last frame has a value of 0.99. As long as the left foot touches the ground at the same normalized time in each clip, say 0.2, and the right foot touches the ground at the same time, say 0.7, then the clips will blend well.

In the following illustration, a walk animation is compared to a run animation. You know that the general movement of alternating arm and leg movements are similar, and that it makes sense that in real time a run loop takes less time than a walk loop, since running is faster than walking. Normalized time accounts for the speed difference and looks at positions at the same relative point (represented as a percentage) in the loop cycle. Notice the difference in real time on the bottom left and normalized time as a percentage on the right (Figure 5-41).

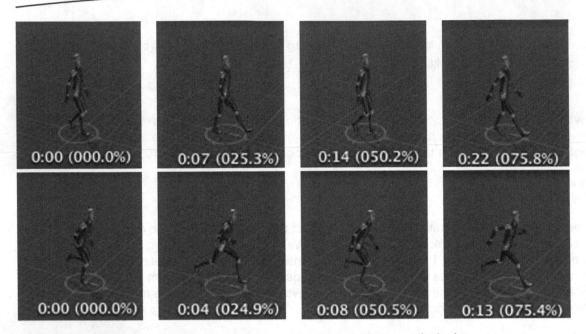

Figure 5-41. Comparison of walk animation (top) and run animation (bottom) at normalized points

You are going to add more movement for the zombie character by creating a blend tree for walking forward, walking forward while turning right, and walking forward while turning left. In the Project window select the ZombieLocomotion controller and open it in the Animator window. Create a new float parameter named Direction in the same way you created the Speed parameter previously.

Select the Walk state, then right-click and select Create new BlendTree in State. Notice the Motion property changed from Walk to Blend Tree in the Inspector. Now double-click the Walk state to open the Blend Tree Graph with the root Blend Tree Node. Notice the Speed parameter with a slider next to it appears on the node. First, change this parameter by selecting the Blend Tree Node and changing Parameter in the Inspector panel from Speed to Direction, then click the minimum value of 0 and change it to –1 (Figure 5-42). When using the Input Manager, by definition an axis has a value from –1 to 1.

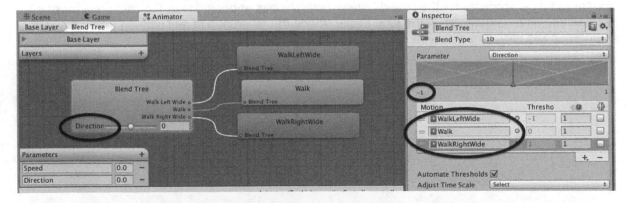

Figure 5-42. Walk Blend Tree in the Animator window and Inspector

Beneath it will be an empty list for Motion. Click the + and Add Motion Field three times to add three motion fields. From the Locomotion Animations folder in the Project panel, drag and drop the WalkLeftWide, Walk, and WalkRightWide into the fields.

The blue pyramids represent each of the motions, the red mark the parameter value at that particular point in the graph, and the height of the pyramids at that point show the relative influence or weight of the child motion in the blend. If you move the slider of the Direction parameter in the Blend Tree Root Node to 0, the graph in the Inspector shows you that the Walk motion is at its greatest weight while WalkTurnRight and WalkTurnLeft are at their minimums. WalkTurnLeft is at its maximum at a Direction parameter value of –1, and WalkTurnRight is at its maximum at a Direction parameter value of 1.

In MonoDevelop, add the following lines of code to the Update() function in the ZombieLocomotion script:

```
animator.SetFloat("Direction", Input.GetAxis("Horizontal"));
var directionInputValue : float = Input.GetAxis("Horizontal");
Debug.Log(directionInputValue);
```

Save the script. In the editor, save the scene. In the Project panel, select the Console tab so you can see the Speed and Direction parameters change in response to your input. Notice that you have to have the W or up arrow key pressed for the zombie character to respond to the right or left arrow keys to turn. This is exactly how you set up the Animator Controller: the WalkTurnRight and WalkTurnLeft clips are part of the Walk blend tree, so the zombie character must be in the Walk state in order to turn.

Don't Reinvent the Wheel

The Mecanim Locomotion Starter Kit asset that you imported is a ready-to-go basic animation rig and controller. While this just scratches the surface of what you can do with Mecanim, now that you have a solid understanding of how animation clips, animator controllers, and scripts work together, you can use this and other similar ready-made assets in your projects by customizing them to your game rather than starting from scratch. Take a closer look at Locomotion now and see what you've learned.

You should be able to identify the parts of the Locomotion animation state machine depicted in Figure 5-43.

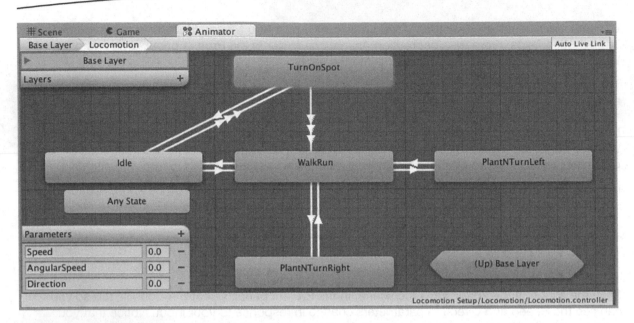

Figure 5-43. Locomotion Animator from Unity's Mecanim Locomotion Starter Kit

Double-click any of these animation states to see the blend trees (Figure 5-44). Though there are more animation clips being blended, the fundamental pieces of the blend tree are the same.

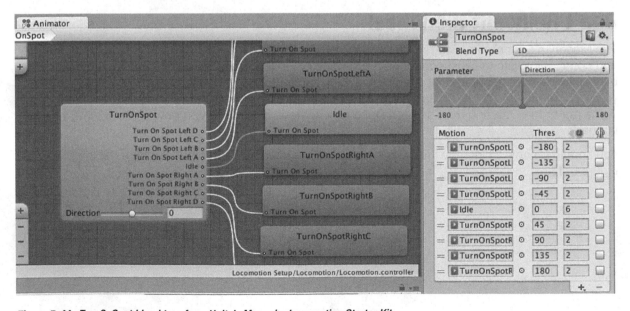

Figure 5-44. TurnOnSpot blend tree from Unity's Mecanim Locomotion Starter Kit

In the Project panel, drill down through Locomotion Setup ➤ Locomotion ➤ Scripts to find the Locomotion script. It happens to be in C# so the syntax is a little different, but with the UnityScript version for comparison here you can decipher it pretty easily:

```
#pragma strict

    private var m_Animator : Animator = null;

    private var m_SpeedId : int = 0;
    private var m_AgularSpeedId : int = 0;
    private var m_DirectionId : int = 0;

    public var m_SpeedDampTime : float = 0.1f;
    public var m_AnguarSpeedDampTime : float = 0.25f;
    public var m_DirectionResponseTime : float = 0.2f;

    function Locomotion(animator : Animator)
    {
        m_Animator = animator;

        m_SpeedId = Animator.StringToHash("Speed");
        m_AgularSpeedId = Animator.StringToHash("AngularSpeed");
        m_DirectionId = Animator.StringToHash("Direction");
    }

    function Do(speed : float, direction : float)
    {
        var state : AnimatorStateInfo = m_Animator.GetCurrentAnimatorStateInfo(0);

        var inTransition : boolean = m_Animator.IsInTransition(0);
        var inIdle : boolean = state.IsName("Locomotion.Idle");
        var inTurn : boolean = state.IsName("Locomotion.TurnOnSpot") || state.IsName("Locomotion.
        PlantNTurnLeft") || state.IsName("Locomotion.PlantNTurnRight");
        var inWalkRun : boolean = state.IsName("Locomotion.WalkRun");

        var speedDampTime : float = inIdle ? 0 : m_SpeedDampTime;
        var angularSpeedDampTime : float = inWalkRun || inTransition ? m_AnguarSpeedDampTime : 0;
        var directionDampTime : float = inTurn || inTransition ? 1000000 : 0;

        var angularSpeed : float = direction / m_DirectionResponseTime;

        m_Animator.SetFloat(m_SpeedId, speed, speedDampTime, Time.deltaTime);
        m_Animator.SetFloat(m_AgularSpeedId, angularSpeed, angularSpeedDampTime, Time.deltaTime);
        m_Animator.SetFloat(m_DirectionId, direction, directionDampTime, Time.deltaTime);
    }
```

This code breaks down as follows:

(1)   private var m_Animator : Animator = null;

Declares an Animator type reference variable with a null value.

```
(2)    private var m_SpeedId : int = 0;
       private var m_AgularSpeedId : int = 0;
       private var m_DirectionId : int = 0;
```

Declares int type variables for parameter IDs, for use as a **hash identifier**. Hash identifiers won't be covered in detail here, but they are another way to reference parameters using integers instead of strings. Using a hash identifier is more efficient, so it contributes to improved performance.

```
(3)    public var m_SpeedDampTime : float = 0.1f;
       public var m_AnguarSpeedDampTime : float = 0.25f;
       public var m_DirectionResponseTime : float = 0.2f;
```

Declares float type variables and set with default values. These are smoothing factors for the various animation transitions.

```
(4)    function Locomotion(animator : Animator)
       {
           m_Animator = animator;

           m_SpeedId = Animator.StringToHash("Speed");
           m_AgularSpeedId = Animator.StringToHash("AngularSpeed");
           m_DirectionId = Animator.StringToHash("Direction");
       }
```

The Locomotion() function accepts an Animator argument and with this sets the values of the previously declared animator and parameter ID variables.

```
(5)    function Do(speed : float, direction : float)
```

The Do() function accepts two float arguments speed and direction.

```
(6)        var state : AnimatorStateInfo = m_Animator.GetCurrentAnimatorStateInfo(0);
```

Declares an AnimatorStateInfo reference variable state and sets it with the state of the Animator. With this you have more detailed information on the current animation state, such as length of the animation state, whether or not it is looping, and more.

Remember   You can use ⌘+' to open the Scripting Reference for more details, such as the complete list of variables and functions available through AnimatorStateInfo.

```
(7)        var inTransition : boolean = m_Animator.IsInTransition(0);
```

Declares the boolean variable `inTransition`. This will be set to `true` if the current Animator is in a transition between animation states and `false` if not.

```
(8)          var inIdle : boolean = state.IsName("Locomotion.Idle");
```

Declares the boolean variable `inIdle` and set to `true` if the current animation state is the Locomotion animator's Idle state.

```
(9)          var inTurn : boolean = state.IsName("Locomotion.TurnOnSpot") ||
state.IsName("Locomotion.PlantNTurnLeft") || state.IsName("Locomotion.PlantNTurnRight");
```

Declares the boolean variable `inTurn`, and set it to `true` if the current animation state is one of the turning animations. Recall that || is the logic OR operator, so this line declares inTurn as a boolean and sets it to `true` if the name of the current animation state is `Locomotion.TurnOnSpot` OR `Locomotion.PlantNTurnLeft` OR `Locomotion.PlantNTurnRight`.

```
(10)         var inWalkRun : boolean = state.IsName("Locomotion.WalkRun");
```

Declares the boolean variable `inWalkRun` and set to `true` if the current animation state is the Locomotion animator's WalkRun state.

```
(11)         var speedDampTime : float = inIdle ? 0 : m_SpeedDampTime;
             var angularSpeedDampTime : float = inWalkRun || inTransition ? m_AnguarSpeedDampTime :
                0;
             var directionDampTime : float = inTurn || inTransition ? 1000000 : 0;
```

These statements are used to set the respective damping factors depending on the state of the animator, whether an animation state or a transition. The syntax here is a very abbreviated form of a conditional that is not as readable as you've seen so far—remember that the less code, the more efficient and so the better performance.

The question mark ? with the subsequent colon is called a **conditional operator**. The condition to be evaluated comes first, before the question mark. If the condition evaluates to `true`, then the result of the first expression—after the question mark and before the colon—is the result of the operation. If `false`, the second expression—after the colon—is the result of the operation.

For example, in the first line of this block of code, the newly declared float variable `speedDampTime` is set to 0 if `inIdle` is true. The character has no speed if it is in the Idle state. If inIdle is false, the character is moving so the speedDampTime is set to the current value of m_SpeedDampTime.

In the second line, the newly declared float variable `angularSpeedDampTime` will be set to the current value of `m_anguarspeeddsmptime` if the animator is in the WalkRun state OR in transition; otherwise it evaluates to `false` and it is set to 0.

Similarly, in the third line, the newly declared float variable `directionDampTime` will be set to 1000000 if the animator is in the Turn state OR in transition; otherwise it evaluates to `false` and is set to 0.

```
(12)         var angularSpeed : float = direction / m_DirectionResponseTime;
```

Declares the `angularSpeed` variable and setting it with the result of the calculation `direction/m_`
`DirectionResponseTime`.

```
(13)        m_Animator.SetFloat(m_SpeedId, speed, speedDampTime, Time.deltaTime);
            m_Animator.SetFloat(m_AgularSpeedId, angularSpeed, angularSpeedDampTime, Time.
             deltaTime);
            m_Animator.SetFloat(m_DirectionId, direction, directionDampTime, Time.deltaTime);
```

Finally, now that you have determined the state of the animator and determined the appropriate
damping factors, you can set the animator's parameters. As you can see in the Scripting reference,
`Animator.SetFloat` accepts as arguments the name of the parameter, the new value for the
parameter, the time allowed for the parameter to reach the value (the smoothing factor), and the
current frame `deltaTime`.

If you want to dig in to more animation, Unity has a number of other examples with more animations,
controllers, and scripts and entire projects with sample scenes available for free on the Asset
Store. These are phenomenal working examples of common uses and best practices in animation.
Experiment with these, and don't be shy about searching for answers to your questions on the Unity
forums.

Summary

Whew—this chapter was pretty intense! You began with moving primitive game objects with scripts
that altered the `transform.position` and `transform.rotation` properties, then added user interaction
to drive the movement. You also learned to smooth these movement transitions with the `Lerp()`
function.

Next you reviewed Unity's Mecanim animation system and learned to animate character models
with animation clips driven with animator controllers. You went on to learn how to transition between
different animation states with Mecanim and corresponding scripts. During this process, you found
and utilized handy ready-made animation assets provided by Unity in the Asset Store.

Unity's Mecanim is a wonderful tool that makes learning and applying animations easier than ever
before. Nevertheless, this was no small endeavor—animating 3D models is still a career field in and
of itself. You definitely deserve a pat on the back for a job well done!

6

Starting with Coding Physics

Working with game physics is fun, and Unity's physics engines make it super easy. Physics defines physical properties of how objects interact with each other or in response to external forces. Unity's powerful physics engines allow you to assign physical properties to your game objects for consistent, realistic gameplay. There are two physics engines, one for 2D and another for 3D. Though they are implemented with different components such as Box Collider 2D and Box Collider 3D, they work much the same way. In this chapter, you will create a simple game to learn how to set up the physical properties of 3D game objects, then add scripting for more complex, interactive behavior.

Rigidbodies

A game object must have a Rigidbody component for the physics engine to recognize it. The physics engine does the calculations on how the object will behave, resulting in a change in the object's Transform. Rather than manipulating the position and orientation of the object directly with the Transform component's translate and rotate properties as you did in Chapter 4, this time you will manipulate the object with physical forces.

> **Note** While you could change the Transform itself, this might interfere with the game engine's calculations and result in unexpected behavior—just don't do it.

Start a new project with a new scene. Add a directional light, a plane with a Transform position of (0, 0, 0), then a Cube game object with a Transform position of (0, 3, 0). Playing demonstrates a static, primitive cube above a plane. Add a Rigidbody component to the Cube either with the top menu by selecting Component ➤ Physics ➤ Rigidbody or in the Inspector with Add Component ➤ Physics ➤ Rigidbody. Play, and the cube falls to the plane because it is now affected by gravity.

Rigidbody Properties

Let's take a closer look at the Rigidbody component and its properties displayed in the Inspector (Figure 6-1).

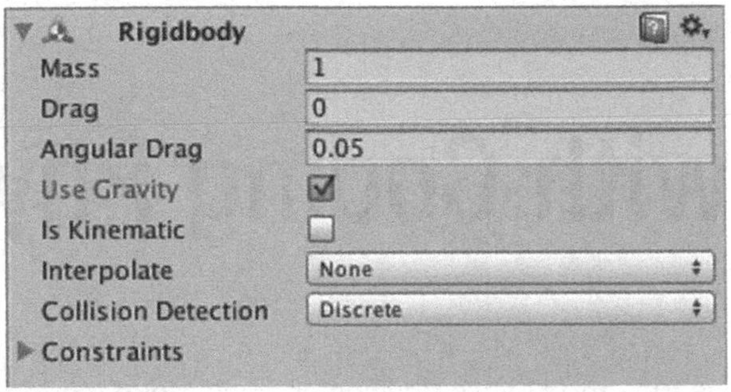

Figure 6-1. Rigidbody component in the Inspector

In physics, **mass** describes the amount of physical matter in an object. This is not the same as weight—weight is the measurement of the pull of gravity on an object. For example, a golf ball on Earth and a golf ball on the Moon have the same mass, but a different weight because of the difference in gravity on the Earth and the Moon.

If you play around with the Mass property right now by changing the mass to 100 and playing, or to 0.1 and playing, the cube appears to fall at the same rate. Gravity is a constant force acting on an object. Without getting into the mathematics, the acceleration (the speeding up) by gravity of two objects with different masses will be the same, if you eliminate other factors such as air resistance. In real terms, this means that a penny will fall at the same rate as a bowling ball. Mass is an important factor in collisions and the application of arbitrary forces.

Drag is an opposing force that works like air resistance. Try changing the value of the Drag property to 10, play, and see the effect it has on the falling cube.

Angular Drag works much the same way as Drag only in opposition to a rotational movement.

Uncheck **Use Gravity** and the cube no longer falls since it is no longer affected by gravity.

There may be situations within your game where you may want to move the game object with its Transform rather than with the physics engine. Enabling **Is Kinematic** means the game object has a Rigidbody component but is no longer driven by the physics engine.

Interpolate is used for smoothing the motion of an object. A general rule of thumb for optimizing performance is not to use this unless you actually see jerkiness in the movement of your game object. The Interpolate option smooths the motion based on the object's Transform in the previous frame, while the Extrapolate option smooths the motion based on the object's estimated Transform in the next frame.

Collision Detection varies the method the physics engine uses to calculate collisions. Discrete is the default value for normal collisions. Continuous is used for fast-moving objects if their collisions are not being detected properly. Game performance can be detrimentally affected when using Continuous collision detection, so use this only if needed. Continuous Dynamic is a combination of Continuous collision detection against other objects using Continuous or Continuous Dynamic detection and against static Mesh Colliders without rigidbodies, but Discrete collision detection for everything else. Since Continuous Dynamic also uses Continuous, it can also have a big effect on performance.

You've seen **Constraints** used for animation Root Motion and they work the same way here. Expanding Constraints and checking a Freeze Position axis stops movement along that axis, while checking a Freeze Rotation axis stops the object from rotating around that axis.

Controlling a Rigidbody with Forces

AddForce() and AddTorque() are the functions you use in scripts to apply forces to a rigidbody. Torque is a type of force that results in a rotational movement.

In the Project panel, create a new folder and name it Scripts. Select the Scripts folder, then Create ➤ Javascript, then name the script Forces. Drag the script to the Cube game object in the Hierarchy to attach it. Double-click the script icon in the Project panel to open it in MonoDevelop for editing. Delete the Start() and Update() functions. Add the following code:

```
public var aForce : float = 5;

function FixedUpdate () {
        rigidbody.AddForce (Vector3.right * aForce);
}
```

Physics calculations depend on discrete increments of time, so the time-based FixedUpdate() function is used instead of the frame-rate-based Update() function. Save, then play in the editor. Notice that as the cube is moving to the right, it is speeding up. This is because the force is applied with every FixedUpdate() call, which occurs at every fixed frame-rate frame. aForce is a factor that you can change in the Inspector to get the response to AddForce exactly the way you want it.

Now change the code in FixedUpdate() to the following:

```
rigidbody.AddTorque (Vector3.right * aForce);
```

Recall (or check the Scripting Reference) that Vector3.right is shorthand for (1, 0, 0). Now instead of moving to the right along the x axis, the cube rotates around the x axis, causing it to move backward.

While that works fine for applying a constant force, what if you would like to control the force during gameplay? Comment out the FixedUpdate() function and add the following code:

```
function OnMouseDown () {
        rigidbody.AddTorque (Vector3.forward * aForce);
    }
```

Play, and click the stationary cube to start it rotating around its z axis. Remember, with OnMouseDown() you must click the game object, in this case the cube, for the code to be executed. Keep clicking and it rotates faster with each click. Exit Play mode.

Select the Cube game object in the Hierarchy. Change its Transform position to (0, 1, 0). Now create a Sphere game object with a Transform position of (0, 2, 0). In the Inspector, select Add Component ➤ Physics ➤ Rigidbody to add a Rigidbody component. Uncheck Use Gravity. From the Scripts folder in the Project panel, drag the Forces script to the Sphere in the Hierarchy to add it; alternatively, select the Sphere in the Hierarchy, then drag the Forces script icon from the Project panel to the bottom of the Inspector to add it as a component to the Sphere game object. Change the OnMouseDown() line of code from AddTorque to AddForce:

```
rigidbody.AddForce (Vector3.forward * aForce);
```

Save the script. Back in the Inspector view of the editor, change the value of aForce to 1000. Enter Play mode and click the sphere; it moves forward along the z axis in a straight line. Check Use Gravity, and now it arcs forward and downward.

What you use only depends on what suits your game. While a magical ball of fire might travel in a straight line, a rubber chicken launched from a trebuchet should probably respond to gravity. But what if you'd like your magical ball of fire to accelerate like a rocket? Or your rocket to accelerate like a rocket?

There are several ways to accomplish this. One is to simply apply the force in FixedUpdate(), where the force is applied continually rather than once with the click of the mouse.

Another is that the AddForce() function takes a second argument after the Vector3, called ForceMode. If not explicitly designated, it defaults to Force. If you're reviewing the Unity documentation as we go, then you may have already found that it also has choices of Acceleration, Impulse, and VelocityChange. The AddTorque() function also has this second optional ForceMode parameter.

You can make the Sphere accelerate by using AddForce.Acceleration as follows:

```
rigidbody.AddForce (Vector3.forward * aForce, ForceMode.Acceleration);
```

Another is not through scripting, but with a handy physics component you can use with rigidbodies called Constant Force.

First, disable the Sphere's Forces script component by unchecking it in the Inspector. Then select Add Component ➤ Physics ➤ Constant Force and it will appear in the Inspector (Figure 6-2).

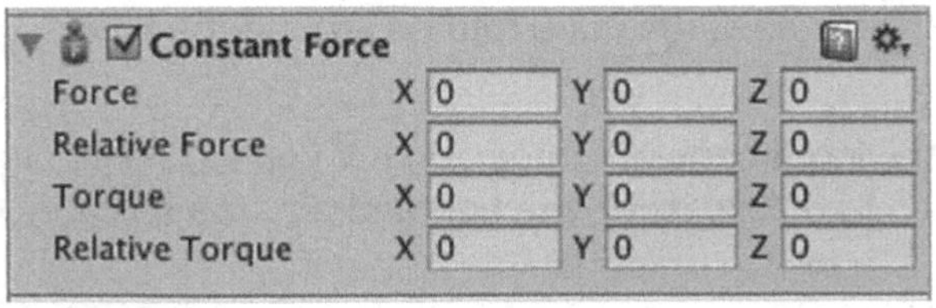

Figure 6-2. Constant Force component in the Inspector

The Force and Torque properties define force vectors relative to world space coordinates, while Relative Force and Relative Torque properties define vectors relative to the object's local space coordinates. For example, while your player character might run around with a rocket launcher and point it in any direction, if you set the z coordinate of the Relative Force to a positive value, the rocket will move forward in the direction that it is pointed. Let's give it a try with a rough prototype.

Select the Cube game object and change its Transform position to (1, 1, 0), rotation to (350, 0, 0) and scale to (1, 1, 3). In the Hierarchy view, create a Capsule game object and set its Transform position to (0, 1, 0). Again in Hierarchy, drag Cube and drop it on the Capsule game object to make it a child object. Notice that the Transform of the Cube has changed; now its position is designated as relative to its parent object, the Capsule, rather than relative to the origin of world space. The Capsule game object represents the player and the Cube game object represents the rocket launcher.

The Sphere game object will represent the rockets being fired. Select the Sphere and delete the Forces script component by clicking the cog icon and Remove Component. Then in the Constant Force component, change the Sphere's Relative Force z coordinate to 35, then its Transform. position to (1, 1, 2). In the Hierarchy view, drag the Sphere onto the Cube to make it a child object of the Cube so it will always launch from the end of the Cube rocket launcher whichever way the player is pointing it.

You'll want to fire more than one rocket, so you need to make the Sphere into a prefab. You'll do this the same way you created the snazzy cube prefab in Chapter 3. Create a Prefabs folder in the Project panel. Drag the Sphere from the Hierarchy to the Prefabs folder, then name the prefab Rocket. Delete the Sphere from Hierarchy view by right-clicking and selecting Delete.

In the Project panel, open the Scripts folder, then select Create ➤ Javascript and name the new script RocketLaunch. Double-click the script icon to open it in MonoDevelop. Edit the code to the following:

```
#pragma strict

public var rocket : GameObject;

function Update () {
        if(Input.GetButtonUp("Fire1")) {
                var rocketInstance : GameObject = Instantiate(rocket);
        }
}
```

All of this should be familiar from previous chapters. First you declare a GameObject type reference variable named rocket. Then, in the Update() function you use the if statement to check for the condition where the default "Fire1" button managed by the Input Manager has been released from being pressed. If this condition is true, then a new instance of the rocket is created. Save the script.

In the editor, drag the RocketLaunch script from the Project panel and drop it onto the Main Camera in the Hierarchy. With the Main Camera selected, you'll see the RocketLaunch script has been added as a component. The Rocket field is empty, so if you were to play now, nothing would happen when you try to launch a rocket. Drag the Sphere prefab from the Prefabs folder in the Project panel and drop it into the Rocket field in the Inspector. Save the scene.

Playtest using the left Ctrl key, which is the default Fire1 button. Yay! You are launching spheres that are accelerating like a rocket. The Drag property of the rigidbody will oppose any of these means of acceleration and can be used to limit the maximum velocity.

Several methods of accomplishing an acceleration effect are presented to you here. Which to use always depends on the context within your game. The important thing here is that Unity often has more than one solution, one of which may be more appropriate for your game context and performance than another. Find these in the documentation, experiment with them, and cross-search in the Unity community forums to rapidly expand your game developer repertoire.

Meanwhile, take a look at what's going on in the Hierarchy—a Sphere(Clone) appears for each new instantiation. Each of these is being tracked by the physics engine, which will ultimately bog it down and detrimentally affect game performance.

In Chapter 4, you addressed this with the `Destroy()` function. Then, you used the `Destroy()` function's time-delay argument. Add `Destroy(rocketInstance, 2);` to the end of the `Update()` function in the RocketLaunch script, save, and play. As expected, the rockets disappear after three seconds. The whole point of firing rockets is to blow something up. How about hitting some targets? Physical interactions between game objects is where colliders come into play.

Colliders

While a rigidbody component enables a game object to respond to physical forces, a collider component enables a game object to react when it comes into contact with other game objects. Unity's primitive objects come with collider components already attached. Select Cube in the Hierarchy, and you'll see the green outline of the Box Collider in the Scene view.

You can add a collider either in the Inspector by selecting Add Component ➤ Physics then selecting the type of collider, or with the editor top menu by selecting Component ➤ Physics, then the collider type.

The Mesh Collider selection will take the shape of the game object's mesh. While it sounds ideal, mesh colliders often have a negative effect on game performance and Unity has a limit on the number of polygons allowed. The solution is to use several primitive colliders to approximate the shape of your 3D model.

> **Note**   Best practices call for using mesh colliders for scene geometry and compound primitive colliders for moving objects.

The collider properties are pretty straightforward (Figure 6-3). Using a collider as a **trigger** will be explained in the Triggers section of this chapter. **Physic Materials** define in more detail the behavior of the object when it collides. You can easily picture how a metal ball, a rubber ball, and a soap bubble would respond differently to collisions with the same object even though each is a simple sphere. Physic Materials will be covered in a section by that name later in this chapter. **Center** is the (x, y, z) coordinates of this collider in local space. This means you can offset the collider from the game object. The size doesn't have to be the same as the game object, either, so the remaining fields pertain to resizing the collider depending on which primitive type you have—Size with x, y, z values for a box; radius and height for a capsule; and radius for a sphere.

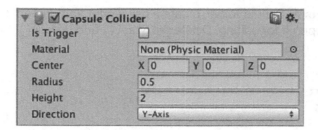

Figure 6-3. *Capsule Collider component in the Inspector*

Stop to playtest after each of the following instructions. First, add a primitive game object cube, name it Target, and change its Transform position to (1.4, 1, 7) and scale to (2, 2, 0.2). At least one of the game objects involved in a collision must have a rigidbody component. In the Inspector, select Add Component ➤ Physics ➤ Rigidbody. Play, and Target falls according to gravity.

In the Rigidbody component, uncheck Use Gravity. Play, and the projectile impacts the cube, then falls under the force of gravity while the cube flies away, the rate of change of its position and rotation governed by the physics engine. Here you see that though you disabled the target cube's response to the force of gravity, with a Box Collider component it still responds to collision forces.

Change the target rigidbody constraints so it will rotate in place when hit. In the Inspector, find the Rigidbody component and expand the Constraints property. Check X, Y, and Z for Freeze Position, which will hold the target in place when struck. Play and the target still responds to being struck by the projectile, but stays in position relative to world space.

Still in the Inspector, check Y and Z for Freeze Rotation. Play, and now the target stays in position and rotates about the x axis. Save the scene and save the project.

The primitive objects provided by Unity come with colliders that match the size and shape of the game object's rendered appearance, but you aren't limited to this. You can offset the collider from the game object, change the size of the collider relative to the game object, or even use a collider with a different shape than the game object for an even wider variety of behaviors. Continue to experiment as you go!

OnCollision

While this is a nice little demo for what the physics engine can do with your game objects, let's get back to scripting and take a look at what is going on behind the scenes. In the frame where the projectile first impacts the target, the physics engine calls the function OnCollisionEnter(). In the subsequent frames where the two objects remain in contact it calls OnCollisionStay(). Finally, when the objects are no longer in contact with each other, OnCollisionExit() is called.

Create a new scene and add a directional light. Create a cube and assign a Transform position of (0, 0.5, 0) and rotation of (0, 0, 10). Create a Sphere with a Transform position of (0, 3, 0) and add a Rigidbody component by selecting Add Component ➤ Physics ➤ Rigidbody. Save the scene and name it.

In the Project panel Assets ➤ Scripts folder, create a new script and name it CollisionColors. Double-click its icon to open it for editing. Delete the Start() and Update() functions, then add the following lines of code:

```
private var red : float;
private var green : float;
private var blue : float;
private var color : Color;

function OnCollisionEnter() {
    Debug.Log("OnCollisionEnter");
    color = GetRandomColor();
    gameObject.renderer.material.color = color;
}

function OnCollisionStay() {
    Debug.Log("OnCollisionStay");
}

function OnCollisionExit() {
    Debug.Log("OnCollisionExit");
    color = GetRandomColor();
    gameObject.renderer.material.color = color;
}

function RandomColorValue() {
    var randomValue : float;
    randomValue = Random.Range(0.000, 1.000);
    return randomValue;
}

function GetRandomColor() {
    red = RandomColorValue();
    green = RandomColorValue();
    blue = RandomColorValue();
    color = Color(red, green, blue);
    return color;
}
```

Save the script, and return to the editor. Drag the script and drop it on the Sphere to attach it, then save the scene. Play, and you'll see the sphere falls to the cube, changes color, and rolls across the slanted top surface of the cube and over the edge, again changing color when it does. In the Console, you'll find one "OnCollisionEnter", multiple lines of "OnCollisionStay", and finally one "OnCollisionExit".

Breaking this down, the color-changing code is familiar to you from Chapter 4. You declare float values to hold the individual color values and a Color type reference variable to hold a randomly generated Color's RGB values. GetRandomColor() calls RandomColorValue() to generate random values for each of the Color RGB values, then assigns them to the color variable.

When the sphere falls under the force of gravity, it will collide with the cube. The physics engine will call OnCollisionEnter(), where "OnCollisionEnter" will print to the console, and a call to GetRandomColor() generates a random color, which is then assigned to the material property of the sphere.

As the sphere rolls across the cube, the physics engine calls OnCollisionStay() in each frame the sphere is in contact with the cube, and "OnCollisionStay" is printed to the Console many times.

Finally, the sphere rolls off of the cube and the colliders are no longer in contact. When this happens, the physics engine calls OnCollisionExit()."OnCollisionExit" will print to the Console, and a new random color is generated and assigned to the sphere.

The Other GameObject

You can also get information about the collision itself, including a reference to the other object the scripted object is colliding with. In MonoDevelop, edit the OnCollisionEnter() as follows:

```
function OnCollisionEnter(other : Collision) {
    Debug.Log("OnCollisionEnter");
    color = GetRandomColor();
    other.gameObject.renderer.material.color = color;
}
```

Save the script. Return to the editor, save the scene, then play. Now the cube rather than sphere changes color on initial impact.

Changing the color is just an example that is easy to follow in the editor. Remember that game objects are made up of components, and you can affect any component's properties through your script. The autocomplete function of MonoDevelop help you out here. Type other.gameObject. to see your options (Figure 6-4).

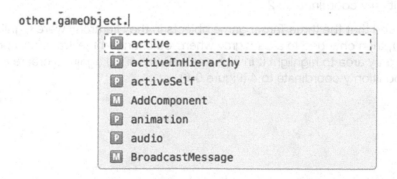

Figure 6-4. autocomplete selections for gameObject

Let's put these pieces together into a simple game prototype, but first take a moment to make sure your project is organized with scripts in the Scripts folder, prefabs in the Prefabs folder, and scenes in the Scenes folder. If you don't have any of these folders, select the Assets folder, then Create ➤ Folder and name it appropriately.

Target Practice

Create a new scene, save it, and name it TargetPractice, then add a directional light. Now, set up a 3 × 3 grid of nine targets. In the Hierarchy, select Create ➤ Cube and make sure its Transform position is (0, 0, 0). Rename it Target and set its Transform scale to (2, 2, 0.2). In the Inspector panel, select Add Component ➤ Physics ➤ Rigidbody. In the Rigidbody component, uncheck the Use Gravity property. Expand the Constraints property and check all three Freeze Position coordinates. Check Y and Z coordinates for Freeze Rotation (Figure 6-5).

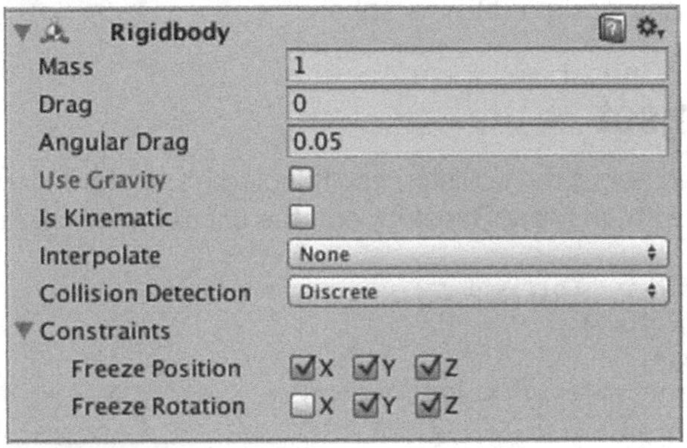

Figure 6-5. Target game object Rigidbody property settings

You can duplicate this game object by selecting it in the Scene view and pressing ⌘+D for Duplicate. Reposition it next to and touching the first (Transform position x of 2), then repeat to place another Target game object on the other side of the original (Transform position x of –2) so you now have a row of three Target game objects. While holding down the ⌘ button, click each of the Target game objects to select the row. Again press ⌘+D, this time duplicating the row. In the Inspector, change the Transform position y coordinate to 2.

You may have noticed that the three Target game objects in the Hierarchy were highlighted blue when first selected, then changed to a dark gray when you changed the Transform position y value. Click once on this gray area to highlight it in blue again. Press ⌘+D again to create a third row, and set its Transform position y coordinate to 4 (Figure 6-6).

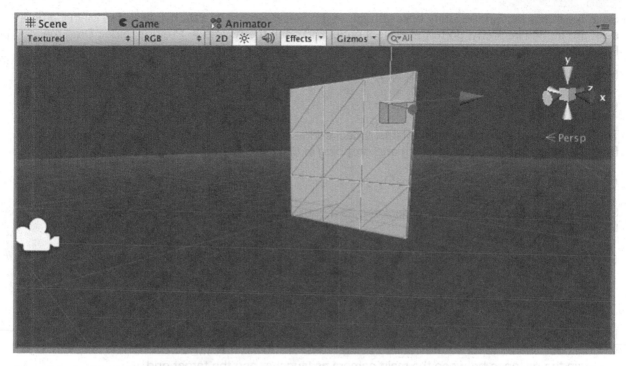

Figure 6-6. 3 × 3 grid of nine Target game objects

Now that the target grid is in place, set up the projectile launcher. We will use the Main Camera as the source for aiming and launching the projectiles. In the Project panel, select the Assets ➤ Scripts folder, then Create ➤ Javascript and name the new script ProjectileLauncher. Double-click to open for editing in MonoDevelop. Edit the ProjectileLauncher script to the following:

```
#pragma strict

public var projectile : GameObject;
public var cameraSpeed : float = 5;

function Update () {
    var horiz : float = Input.GetAxis("Horizontal") * Time.deltaTime * cameraSpeed;
    var verti : float = Input.GetAxis("Vertical") * Time.deltaTime * cameraSpeed;

    transform.Translate(horiz, verti, 0);

    if(Input.GetButtonUp("Fire1")) {
        var projectileInstance : GameObject = Instantiate(projectile, transform.position,
transform.rotation);
        Destroy(projectileInstance, 2);
    }
}
```

Save the script, and in the Unity editor drag it to the Main Camera to attach it. With the Main Camera selected in the Hierarchy, go to the Project panel and open the Assets ➤ Prefabs folder. Drag the Rocket prefab to the Projectile property in the Rocket Launcher script component in the Inspector.

Most of this code should be familiar to you in the following breakdown:

(1)   ```
public var projectile : GameObject;
```

The GameObject type reference variable is declared as a public variable, allowing you to access it from the Inspector for easy dragging and dropping in different prefabs.

(2)    ```
public var cameraSpeed : float = 5;
```

Similarly, the cameraSpeed factor is declared as a public variable to be available through the Inspector.

(3)   ```
var horiz : float = Input.GetAxis("Horizontal") * Time.deltaTime * cameraSpeed;
var verti : float = Input.GetAxis("Vertical") * Time.deltaTime * cameraSpeed;

transform.Translate(horiz, verti, 0);
```

In the Update() function, first the player input is processed to determine the new horizontal and vertical coordinates to move the camera using transform.Translate. The z coordinate is held at 0 to maintain the distance between the main camera as launcher and the target grid.

(4)    ```
if(Input.GetButtonUp("Fire1")) {
        var projectileInstance : GameObject = Instantiate(projectile, transform.position,
transform.rotation);
        Destroy(projectileInstance, 2);
}
```

Next, the Update() function tests to determine if the default Fire1 button has been released and, if true, creates an instance (instantiates) of a new projectile game object. It then sets the condition for the projectile instance to be destroyed after two seconds.

The projectile game object also needs a script. In the Project panel, go back to the Assets ➤ Scripts folder and select Create ➤ Javascript, then name the new script Projectile. Double-click the script icon to open it for editing in MonoDevelop. Edit the code to the following:

```
#pragma strict

public var aForce : float = 500;
private var redColor : Color = Color (1, 0, 0);
private var greenColor : Color = Color (0, 1, 0);

function FixedUpdate () {
        rigidbody.AddForce (Vector3.forward * aForce);
}
```

```
function OnCollisionEnter(other : Collision) {
        var checkColor : Color = other.gameObject.renderer.material.color;

        if (checkColor == greenColor) {
                other.gameObject.renderer.material.color = redColor;
        } else {
                other.gameObject.renderer.material.color = greenColor;
        }
}
```

Save the script and attach it to the Rocket prefab by opening the Assets ➤ Prefabs folder in the Project panel and selecting the Projectile prefab. In the Inspector, select Add Component ➤ Scripts, then find the Projectile script in the drop-down menu and select it. The Projectile script should appear in the Inspector as a new component for the Rocket prefab.

This code breaks this down as follows:

```
(1)     public var aForce : float = 500;
        private var redColor : Color = Color (1, 0, 0);
        private var greenColor : Color = Color (0, 1, 0);
```

The aForce variable used to determine the launch force on the Projectile game object is declared as public to allow for adjustment through the Inspector, and assigned an initial value. The redColor and greenColor variables of type Color are assigned the corresponding RGB values for red and green.

```
(2)     rigidbody.AddForce (Vector3.forward * aForce);
```

In the FixedUpdate() function, a forward-directed force is applied to the projectile.

```
(3)     var checkColor : Color = other.gameObject.renderer.material.color;

        if (checkColor == greenColor) {
                other.gameObject.renderer.material.color = redColor;
        } else {
                other.gameObject.renderer.material.color = greenColor;
        }
```

When the Rocket prefab projectile collides with a target, the onCollisionEnter() function is called and the target will change color. The Color type reference variable checkColor is declared and assigned the value of the target game object. The target object color is then tested arbitrarily to see if it is green; if true it is changed to red. If false, meaning the target object is not green, then it is changed to red.

In the editor, save the scene, save the project, then enter Play mode to test it out (Figure 6-7). There you have it—your first game prototype!

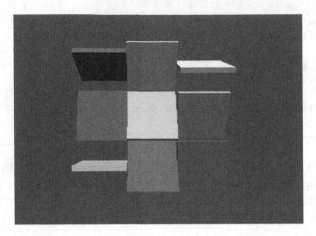

Figure 6-7. Target Practice in the Game view

Physic Materials

You can further refine the collision behavior of your game objects in collisions by using Physic Materials. Physic Materials are assets that define the bounciness and surface friction properties. Two objects sliding against each other lose energy through friction, and a bouncing object also loses energy when it strikes another surface with each bounce.

This scene is a way to test physic materials. First, you are going to test pushing a cube on a flat surface. Create a new scene and name it PhysicMaterialsTest, and as always, add a directional light. Select the Main Camera and change its Transform position to (0, 1, −7). Create a plane, then create a Cube game object with a Transform position of (0, 0.5, 0). Add a Rigidbody component to the Cube with Add Component ➤ Physics ➤ Rigidbody in the Inspector or Component ➤ Physics ➤ Rigidbody from the top menu.

In the Project panel, first select Assets, then Create ➤ Folder and name the folder Physic Materials. With the Physic Materials folder selected, now choose Create ➤ Physic Material. You may have to scroll down a bit to find it. Name the new physic material Icy (Figure 6-8).

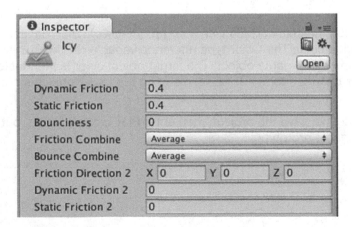

Figure 6-8. Physic Material asset in the Inspector

The **Dynamic Friction** property is used when the object is already moving. A value of 0 means no loss of energy—that is, it is the most slippery so the object will slide a good distance. A value of 1 is the opposite end of the scale: the moving object will stop moving quickly.

Static Friction is when the object is at rest. This is the friction that must be overcome in order to get the object moving. This property has the same scale of 0 to 1 where 0 is virtually frictionless and 1 takes a lot of force to get the object moving.

Bounciness also has a scale of 0 to 1, where 0 means all energy is lost—no bounce—while 1 means no energy is lost and the object is super bouncy.

Friction Combine and **Bounce Combine** give you options for how to combine the frictions of the two colliding game objects. You have the choice of Average for averaging the two values, Minimum to use the smallest value, Maximum for the greatest value, and Multiply to multiply the two values.

Friction Direction 2 allows you to create a different friction for the game object in a different direction across its surface. An example would be going with or against the grain of wood. If you choose to have this second directional friction, you modify the behavior with **Dynamic Friction 2** and **Static Friction 2** just like you did with Dynamic Friction and Static Friction.

Time to give it a try. With the Ice physic material asset selected, change Dynamic Friction and Static Friction both to 0. Now apply this physic material to the cube and the plane game objects by dragging and dropping it from the Project panel onto the objects in the Scene view, or in the Inspector by using the circle selection button to the right of the Material property field of the Collider component and choosing it from the menu that appears.

The last thing you need for testing is the ability to apply a force to the cube. In the Project panel select Create ➤ JavaScript and name the new script Push. Double-click it to open for editing in MonoDevelop. Delete the `Start()` and `Update()` functions, then add the following code:

```
public var aForce : float = 50;

function OnMouseDown () {
    rigidbody.AddForce (Vector3.forward * aForce);
}
```

You've used this code before. You can adjust the amount of force of the push in the Inspector with the public variable `aForce`. In the `OnMouseDown()` function, you apply `aForce` to the rigidbody component of the game object that the physics engine is tracking. Save the script and attach it to the Cube game object. Save the scene. Play to test and when you click the cube, it begins sliding.

Since both it and the plane are essentially frictionless, it will continue to slide until it falls off. Test changing the Dynamic and Static Friction values of the Icy physic material, then push the Cube game object in Play mode. When you are finished experimenting, reset the Dynamic Friction and Static Friction properties of the Icy physic material to 0.

Bounciness

To test out bounciness, add a Sphere game object to the Scene with a Transform position of (0.5, 2, 0). Add a Rigidbody component to it just as you did for the Cube game object. Save the scene and Play. The sphere falls and impacts the edge of the cube, then falls to the plane. The movement of the sphere and the cube are calculated by the physics engine according to each game object's physical properties. The cube responds to the impact of the falling sphere by sliding in one direction while the sphere rolls away in the other. Notice that the sphere doesn't bounce at all.

Unity does provide a few basic physic materials in its Standard Assets package. In the top menu of the editor, select Assets ➤ Import Package ➤ Physic Materials. Go ahead and import all of them so you have them in your project to experiment with.

> **Note** At the time of this writing, Unity's Standard Assets and Sample Assets (beta) are being combined. If the Physic Materials here don't import properly, download and import the Sample Assets (beta) package from the Asset Store then use the search bar in the Project panel to find the Bouncy physic material.

Drag Bouncy from the Standard Assets ➤ Physic Materials folder in the Project panel to the Sphere's Material property of the Sphere Collider component in the Inspector. Save the scene. Now when you playtest, the Sphere game object has some distinct bounciness to it when it collides with the Cube and then the Plane.

The physic materials in the Standard Assets package are meant to be starting points. For your game and your game objects to be distinctive, you should further customize and refine their physical characteristics.

LookAt

Take a step away from the topic of Physics for a moment. Now that you have objects moving around, you may find you'd like your camera to keep pointing at an object as it moves. LookAt is the handy function that does just that. Still using your PhysicMaterialsTest scene, in the Project panel create a new script with Create ➤ Javascript, and name it PointCamera. Double-click to open in MonoDevelop and edit the contents as follows:

```
#pragma strict

var cameraTarget : Transform;

function Update () {
    transform.LookAt(cameraTarget);
}
```

Save the script and attach it to the Main Camera. Breaking this down:

```
(1)    var cameraTarget : Transform;
```

If you don't specify public or private scope the Transform type variable cameraTarget you declare here will by default be a public variable available to you through the Inspector.

```
(2)    transform.LookAt(cameraTarget);
```

Within the `Update()` function, the Transform of the game object to which the script is attached, in this case the Main Camera, is rotated so its forward vector position points at the `cameraTarget`'s position.

In the Inspector, assign the Sphere game object to the Camera Target property with the circle selection button to the right of its field. Save and play. The camera follows the sphere as it falls onto the cube, bounces across the plane, then falls away. The camera position doesn't change as it follows the movement of the Sphere. Now try following the Cube instead.

Accessing Other Game Objects

You've used `OnCollision()` to make changes to either game object involved in a collision. You can also write script for one game object to have an effect on any other game object. In this example, when the Sphere game object strikes the Cube game object, your script will tell the Main Camera to follow the Cube rather than the Sphere.

In the Project panel, create a new script with Create ➤ JavaScript and name it ChangeCameraTarget. Double-click to open it in MonoDevelop and edit to the following:

```
#pragma strict

function OnCollisionEnter() {
    var cameraScript : PointCamera = GameObject.Find("Main Camera").GetComponent(PointCamera);
    cameraScript.cameraTarget = GameObject.Find("Cube").transform;
}
```

This code breaks down as follows:

(1)   `var cameraScript : PointCamera`

Declares the `cameraScript` reference variable of type PointCamera, the script attached to the Main Camera game object that directs it to follow the Sphere game object.

(2)   `= GameObject.Find("Main Camera").GetComponent(PointCamera);`

The `cameraScript` variable was declared as a script reference. Since this script is attached to the Sphere game object, you use the `GameObject.Find` function to find any object with the name Main Camera. Then with dot notation, drill down to the Main Camera game object's PointCamera script component to assign it to `cameraScript`.

(3)   `cameraScript.cameraTarget`

Using dot notation to identify the `cameraTarget` public variable,

(4)   `= GameObject.Find("Cube").transform;`

change the target of the Main Camera by assigning the Cube game object transform.

Save the script and attach it to the Sphere game object. Save the scene and playtest. The camera follows the Sphere down, then on impact switches to following the Cube.

Triggers

The physics engine automatically adjusts the position and rotation of game objects according to the physical characteristics you assign to them. The OnCollision() function calls allow you to direct what happens at the beginning, during, and at the end of the collision. There are many scenarios in games where you want to direct the game action when one game object reaches a particular location. It may be for a door to automatically open as your game object approaches, to spring a trap as your game object travels through the doorway, or perhaps to end the scene when your game object leaves the doorway and enters the room. At no point does your game object actually collide with a physical object, so in these scenarios you would use a trigger collider.

> **Note**   Best practices call for the game object with the trigger collider to be a static object. The game object with the Rigidbody component that is governed by the physics engine passes through the trigger collider.

Is Trigger is a property of the Collider component. When the Is Trigger box is checked, the collider will detect a collision but call a different series of methods: OnTriggerEnter(), OnTriggerStay(), and OnTriggerExit(). No physical collision occurs with the rigidbody passing through the volume of the trigger collider. You use these methods much like OnCollisionEnter(), OnCollisionStay(), and OnCollisionExit().

OnTrigger

In the Project panel Assets ➤ Scene folder, create a new scene, name it TriggerTest, and save it. Add a directional light, and a Plane with a transform position of (0, 0, –5). Create a Sphere game object with a Transform position of (0, 0.5, –7). You are going to push the Sphere game object so that it rolls through the trigger collider. From your Scripts folder in the Project panel, drag the Push script and drop it onto the Sphere game object. A game object must have a rigidbody for physical forces to act on it, so select the Sphere game object in the Hierarchy and in the Inspector select Add Component ➤ Physics ➤ Rigidbody.

Back in the Hierarchy, create a Cube game object and name it Trigger. Give it a Transform position of (0, 0.5, –3) and a Transform scale of (3, 3, 1). Now set up a couple of goalposts on either side of the Trigger game object by creating a Cube game object named Cube1, with a Transform scale of (1, 3, 1). Give Cube1 a Transform position of (2, 0.5, –3). Duplicate it by selecting Edit ➤ Duplicate in the top menu or pressing ⌘+D, name the new game object Cube2, and give it a Transform position of (–2, 0.5, –3).

Save the scene and playtest. Give the sphere a push and you'll see that it bounces off of the Trigger game object. Remember that only one object needs to have a rigidbody for a collision to be detected. Exit Play mode.

Select the Trigger game object and, in the Inspector, check Is Trigger in the Box Collider component. Save and playtest. This time, no physical reaction occurs and the sphere rolls right through the Trigger game object after you push it.

In the Project panel, create a new script named TriggerScript. Edit with the following code:

```
#pragma strict

function OnTriggerEnter() {
    Debug.Log("OnTriggerEnter");
}

function OnTriggerStay() {
    Debug.Log("OnTriggerStay");
}

function OnTriggerExit() {
    Debug.Log("OnTriggerExit");
}
```

Save the script. In the Unity editor, attach the TriggerScript to the Trigger game object. Select the Console tab in the Project panel. Play, and click the sphere to move it forward. In the Console panel you will see a similar result to OnCollision(), where there is one OnTriggerEnter() call, many OnTriggerStay() calls as the sphere rolls through the volume of the Trigger game object's trigger collider, and finally one OnTriggerExit() call.

While testing OnCollision() functions, you changed the property of a game object's component by changing the Color property of the Renderer. You can also enable and disable entire components. Edit the OnTriggerEnter() function to the following:

```
function OnTriggerEnter() {
    var triggerRenderer : Renderer = GetComponent(Renderer);
    triggerRenderer.enabled = false;
}
```

This code breaks down as follows:

(1)   var triggerRenderer : Renderer = GetComponent(Renderer);

Declares a Renderer reference type variable named triggerRenderer, then assigns to it the reference to the Trigger game object Renderer component.:

(2)   triggerRenderer.enabled = false;

Disables the Renderer component by setting its boolean enable property to false.

Save and play. As expected, the Trigger game object disappears from view as the Sphere game object's collider comes in contact with the Trigger game object's trigger collider.

Oftentimes in the course of a game you may want to change a boolean value to its opposite. Rather than explicitly assigning it a value of true or false, you can use the ! logic operator instead.

Change the second line of code in the OnTriggerEnter() function to:

```
triggerRenderer.enabled = !triggerRenderer.enabled;
```

Here you are reassigning the opposite boolean value to the Renderer component's enabled state. If it is currently true it will be changed to false, and if it is currently false it is changed to true.

Save and playtest, and you will see that the Trigger game object disappears just as before. Now copy this code to OnTriggerExit():

```
function OnTriggerExit() {
    var triggerRenderer : Renderer = GetComponent(Renderer);
    triggerRenderer.enabled = !triggerRenderer.enabled;
}
```

Save and playtest again. Push the sphere and now the Trigger game object disappears as the Sphere game object enters the trigger collider volume, then reappears when the Sphere game object exits the trigger collider volume.

Now for some code to do something with the game object that collided with the Trigger game object. After #pragma strict, declare a public float variable named triggerForce and assign it a value of 10:

```
public var triggerForce : float = 10;
```

Now edit your OnTriggerStay() function to the following:

```
function OnTriggerStay(other : Collider) {
    other.rigidbody.AddForce(Vector3.up * triggerForce);
}
```

This is a remix of what you've done with OnCollision(), where the other parameter refers to the other game object involved in the collision with the trigger collider, in this case the Sphere game object. An upward force is applied to the Sphere while it is within the trigger collider's volume.

Save and playtest. The Trigger game object still disappears and reappears as the Sphere enters and exits its volume, but now it moves up from the force applied to it in OnTriggerStay(). The Sphere will still have a forward motion from the initial push that you gave it, so after a few bounces it will pass beyond the boundary of the trigger collider.

As you review the OnTriggerStay() function in the Scripting Reference, you notice that the force is applied from within a conditional (Figure 6-9).

Collider.OnTriggerStay(Collider)

Description

OnTriggerStay is called *almost* all the frames for every Collider **other** that is touching the trigger.

This message is sent to the trigger and the collider that touches the trigger. Note that trigger events are only sent if one of the colliders also has a rigidbody attached.

Note: OnTriggerStay function is on the physics timer so it wont necessary run every frame.

```
// Applies an upwards force to all rigidbodies that enter the trigger.

function OnTriggerStay (other : Collider) {
    if (other.attachedRigidbody) {
        other.attachedRigidbody.AddForce(Vector3.up * 10);
    }
}
```

Figure 6-9. Unity Scripting Reference for the OnTriggerStay() function

As you start dissecting sample projects, you will see this kind of check fairly often. If some other game object without a Rigidbody component incidentally passed through the trigger collider, you would get an error because your code tells the physics engine to apply an upward force, but without a rigidbody it cannot. By adding this conditional, the game engine checks for a Rigidbody component and if there is none, avoids the error by skipping this line of code.

You are getting a good feel for the general mechanics of Unity: In the course of gameplay the Unity game engine makes calls to functions such as Awake(), Start(), and Update() while the physics engine makes calls such as OnCollision() and OnTrigger(). Within these calls you write code to direct the gameplay. Your code can take an action on the game object the script is attached to, a different game object that is interacting physically, or any other game object. Since scripts are also components, the script from one game object can interact with the script attached to a different game object.

Rapid Prototyping

At the time this is being written, Unity has just added a plethora of goodies for you in its Sample Assets (beta) package in the Asset Store. Beta testing is when a software version is released for testing by users outside of the original programming team. This can be small groups of people or even the general public, where the intention is to get feedback for some polishing of the product before the official version is released.

If the Sample Assets is still a beta version when you read this and you find anything from "doesn't work" to "unexpected behavior" or even "I wish it did this," let the folks at Unity know in the comment thread at the bottom of the product page on the Asset Store (Figure 6-10).

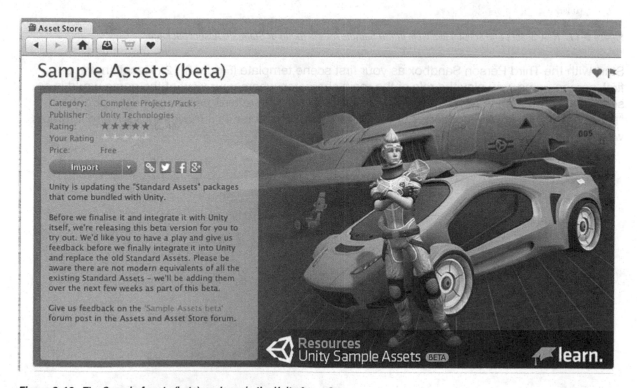

Figure 6-10. The Sample Assets (beta) package in the Unity Asset Store

You've accomplished a great deal so far. You have a basic understanding of programming concepts and syntax, the Unity editor, game objects, animation, and physics. Rather than starting from the drawing board each time, you can more rapidly advance your game development by using ready-made assets and customizing them to your needs. It's a great way to learn best practices and different approaches to common problems.

Those nice folks at Unity designed these new assets with you in mind—rather than pulling parts out of one large, specifically themed project, Unity designed these assets for easy use either out of the box or as solid, easily customizable starter kits.

Download and import the Sample Assets (beta) package to your project. If you can't find it, then it's probably no longer a beta version and the assets have been migrated into the Standard Assets package that comes with the Unity editor. Take a look at all this great stuff! (Figure 6-11)

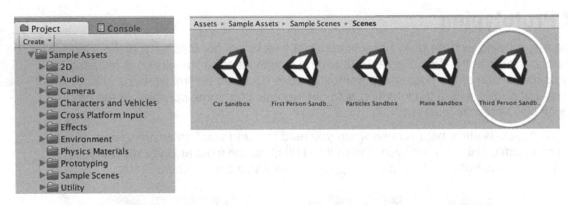

Figure 6-11. New assets and scenes available in the Sample Assets (beta) or Standard Assets package

Start with the Third Person Sandbox as your first scene template (Figure 6-12). Recall that in a first-person game, you play the role of the main character, where your view of the game world is as seen directly through the eyes of the player character, while in a third-person game you are the "third person," an invisible observer of the game's main character as it moves through and interacts with the game world.

Figure 6-12. Third Person Character sample scene from the Unity Sample Assets (beta) package

In the Project panel, drill down to the Sample Scenes folder and double-click the Third Person Sandbox (SceneAsset). In the editor top menu, select File ➤ Save Scene As and name it MyFirstPrototype, and save it in your Assets ➤ Scenes folder.

Unity only shows one scene at a time. The MyFirstPrototype scene should be the active scene now, but just glance at the top of the editor to make sure. You want to leave the Third Person Sandbox scene alone to maintain it as an unmodified template that you can copy again for future projects.

First, take a look at the contents of the Scene view in the Hierarchy.

The **Floor_Tile** is pretty basic with the mandatory Transform component and a Collider component for physical interactions with other game objects. Expand it to take a look at prototype_floor, which has the renderer and shader that you can modify to change the appearance of the floor.

Expand the **Free Look Camera Rig** to find the Main Camera. The components of the rig define how the camera operates in the game. The attached scripts specifically describe the behavior of the camera, while a rigidbody is a clue that the camera has a physical presence in the game.

There are two **Lights**: a Main Directional light that provides a basic white light from above, and an Ambient Directional light that shines a soft blue light from below, enhancing the 3D characteristics of the game objects. This second light makes a big difference to the appearance of the game. In the real world, light is reflected from the ground, walls, windows, and any other object to some extent. The color of the light is very important for both the look and mood of your game.

The **Mobile Character Control Rig** is largely made up of scripts that address the different methods of input for mobile devices and shader replacements that address the reduced graphic processing capabilities of mobile devices.

Obstacles expands to show a long list of the individual block, cube, platform, and ramp building blocks used in this scene. You can find these and more for you to use for your own prototype environment in the Prototyping ➤ Prefabs folder.

The **Third Person Character** is vastly improved (Figure 6-12). It used to be a simple Capsule game object representing your player character, but now it comes with Unity's Mecanim-based Ethan model complete with root-motion-embedded animations. You can easily change out Ethan for your own humanoid-rigged model.

Before making modifications, take a few minutes to play the template version and get a feel for its capabilities. In addition to using the standard inputs for moving forward, back, left, and right at a run and (while also pressing the Shift key) to walk, the Ethan character can move while crouching if the C key is pressed, and jump by pressing the spacebar.

Spawning and Spawn Points

Spawning is the creation of a character or game object during gameplay. The location in which the game object appears is the **spawn point**. Spawning is a common function in many games, though in this template scene the player character is already present from the initialization of the game.

While it's fun to run the character around the scene to check it out, it's not exactly a game. A game needs some kind of endpoint, whether it's an objective achieved, points earned, the timer running out, or the like. Let's say the goal here is for the player to get to the top of the tallest of the blue cubes. In the template it's pretty simple: the character can either jump up each successively taller cube or jump across from the yellow platform. Make it a little more difficult by raising the blue cube so its bottom face is resting on the top face of the next lower cube (Figure 6-13).

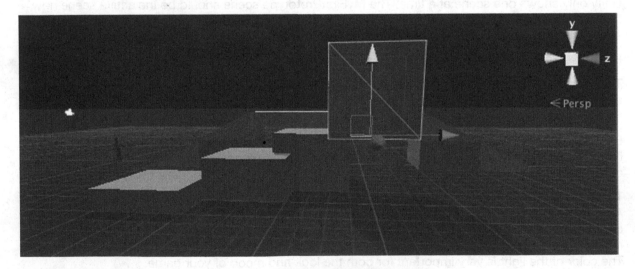

Figure 6-13. Move the tallest cube up to rest on its neighbor using the Transform widget

If you playtest now, the cube is too tall to jump to from either the blue cube or the platform. An unbeatable game is not very fun, so you will create a trigger collider that will send your player character to a spawn point at the top of the cube.

First, designate the spawn point. Create an empty game object using the top menu Game Object ➤ Create Empty and position it on top of the cube. Rename it SpawnPoint01.

Second, create a trigger point for the character to respawn on top of the cube. Again use the top menu Game Object ➤ Create Empty, then in the Inspector select Add Component ➤ Physics ➤ Sphere Collider. Check Is Trigger and change Radius to 1. Name it RespawnPoint01Trigger01. That's a pretty long name, but if you choose to add more respawn points and more triggers, each will have a unique descriptive name. Now position the game object on the yellow platform.

In the Project panel, select Create ➤ Javascript, name the new script Respawn01, and open it in MonoDevelop for editing. Delete the Start() and Update() functions, then add the following code:

```
#pragma strict

public var respawnPosition: Transform;

function OnTriggerEnter(other : Collider) {
    other.gameObject.transform.position = respawnPosition.position;
}
```

This breaks down as follows:

```
(1)     public var respawnPosition: Transform;
```

Declares a public Transform type reference variable named respawnPosition.

```
(2)     other.gameObject.transform.position = respawnPosition.position;
```

In this case the other object impacting the trigger collider is the player character. Here you assign the position reference held by the respawnPosition variable to the player character game object's transform position.

Save the script and attach it to the RespawnPoint01Trigger01 game object. With the RespawnPoint01Trigger01 game object selected in the Hierarchy, drag the SpawnPoint01 game object from the Hierarchy and drop it into to the Respawn Position field of the Respawn01 script component. This assigns the SpawnPoint01 transform.position (x, y, z) coordinate values to the respawnPosition variable.

Save the scene and play. Run the character around the platform until it trips the trigger and disappears from the platform, only to instantly respawn at the designated point on top of the highest blue cube. Success!

Your player audience would have no idea that there might be a magical solution to get to the top of the cubes, so you want to give some kind of cue. In the Project panel, drill down to the Prototyping ➤ Prefabs folder and open it up. Drag a Question Coin to the Scene and position it over the RespawnPoint01Trigger01 trigger collider. Do not click Apply in the Inspector as you do not want these changes applied to all Question Coin prefabs. In the Hierarchy rename it Question Coin 01.

The Question Coin will really catch the player's eye if it is moving. In the Project panel, create a new script and name it SpinCoin. Double-click to open it in MonoDevelop and edit the code to the following:

```
#pragma strict

public var spinSpeed : float = 50;

function Update () {
    transform.Rotate(Vector3.up * spinSpeed * Time.deltaTime);
}
```

This is a simple rotation animation that you've been introduced to before. It breaks down as follows:

(1)   `public var spinSpeed : float = 50;`

Declares a public `spinSpeed` float variable that you can access through the Inspector at runtime to adjust the rate of rotation of the Question Coin game object.

(2)   `transform.Rotate(Vector3.up * spinSpeed * Time.deltaTime);`

Each frame, update the Question Coin's Transform.rotation around the `Vector3.up` axis (the y axis) multiplied by the `spinSpeed` factor and smoothed with `Time.deltaTime`. If there was no `spinSpeed` factor, the coin would rotate at a rate of one degree per second.

Save the script and attach it to the Question Coin. Save the scene and play. Now the coin definitely stands out as an object of interest as it spins in place.

If you dig a little deeper into the Prototyping ➤ Prefabs folder, you will come across the Compound Prefabs folder (Figure 6-14). This has some box piles and smash platforms where the player character and boxes respond to collisions with each other, and super-cool tracks, ramps, and steps.

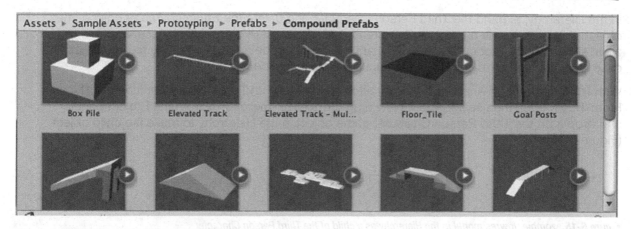

Figure 6-14. Compound Prefabs in the Sample Assets package

Have a little fun with the scene and see how these work—for example, by adding a Loop and seeing if your character can make it all the way around.

Changing the Character Model

The purpose of a prototype is to be able to test game mechanics in terms of layout and flow, while the final artwork comes later in the production process. You see how you could quickly put together a maze for your character to run through, using colliders and triggers as obstacles, collectables, and so forth. You, the game developer, have a clear picture of the look of your game: dark and post-apocalyptic, bright and cheery cartoon-y, or whatever suits your tastes. Your family members and friends most often have a much murkier view. After hearing you excitedly talk about your game design for weeks, they might seem less than impressed by the prototype.

Don't be disappointed; this happens all the time, and not just to the new indie-game developers, either. In one instance I was working on game prototypes with one of the top electronic device manufacturers in the world. When we presented the various prototype versions, the project manager expressed her disappointment in the minimalistic placeholder art—even though she was the person responsible for obtaining the final art from the subcontracted studio!

This really speaks to the power of the visual impression of today's games. Beautifully detailed high-resolution graphics set the bar high for user expectations, so a bare-bones functional prototype might be a new concept. Take your time to walk them through the game design concept and be sure they understand that the focus at this point is on gameplay mechanics rather than looks.

That being said, if you have your character models ready to go, why not put them in there? Animated models need testing too, from making sure the mesh is properly responsive to the animations to making sure that oddball appendages, props, and the like behave appropriately for your character. For example, if you are mixing and matching animations and props from the Asset Store, you may find that some swordplay animation appears to make the character slice his own limbs if the prop sword is too long.

In the Hierarchy, expand the Third Person Character and delete the Ethan character child game object. If it's not in your current project already, select Assets ➤ Import New Asset and find the zombie_lowres.fbx model you used in Chapter 5. It should be rigged and ready to go, but just in case, select it in the Project panel and take a look in the Inspector.

With Rig selected, the Animation Type should be Humanoid and the Avatar Definition set at Create From This Model, then select Apply. Now drag the zombie_lowres.fbx from the Project panel and drop it on the Third Person Character game object in the Hierarchy to make it a child object (Figure 6-15).

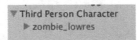

Figure 6-15. zombie_lowres model in the Hierarchy as a child of the Third Person Character

Select Third Person Character, then in the Inspector scroll down to the Third Person Character script (Figure 6-16).

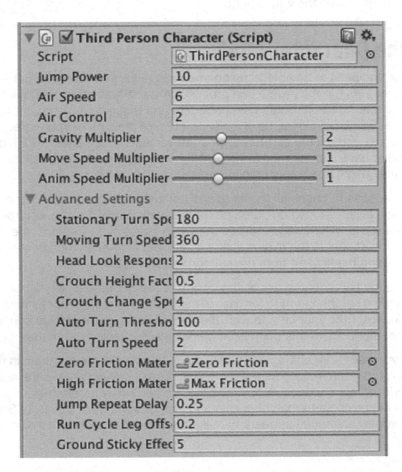

Figure 6-16. Third Person Character script component in the Inspector

Expand Advanced Settings to reveal a large number of properties available to you for customizing the behavior for your particular character.

If you click the book icon to access the reference, the Scripting Reference opens up with the MonoBehavior parent class description. The Scripting Reference contains information about the classes and functions used in scripting rather than the contents of any particular script. Even with the addition of a new function, the reference documentation might not reflect the new content from a beta version because it is still subject to change.

This is a great example of the importance of developing good habits with naming conventions and documenting your scripts with comments as you go. The properties listed in the Inspector are descriptively named, so you can take a pretty good guess at what they do. If you open the script itself, you will find that the Unity team did an outstanding job breaking down the script variables and functions with extensively detailed comments (Figure 6-17).

```
   ThirdPersonCharacter ► No selection
 1 ⊟ using UnityEngine;
 2 └ using System.Collections;
 3
 4 ⊟ public class ThirdPersonCharacter : MonoBehaviour {
 5
 6       [SerializeField] float jumpPower = 12;                                    // determines the jump force applied when jumping (and therefore the jump heig
 7       [SerializeField] float airSpeed = 6;                                     // determines the max speed of the character while airborne
 8       [SerializeField] float airControl = 2;                                   // determines the response speed of controlling the character while airborne
 9       [Range(1,4)] [SerializeField] public float gravityMultiplier = 2;        // gravity modifier - often higher than natural gravity feels right for game c
10       [SerializeField] [Range(0.1f,3f)] float moveSpeedMultiplier = 1;         // how much the move speed of the character will be multiplied by
11       [SerializeField] [Range(0.1f,3f)] float animSpeedMultiplier = 1;         // how much the animation of the character will be multiplied by
12       [SerializeField] AdvancedSettings advancedSettings;                      // Container for the advanced settings class , thiss allows the advanced setti
13
14
15       [System.Serializable]
16 ⊟     public class AdvancedSettings
17       {
18           public float stationaryTurnSpeed = 180;                             // additional turn speed added when the player is stationary (added to animation root rota
19           public float movingTurnSpeed = 360;                                 // additional turn speed added when the player is moving (added to animation root rotation
20           public float headLookResponseSpeed = 2;                             // speed at which head look follows its target
21           public float crouchHeightFactor = 0.6f;                             // collider height is multiplied by this when crouching
22           public float crouchChangeSpeed = 4;                                 // speed at which capsule changes height when crouching/standing
23           public float autoTurnThresholdAngle = 100;                          // character auto turns towards camera direction if facing away by more than this angle
24           public float autoTurnSpeed = 2;                                     // speed at which character auto-turns towards cam direction
25           public PhysicMaterial zeroFrictionMaterial;                         // used when in motion to enable smooth movement
26           public PhysicMaterial highFrictionMaterial;                         // used when stationary to avoid sliding down slopes
27           public float jumpRepeatDelayTime = 0.25f;                           // amount of time that must elapse between landing and being able to jump again
28           public float runCycleLegOffset = 0.2f;                              // animation cycle offset (0-1) used for determining correct leg to jump off
29           public float groundStickyEffect = 5f;                               // power of 'stick to ground' effect - prevents bumping down slopes.
30       }
31
32       public Transform lookTarget { get; set; }                               // The point where the character will be looking at
33
34       bool onGround;                                                          // Is the character on the ground
35       Vector3 lookPos;                                                        // The position where the character is looking at|
36       float originalHeight;                                                   // Used for tracking the original height of the characters capsule collider
37       Animator animator;                                                      // The animator for the character
38       float lastAirTime;                                                      // USed for checking when the character was last in the air for controlling jumps
```

Figure 6-17. Extensive documentation within the ThirdPersonCharacter script

In the Project panel, find the Smash Boxes Platform in the Sample Assets ➤ Prototyping ➤ Prefabs ➤ Compound Prefabs folder. Drag a Smash Boxes Platform into your scene.

Move your SpawnPoint01 game object to get your character onto the Smash Boxes Platform, then try to jump to the top of the stack. Try making more spawn points and triggers. Reposition the SpawnPoint01 game object on top of the platform in front of the boxes.

Save the scene and play to get your character up on the platform to check out some additional behaviors. If you try to walk your character into the spaces between the boxes, you'll find that it automatically crouches to move through the small space. If you walk your character into a box, unlike the static platform these white boxes will respond to collisions with your player character. See if you can get your character to the top of the stack of boxes without knocking it over. Good luck!

Summary

You've accomplished a great deal in this chapter, learning about Rigidbodies and the physics engine, customizing game object behavior with Physic Materials, and game object interaction with Colliders and Triggers.

The OnCollision() and OnTrigger() functions are new additions to your scripting knowledge base, along with functions for applying forces to the game object, directing the camera to follow a game object, changing the game object the camera is following, changing the properties of a component, enabling/disabling a component, using the ! logic operator to flip boolean values, and avoiding errors by using conditionals.

You've expanded the application of your script code from the game object the script is attached to, onward to affecting a secondary object co-involved in a collision and beyond, to accessing any game object in your scene.

Best of all, you're taking what you've learned so far and starting down the path of designing functional game prototypes. Great job! There's more great stuff ahead, including more physics with joints and ray casting, special effects like explosions and sound, and pulling all this together within the rules of a game to go from playing around with a scene to playing and winning a fully functional game. Woo!

Using Advanced Physics Concepts

In this chapter, you will start building an obstacle course using what you've learned so far and adding new physics concepts, including using joints in the obstacle course, ragdoll physics for the player, and of course new functions and scripts to bring it all together.

Setting Up the Obstacle Course

In the Project panel, select Assets ➤ Sample Assets ➤ Sample Scenes ➤ Scenes and open Third Person Character. In the editor top menu, select File ➤ Save Scene as; name the new scene Obstacle Course. In the Hierarchy, delete the Obstacles parent game object, which also deletes all of its children. In the Scene view at this point you have only the player character standing on the floor.

In the Project panel's Assets ➤ Sample Assets ➤ Prototyping ➤ Prefabs ➤ Compound Prefabs folder, find the Elevated Track, drag it to the Scene view, and set its Transform Position coordinates to (0, 0, 22). Your player character should already have a position of (0, 0, 0) and be facing the ramp of the Elevated Track when you select Play (Figure 7-1).

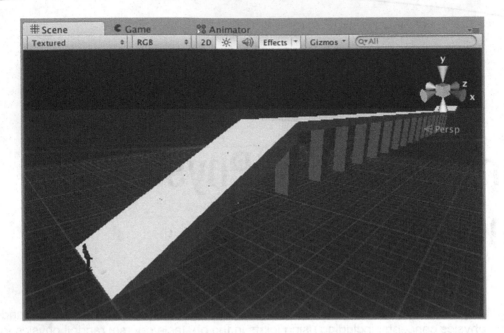

Figure 7-1. The Elevated Track prefab for the obstacle course

Lowering Platform Obstacle

Now that you have a nice elevated track that your character can easily run from start to finish, the easiest obstacle to begin with is to eliminate a portion of the track. Delete the third Platform 8 × 1 × 8 game object and its supporting pillar (Pillar 8 × 2 × 8). You can select the game object and right-click it in the Hierarchy to select Delete from the context menu that pops open, or you can select the game object in the Hierarchy, then select Edit ➤ Delete from the editor top menu (Figure 7-2).

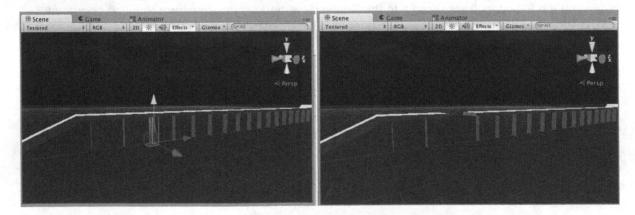

Figure 7-2. Delete the third Platform 8 × 1 × 8 platform prefab and its supporting pillar

If you run the course now, your character can't make it across the gap. Impossible obstacles in an unwinnable game are no fun. To address this gap, in the Project panel's Assets ➤ Sample Assets ➤ Prototyping ➤ Prefabs folder find the Platform 4 × 1 × 4 prefab, and drag and drop it into the Scene view. Give it a Transform Position of (0,12, 38). This places it in the middle of the gap, slightly higher than the elevated track. Playtest now, and you can guide the player character across the gap using the spacebar to jump to the platform and off again on the far side back to the elevated track.

A helpful stepping stone is necessary to fill the gap for the player to be able to continue onward, but it can be a more challenging obstacle by moving up and down. In the Project panel's Assets ➤ Scripts folder, create a new script named MovePlatform. Open it in MonoDevelop and edit the code as follows:

```
#pragma strict

private var platformStartPosition : Vector3;
private var platformEndPosition : Vector3;
public var lowLevel : float = 6;
public var duration : float = 5.0f;
private var step : float = 0.0f;
private var movingBack : boolean = false;

function Start () {
        platformStartPosition = transform.position;
        platformEndPosition = (transform.position - Vector3(0, lowLevel, 0));
}

function FixedUpdate() {
    var delta : float = (Time.deltaTime / duration);
    if(movingBack) step -= delta;
    else step += delta;
    step = Mathf.Clamp01(step);
    rigidbody.MovePosition(Vector3.Lerp(platformStartPosition, platformEndPosition, step));

    if(step == 1.0f) movingBack = true;
    else if(step == 0.0f) movingBack = false;
}
```

There are many ways you could have written this script. Essentially you want the platform to move from point A to point B and back again. However, you also want to take into account other factors such as the reusability of a script and ease of testing/tweaking behavior.

With this in mind, this script breaks down as follows:

```
(1)    private var platformStartPosition : Vector3;
       ...
       function Start () {
               platformStartPosition = transform.position;
       ...
```

Rather than assign explicit coordinates to platformStartPosition with the variable declaration, your script assigns whatever the position of the platform game object is in the Start() function. By writing it this way, you can reposition the platform in the Scene view without having to come back and edit the script to update the start position coordinates.

```
(2)      private var platformEndPosition : Vector3;
         public var lowLevel : float = 6;

         function Start () {
                 ...
                 platformEndPosition = (transform.position - Vector3(0,
                 lowLevel, 0));
         }
```

In the same fashion, the platformEndPosition variable is declared but not assigned explicit coordinates. The platform will move straight down along the Y-axis for the distance designated by the lowLevel variable. A value of 6 is explicitly assigned to lowLevel to begin with, but more importantly the lowLevel variable is public so you can adjust the range of the platform's movement directly in the editor. The platformEndPosition is assigned in the Start() function the result of subtracting the lowLevel value from the y coordinate of the platformStartPosition.

```
(3)      public var duration : float = 5.0f;
```

The duration variable determines how fast the platform moves from platformStartPosition to platformEndPosition, so making it public allows you to adjust the speed of the platform movement directly from the editor.

```
(4)      private var step : float = 0.0f;
         private var movingBack : boolean = false;
```

Both step and movingBack are used for changing the direction of the platform to maintain a repeating up-and-down movement during gameplay.

```
(5)      function FixedUpdate() {
```

Since this is physics-based rigidbody movement, the FixedUpdate() function is used instead of Update(). A common beginner mistake is to forget the Rigidbody component for the game object. Make sure the Platform 4 × 1 × 4 has a Rigidbody component. If not, select it in the Hierarchy, then in the Inspector select Add Component ➤ Physics ➤ Rigidbody. When the Rigidbody component appears in the Inspector, uncheck Use Gravity since this isn't needed and check Is Kinematic so the platform movement is unaffected by the player character jumping onto it.

```
(6)      var delta : float = (Time.deltaTime / duration);
```

Time.deltaTime is the time in seconds it took to complete the last frame, so dividing by duration assigns a normalized fraction to delta so that

```
(7)      if(movingBack) step -= delta;
```

if the boolean movingBack is true, then the normalized fractional amount delta is subtracted from step, otherwise

(8)   else step += delta;

the normalized fractional amount delta is added to step.

(9)   step = Mathf.Clamp01(step);

Mathf.Clamp01 is a function that "clamps" a value between 0 and 1 and returns a float value. In this case, if step -=delta ever drops below 0, Mathf.Clamp01 would simply return 0. If step += delta is greater than 1, Mathf.Clamp01 would simply return 1. For any value between 0 and 1, Mathf.Clamp01 returns the same value.

(10)   rigidbody.MovePosition(Vector3.Lerp(platformStartPosition,
         platformEndPosition, step));

Instead of moving the platform game object by setting its Transform position, Rigidbody.MovePosition tells the physics engine to move the game object to the new position. By using the physics engine, any other objects will be pushed aside according to their physical properties, maintaining consistent behavior as this game object is moved. Using Vector3.Lerp smooths the movement of the game object.

(11)   if(step == 1.0f) movingBack = true;

Recall that if movingBack is false, the value of step is increased by the value of delta, then in (9) step = Mathf.Clamp01(step) returns 1 if the value of step is equal or greater than 1. When step reaches the value of 1, movingBack is reassigned as true, so when the next fixedUpdate() call reaches (7) the platform will begin to move in the opposite direction.

(12)   else if(step == 0.0f) movingBack = false;

This is the reverse of (11). When step is decremented to 0 the boolean value of movingBack is reassigned to false, so when the next fixedUpdate() call reaches (8) the platform will reverse direction again. Save the script, attach it to the Platform 4 × 1× 4 game object, and Play. Try changing duration and lowLevel until you feel it is a sufficiently challenging obstacle. Save the scene and save the project (Figure 7-3).

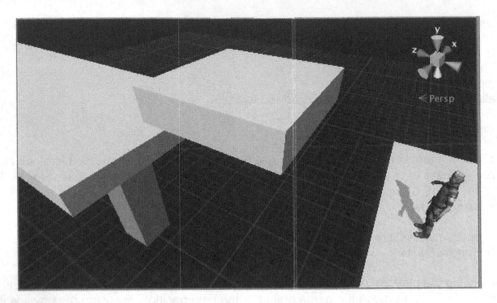

Figure 7-3. Player character and the moving platform obstacle

Note that because of the way the script is written, you could delete another section of the Elevated Track and put in another moving platform obstacle using this same script. Before you do that, read onward for more obstacles!

Joints and the Pendulum Obstacle

A **joint** is merely a point at which two objects come together. Whereas parent–child relationships also link two or more game objects with Transform, joints link two objects using physics. This is another case of Unity offering you more than one solution to choose from when constructing your game to get the precise behavior that you want.

Fixed Joint

A Fixed Joint is the simplest of the joints. It ties one game object's movement to another game object's movement much like parenting, only through the use of the physics engine instead of the parent–child Transform relationship. In the Hierarchy, create a Sphere game object and give it a Transform position of (11.4, 20.3, 60) and a Transform scale of (11, 11, 11). Rename it Pendulum Sphere. Remember that any game object first needs a Rigidbody component to be recognized by the physics engine, so in the Inspector select Add Component ➤ Physics ➤ Rigidbody. Set the Mass property to 20. Again in the Inspector, select Add Component ➤ Physics ➤ Fixed Joint (Figure 7-4).

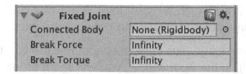

Figure 7-4. The Fixed Joint component in the Inspector

The **Connected Body** property holds the reference to the game object the sphere is connected to with the Fixed Joint. If left empty, the joint is connected to the game world. The Fixed Joint has physical characteristics, including the possibility that it could break. **Break Force** and **Break Torque** tell the physics engine the amount of force or torque required to break the joint. The default values of Infinity instruct the physics engine that the joint is unbreakable.

Now create a Cube game object with a Transform position of (6.5, 24, 60) and rename it Link01. Add a Rigidbody component. In the Hierarchy, select the Pendulum Sphere. Drag the Link01 game object from the Hierarchy and drop it into the Fixed Joint component Connected Body field in the Inspector, or use the circle selection button to the right of the field, then select Link01. Now the Pendulum Sphere and Link01 game objects are connected by a Fixed Joint.

Hinge Joint

The Hinge Joint is just what you would expect by the name: a joint connecting two game objects that allows movement around a single axis, just like the hinge on a door. Select the Link01 game object in the Hierarchy, then select Add Component ➤ Physics ➤ Hinge Joint in the Inspector (Figure 7-5).

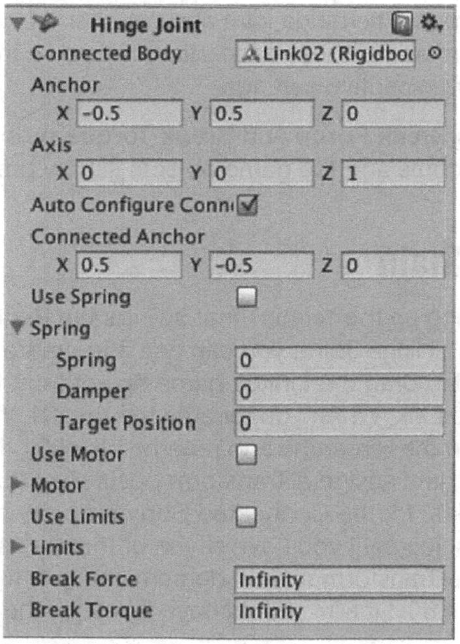

Figure 7-5. Hinge Joint component in the Inspector

The **Connected Body** is the same as with a Fixed Joint. The None default connects it to the world, or you can select a specific game object to which to connect the joint.

The **Anchor** is the position of the hinge axis in local space. For the Link01 game object, set the Anchor position to (–0.5, 0.5, 0). In the Scene view, you will see a small orange arrow representing the hinge joint (Figure 7-6).

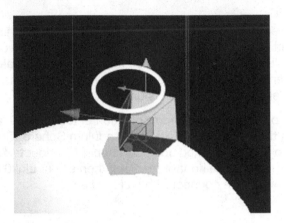

Figure 7-6. *Orange arrow representing the Hinge Joint location and axis*

The connected game object swings around the **Axis** of the hinge joint. Set the axis of the Link01 Hinge Joint to (0, 0, 1).

The Hinge Joint can behave as if it is spring-loaded with **Use Spring**. The game object will swing around the joint automatically as if motor-powered with **Use Motor**. **Limits** allows you to constrain how far the object can rotate around the hinge joint and whether it bounces when it reaches the limit. The pendulum links won't require any of these properties, but you can select the blue book icon to read more about them and their respective settings.

Finally, the Hinge Joint also has **Break Force** and **Break Torque** properties that determine the force at which the joint action is overcome and the game objects simply break apart from each other.

Build the Pendulum Chain

Link01 is the first of seven making up the "chain" that swings the Pendulum Sphere. Now that it has a Rigidbody component and Hinge Joint, you can use it to create a Prefab. In the Project panel, open the Assets ➤ Prefabs folder. Drag the Link01 game object from the Hierarchy to the Prefabs folder and name the new prefab Link. When you rename the prefab, the original Link01 game object also changes to Link. Select it in the Hierarchy and rename it Link01. Now drag the Link prefab to the Scene view, name it Link02, and assign a Transform position of (5.5, 25, 60). Select Link01, then in the Inspector select Link02 for the Connected Body property of the Hinge Joint component. Continue to add links in this fashion until you have seven of them as seen in Figure 7-7. Note that for each new Link the x value of the Transform should decrement by 1, the y value should increase by 1, and the z value should remain at 60. Link07 should have None for the Connected Body property.

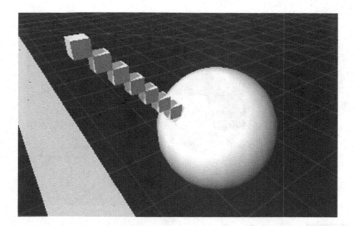

Figure 7-7. *The Pendulum Sphere and "chain"*

Save the scene and try it out. Notice how Link07, with a Hinge Joint Connected Body property of None, is automatically suspended from a fixed point in the world. Exit Play mode.

In the Scene view, with the left mouse button pressed, drag the cursor across all of the cube chain links and the Pendulum Sphere game object to select them. Press ⌘ +D to duplicate the entire pendulum structure, then drag the duplicate pendulum to a Transform Position z coordinate of 72. Repeat these steps to place a third pendulum at a Transform Position z coordinate of 84.

Take a look at the Hierarchy. Now you have three each of the numbered link game objects from 1 to 7, and three Pendulum Spheres—what a mess. This is a great example of the need to maintain organization as you develop your game. In the editor top menu, select Game Object ➤ Create Empty and name it Pendulum_01. In the Hierarchy, find each of the links to the first pendulum along with the sphere and drag and drop them into the Pendulum_01 game object. In the same fashion create Pendulum_02 and Pendulum_03 empty game objects to hold the game objects that comprise the second and third pendulum obstacles. Much better—now your Hierarchy has easily identifiable, numbered, pendulum parent game objects that can be expanded as needed for further adjustment of the pendulum child game object building blocks.

To vary the obstacles, move the second pendulum to begin its swing from the left side of the obstacle course. Change the sign of the Transform Position x coordinates of all of the link and Pendulum Sphere game objects to negative (Figure 7-8).

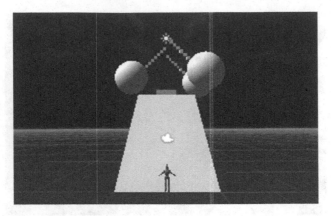

Figure 7-8. The pendulum obstacles

Save the scene and give it a try. Less synchronized pendulum swings add to the challenge of these obstacles. You could reposition their start point, or for a quick test adjust the mass settings on the Pendulum Sphere game objects.

Character Joint

Character Joints allow you to put limits on the joints of your character. Right now your character's body movements are driven by the Animator. The physics engine tracks on the Rigidbody and Capsule Collider when the character as a whole collides with another game object. Character Joints are more commonly used for Ragdoll effects, when your character's body and limbs are controlled entirely by the physics engine rather than the Animator component. The joint itself works like an extended ball-and-socket joint that can rotate (twist) in place and bend (swing), giving it a huge range of movement that you customize by setting the various limit properties (Figure 7-9).

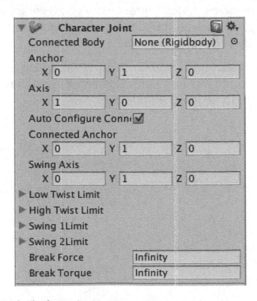

Figure 7-9. Character Joint component in the Inspector

The **Connected Body** property refers to the rigidbody to which the Character Joint is attached. If its value is None, then the joint connects to world space as seen with the Hinge Joint. The joint rotates around the **Anchor** point in the game object's local space. As a ball-and-socket joint, it has an **Axis** to twist around and a separate **Swing Axis** to "swing" or bend around.

Use the **Low Twist Limit** and **High Twist Limit** properties to constrain the twisting movement of the joint around the Axis, and the **Swing 1 Limit** and **Swing 2 Limit** properties to constrain the movement around the Swing Axis.

Break Force and **Break Torque** determine the amount of force required to break the joint, where Infinity means the joint cannot be broken.

Ragdoll Physics

You may have noticed that when a pendulum strikes the player character, it might push the player around a little bit, but that's all. A massive pendulum ought to have a bigger effect on the character, like whacking him senseless so he collapses in heap like—you guessed it—a ragdoll.

Your player character has a rigidbody and simple Capsule Collider components so it can interact with other game objects. For the physics engine to give your character's body and limbs realistic physical properties, each discrete body part needs to have its own rigidbody and collider. In its ever-helpful way, Unity provides a Ragdoll Wizard to assist you in creating these child rigidbodies and colliders. Once your ragdoll is configured, you will save it as a prefab for reuse later.

First, in the Hierarchy select the Third Person Character and rename it Third Person Character Ragdoll. Expand everything so you can see all the child body parts (Figure 7-10). (You may find that using the cursor keys rather than the mouse is easier to navigate and expand the tree hierarchy.)

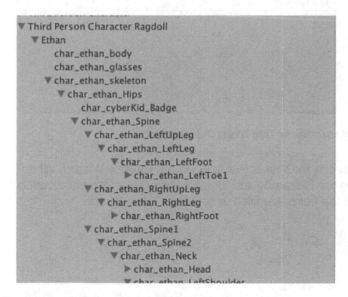

Figure 7-10. Third Person Character Ragdoll game object expanded in the Hierarchy view

In the editor top menu, select Game Object ➤ Create Other ➤ Ragdoll... to open the Ragdoll Wizard. Drag and drop the respective body parts to the Ragdoll Wizard. In this case use char_ethan_Hips for Root, and the rest according to Fig 7-10. Notice the helper statements at the top of the Ragdoll Wizard window. If it isn't already, you can put the character in T-Stand configuration by selecting the Third Person Character Ragdoll in the Hierarchy, moving the mouse cursor to the Scene view, then pressing the F key (Figure 7-11).

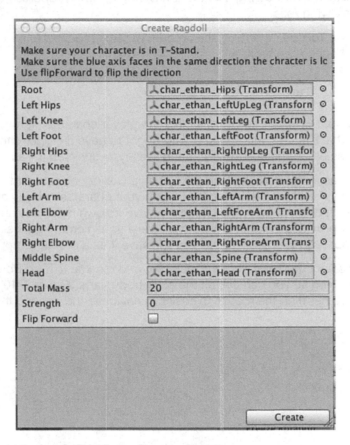

Figure 7-11. *Ragdoll Wizard selections for Third Person Character Ragdoll*

Not all of the names match the respective fields in the Ragdoll Wizard. When in doubt, select the body part of interest in the Hierarchy and look for the orange arrow indicating the location of the joint (Figure 7-12). Once all the fields are filled, select the Create button.

Figure 7-12. Orange arrow indicates joint location at elbow for char_ethan_LeftForeArm

That's it for creating a ragdoll. If you had a freshly imported character model and followed these steps, at this point when you press Play the character would collapse like a ragdoll as expected. However, the Third Person Character Ragdoll already has a number of other components attached, including scripts governing animation, so if you press Play now, you will get some really strange behavior from your player character.

The Third Person Character already has a rigidbody and Capsule Collider attached to it. The Third Person Character script has a function check to see if the character can fit underneath an object it has collided with by going into a crouch. You may have seen this when the pendulum swung over your character. The strange behavior here is the interaction of the original player character Capsule Collider, the ThirdPersonCharacter script, and the new ragdoll rigidbodies/colliders (Figure 7-13).

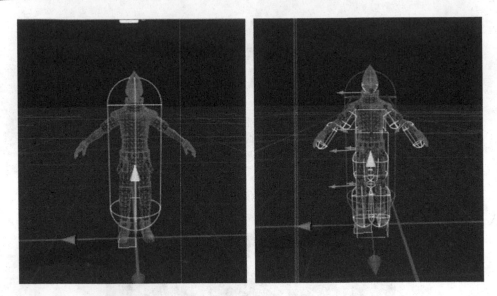

Figure 7-13. Original Capsule Collider (left) and Ragdoll colliders (right)

In the Hierarchy, select each of the child body parts used for the Ragdoll Wizard in turn and uncheck to disable the Collider components in the Inspector, and for each of the new Rigidbody components check the Is Kinematic box. Leave the parent Third Person Character Ragdoll Rigidbody and Capsule Collider components enabled. The player character functions normally in Play mode again.

To go from normal player-controlled animations and movement to a physics-engine-driven ragdoll state requires a script. In the Project panel's Assets ➤ Scripts folder, select Create ➤ Javascript and name the new script GoRagdoll. Add the following code:

```
#pragma strict

private var childRigidBodies : Rigidbody[];
private var childColliders : Collider[];

function Start ()
{
        childRigidBodies = gameObject.GetComponentsInChildren.<Rigidbody>();
        childColliders = gameObject.GetComponentsInChildren.<Collider>();
}

function GotoRagdoll ()
{
        if (childRigidBodies != null)
        {
                for (var childRigidBody : Rigidbody in childRigidBodies)
                {
                        childRigidBody.isKinematic = false;
                }
        }
```

```
            if (childColliders != null)
            {
                    for (var childCollider : Collider in childColliders)
                    {
                            childCollider.enabled = true;
                    }
            }

        gameObject.collider.enabled = false;
        gameObject.rigidbody.isKinematic = true;
        gameObject.GetComponent(Animator).enabled = false;
        gameObject.GetComponent(ThirdPersonCharacter).enabled = false;
        gameObject.GetComponent(ThirdPersonUserControl).enabled = false;
}
```

This script breaks down as follows:

```
(1)     private var childRigidBodies : Rigidbody[];
(2)     private var childColliders : Collider[];
```

Here you are introduced to another programming concept: an **array**. An array is a set of the same type of items, called **elements**. In (1), a private reference variable for an array named childRigidBodies is declared that will hold elements of type Rigidbody. The square brackets [ ] are the syntax that makes this an array as opposed to a singular Rigidbody variable declaration. In this example, the childRigidBodies array will hold as elements the child rigidbodies of the ragdoll.

Similarly in (2) a private reference variable for an array named childColliders is declared that will hold elements of type Collider, in this case the child colliders of the ragdoll.

In the Start() function:

```
(3)     childRigidBodies = gameObject.GetComponentsInChildren.<Rigidbody>();
```

GetComponentsInChildren is aptly named as it returns all components of the designated type of both the game object and any of its children. Here the rigidbody components of the character and child rigidbodies created by the Ragdoll Wizard are assigned as elements of the childRigidBodies array.

```
(4)     childColliders = gameObject.GetComponentsInChildren.<Collider>();
```

Likewise, the Third Party Character Ragdoll game object's Collider component and the child collider components created by the Ragdoll Wizard are assigned as elements of the childColliders array.

In the GotoRagdoll() function:

```
(5)     if (childRigidBodies != null)
```

Tests to make sure the childRigidBodies contains any elements. No elements would equal a "null" state.

```
(6)      for (var childRigidBody : Rigidbody in childRigidBodies)
         {
                 childRigidBody.isKinematic = false;
         }
```

This is a for loop in action, where for each element in the array childRigidBodies, a reference variable childRigidBody of type Rigidbody is created, then its isKinematic property is set to false. Setting isKinematic to false means the rigidbody is now recognized by the physics engine.

```
(7)      if (childColliders != null)
```

Tests to make sure the childColliders contains any elements.

```
(8)      for (var childCollider : Collider in childColliders)
         {
                 childCollider.enabled = true;
         }
```

Another for loop, where for each element in the array childColliders, a reference variable childCollider of type Collider is created then enabled.

```
(9)      gameObject.collider.enabled = false;
(10)     gameObject.rigidbody.isKinematic = true;
(11)     gameObject.GetComponent(Animator).enabled = false;
(12)     gameObject.GetComponent(ThirdPersonCharacter).enabled = false;
(13)     gameObject.GetComponent(ThirdPersonUserControl).enabled = false;
```

(7) and (8) activate the ragdoll child objects to be accessible by the physics engine, but the Animator and scripts that were running the player character animations and movements also need to be deactivated.

(9) and (10) are simple dot notation property-changing statements where the parent Capsule Collider component of the Third Person Character Ragdoll is disabled and the parent Rigidbody component is set to isKinematic—meaning not recognized by the physics engine.

(11), (12), and (13) are slightly different syntax, because the Collider and Rigidbody classes inherit directly from the gameObject class. Animators and Scripts belong to the MonoBehavior class, so must be obtained by name using the GetComponent function to access their properties and disable them.

Save the GoRagdoll script and attach it to Third Person Character Ragdoll.

Note   If the Sample Assets (beta) assets are integrated into your Standard Assets folder already, you can skip the following step.

If you are working with the Sample Assets (beta) package, you will get an "Unknown identifier: Third Person Character" error. The compiler compiles JavaScript files first so it does not recognize the references to "Third Person Character" or the "Third Person User Control" C# scripts not yet compiled being called from our GoRagdoll script in the GotoRagdoll() function.

There is an exception to this rule; the scripts in the Standard Assets folder are compiled even before the JavaScript files. The quick solution here is in the Project panel: move the Sample Assets ➤ Characters ➤ Third Person Character folder by dragging and dropping it into the Standard Assets folder, and also dragging and dropping the Sample Assets ➤ Cross Platform Input folder into the Standard Assets folder. Next, in the Project panel search bar find the CrossPlatformInputInitialize script and delete it. Recall that at the time of this writing, Sample Assets (beta) is a separate folder, but eventually these assets will be integrated into Standard Assets. If this is the case for you, then you can skip this step.

In the Project panel, open your Assets ➤ Prefabs folder. Drag the Third Person Character Ragdoll from the Hierarchy to the Assets ➤ Prefabs folder to save it as a prefab.

Now to write a script for activating the ragdoll physics when the player character is impacted by a pendulum.

In the Project panel's Assets ➤ Scripts folder, select Create ➤ JavaScript, name it KillOnCollision, and open it in MonoDevelop. Edit the code to the following:

```
#pragma strict

function OnCollisionEnter(other : Collision) {
        if (other.gameObject.name == "Third Person Character Ragdoll")
        {
        other.gameObject.GetComponent(GoRagdoll).GotoRagdoll();
        }
}
```

This is all familiar from Chapter 6. The code breaks down as follows:

(1)   `function OnCollisionEnter(other : Collision)`

When the Collider component of the game object to which this script is attached detects a collision, the `OnCollisionEnter` function is called, and passes in a reference `other` to the game object it has collided with (the player character).

(2)   `if (other.gameObject.name == "Third Person Character Ragdoll")`

Check to see if it was the Third Person Character Ragdoll game object that was collided with.

(3)   `other.gameObject.GetComponent(GoRagdoll).GotoRagdoll();`

Use the `GetComponent` function to access the GoRagdoll script and then call the `GotoRagdoll()` function.

In this particular case, the conditional is necessary because sometimes when the player character gets taken out by a pendulum, the pendulum will continue to collide with one or more of the ragdoll colliders, which would cause an error. The same thing would happen if you had moving objects other than the player character that ran into the pendulum.

Save the script and attach it to each of the three Pendulum Spheres. Save the scene, save the project, and playtest. Now THAT is a satisfying response to getting smacked by a pendulum! (See Figure 7-14.)

Figure 7-14. The player character collapsed according to ragdoll physics

If you look closely, you will notice that the head and heels of the player character appear to sink into the surface he is lying on. You can fine-tune this for your game's player character model by adjusting the size and position of the individual ragdoll colliders.

Kill Zone

You can also write a KillOnTrigger script to use for invisible kill zones. Since the obstacle course is an elevated track, something dire should happen to the player if he falls off, such as an invisible kill zone over the floor that kills the player character on impact. In the Assets ➤ Scripts folder in the Project panel, select Create ➤ JavaScript, name the new script KillOnTrigger, and open it in MonoDevelop. You can cut and paste the code from KillOnCollision, then change the function name from OnCollisionEnter(other : Collision) to OnTriggerEnter(other : Collider) as follows, then save the script:

```
#pragma strict

function OnTriggerEnter(other : Collider) {
        if (other.gameObject.name == "Third Person Character Ragdoll")
        {
        other.gameObject.GetComponent(GoRagdoll).GotoRagdoll();
        }
}
```

In the Hierarchy select Create ➤ Cube and name it KillZone_Floor. In the Inspector, give it a Transform position of (0, 0, 120) and a scale of (30, 1, 200). Uncheck the Mesh Renderer component to disable it, making the kill zone invisible. Check Is Trigger in the Box Collider component. Select Add Component ➤ Scripts and choose KillOnTrigger. Save the scene, save the project, and playtest. When your player falls off the elevated track, the ragdoll physics take effect just before he hits the floor.

Spring Joint

A Spring Joint attaches two rigidbodies, where their respective movement is as if they were connected by a spring. A spring has an equilibrium position where it is at rest. If the two rigidbodies are pulled apart, the spring opposes this movement by pulling back. You can see the Spring Joint component properties in Figure 7-15.

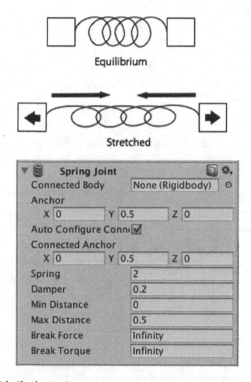

Figure 7-15. Spring Joint component in the Inspector

The **Connected Body** for the Spring Joint property again indicates the rigidbody the spring joint is attached to; if this is None, then it is connected to world space. The **Anchor** is the center of the joint relative to the game object's local space, while the **X**, **Y**, and **Z** properties are the joint's local center. You can see how these values change as you add a Connected Body.

The **Spring** property sets how hard the spring pulls back against an opposing force. **Damper** opposes Spring much like Drag opposes a force. The higher the Damper value, the fewer oscillations or "bounces" before the spring comes to rest.

Min Distance and **Max Distance** set a range within which the spring action will not activate, such that the spring joint will not pull back until the rigidbody moves outside of this range. **Break Force** and **Break Torque** determine the forces necessary to break the spring joint.

Configurable Joint

A configurable joint is a super-customizable joint that is beyond the scope of this book. The Unity Component Reference documentation is the best place to start for more information. You can view the Configurable Joint component properties in Figure 7-16.

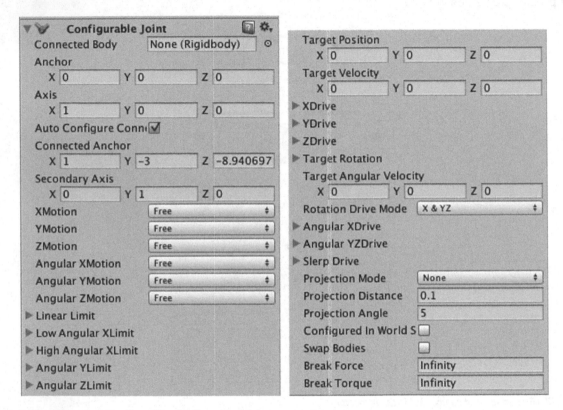

Figure 7-16. The many properties of the Configurable Joint component

Raycasting

Raycasting is a technique for extending a ray from your game object into the world to see if any colliders are in its path. It is commonly used for aiming, calculating distances, and more. The name comes from its coordinate geometry roots where a ray is a type of line where one end has a specific point in space and the other can extend to infinity.

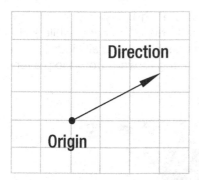

The Ray struct contains the origin point as a Vector3 and the direction as a Vector3.

In the Unity editor Project panel, open the Assets ➤ Sample Assets ➤ Sample Scenes ➤ Scenes folder and open the Third Person Character scene. In the top menu select File ➤ Save Scene as… and save the scene as RaycastTest.

Again in the Project folder, select the Assets ➤ Scripts folder, then select Create ➤ Javascript, name the new script RaycastFun, and open it in MonoDevelop. In normal gameplay you aren't going to see the rays, but `Debug.DrawRay(origin, direction, color)` is a great help during development. Edit the code to the following:

```
public var rayLength : float = 2;

function Update () {
        Debug.DrawRay(transform.position + Vector3(0, 0.5, 0), transform.forward * rayLength, Color.white);
}
```

Breaking this down:

```
(1)     public var rayLength : float = 2;
```

Declare the float variable rayLength as public to make it accessible from the Inspector.

```
(2)     Debug.DrawRay(transform.position + Vector3(0, 0.5, 0),
        transform.forward * rayLength, Color.white);
```

Uses the game object's `transform.position` as the origin of the ray, then adds 0.5 to the y coordinate to raise it from the floor a little. The ray's direction is where the player character is facing, so this is the game object's local `transform.forward`, with the length adjusted by the factor rayLength. You can change the color of the ray for optimal visibility. There are a few more parameters we won't be using, such as the time the ray is visible and how it is drawn relative to other game objects. ⌘+' on DrawRay for the full Scripting Reference.

Save the script, attach it to Third Person Character Ragdoll, save the scene, and playtest. Depending on your editor settings, you might not see anything different. If this is the case, while still in Play mode select the Gizmos button at the top of the Game view. Playtest now and all kinds of things are visible, including the thin white line representing the ray extending forward from the player character (Figure 7-17).

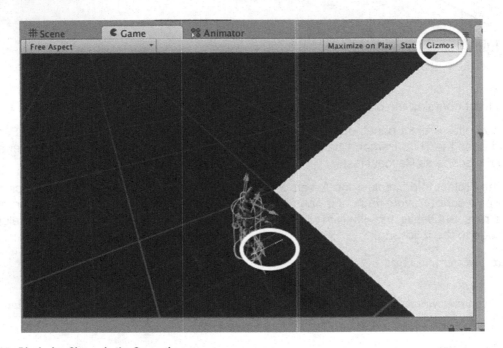

Figure 7-17. Displaying Gizmos in the Game view

The little arrow on the Gizmos button reveals a context menu of Gizmos by type so you can control what you do and do not want to see while testing (Figure 7-18).

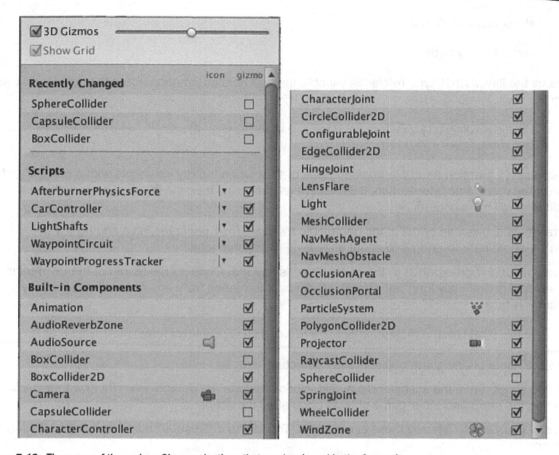

Figure 7-18. The menu of the various Gizmo selections that can be viewed in the Game view

The various Raycast methods give you control over which colliders the ray can hit, and whether or not you want information back regarding the collider hit by the raycast.

In the editor, turn the player character around by changing the Transform.rotation y coordinate to 180. Create five primitive sphere objects and give them transform.positions of (0, 0.5, –5), (4, 0.5, 5.5), (0.7, 0.5, –4), (–3, –0.5, –11) and (–4, 0.5, –2). Using standard naming conventions, name them sequentially Sphere_001 to Sphere_005. In MonoDevelop edit your RaycastFun script to the following:

```
function Update () {
        var hit : RaycastHit;
        if(Physics.Raycast(transform.position + Vector3(0, 0.5, 0), transform.forward, hit))
        {
                print ("Collided with game object " +
                hit.collider.gameObject.name);
        }
}
```

This breaks down as follows:

```
(1)      var hit : RaycastHit;
```

Declares the `RaycastHit` type reference variable that will hold information about the collider that was hit by the ray.

```
(2)      if(Physics.Raycast(transform.position + Vector3(0, 0.5, 0),
         transform.forward, hit))
```

The `Raycast()` function returns a boolean value of `true` when the ray intersects with a collider and `false` when there is no intersection. If `Raycast()` returns `true`, then the block of code within the conditional will be executed.

The ray itself is given an origin of the game object's `transform.position`, plus adding 0.5 to the origin's y coordinate to bring it to about knee level of the character.

The ray direction corresponds to the game object's forward. Omitting the length of the ray means it defaults to an infinitely long ray, so you will get hit information from any game object the player character is facing.

```
(3)      print ("Collided with game object " + hit.collider.gameObject.name);
```

Prints the name of any game object the ray detects.

Save the script. Save the scene and playtest. Notice that the ray detects everything with a collider, including the ramp and other game objects populating the scene.

Let's say you want to destroy these evil spheres. Try adding a "Destroy" command to your `Update()` function:

```
function Update () {
    var hit : RaycastHit;
        if(Physics.Raycast(transform.position+ Vector3(0, 0.5, 0),
        transform.forward, hit)) {
                print ("Collided with game object " +
                hit.collider.gameObject.name);
                Destroy(hit.collider.gameObject);
        }
}
```

Save the script and playtest. Run your character around and destroy the evil spheres. But watch out—you also destroyed the lower ramp and obstacle game objects that the ray collided with.

You have used `gameObject.name` in conditionals to test for a game object, but now you have five evil spheres to contend with. You could destroy the spheres using this approach:

```
function Update () {
    var hit : RaycastHit;
        if(Physics.Raycast(transform.position+ Vector3(0, 0.5, 0), transform.forward, hit)) {
                print ("Collided with game object " + hit.collider.gameObject.name);
```

```
        if (hit.collider.gameObject.name == ("Sphere_001"))
        {
                Destroy(hit.collider.gameObject);
        } else if (hit.collider.gameObject.name == ("Sphere_002"))
        {
                Destroy(hit.collider.gameObject);
        } else if (hit.collider.gameObject.name == ("Sphere_003"))
        {
                Destroy(hit.collider.gameObject);
        } else if (hit.collider.gameObject.name == ("Sphere_004"))
        {
                Destroy(hit.collider.gameObject);
        } else if (hit.collider.gameObject.name == ("Sphere_005"))
        {
                Destroy(hit.collider.gameObject);
        }
    }
}
```

But you see how tedious and bulky the code gets with only a few evil spheres. What if you had a much bigger number of evil spheres?

Tags

Tags are an important scripting tool that allow you to sort and identify groups of game objects such as evil spheres, which in turn simplifies your code.

In the Hierarchy, select Sphere_001 and take a look at the Inspector, where you'll see an option for Tag near the top, just below the game object name (Figure 7-19).

Figure 7-19. Tag drop-down menu selector in the Inspector

Open the Tag drop-down menu and you'll see a list of commonly used tags. While some built-in tags appear, you want to create one called Enemy, so select Add Tag... at the bottom of the menu to open the Tag Manager in the Inspector (Figure 7-20).

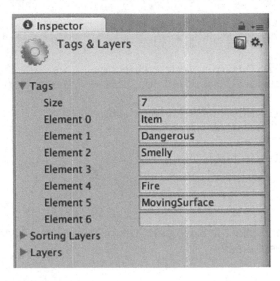

Figure 7-20. Tag and Layer Manager in the Inspector

If none of the Elements are empty, you can increase the value of Size. Bear in mind that a game object can only have one tag, but you can create as many different tags for your game as you like. Add Enemy to an empty element in the Tag list, then reselect Sphere_001 in the Hierarchy. Now when you select the Tag drop-down menu in the Inspector, Enemy appears as a choice, so go ahead and select it. Tag the other four Sphere game objects as Enemy as well.

In MonoDevelop, edit your `Update()` function to the following:

```
function Update () {    var hit : RaycastHit;
        if(Physics.Raycast(transform.position+ Vector3(0, 0.5, 0), transform.forward, hit)) {
                print ("Collided with game object " + hit.collider.gameObject.name);
                if (hit.collider.gameObject.tag == ("Enemy"))
                {
                        Destroy(hit.collider.gameObject);
                }
        }
}
```

Save and playtest, and now any evil sphere the ray intersects with is destroyed. Run the player character around in all directions, and notice that the platform and block obstacles are not destroyed, only the spheres.

Tags aren't specific to raycasting; they are for easier management of groups of game objects in your scripts.

Layers

Whereas tags reduce bulky code by addressing groups of game objects, Layers also address groups of game objects. They help in terms of game performance because they are most commonly used as a constraint to selectively ignore groups of game objects or areas of the scene, which reduces the processing load.

Layers can be used to limit which part of a scene will be rendered by a camera, for layer-based collision detection, or to determine which areas of a scene will be illuminated, again reducing the processing load. Unlike Tags, the first seven layers are required by Unity and you are limited to a total of 31 layers.

If you comment out or edit your code in the RaycastFun script's Update() function to the following:

```
function Update () {
    var hit : RaycastHit;
        if(Physics.Raycast(transform.position+ Vector3(0, 0.5, 0),
        transform.forward, hit)) {
                print ("Collided with game object " +
                hit.collider.gameObject.name);

                Destroy(hit.collider.gameObject);
        }
}
```

once again the platform and block obstacles the ray detects are destroyed along with the spheres. Select Obstacles in the Hierarchy. In the Inspector, to the right of the Tag menu select the Layer drop-down menu and choose Ignore Raycast (Figure 7-21).

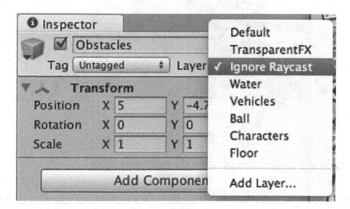

Figure 7-21. Select Ignore Raycast in the Layer drop-down menu

A pop-up window will ask if you want to set the layer to Ignore Raycast for all child objects. Select Yes, change children so all the smaller prefab blocks making up Obstacles will be included in the Ignore Raycast layer.

Save the scene and playtest. Again only the evil spheres disappear when the ray detects their colliders. The difference now is that the game engine does not have to check every collider the ray intersects, but literally ignores any colliders on the Ignore Raycast layer.

Character Controller

You've moved game objects with scripts, animations, and physical forces. You have spent some time using Unity's Sample Assets controllers like the Third Person Character, but you can also make your own controller using the Character Controller component. For first-person or third-person characters that you do not want affected by rigidbody physics, the Character Controller component may be just the thing.

In the editor, create a new scene, and add a Plane and a Directional light. In the Hierarchy select Create ➤ Cube. Notice that the primitive game object Cube does not have a Rigidbody component. Recall that rigidbody movement is controlled by the physics engine, so a Character Controller component also trying to control movement and a Rigidbody component on the same game object would result in odd behavior.

Notice that the Cube game object already has a Box Collider. The Character Controller is essentially a Capsule Collider whose movement can be controlled by a script. It inherits from the `Collider` class, which means that it contains the `Collider` class capabilities and builds on them with more customized functions. With the Cube game object selected in the Hierarchy, in the Inspector select Add Component ➤ Physics ➤ Character Controller. In the Scene view, you'll see the Capsule Collider gizmo appear within the Cube game object (Figure 7-22).

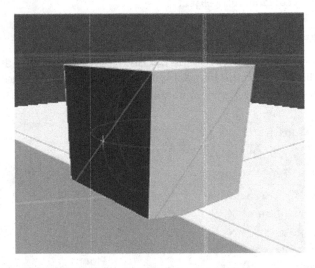

Figure 7-22. The Character Controller Capsule Collider within the Cube game object

In the Inspector you will find the Character Controller. The controller cannot climb a slope steeper than the **Slope Limit**. The **Step Offset** is a similar vertical constraint that determines how high from the ground the controller can climb stairs. **Skin Width** sets the margin within the surface that another collider can penetrate into the controller's collider before detecting a collision. A general rule of thumb is 10% of the character controller's radius, so change this to 0.1. To reduce jitter, if the controller is told to move a distance less than the **Min Move Distance**, it will stay in place. The higher the number, the more control input required. Like a standard collider, the Capsule Collider can be offset using **Center**, and adjusted in size using **Radius** and **Height** (Figure 7-23).

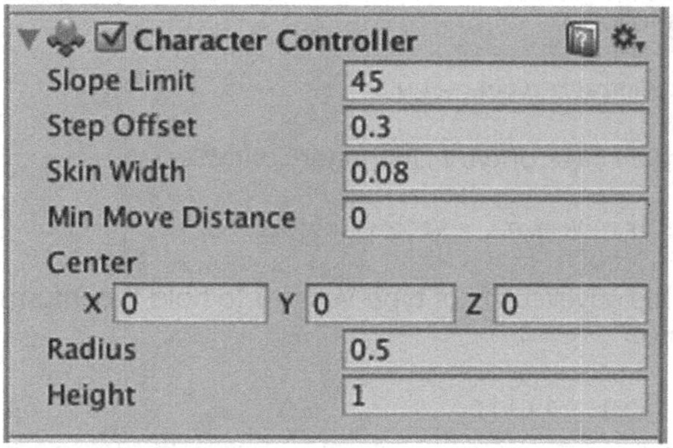

Figure 7-23. The Character Controller component in the Inspector

To test some of these properties you will need to populate the scene with a few more items. In the Project panel, select the Assets ➤ Sample Assets ➤ Prototyping ➤ Prefabs folder and add a Loop to the scene. Give the Loop a y-rotation of 90. The Loop and Plane should each have Transform positions of (0, 0.5, 0) while the Cube should have a Transform position of (0, 0, 0). Give the Plane a scale of (20, 20, 20), and add a little contrast by dragging the prototype_grey_dff texture from the Assets ➤ Sample Assets ➤ Prototyping ➤ Prefabs ➤ Textures folder and dropping it on the Plane in the Scene view. Drill down one more folder into Compound Prefabs and drag a Box Pile into the scene; give it a Transform position of (2, 0, –8).

Finally, in the Assets ➤ Standard Assets ➤ Scripts ➤ Camera Scripts folder, find the Mouse Orbit script. If the folder isn't there, in the top menu select Assets ➤ Import Package ➤ Scripts to obtain it. Drag and drop it onto the Main Camera. Select Main Camera in the Hierarchy. Drag the Cube game object from the Hierarchy to the Main Camera ➤ Mouse Orbit Script component and drop it into the Target property field.

The scene is set up and the Character Controller properties are set. Now for a script to get the Cube game object moving. In the Project panel select the Assets ➤ Scripts folder, then Create ➤ New Script ➤ Javascript. Name it CCScript and open it in MonoDevelop. Edit the code to the following:

```
#pragma strict

private var contr : CharacterController;
private var moveVector : Vector3 = Vector3.zero;
public var speed : float = 10.0f;

function Start () {
        contr = gameObject.GetComponent.<CharacterController>();
}

function Update () {
                moveVector.x = Input.GetAxis("Horizontal") * speed;
                moveVector.z = Input.GetAxis("Vertical") * speed;
                contr.Move(moveVector * Time.deltaTime);
}
```

This code breaks down as follows:

(1)   `private var contr : CharacterController;`

Declares a reference variable `contr` of type CharacterController.

(2)   `private var moveVector : Vector3 = Vector3.zero;`

Declares a reference variable `moveVector` of type Vector3 to hold the information on how far to move the game object each frame.

(3)   `public var speed : float = 10.0f;`

Declares a public float variable `speed` for adjusting the speed of the game object in the Inspector.

```
        function Start () {
(4)      controller = gameObject.GetComponent.<CharacterController>();
        }
```

Accesses the CharacterController component reference and assigns it to controller.

```
        function Update () {
(5)          moveVector.x = Input.GetAxis("Horizontal") * speed;
(6)          moveVector.z = Input.GetAxis("Vertical") * speed;
        }
```

Here the input from the user is multiplied by the `speed` factor and stored in the respective x-axis and z-axis components of the Vector3 variable `moveVector`.

(7)   `controller.Move(moveVector * Time.deltaTime);`

First the `moveVector` information is multiplied by the `Time.deltaTime` smoothing factor, then passed to the Controller Character `Move()` function.

The `Move()` function moves the game object, and returns information regarding any collisions from the move in a `CollisionFlags` variable. This information can give you a general idea about where the collisions occurred. The `CollisionFlags` variable is a bitmask, the explanation of which is beyond the scope of this text. However, you can ⌘+' `CollisionFlags` in MonoDevelop to open the Scripting Reference and get an idea of how to filter `CollisionFlags` information (Figure 7-24).

CollisionFlags.None

Description

CollisionFlags is a bitmask returned by CharacterController.Move.

It gives you a broad overview of where your character collided with any other objects.

```
function Update () {
        var controller : CharacterController = GetComponent(CharacterController);
        if (controller.collisionFlags == CollisionFlags.None)
                print("Free floating!");

        if (controller.collisionFlags & CollisionFlags.Sides)
                print("Touching sides!");

        if (controller.collisionFlags == CollisionFlags.Sides)
                print("Only touching sides, nothing else!");

        if (controller.collisionFlags & CollisionFlags.Above)
                print("Touching sides!");

        if (controller.collisionFlags == CollisionFlags.Above)
                print("Only touching Ceiling, nothing else!");

        if (controller.collisionFlags & CollisionFlags.Below)
                print("Touching ground!");

        if (controller.collisionFlags == CollisionFlags.Below)
                print("Only touching ground, nothing else!");
}
```

Figure 7-24. CollisionFlags in the Unity Scripting Reference has example boolean logic conditionals for extracting the collision information of interest

Save the script and attach it to the Cube game object. Save the scene and play. Try moving the Cube up the loop. Once the slope of the loop exceeds the Slope Limit value the Cube cannot proceed. You can also see the effect of the Skin Width setting by how much of the corner of the Cube nearest the loop is obscured.

You'll also find the Cube runs into the Box Pile and stops, but the Box Pile doesn't react to the impact. For this type of interaction you'll have to manually add this functionality to your script. In MonoDevelop, add a variable declaration to the others:

```
public var pushPower : float = 2.0;
```

This gives you a factor for adjusting the effect of the impact through the Inspector.

Add the following function below the Update() function:

```
function OnControllerColliderHit (hit : ControllerColliderHit) {
        var body : Rigidbody = hit.collider.attachedRigidbody;

        if (body == null || body.isKinematic)
                return;
        if (hit.moveDirection.y < -0.3)
                return;

        var pushDir : Vector3 = Vector3 (hit.moveDirection.x, 0,
        hit.moveDirection.z);
        body.velocity = pushDir * pushPower;
}
```

This code breaks down as follows:

(1)   `function OnControllerColliderHit (hit : ControllerColliderHit) {`

The Character Controller component has an OnControllerColliderHit function that is called if the capsule hits another collider during a Move. ControllerColliderHit provides more detailed information about the collision.

(2)   `var body : Rigidbody = hit.collider.attachedRigidbody;`

Declares a Rigidbody type variable body to hold a reference to the rigidbody of the game object the Cube collided with.

(3)   `if (body == null || body.isKinematic)`
                `return;`

Checks to see if in fact the other object has a rigidbody component OR if it is set to Is Kinematic. If either of these is true, then the Cube cannot push it around, so the function is exited via the return statement.

(4)   `if (hit.moveDirection.y < -0.3)`
                `return;`

This conditional is for checking the collision direction to prevent pushing any objects below the Cube.

(5)   `var pushDir : Vector3 = Vector3 (hit.moveDirection.x, 0,`
        `hit.moveDirection.z);`

Declares a Vector3 type reference variable pushDir to hold the moveDirection information from the collision in the x and z axes.

(6)   `body.velocity = pushDir * pushPower;`

The final response to the Cube's push is calculated by multiplying the push direction by your pushPower factor and applying this velocity to the impacted object's rigidbody.

Save the script and playtest. This time when you run the Cube into the Box Pile, the boxes respond to the impact of the Cube (Figure 7-25).

Figure 7-25. *The smaller game object Cube pushing the Box Pile cubes*

As always, have fun and experiment with the properties to see how the Cube's behavior changes.

Summary

In this chapter you began the construction of an obstacle course, using what you've learned so far for the first obstacle. You added joints to your Physics knowledge base and designed some pendulum obstacles. With your basic understanding of rigidbodies, colliders, joints, and animation you learned to use the Ragdoll Wizard to apply ragdoll physics to your player character for a satisfying, realistic demise. You've also added the Character Controller component to your menu of options for controlling the player game object. In each of these categories you've learned about the corresponding functions and variables, and how to use them in basic scripts. You've also added the use of Tags and Layers to your general game development skill set.

That's quite an accomplishment! Hang in there, it's going to get even more fun and exciting as we integrate these new physics capabilities with particle emitters and special effects in the next chapter.

Chapter 8

Particle Emitters and Special Effects

The Shuriken Particle System Engine

Unity introduced the Shuriken Particle System Engine with version 3.5. While 3D models and animations must be created outside of Unity, the Shuriken particle engine enables you to make your own particle effects like fire, rain, and more. In this chapter you will learn how to create special effects with particle systems, and then move on to using them with scripts.

Particle systems are very visually dynamic. You definitely want to have the editor open to see the particles in action and how they change in response to the system's module settings (Figure 8-1).

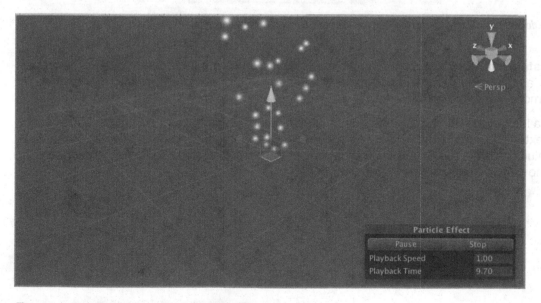

Figure 8-1. Default particle system in the Scene View

In the Unity editor, open the Obstacle Course scene. From the top menu select Game Object ➤ Create Other ➤ Particle System. In the Scene view, the newly created particle system appears and immediately begins emitting particles according to the default settings.

You'll notice the particle system controls appear in the lower right corner of the Scene view as well. The pause and stop buttons are self-explanatory. Watch the difference when you change the Playback Speed to 10, then 0.1, then back to 1.00. Playback time is helpful in coordinating systems that make up particle effects and general fine-tuning.

Before going any further, first a little terminology. **Particles** are the objects emitted in groups by a particle system. They are typically composed of a texture of a simple shape, emitted as 2D billboards. A **billboard** is a plane with a texture that always faces the camera, giving a 3D effect with a 2D object.

Remember that game performance depends on how "busy" or "heavy" a scene gets. Particles can be 3D or even animated using the Texture Sheet Animation module, depending on the needs of the game (Figure 8-2). As fun as they are to experiment with, use them in your game where they make sense: employ just the particles you need, just for how long you need them.

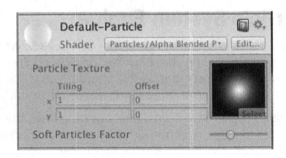

Figure 8-2. The default particle displaying its texture on the right, as seen in the Inspector

A particle **system** is the component that emits the particles. It has a number of modules and settings that allow for a huge variety of effects. Particle systems can in turn be combined into groups that create even more complex **particle effects**.

As you take a look at the Particle System component in the Inspector (Figure 8-3), you can see that it gives you extensive editing capabilities. As you read the property descriptions, take the time to adjust the values and use the Simulate/Stop buttons of the particle system controller in the Scene view to see how the default particle system responds.

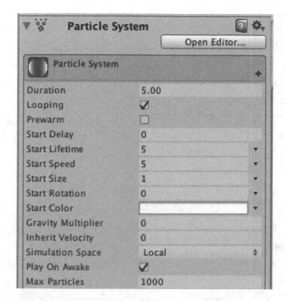

Figure 8-3. The Initial module of the Particle System component in the Inspector

The first few properties control particle emission by the particle system. **Duration** is the time in seconds the particle system will emit particles. For a continuous effect you can check the **Looping** box. If you are using Looping and check the **Prewarm** box, particles will appear in place as if particle emission was ongoing. If instead you want a delay before particle emission begins, use **Start Delay** with Prewarm unchecked to designate the time in seconds before emitting particles.

The next group of properties control behavior of the individual particles. You can designate the lifetime of each particle in seconds with **Start Lifetime. Start Speed**, **Start Size**, and **Start Rotation** are just as they sound: the initial velocity, size, and rotation of the particles when first emitted. All four of these can be designated with a numerical value in the corresponding field, or further customized with random ranges or curves.

Start Color is just that, with more controls to vary the color of the particles, including the alpha value for opacity, over their lifetime.

You can have effects like smoke that floats upward or fluid splashes that fall to the ground by using the **Gravity Multiplier**.

Particle systems like any other game object can be in motion. When they are moving you can use **Inherit Velocity** to determine how much of this velocity should be inherited by the particles.

Simulation Space allows you to choose between Local or World space. When checked, **Play on Awake** tells the particle system to start automatically upon creation. Finally, **Max Particles** is the total number of particles emitted by the system for one cycle.

The remaining items in the Inspector are more modules. Click each to see its own controllable properties (Figure 8-4). Bear in mind that while individual particle systems don't use each module every time, Shuriken gives you plenty of options (Table 8-1).

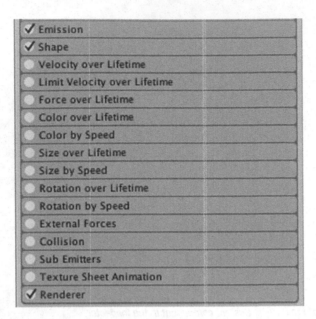

Figure 8-4. More modules of the Particle System component in the Inspector

Table 8-1. Additional Shuriken Particle System Modules in the Inspector

Module	Description
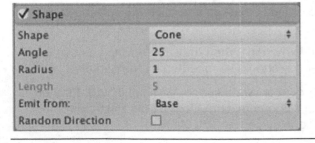	**Emission module** Rate: Number of particles per second. Also an alternative option for particles/meter. Bursts: Designates the time in seconds and the number of particles to be emitted within that time. Use the + to add more bursts. **Shape module** Emitter shape options: Sphere, Hemisphere, Cone, Box, and Mesh. Depending on the shape there are more adjustable parameters to further refine the direction of emission for the particles. Each shape also has a Random Direction option.

(continued)

Table 8-1. (continued)

Module	Description
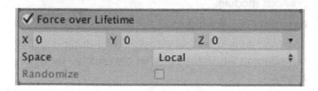	**Velocity over Lifetime module** Can control the velocity over the lifetime of the particle in each axis.
	**Limit Velocity over Lifetime module** Velocity limit is another term for dampening or drag. The Speed limit is the threshold at which the particle is affected by the amount of dampening.
	**Force over Lifetime module** Apply forces along any axis using constant values or curves, or check the Randomize box at the bottom of the module. Can designate Local or World space.
	**Color over Lifetime module** Gives a choice of Gradient or Random Between Two Gradients. Clicking on the field will open up the Gradient Editor.
	Color by Speed module Displaying color based on speed effectively mimics Doppler imaging. Set the color gradient with the Color property, where the min speed represents the left margin of the color gradient and the max speed represents the right side of the color gradient, and the color gradient is mapped to the speed scale proportionally.
	Size over Lifetime module You have the option of using a curve editor, or choosing randomization between two constants or two curves.
	Size by Speed module Same options as Size over Lifetime of using a curve editor, or choosing randomization between two constants or two curves.

(continued)

Table 8-1. (*continued*)

Module	Description

Rotation over Lifetime module

Designate the angular velocity of the particles over their lifetime with a constant or a curve. Also has options for randomization between two constants or two curves.

Rotation by Speed module

Same options as Rotation over Lifetime, though you must designate the range of speeds since it is not predetermined by the Duration property as in the previous module.

External Forces module

This module is specifically designed for designating the extent to which the particles are affected by wind zones.

Collision module

First select whether the particles will recognize collisions with every game object or be limited to planes. Using planes whenever possible is the most efficient for game performance.

Visualization of the planes lets you choose between using wireframe-like or solid grids. The remaining parameters affect particle behavior similarly to Rigidbody and Physic Materials.

Send Collision Messages calls the OnParticleCollision() function when checked.

Sub Emitters module

Particles can be designated to convert to another Particle System either on collision or at the beginning or end of its lifetime. Using the Collision option requires enabling of the Collision Module. You can find an excellent example of sub emitters at work with the fireworks in the Particle Sandbox scene of the Sample Assets particle system demo.

(continued)

Table 8-1. (*continued*)

Module	Description
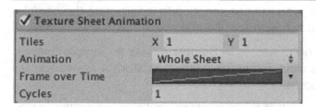	**Texture Sheet Animation module** Particles can be animated with an array of images that are contained on one Texture Sheet file. See the part_fireball_sheet_dff particle texture in the Sample Assets package.
	Renderer module This module holds the ParticleSystemRenderer properties that determine how the particles are drawn or rendered. The simplest mode, Billboard, uses a 2D graphic that turns so it always faces the camera. The other Billboard selections provide for some enhanced visual effects without the overhead of true 3D particles (Mesh is a true 3D particle). The properties affecting material, lighting, shadows and drawing order apply to all of the Renderer Module modes. Manipulating these settings is beyond the scope of this book.

The Grand Entrance

This example will add pizzazz to the scene by having the player make a Nordic-god-like grand entrance in a flash of energy (Figure 8-5).

Figure 8-5. The player arrives with a grand entrance at the start of game play

To get an idea of where you are headed, first you will check out a variety of particle effects from Unity's Sample Assets. For your first particle system you will start with a Sample Asset prefab and modify it. You will move on to create a custom particle system from scratch, and ultimately combine these systems into a complex particle effect. Finally, you will use scripting to incorporate the particle effects and interaction with other game objects into the Obstacle Course scene.

To get straight to the fun stuff, in the Project panel go to Assets ➤ Sample Assets ➤ Sample Scenes ➤ Scenes, open up the Particles scene, and give a whirl. Explosions, fire, dust storms, fireworks, water sprays and more all at your fingertips—awesome!

Okay, when you are ready to proceed, take a closer look at the dust storm and notice how the entire area is involved. This is one simple particle system, with a distinct difference in the use of the size of the emitter.

In the Hierarchy, select Particle Systems ➤ DustStorm. Next, in the Inspector expand the Shape module of the Particle System component. Notice it is a box shape—a really big one with x and z values of 100. This entire 100 × 100 box is the particle emitter, emitting the entire dust storm over the surface area of the box so it appears to cover the scene when played.

You are going to build your particle effects in the Obstacle Course scene. Go ahead and reopen the Obstacle Course scene in the editor and delete the default particle system.

In the Project panel, select the Assets ➤ Sample Assets ➤ Effects ➤ Particle Systems ➤ Prefabs folder, drag a copy of the DustStorm particle system prefab into the scene, and rename it DustPuff. The landing of the player character will be emphasized by a puff of dust. We will start with it since it is the simplest.

Puff of Dust

The goal here is a sudden burst of dust to emphasize the force of the player's impact. With DustPuff selected, turn your attention to the Particle System component in the Inspector (Figure 8-6).

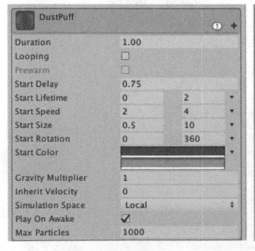
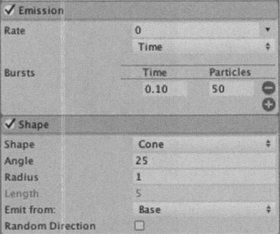

Figure 8-6. DustPuff particle system component settings

The timing is that the burst of energy will appear first, the player falls through it to the ground, landing on his feet, and the dust puffs up at this moment of impact.

For a single short burst of dust, set the Duration to 1 second and uncheck Looping. Set Start Delay to 0.75. This will allow some time for the energy burst and player's appearance, specifically to coincide with the player landing on the ground.

Open the drop-down menu for Start Lifetime and select Random Between Two Constants, and enter 0 and 2 into the respective fields. Introducing some randomness to the particle Start Lifetime, Start Speed and Start Size adds a more "natural" look to the particle system. Change the values for Start Size to 0.5 and 10.

Rather than blowing dust, for the dust to puff up and then fall back to the ground change the Gravity Multiplier to 1. If you were going for a smoke- or steam-like effect, you could make this a negative value for the particles to float up and away.

For the burst effect, in the Emission module change Rate to 0. Now in Bursts, select the +, then set Time to 0.10 and Particles to 50.

Use the Shape module to make the puff of dust more localized around the player character's landing area. Select Cone for the Shape property, which should have an Angle of 25, a Radius of 1, and Base for the Emit from: property.

Test the DustPuff particle system as you make changes with the Simulate and Stop buttons in the Scene view. Now move the Third Person Character Ragdoll's `Transform.position` to (0, 4, 0) and make sure that the DustPuff's `Transform.position` is (0, 0, 0) and the `Transform.rotation` is (90, 0, 0). Save the scene and playtest.

Energy Burst

The next particle system to add to the Grand Entrance is the energy burst (Figure 8-7). In the editor top menu select Game Object ➤ Create Other ➤ Particle System and name it EnergyBurst. Change the `Transform.position` to (0, 4, 0) for the burst to come from above the final landing site of the player character.

Energy Burst		
Duration	1.00	
Looping	☐	
Prewarm	☐	
Start Delay	0	
Start Lifetime	5	
Start Speed	5	
Start Size	1	
Start Rotation	0	
Start Color		
Gravity Multiplier	1	
Inherit Velocity	0	
Simulation Space	Local	
Play On Awake	☑	
Max Particles	1000	

✓ Emission		
Rate	200	
	Time	
Bursts	Time	Particles
✓ Shape		
Shape	Box	
Box X	0.2	
Box Y	1	
Box Z	0.2	
Random Direction	☐	

Figure 8-7. EnergyBurst particle system component settings

Only a few of the settings of the Initial module in the Inspector need to be changed. While this won't be a truly instantaneous burst of energy, it will be a short, one-time emission of particles to produce a plasma-like stream of light. Change the Duration to 1 second and uncheck Looping. Increase the Gravity Multiplier to 1, otherwise the player character will fall through the particles more quickly than they can reach the ground.

In the Emission module, change the Rate to 200. Next, in the Shape module, select Box. For a more condensed stream of particles, change the Box X and Box Z settings to 0.2.

Finally, check and expand the Color Over Lifetime module. Double-click the Color field to open the Gradient Editor (Figure 8-8). Select and move the various cursors and change their colors and alpha values according to Figure 8-8, in which the bottom left cursor starts with a light electric blue, and transitions to a faint lavender at the second cursor on the bottom right. The top cursor on the left has an alpha value of 100% and that on the upper right has an alpha value of 0%. You can also click to add more cursors as needed for more variation.

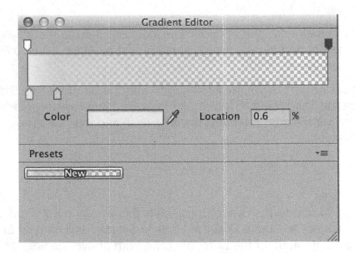

Figure 8-8. Gradient Editor for the Color property of the Color Over Lifetime module

While the examples in this book are using ready-made assets, for a more lightning-like look, you would want to create a material that uses a spikier-shaped texture. To make a particle material, create a new material in the Project panel, then with the Shader property use its drop-down menu to change from the default of Diffuse to select one from Particles (Figure 8-9).

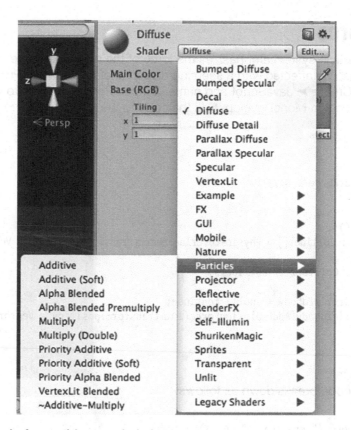

Figure 8-9. Selecting a shader for a particle system in the Inspector

For more examples of custom materials and textures for particle systems, open the Assets ➤ Sample Assets ➤ Effects ➤ Particle Systems folder and take a look at the contents of the Materials and Textures folders.

Particle Effect

To combine the DustPuff and EnergyBurst particle systems into a single particle effect, in the editor top menu select Game Object ➤ Create Empty. Name it GrandEntrance and set its Transform.position to (0, 4, 0). In the Hierarchy, drag and drop the DustPuff and EnergyBurst particle systems onto the GrandEntrance game object.

Double-check their positions, which as child game objects are now relative to the parent game object. The Transform.position for DustPuff should be (0, –4, 0) and that of EnergyBurst (0, 0, 0). Save the scene and save the project.

Land With Force

While the DustPuff particle system emphasizes the force of the player character's landing visually, nearby objects can also be affected with a seeming dispersal of force. In the Project panel Assets ➤ Scripts folder, select Create ➤ JavaScript and name it ImpactForce. Attach it to the GrandEntrance game object, then open it in MonoDevelop. Edit the code to the following:

```
#pragma strict

function Start () {
        Invoke ("ImpactForce", 0.75);
}

function ImpactForce () {
        var colliders : Collider[] = Physics.OverlapSphere(transform.position - Vector3(0, 4, 0), 10);

        for(var cldr : Collider in colliders)
        {
                if(cldr.rigidbody == null) continue;
                cldr.rigidbody.AddExplosionForce(10, transform.position - Vector3(0, 4, 0), 10, 0,
ForceMode.Impulse);
        }
}
```

Save the script. This code breaks down as follows:

```
        (1)      Invoke ("ImpactForce", 0.75);
```

1. The Invoke function lets you call functions with a time delay before the function is implemented. It takes two arguments: the function to be called, and the time delay in seconds. In this example the force should coincide with the player character landing on the ground and the start of the DustPuff particle system emission, which you know from its Start Delay is 0.75 seconds.

```
        (2)              (3)
        var colliders : Collider[] =

            (4)                                (5)                (6)
        Physics.OverlapSphere(transform.position - Vector3(0, 4, 0), 10);
```

Within the ImpactForce() function,

2. Declare a reference variable colliders

3. for an array of type Collider.

4. Assign any colliders found within the boundaries of the Physics.OverlapSphere

5. that has a position of the GrandEntrance game object it is attached to, minus 4 from its y coordinate value to position it on the ground centered in the DustPuff particle system emission,

6. and a radius of 10.

```
(7)      for(var cldr : Collider in colliders)
```

7. This for loop will iterate through the array of colliders

```
(8)      if(cldr.rigidbody == null) continue;
```

8. Check for a rigidbody attached to the collider. Remember a rigidbody is required when using physics forces. If there is no rigidbody, continue means do not execute the following block of code, and instead move on to the next item in the for loop.

```
.           (9)               (10)        (11)
cldr.rigidbody.AddExplosionForce(10, transform.position - Vector3(0,

        (12)(13)      (14)
4, 0), 10, 0, ForceMode.Impulse);
```

9. If there is a rigidbody attached, apply an AddExplosionForce

10. of force 10

11. from the same position as the DustPuff particle system emission

12. with an explosion radius of 10

13. no extra upward force (use this when you want a little more upward "pop")

14. using ForceMode.Impulse, which applies all of the force instantaneously rather than over a period of time. This force decreases with distance from the designated position and reaches zero at the designated radius.

If you playtest now, nothing happens because there are no game objects within the radius of the Physics.OverlapSphere. To see this in action, in the Project panel drill down to the Assets ➤ Sample Assets ➤ Prototyping ➤ Prefabs ➤ Compound Prefabs folder. Drag a Smash Boxes prefab into the Scene view, then give it a Transform.position of (–5, 0, –5) and a Transform.rotation of (0, 90, 0).

Create a duplicate of this game object by using Ģ+D in the Hierarchy, then place this duplicate at a Transform.position of (8, 0, –5). Create a third duplicate, this time with a Transform.position of (0, 0, –11) and a Transform.rotation of (0, 0, 0). Save the scene, save the project, and playtest.

Boom! Notice how the first Smash Boxes pile is completely blown away, while the second has its farthest box components barely touched, and the third Smash Boxes pile isn't touched at all. This is because of their placement relative to the explosion radius of 10 designated in the ImpactForce script.

As far as game design and style goes, this is a pretty overdone entrance for our player, but it serves as a great exercise for building particle effects.

Bomb Obstacle

Dramatic fiery explosions are created much the same way, only with fire and smoke particle systems along with additional special touches like adding light and sound. The Sample Assets package has a fantastic explosion example complete with fire and smoke materials and textures.

The Ball prefab in the Sample Assets package looks dark and ominous, so it will make a great bomb. Drag it from the Assets ➤ Sample Assets ➤ Vehicles ➤ Rolling Ball ➤ Prefabs folder onto the scene, name it Bomb, set Tag to Untagged, and give it a `Transform.position` of (0, 9.5, 20). Remove the Ball and Ball User Control Script components by clicking on the gear icon and selecting Remove Component from the drop-down menu.

In the Project panel Assets ➤ Scripts folder, create a new script named BombExplosion and open it in MonoDevelop. Edit the code to the following:

```
#pragma strict

public var victim : GameObject;
public var prefab : GameObject;

function Start () {
        victim = GameObject.Find("Third Person Character Ragdoll");
}

function OnCollisionEnter (collision : Collision) {
        if (collision.gameObject.name == "Third Person Character Ragdoll") {
                Explosion();
        }
}

function Explosion () {
        victim.GetComponent(GoRagdoll).GotoRagdoll();
        Instantiate (prefab, transform.position, Quaternion.identity);
        Destroy(gameObject);
}
```

Save the script and attach it to the Bomb game object. Breaking it down:

> (1)   `public var victim : GameObject;`
> `public var prefab : GameObject;`

1. Declare two reference variables, `victim` and `prefab`, of type `GameObject`.

> (2)   `victim = GameObject.Find("Third Person Character Ragdoll");`

2. In the `Start()` function, assign the Third Person Character Ragdoll reference to `victim`.

> (3)   `if (collision.gameObject.name == "Third Person Character Ragdoll") {`
> `Explosion();`
> `}`

3. If the player character collided with the bomb, call the `Explosion()` function.

```
(4)    victim.GetComponent(GoRagdoll).GotoRagdoll();
(5)    Instantiate (prefab, transform.position, Quaternion.identity);
(6)    Destroy(gameObject);
```

Within the `Explosion()` function,

4. Convert the player character to its ragdoll,

5. Instantiate a new Explosion prefab at the `transform.position` and rotation of the bomb, then

6. Destroy the bomb game object.

If you playtest now, the player character will collapse and the bomb will roll according to the collision with the player character but without the explosion effect, because it hasn't yet been assigned as the prefab to be instantiated in the Explosion function. In the Console you will see a UnassignedReferenceException warning you that the prefab variable has not been assigned and suggesting that you do so.

With the Bomb game object selected, in the Inspector find the BombExplosion script component and notice the field for the Prefab property is None. In the Project panel Assets ➤ Sample Assets ➤ Effects ➤ Particle Systems ➤ Prefabs folder find the Explosion prefab. Drag and drop it into the Prefab property field in the Inspector.

Save the scene and save the project. Playtest and run the player character into the bomb. Nice! You will be using more bombs later, so drag the Bomb game object from the Hierarchy into the Project panel's Assets ➤ Prefabs folder.

Blizzard Obstacle

This simple obstacle serves as a demonstration for using particle collisions. In the editor top menu, select Game Object ➤ Create Other ➤ Particle System and name it Blizzard. Set its `Transform.position` to (–11, 11.5, 106) and `Transform.rotation` to (0, 90, 0).

In the Blizzard Particle System Initial module, use the Start Size drop-down menu to select Random Between Two Constants. Leave the default settings of 0 and 1. In the Emission module, make sure the Rate is set to 10.

The idea is for the player to have a larger volume of particles to contend with. Select Box in the Shape module and alter its proportions to a Box X and Box Y of 5.

Check the Collision module and expand it. **World** means the particles will collide off any object. Be mindful that this setting is more costly to game performance than the use of planes. Leave all the other default settings as they are except check the **Send Collision Messages** box (Figure 8-10).

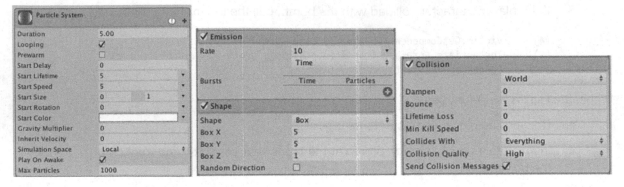

Figure 8-10. Blizzard particle system settings

In the Project panel Assets ➤ Scripts folder, find the KillOnCollision script and open it in MonoDevelop. Add the following function:

```
function OnParticleCollision(other : GameObject)
{
        if (other.gameObject.name == "Third Person Character Ragdoll")
        {
        other.gameObject.GetComponent(GoRagdoll).GotoRagdoll();
        }
}
```

The OnParticleCollision() is called when the Send Collision Messages box in the particle system Collision module is checked. The block of code within the function checks to see if it is the player character that was the other game object in the collision, and if so calls the player character's GotoRagdoll function.

Save the script and attach it to the Blizzard game object. As with the Bomb, drag and drop the Blizzard particle system into the Assets ➤ Prefabs folder in the Project panel. Save the scene (Figure 8-11) and save the project. Playtest and dodge the deadly snowflakes!

Figure 8-11. The player character facing the blizzard obstacle

Laser Obstacle

For the laser obstacle you will learn to use the Line Renderer (Figure 8-12). The Line Renderer does just that—draws a line between two points. It can also use an array of points, drawing segments between each for more complex patterns.

Figure 8-12. The player character and the laser obstacle

The line itself is a 2D billboard just like the particle textures, so depending on your scene it can appear to have a little motion as it rotates to stay facing the camera. You can adjust its width and color, and even use a texture.

This obstacle consists of a laser emitter above the obstacle course, firing a laser downward to the surface of the elevated track as it moves back and forth.

Laser Emitter

To simulate a laser emitter, create a primitive Cube game object in the Hierarchy, name it LaserCube, and give it a Transform.position of (–3.8, 12, 100) and a Transform.scale of (0.2, 1, 0.2).

The LaserCube game object needs a simple script to add the movement to it. In the Project panel Assets ➤ Scripts folder, select Create ➤ JavaScript, name it MoveLaser, and open it in MonoDevelop. Edit the code to the following:

```
#pragma strict
public var speed : float = 1;
public var offset : float;

function Start () {
        offset = transform.position.x - 0.2;
}
```

```
function Update () {
        transform.position = Vector3(Mathf.PingPong(Time.time * speed, 8) + offset,
transform.position.y, transform.position.z);
}
```

Save the script and attach it to the LaserCube.

This code breaks down as follows:

(1)   ```
        public var speed : float = 1;
        public var offset : float;
        ```

1.  First, declare variables: a public float variable that will allow you to adjust the speed of the LaserCube from the Inspector, and an offset variable for properly positioning the LaserCube as it moves.

(2)     `offset = transform.position.x - 0.2;`

2.  In the Start() function, assign the position of the LaserCube game object minus its width to offset so the laser beam starts at the exact edge of the elevated track.

(3)     ```
        transform.position = Vector3(Mathf.PingPong(Time.time * speed, 8) + offset,
        transform.position.y, transform.position.z);
        ```

3. You have changed the Transform.position of a game object before. This example introduces using the Mathf.PingPong() function for the Vector3 x coordinate value to get a back-and-forth movement.

Mathf.PingPong takes two floats, and returns a value that moves back and forth between 0 and the second value, adjusted by the offset value and assigns the result to the x coordinate of the LaserCube Transform.position.x. Without getting into the math behind it, the first float must change with each frame to get the ping-pong movement, so Time.time is commonly used. Time.time is simply the time in seconds since the game started.

Laser Beam

The laser beam is created with a Line Renderer. The Line Renderer cannot be used with a game object that is already using a renderer, so best practice is to create an Empty game object to hold the Line Renderer, then attach it as a child game object to the LaserCube.

In the editor top menu select Game Object ➤ Create Empty. In the Hierarchy, name it LaserBeam, then drag it on top of the LaserCube game object to nest it as a child game object and give it a Transform.position of (0, –0.5, 0). Since it is a child object, this Transform.position puts it slightly below the parent LaserCube game object on the y axis. With the empty Game Object still selected, in the Inspector select Add Component ➤ Effects ➤ Line Renderer (Figure 8-13). You will notice a magenta line appear in the Scene view at the world origin. You will use a script for coordinating the rendered line and the moving laser emitter during gameplay.

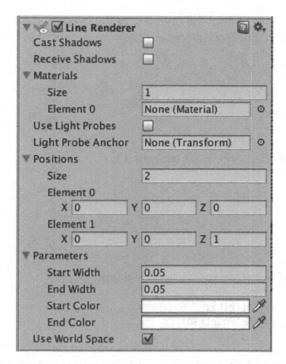

Figure 8-13. The Line Renderer component in the Inspector

In the Inspector, uncheck Cast Shadows and Receive Shadows. The basic version of Unity doesn't use shadows so leaving these checked would not add shadows.

Materials indicates the material to be used for drawing the line. If None, the default is the magenta line you see in the Scene view. You must have a material in order to change the color of the laser beam. In the Project panel select Create ➤ Material and name it SimpleLaser. Drag the SimpleLaser material into the Element 0 property in the Inspector. With this material selected, in the Inspector use the Shader drop-down menu to select Particles ➤ Alpha Blended. The Line Renderer uses Particles materials; otherwise you would just get a black line.

Reselect the LaserBeam game object to display its properties in the Inspector again. **Light Probes** are another Unity Pro feature. **Positions** designates the points the line is drawn between. A line needs a minimum of two for the start and end points, but you can add additional points by increasing the value of the **Size** property.

Expand **Parameters** for more customization options. Change the values of **Start Width** and **End Width to** 0.05 to make the line thinner, change **Start Color** and **End Color** to a bright red, and check **Use World Space**.

From here you'll need a script to control the behavior of the laser. In the Project panel Assets ➤ Scripts folder, select Create ➤ JavaScript, name it Laser, and open it in MonoDevelop. Edit the code to the following:

```
#pragma strict

public var line : LineRenderer;

function Start () {
        line = gameObject.GetComponent.<LineRenderer>();
}

function Update () {
        ShowLaser();
}

function ShowLaser () {
        var ray : Ray = Ray(transform.position, -transform.up);

        line.SetPosition(0, ray.origin);
        line.SetPosition(1, ray.GetPoint(50));
}
```

Save the script, attach it to the child empty game object, and playtest. You'll see that the LaserCube moves side to side, emitting a red laser.

This code breaks down as follows:

(1)   `public var line : LineRenderer;`

1. Declares a reference variable `line` of type `LineRenderer`.

(2)   `line = gameObject.GetComponent.<LineRenderer>();`

2. Gets the reference to the Line Renderer component and assign it to the `line` variable.

(3)   `ShowLaser();`

3. In previous examples the code samples have been largely written in the `Update()` function. With this example, better code writing practices are employed, where the code is broken down into smaller modules. Here the `ShowLaser()` function that contains just the laser-drawing code is called.

(4)   `var ray : Ray = Ray(transform.position, -transform.up);`

4. Within the `ShowLaser` function, a reference variable Ray is created and assigned the game object's `transform.position` as its origin and `-transform.up` for a downward direction.

      (5)   `line.SetPosition(0, ray.origin);`

5.   The first point for the Line Renderer, Element 0, is set with the position of the ray origin.

      (6)   `line.SetPosition(1, ray.GetPoint(50));`

6.   The second point for the line to be drawn to, Element 1, is set with the position of 10 units further down along the ray.

That's a good start, but the laser is going straight through the elevated track, so it's not very realistic. Edit the Laser script ShowLaser() function as follows:

```
function ShowLaser () {
        var ray : Ray = Ray(transform.position, -transform.up);
        var hit : RaycastHit;
        line.SetPosition(0, ray.origin);
        if(Physics.Raycast(ray, hit, 50))
        {
                line.SetPosition(1, hit.point);
        } else {
                line.SetPosition(1, ray.GetPoint(50));
        }
}
```

Save the script. Now when you playtest, you'll see the laser stops at the surface of the track.

This code breaks down as follows:

      (1)   `var hit : RaycastHit;`

1.   Declare a reference variable hit of type RaycastHit.

      (2)   `if(Physics.Raycast(ray, hit, 50))`

2.   Test to see if the raycast detects a collider within 10 units.

      (3)   `line.SetPosition(1, hit.point);`

3.   If a collider is detected, set the second point for the line to be drawn where the raycast detected the collider.

      (4)   `} else {`
                `line.SetPosition(1, ray.GetPoint(50));`

4.   Otherwise, as before draw the line 50 units further along the ray.

For now the only thing to see is that the laser ends when it hits the track. By using a raycast, if any other game object with a collider intersects the raycast, the laser will end wherever that intersection occurs on the surface of the game object. To test this, playtest and put the player character in the path of the laser beam.

The laser would look more realistic and intimidating with the addition of a particle system. In the Project panel, open the Assets ➤ Sample Assets ➤ Effects ➤ Particle Systems ➤ Prefabs folder. Find the Flare prefab, drag a copy to the Hierarchy, and make it a child object to LaserCube by dropping it on LaserCube.

In MonoDevelop, edit the Laser script to add the three lines of code as follows:

```
#pragma strict

public var line : LineRenderer;
public var sparks : GameObject;

function Start () {
        sparks = GameObject.Find("Flare");
        line = gameObject.GetComponent.<LineRenderer>();
}

function Update () {
        ShowLaser();
}

function ShowLaser () {
        var ray : Ray = Ray(transform.position, -transform.up);
        var hit : RaycastHit;

        line.SetPosition(0, ray.origin);
        if(Physics.Raycast(ray, hit, 50))
        {
                line.SetPosition(1, hit.point);
                sparks.transform.position = hit.point;
        } else {
                line.SetPosition(1, ray.GetPoint(50));
        }
}
```

Save the script and playtest. Now THAT is a laser!

The code breaks down as follows:

> (1)   `public var sparks : GameObject;`

1. Declare a reference variable sparks of type GameObject.

> (2)   `sparks = GameObject.Find("Flare");`

2. Find the reference to the Flare particle system prefab and assign it to sparks.

> (3)   `sparks.transform.position = hit.point;`

3. Assign the position of the sparks particle system at the point where the laser raycast detects a collider.

Super cool, right? Notice that when playtesting, if the player character is struck by the laser, sparks fly off him as if he is indestructible. While this might be awesome in another setting, here the laser obstacle is meant to be more lethal.

In the Laser script, add the following to the variable declarations:

```
public var victim : GameObject;
```

This is declaring a reference variable victim of type GameObject.

To assign the reference to the player character, in the Start() function, add the following line of code:

```
victim = GameObject.Find("Third Person Character Ragdoll");
```

Finally, in the ShowLaser() function, insert the following lines of code:

```
        function ShowLaser () {
    var ray : Ray = Ray(transform.position, -transform.up);
    var hit : RaycastHit;

    line.SetPosition(0, ray.origin);
    if(Physics.Raycast(ray, hit, 50))
    {
            line.SetPosition(1, hit.point);

            if (hit.collider == victim.collider) {
                    victim.GetComponent(GoRagdoll).GotoRagdoll();
            }
    sparks.transform.position = hit.point;
    } else {
    line.SetPosition(1, ray.GetPoint(50));
    }
}
```

If the raycast detects a collider, it checks to see if the collider is that of the player character. If so, the player character's GotoRagdoll() function is called to eliminate the player.

Save the script. In the Project panel open the Assets ➤ Prefabs folder. Drag the LaserCube from the Hierarchy and drop it into the Prefabs folder for future use. Now go ahead and playtest.

For this obstacle a simple material and red color is sufficient, but a sample code snippet for setting colors from the script would be to put the following lines of code in the Start() function:

```
line.material = new Material (Shader.Find("Particles/Additive"));
line.SetColors(Color.green, Color.blue);
```

Here you are making a new simple material, then setting the start and end colors of the line.

Tracer Fire Obstacle

Another nifty renderer for visual effects is the Trail Renderer component (Figure 8-14). Aptly named, it simply draws a trail behind a moving game object. It is typically used as a visual cue to indicate speed as with an aircraft contrail, or even a combination of speed and realistic imagery such as tracer fire. The tracer fire obstacle will be random tracer fire across the path of the player along the elevated track.

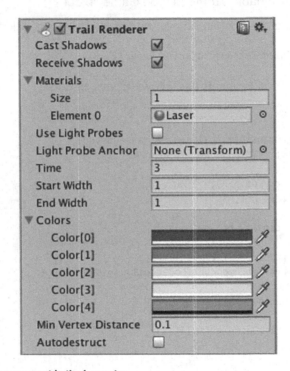

Figure 8-14. The Trail Renderer component in the Inspector

For a quick demonstration, in the Hierarchy select Pendulum_01. In the Inspector, choose Add Component ➤ Effects ➤ Trail Renderer.

The Trail Renderer can use an array of different materials for a variety of effects. Like the Line Renderer, the Trail Renderer uses Particles materials. Leave the size of the Materials array indicated by the **Size** property as 1. For Element 0, select the SimpleLaser material you created for the laser obstacle.

Time is the time in seconds the trail is to last. **Start Width** and **End Width** adjust the width of the trail, which similar to the Line Render is also a 2D billboard. If you have colors in your material you can leave the elements of the **Colors** property as is. Since our Laser material is white, go ahead and make a colorful spectrum by choosing colors for all five elements.

If the game object is not moving for the period of time designated in **Time**, and **Auto Destruct** is checked, the game object will be destroyed.

When you are finished experimenting with the pendulum's trail (Figure 8-15), disable or delete the Trail Renderer component.

Figure 8-15. Trail rendered behind the swinging pendulum obstacle

Projectile Prefab

Create a primitive sphere game object and name it Projectile. Give it a `Transform.position` of (0, 0, 0), `Transform.rotation` of (0, 0, 0), and scale it to (0.05, 0.05, 0.05). In the Inspector, add a Rigidbody component by selecting Add Component ➤ Physics ➤ Rigidbody.

Next, add a Trail Renderer component by selecting Add Component ➤ Effects ➤ Trail Renderer. In the Materials property leave Size as 1. Use the circle select button to the right of the Element 0 field to locate and select the part_afterburner material. This is a particle material from the Sample Asset package. Set Time to 0.5 and both the Start Width and End Width to 0.1. In the Colors property, assign a light yellow color to Color[0]. Choose successively darker yellow to orange colors for the remaining color elements.

To make this is a more deadly obstacle, the player character should be killed when struck by the projectile. You can use the same KillOnCollision script that you used for the pendulum obstacle by selecting Add Component ➤ Scripts ➤ KillOnCollision.

Finally, make the Projectile game object a prefab by dragging it from the Hierarchy to the Assets ➤ Prefabs folder in the Project panel. Now you can safely delete the Projectile game object from the Scene view.

Projectile Launcher

Create a primitive cylinder game object and name it Cannon. Give it a `Transform.position` of (4, 10.5, 95), a `Transform.rotation` of (0, 0, 90), and a `Transform.scale` of (0.2, 0.2, 0.2). Now create an empty game object and name it Launcher. The empty game object will be where the projectiles are instantiated. In the Hierarchy drag Launcher on top of Cannon to make it a child of Cannon. Now its Transform coordinates are relative to the Cannon game object rather than the world. Give it a `Transform.position` of (0, 1.25, 0) and a `Transform.rotation` of (270, 270, 0), and its scale should have reset to (5, 5, 5).

In the Project panel Assets ➤ Scripts folder, create a script named LaunchProjectile. Attach it to the Launcher game object, then open it in MonoDevelop. Edit the code to the following:

```
#pragma strict

public var projectile : GameObject;
public var force : float = 25;
public var frequency : float = 2.0;
private var nextLaunch : float = 0.0;

function Update () {
    if (Time.time > nextLaunch) {
    nextLaunch = Time.time + frequency;
        var projectileInstance : GameObject = Instantiate(projectile, transform.position,
transform.rotation);
        projectileInstance.rigidbody.AddForce (projectileInstance.transform.forward * force,
ForceMode.Impulse);
      Destroy(projectileInstance, 2);
    }
}
```

Save the script. This breaks down as follows:

```
(1)    public var projectile : GameObject;
       public var force : float = 25;
       public var frequency : float = 2.0;
       private var nextLaunch : float = 0.0;
```

1.   The variable declarations; projectile to hold a reference to a GameObject, while the float variables force and frequency are for you to fine-tune the projectile behavior from the Inspector. The float variable nextLaunch tracks the time between each projectile launch.

```
(2)    if (Time.time > nextLaunch)
```

2.   Time.time is the number of seconds since the game began. The if conditional tests to see if the time passed is greater than the calculated time for the next launch of a projectile. If so,

```
(3)    nextLaunch = Time.time + frequency;
```

3.   nextLaunch is reset to the currently elapsed game playing time plus the seconds between each launch designated by the float variable frequency.

```
(4)    var projectileInstance : GameObject = Instantiate(projectile,
       transform.position, transform.rotation);
```

4.   Instantiate a clone of the projectile Prefab game object, at the transform. position and transform.rotation of the parent Launcher game object this script is attached to.

```
(5)    projectileInstance.rigidbody.AddForce
       (projectileInstance.transform.forward * force,
       ForceMode.Impulse);
```

5. Add a force to the Projectile prefab's rigidbody using the `AddForce()` function, giving it a Vector3 forward direction with a magnitude of the adjustable `force` factor, using `ForceMode.Impulse`, which applies all of the force instantaneously.

```
(6)    Destroy(projectileInstance, 2);
```

6. For performance purposes you don't want these Projectile game objects piling up out of view, so each clone will be destroyed after two seconds.

Select the Launcher game object in the Hierarchy. Drag the Projectile prefab from the Assets ➤ Prefabs folder and drop it into the Projectile property field of the LaunchProjectile script. The Tracer Fire obstacle is finished. Drag the Cannon game object from the Hierarchy to the Assets ➤ Prefabs folder in the Project folder to make it a prefab asset. Save the script, save the scene, and save the project. Playtest, and now you have a killer projectile Tracer Fire Obstacle. Great job!

Summary

Now you have a handle on creating particle systems and effects using Shuriken, and you're beginning to imagine how your obstacle course will shape up into a game. You've added LineRenderer and TrailRenderer to your bag of visual effects as you created a number of new obstacles prefabs for the Obstacle Course scene.

Before dispersing these obstacles randomly along the course, in the next chapter, among other things, you will be introduced to the theories of game design, which will in turn give you guidance on the hows and whys behind designing scene layouts like the obstacle course.

Chapter **9**

Game Design and Logic—The Blueprint

The most common advice you'll hear for beginning developers is, "To get better at making games, make more games." An equally common response is, "Yes, but where do I start?"

Before sitting down at your computer, first you must have a blueprint of the game you are building. Game design is the process of creating this blueprint. Now that you are comfortable with the Unity editor and have some scripting under your belt, it's time to take a look at game design and the game production process.

> **Note** Before anything else, preparation is the key to success. —Alexander Graham Bell

Game

What is a game anyway? For practical purposes the basic requirements for a game are the following:

1. *A player*: Other forms of video entertainment such as movies and TV shows can be shown to an audience of one to many, or even to an empty room, but a game requires interaction and input from at least one player.

2. *Rules*: These define how a game is to be played, both in terms of what a player can do and constraints for what they cannot.

3. *A goal*: Determines how the game ends. It can be an objective that if achieved is a win, or if not achieved is a loss. It could also be successfully completing a task or attempting an activity in a specific period of time.

Take a look at the obstacle course scene you've been building in the past few chapters as an example. Is it a game?

1. *Player*: Yes, a player's input is required for gameplay.

2. *Rules*: Yes: The player always begins the game at the lowest end of the course. The player can walk, run, jump, and crouch. Hazards kill the player. Falling or jumping off the elevated track kills the player.

3. *A goal*: No. "Not dying" is not a goal. At least it's not a very good one for a game. The player could accomplish that by never moving the character, or simply running away from the elevated track without ever playing the intended game of negotiating the obstacle course. "Reach the far end of the obstacle course" is a goal.

No one definition is all-encompassing. For example, puzzles also meet this criteria and are a genre of games, with a slight difference in that puzzles typically have one right answer, while a non-puzzle game's outcome is unpredictable each time it is played. Rare exceptions aside, these three ingredients are generally found in games of all types and serve as a practical starting point for basic game design.

Games, Minigames, and Microgames

Games can take any length of time. At one end of the scale are games such as *World of Warcraft* that potentially could never end, while at the other end are microgames that can be played in seconds.

Popular, robust console and PC games have hours of pure gameplay, not counting menus, cutscenes, instructions, dialogue, and the like. More content is always better, but the final size of any particular project will be determined by budget and publishing deadlines.

The current rising trend in "casual gaming" is often remarked upon but ill-defined. Influenced by the increased use of mobile devices as game platforms, casual games are typically playable in minutes rather than hours. The gameplay itself may vary greatly but casual games typically have well-defined levels, linear progression, and a simple scorekeeping system.

Minigames are shorter games, on the order of 5- to 10-minute intervals of gameplay, and are often similar to classic arcade games. They can stand alone, or be used inside of larger games. Within bigger games, they have a wide variety of uses. Unlocked as a reward, they can be separate activities to earn rewards; they can be used to introduce a new item or how to use a new feature; or they can simply be bonus content after the main game is completed. Minigames don't have to be required in order to complete the parent game. When found within a larger game like *Legend of Zelda*, they usually are simpler in terms of control and complexity. Even so, a minigame still has the same three basic requirements of a player, rules, and an endpoint.

Microgames are meant to be played in seconds rather than minutes. *Wario Ware* is the classic example of a collection of microgames. They provide a unique challenge in both gameplay and design, where the challenge is both to figure out and then win the game in such a short time period.

Game Design Considerations

When designing any game there are several considerations that you should make.

Target Audience and ESRB Ratings

The Entertainment Software Rating Board (ESRB) is the self-regulatory industry organization that defines and enforces the rating system.

The target age of your audience and the corresponding ESRB ratings can have an influence on your game design. The extent of sensitive content including blood, violence, nudity, and profanity will affect the rating of your game, which could potentially exclude it from the audience you intended to reach if you aren't aware of these standards.

There are three parts to the rating system:

1. *Rating categories*: Similar to movie ratings, these are used to suggest age appropriateness (Figure 9-1).

Figure 9-1. ESRB rating category depictions

2. *Content descriptors*: These provide more specific information on the particular content of the game that earned the rating. For example a game may have a rating of E10+ that "may contain more cartoon violence." If you think this is pretty vague, the ESRB content descriptors tells you exactly what they mean by terms such as "cartoon violence" (Table 9-1).

Table 9-1. ESRB Video Game Content Descriptors

Content Descriptor	Definition
Alcohol Reference	Reference to and/or images of alcoholic beverages.
Animated Blood	Discolored and/or unrealistic depictions of blood.
Blood	Depictions of blood.
Blood and Gore	Depictions of blood or the mutilation of body parts.
Cartoon Violence	Violent actions involving cartoonlike situations and characters. May include violence where a character is unharmed after the action has been inflicted.

(continued)

Table 9-1. (continued)

Content Descriptor	Definition
Comic Mischief	Depictions or dialogue involving slapstick or suggestive humor.
Crude Humor	Depictions or dialogue involving vulgar antics, including "bathroom" humor.
Drug reference	Reference to and/or images of illegal drugs.
Fantasy violence	Violent actions of a fantasy nature, involving human or nonhuman characters in situations easily distinguishable from real life.
Intense violence	Graphic and realistic-looking depictions of physical conflict. May involve extreme and/or realistic blood, gore, weapons, and depictions of human injury and death.
Language	Mild to moderate use of profanity.
Lyrics	Mild references to profanity, sexuality, violence, alcohol, or drug use in music.
Mature Humor	Depictions or dialogue involving "adult" humor, including sexual references.
Nudity	Graphic or prolonged depictions of nudity.
Partial Nudity	Brief and/or mild depictions of nudity.
Real Gambling	Player can gamble, including betting or wagering real cash or currency.
Sexual Content	Nonexplicit depictions of sexual behavior, possibly including partial nudity.
Sexual Themes	References to sex or sexuality.
Simulated Gambling	Player can gamble without betting or wagering real cash or currency.
Strong Language	Explicit and/or frequent use of profanity.
Strong Lyrics	Explicit and/or frequent references to profanity, sex, violence, alcohol, or drug use in music.
Strong Sexual Content	Explicit and/or frequent depictions of sexual behavior, possibly including nudity.
Suggestive Themes	Mild provocative references or materials.
Tobacco Reference	Reference to and/or images of tobacco products.
Use of Alcohol	The consumption of alcoholic beverages.
Use of Drugs	The consumption or use of illegal drugs.
Use of Tobacco	The consumption of tobacco products.
Violence	Scenes involving aggressive conflict.
Violent References	References to violent acts.

3. *Interactive elements*: This includes notification of location sharing, other information sharing with third parties, and interactivity with other users that by its nature is often uncensored (Figure 9-2).

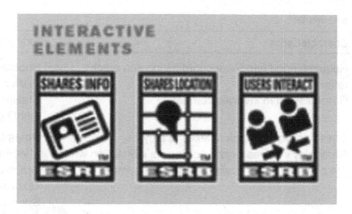

Figure 9-2. ESRB interactive element depictions

Be aware that while the AO rating appears to differ from M by one year of age appropriateness, it's the software entertainment version of the X rating for films and has the same stigma to publishers and consumers alike.

Game Genres

What kind of game should you make? Make one you would enjoy—this is supposed to be fun, after all. Whether you have an existing concept you are working on or not, understanding existing genres and their respective styles of gameplay can help you flesh out a game design and further refine it with your greater understanding of user expectations.

A good place to begin would be a simple example from the game genre you enjoy in order to focus your learning on the most similar game behavior. You certainly don't have to force your game to fit any particular categorization. Action games are a genre. Adventure games are a genre. Some sources call Action-Adventure a genre, while others would call these hybrids.

Essentially duplicating an existing game and publishing it could possibly lead to legal trouble. Studying, dissecting, and learning how to reconstruct an existing game to build your skills, however, is fine.

Table 9-2 lists some broad categories of game genres. There are many more genres including party, music, educational, and trivia. You can probably think of a number of games that are hybrids of genres, or that compile a variety of genres.

Table 9-2. Video Game Genres

Genre	Characteristics	Examples
Action	Requires good hand-eye coordination and quick reflexes to play Gameplay often involves combat	Shooters Platformers Stealth Fighting games
Adventure	Does not require quick reflexes to play Gameplay involves puzzle solving via interaction with the characters and environment of the game	Role-playing MMORPG* Graphic based Text based Survival Horror
Strategy	Requires careful long-term thinking and planning Player typically has a "godlike" view	Turn-based strategy Real-time strategy Tower defense Wargames
Sports	Gameplay based on an athletic competition or sport	As player As coach/manager Racing
Simulation	Gameplay simulates reality	Vehicle Life Pet Construction Management
Puzzle	Gameplay based on problem solving	logic pattern completion word games

MMORPG = massively multiplayer online role-playing game.

Themes

The primary basis of a theme choice might be based on a certain time period, environment, technology, or character type.

Time Period	Environment	Technology	Character Types
Medieval	Amusement park	Medieval	Angels
Victorian	Jungle	Science fiction	Dinosaurs
Present	Dungeon	Fantasy/magical	Robots
Alternate history	School	Steampunk	Organized crime

(continued)

(continued)

Time Period	Environment	Technology	Character Types
Post-apocalyptic	Party Space station Alien world	Time travel	Ninjas Pirates Cowboys Demons Superhero Detective Zombies Animals Diseases

Determining the game's target audience with its corresponding ESRB rating, its genre, and its theme will in turn guide your choices for other game design elements such as color schemes, music, character names, clothing, and gear, as well as types of treasure, abilities, weapons, and hazards.

Fun and the Game Experience

If it were simple to define what "fun" is and apply it, game design would be easy. Unfortunately, "fun" is subjective—what is fun to you may not be fun to anyone else. You may not even find the same game to be fun after you've played it many times. The simple truth is that you cannot predict if the game-playing masses will think your game is fun.

While there is no specific formula for fun, there are well-known tools you can use to avoid common problems in gameplay mechanics that would otherwise definitely lower the game's fun potential.

Maps

A good place to start is by mapping out your game on a piece of paper or with your favorite drawing tool. To see how a map can help you find game design problems, let's take a look at a map of the Obstacle Course scene (Figure 9-3).

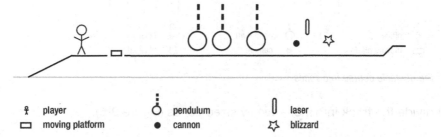

Figure 9-3. Initial map of the obstacle course

Now you can easily see the player, the elevated track from start to finish, and the various obstacles all together.

A map should be drawn to scale to be most effective. In this example the player is too big relative to the obstacles and track. The player icon adds more information to the map by also designating the player's start point (Figure 9-4).

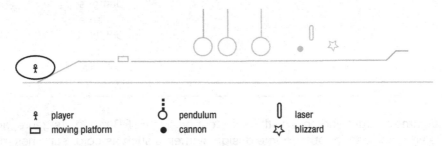

| ♀ | player | ⊙ | pendulum | ◗ | laser |
| ▭ | moving platform | ● | cannon | ☆ | blizzard |

Figure 9-4. Obstacle course map with player character drawn to scale

Now that the player icon on the map is scaled, take a look at the overall layout of the obstacle course with a critical eye.

There is quite a bit of empty space along the track where the player has nothing to do but walk. This is no good—just walking is boring. An obstacle course without very many obstacles is boring. Boring isn't fun.

After the pendulums, the cannon, laser, and blizzard obstacles are all crammed together into a clump. Divide the track into zones on your map and the clumping becomes even more obvious (Figure 9-5).

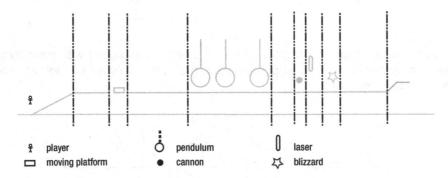

| ♀ | player | ⊙ | pendulum | ◗ | laser |
| ▭ | moving platform | ● | cannon | ☆ | blizzard |

Figure 9-5. Divide the obstacle course into zones

To fix this, first divide the track into more evenly sized zones (Figure 9-6).

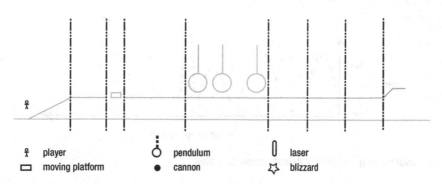

♀ player	♂ pendulum
▭ moving platform	● cannon

laser

blizzard

Figure 9-6. *The obstacle course redivided into zones of similar size*

The moving platform doesn't need a larger zone, and the pendulums are bigger obstacles in a fairly reasonable size zone, so these obstacles and their zone boundaries can stay as is.

Now that the zones are marked, it makes more sense for a number of reasons to have zones of obstacle types rather than just one of each kind. Using zones populated with similar obstacles is a more efficient use of time and assets. In this case, you can use a collection of cannons and lasers in their respective zones, while the blizzard can simply be resized to fit a zone. Before assigning these zones, there are a few more game design factors to consider.

Pacing

Human brains are pretty good at adjusting to just about anything. Even if you design a game to be a mind-blowing warp-10 hair-on-fire action-packed experience from start to finish, once the player's brain has adjusted to the pace, it may be perceived as boring because it feels "flat" (Figure 9-7).

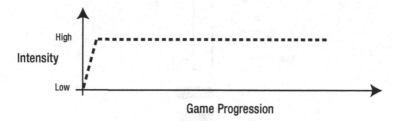

Figure 9-7. *Continuous high intensity appears flat over time*

The player's mind will be more involved and stimulated the more it has to adjust, so you want to integrate emotionally intense highs and lows into the game experience (Figure 9-8).

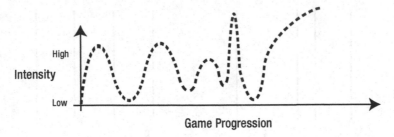

Figure 9-8. Gameplay with varying emotional intensity levels over time

In the obstacle course example, each of the zones within the obstacle course can be a distinct level of intensity, separated by a checkpoint where you provide just enough room for the player to stand and assess the next obstacle. This breathing space allows the player to come down emotionally, resetting the perceived intensity downward before the player dives into the relatively higher intensity of the next zone.

Balance

Since this sample project is an obstacle course of mechanical hazards, obstacles that are similar shouldn't be placed one after another. This concept is based on the same reasoning as pacing—the more the brain has to adjust, the greater the perceived difference.

At one end of the extreme, imagine a cannon zone and blizzard zone that are very similar. The cannons are spaced approximately equal to the concentration of the blizzard "snowflakes," the projectiles are the same speed, and both zones' projectiles travel from right to left horizontally (Figure 9-9).

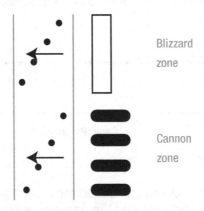

Top view of elevated track

Figure 9-9. Cannon zone and blizzard zone look like similar obstacles

From the player's perspective, the brainpower for pattern recognition and subsequent character control required to negotiate the two zones is almost identical as the player transitions from the cannon zone to the blizzard zone.

At the other end of the extreme, imagine the cannon zone first. It is an array of cannons, where each cannon fires a projectile at a specific frequency, the cannons have a regular spacing between them, and the projectiles are traveling from right to left.

In this case, the regular spacing and frequency of the projectiles means successfully negotiating this zone is based on pattern recognition—that is, analyzing the projectile firing pattern to find the safe path forward.

If the cannon zone is followed instead by the pendulum zone, now the player has to adjust to a new hazard with a different mechanical pattern, and adjust again to the laser zone that follows the pendulum zone (Figure 9-10).

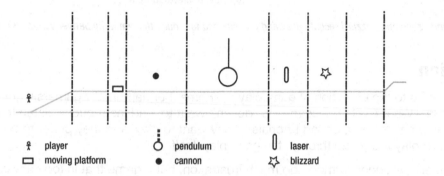

Figure 9-10. Distribute obstacle zones so similar obstacles are not adjacent

After the laser zone, the player finally reaches the blizzard zone, which in this scenario emits the snowflake projectiles with random sizes so they look different, within a range of random speeds, generated from a random starting point. Although they move horizontally, this time they traverse the track from left to right.

Once again the player has to make another major assessment and adjustment in strategy from the laser zone to survive the blizzard zone. Since the player has made three major adjustments since completing the cannon zone, and the details of the blizzard projectile attributes are now different from the cannon projectiles, he perceives a much greater difference in gameplay mechanics between the cannon and blizzard zones than when they had mechanically similar details and were placed one immediately after the other (Figure 9-11).

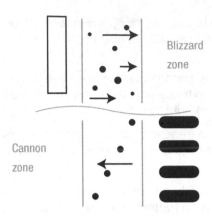

Top view of elevated track

Figure 9-11. Cannon zone and blizzard reconfigured and repositioned to reduce the similarity between these two obstacles

Progression

Progression refers to the evolution of gameplay over time. Fundamentally gamers want to play, and they want to win. "Want to play" also means "doesn't want to read instructions, listen to long-winded NPCs (non-player characters), or find tutorials." They want to play, and they prefer to be able to figure out how to play the game through the gameplay itself.

They want to feel challenged without too much frustration, but a game that is too easy can quickly become boring. Winning should be achievable and feel like a well-earned accomplishment to the player, not a gimmie. The art of game design is to find the right balance for the majority of people in your target audience.

The most straightforward gameplay progression is when the player begins the game with no skills or abilities. The initial challenges—puzzles, enemies, obstacles—allow for the learning curve of the player. In the obstacle course example project, the player must learn how to control the camera and move the character, including discovering the character can crouch, and getting a feel for how high and far the character can jump or how fast she can run.

Using the obstacle course as our example, since the player is learning how to move the camera and character, simple stationary obstacles like land mines are a good choice for the first zone. These give the player deadly obstacles to be avoided, but only require simple controller movements. The player simply has to learn to move and turn the player character to successfully cross this zone.

If the player is more adventuresome he may already have discovered the ability to jump. If not, the moving platform obstacle of the second zone forces this, as correctly gauging a jump to the platform, then another to the elevated track, is the only way to cross.

As the player advances along the elevated track, successive obstacle zones require better pattern recognition and character control. Finally, the blizzard zone introduces elements of randomness such that pattern recognition is not as helpful as better hand-eye coordination.

As the final grand challenge for the level, the last zone introduces true enemies with script-controlled AI elements that track and respond to player movement (Figure 9-12).

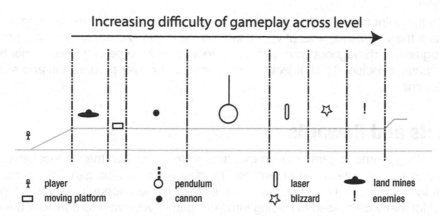

Figure 9-12. *Obstacles distributed in increasing order of difficulty*

The previous example demonstrated progression from the start to finish of one level. Progression can be applied to subsets within levels such as the zones in the obstacle course (Figure 9-13).

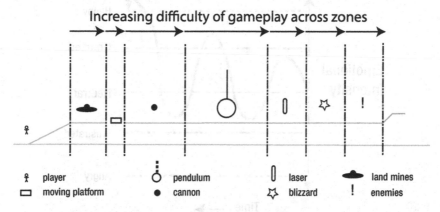

Figure 9-13. *Obstacles distributed within each zone in increasing order of difficulty*

For example, you can apply progression within each zone of the obstacle course by making the obstacles within a zone bigger, faster, or closer together as the player advances through the zone.

Progression also refers to the evolution of gameplay from one level to the next (Figure 9-14).

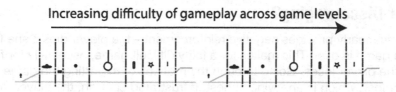

Figure 9-14. *Increasing difficulty throughout the game from one level to the next*

When you get to the point that you are creating multiple levels, you will find that a simple spreadsheet can help you track the various aspects of your game across levels and apply the same concepts of balance and progression throughout your game. Depending on the type of game, elements to consider tracking for comparison include level objectives, play time, and player progression and abilities vs. enemies and hazards.

Punishments and Rewards

Balance is a recurring theme in game design that applies to more than the physical layout of the game. Another area to consider is reinforcement. The player wants a fun game they can win, and that they hopefully enjoy enough to play again and tell their friends about it. As you integrate the varying levels of intensity discussed in Pacing into your game, you want to consider the *quality* of the emotional experience you provide to the player. Consider a range of emotions your player might experience throughout the game (Figure 9-15).

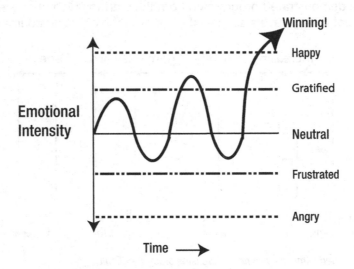

Figure 9-15. The player experiences varying levels of emotional intensity over time

While emotional ups and downs add to the overall game experience, frustration and anger definitely fall into the category of Not Fun for most players.

Challenging or Discouraging?

The obstacle course clearly provides negative reinforcement—the player dies if she fails to clear an obstacle, then the game is over. This makes for a fairly difficult game, especially for first-time players: one mistake and the player loses. Going through the motions of restarting the game emphasizes the fact that the player lost, which is annoying at best. If frustrated enough, the player may choose to move on to another game rather than risk more frustration.

What if you provided the player with more lives? Though the player still dies if she fails to clear an obstacle, with no effort on the player's part the player character respawns, ready for another go.

This time, the "death" is merely a setback rather than a complete loss, and doesn't generate as intense a negative emotional response for the player. Meanwhile, respawning encourages the player to try again by putting them right back into the game.

Another way to accomplish this would be to allow the player character to lose health points with each hit, so it takes an accumulation of hits to finally kill the player character. The player can thus afford to make a few mistakes as they attempt the obstacles.

Positive Reinforcement

Relief from negative consequences turns the direction of emotions into the positive, but might only go so far and leave the player in the neutral zone. Neutral is, well, neutral. Bland. Boring. Better than angry or frustrated, but not particularly fun.

Positive reinforcement is fun, and it can come in many forms. The most common is earning points toward the classic achievement of a high score. Unlocking a minigame or new level, collecting loot or money, achieving a higher skill level, obtaining a more powerful weapon or better gear, earning achievements, and activating power-ups are all forms of positive reinforcement. Depending on the nature of your game you might find a place for some comic relief or just plain silliness.

Easter eggs get their name from the classic Easter egg hunt where the egg, once found, contains a surprise. The surprise could be anything: an extra power, a joke, a secret message, a funny image or video clip, a cheat code, or anything you like. Easter eggs add to the fun, but don't necessarily positively reinforce anything having to do with the gameplay. In fact, since by their nature Easter eggs are hidden in unusual locations in the game environment, the player may explore seemingly uninteresting corners on the off chance they might come across one.

Explicit praise is also positive reinforcement—who doesn't like to hear how awesome they are? Praise can be text, dialogue, a response from an NPC, or come in other forms such as sound and particle effects.

In our obstacle course example, positive reinforcement might take the form of collecting coins (since we have a coin asset readily available in the Sample Assets), where obtaining a certain number of coins means adding an extra life or more health. Underneath the ramp is a perfect place to hide an Easter egg.

The Game Design Document

The game design document (GDD) is the actual blueprint for the game. How did we get from scripting all the way over to the game design document? The GDD describes gameplay—that is, how the player interacts with the game. "Gameplay" is similar to "fun" in terms of the difficulty in finding a clear, all-encompassing description. Definitions include factors such as the choices and tasks presented to the player, the emotional connection and responses while playing, the storyline, and the overall experience while playing, but most agree on player interaction as the fundamental component of gameplay. Since player interaction is governed by scripting, the GDD explains what the game designer wants as the outcome of the code that you, the programmer, will create.

The GDD describes everything about the game. It doesn't have a specific format, but it typically has three parts: a summary, a conceptual overview, and the nitty-gritty details. It conveys the gameplay experience along with the components the development team requires to pull it all together, and can be used to pitch the game to potential investors or publishers.

Before diving into the GDD, here is a brief description of the roles of your fellow game development team members, who along with you will be working from the GDD.

The Game Development Team

The game design document serves to communicate the vision of the game design to the game development team. A typical team includes the game designer, the developer, and the artist.

The **game designer** is usually the originator of the game itself—the original concept, rules, and vision of the play experience. The designer is also the person responsible for creating the game design document and using it to keep the other team members coordinated.

The GDD is a dynamic document—it is normal that much about the game design may change over the course of production. This might be in response to team member input or tester feedback or because of budget restrictions. The game designer steers the changes to conform to the overall vision of the game and updates the GDD to communicate any changes to the rest of the team, as a change in one area commonly requires corresponding adjustments by other team members.

The **artist** creates the visual elements of the game. This includes the characters, animations, the terrain and objects in the game world, and GUIs.

The **programmer** might also be called the **engineer** or **developer**. All interactions between the player and the game are defined by the code the programmer writes. This interaction includes mapping the game controller to character action, controlling the camera, defining the AI for enemies, and even writing the "cheat code" for testing certain aspects of the game. Fundamentally, the programmer writes the code that implements the game designer's vision of gameplay.

Testers come in different varieties of bug testers and play testers. Bug testers are also known as quality assurance, the people who test the products of the other team members to ensure they get the desired results specified in the GDD. Whereas quality assurance screens for technical accuracy, play testers test the game experience—just because a game is bug free and meets the GDD description still doesn't guarantee that it is fun.

As the team gets bigger, it will have more specialized roles in each category. Level designers, enemy-AI developers, and riggers and animators are just examples of the many specialty areas involved in large game development projects.

While you might be your whole team and wear each hat when necessary, creating a game design document will be helpful to you for a number of reasons. First, a GDD will help you clarify your game concept and provide a structure from which you can further flesh out the idea. As you build your game design on paper, you will see the sheer number of details involved in even a relatively simple game. The GDD helps you keep track of the details. Reducing certain desired features due to time or budget constraints is a common occurrence, but you will still have a record of the original concept that may be handy as an upgrade or complete sequel to the original game.

At some point you may end up bringing someone into the development process, and you can quickly get them up to speed via the GDD. When you reach this point, you will learn a lot about what you meant to say in your GDD compared to how it can be interpreted by others. The alternate interpretations might be better or worse than your original version, so be open to outside ideas.

The flip side of this is that when you are the team programmer, you want to be active and communicative in team meetings to ensure that you have a good grasp on the game designer's intent. Game development is very much a team sport where active collaboration and communication makes for the best game development environment.

If your intent is to pitch your game to a publisher, you definitely need a professional-grade GDD that immediately catches their interest, then effectively and concisely communicates the game concept. Practice makes perfect, so you may as well incorporate GDD writing early in your game development skill-building plan.

While there is no specific format for a game design document, there are three general sections with increasing levels of detail: the one-sheet, the concept overview, and then the detailed contents of the GDD itself.

The One-Sheet

The one-sheet is the first page of the GDD, and is a brief summary of the game concept. Though it doesn't have to be limited to one page, having an interesting, attention-getting presentation of your game idea on one page makes it easy for readers to understand your vision. If you capture their attention with your one-sheet, they will want to turn the page to learn more in the concept overview.

A one-sheet typically contains the following:

- The title
- The genre
- The target audience and ESRB rating
- A few paragraphs summarizing the game concept with an emphasis on gameplay
- Platforms
- Licenses (if any)
- Unique features
- Marketing summary

You have to present your game concept in a way that gets people excited, be they potential investors or publishers, team members, marketers, or anyone else in the production process. If you are going it alone, you absolutely need to be able to grab the attention of your target game-playing audience. Either way, you must be able to convey the gameplay experience in a compelling fashion.

You can do a quick Internet search to find many examples of GDDs. An alternative place to find examples of real game pitches is on Kickstarter. Projects are presented with both a written and video description. An interesting exercise is to compare the pitches of the successfully funded projects in comparison to the unfunded projects. Watch the videos and take note of your reaction. Do they draw you in or do you yawn and roll your eyes? What captures your attention, what makes you want to play that game, or what aspect turned you off? Was it the game concept itself or the manner in which it was presented? What did you think of the concept art and the development team (if introduced), and what did you find appealing about the presenter?

While starting with the one-sheet summary and then fleshing out your game idea is one approach, there are times when a simple summary seems elusive. This may be a sign your concept needs more refinement. If you find yourself stuck, you can always skip to the concept overview section to get your thoughts organized, and your game idea fleshed out a little, then go back and summarize the result.

The Concept Overview

You caught attention with your one-sheet, and now your audience is turning the page to learn more. This section of the GDD adds details to the initial content of the one-sheet while still maintaining a broad perspective. The goal is to keep readers interested without overwhelming them with a mass of small details. Keep it brief and easy to understand. It is okay to use visuals—images, diagrams, storyboard or wireframe excerpts, brief Flash animations and the like—if they are pertinent and do a better job of conveying information. When providing examples of comparative games, use recently successful titles that are easily recognized.

Core Game Concept

Briefly describe the story outline of your game from start to finish. This should include define the player's goals (remember, you must have a victory condition), expand on the player character and other characters, describe the environments, and show how gameplay is integrated into the story through the use of challenges, rewards, skills, acquisitions, combat, vehicles, and the like.

Player Character and Controller

Here you describe the character, much like a bio but including more about their personality in addition to stats such as age and gender. You can provide backstory here, along with any character development through the course of the game. Demonstrate how the character's personality and bio relate to the gameplay, including unique skills, use of weapons, and any other gameplay the character implements throughout the game.

Include a diagram that maps out the particulars of the controls for character movement, including combat moves; how the character interacts with other characters and objects in the world; and the use of inventory lists, HUDs, and maps as appropriate.

Gameplay Description

"Gameplay" is a fairly general term that includes the smallest game objects and interactions, the flow from one set of interactions to the next, on up to the larger context of the game in its entirety based on the three fundamental components of player, rules, and goal. Whether you are looking at the microscopic view or the bird's-eye view, you should be able to describe what is fun about the gameplay.

A **set piece** is that carefully planned high point of a scene designed to awe the player, without which the game would be incomplete. The goal here is to capture the reader's imagination, so use a set piece and unique gameplay features here to pull them in and keep them reading.

World/Levels

Describe the physical layout of the game world. Depending on your game you may want to use images in the overview that portray the environments or levels contained in the game world, along with how they tie into the game story and how the player will find his way and progress through the game.

Level Walkthrough

Just like it sounds, you are walking the reader through a level of the game. This is where you describe the gameplay experience through the fusion of story and gameplay. This section may take a couple of pages to cover the important actions, challenges, and advancement of the player. Include how the use of the camera, sound, special effects, and cutscenes contributes to the gameplay and the overall experience.

Obstacles and Enemies

List the hazards, enemies, puzzles, and anything else the player must resolve or overcome to complete the game.

Rewards and Collectables

List achievements, power-ups, and inventory items, including how the player acquires them and how they contribute to gameplay. If the game world uses money or some other form of trade, include a description of how the game world economy functions.

Cutscenes

If your game uses video sequences or cutscenes, describe how they are used in the context of the game.

Audio

List the audio requirements of the game including music, sound effects, and voice-over dialogue.

Concept Art

Do not limit your art to this section only. As mentioned, visuals add to the impact of your presentation and often effectively communicate a concept alone or with a supporting written description. Concept art can be images, storyboards, diagrams, maps, and even brief animations. It can portray characters, inventory items, the game world and level maps, GUIs, and menus.

Conclusion

This is where you wrap it all up into the final pitch for your game.

The GDD

The one-sheet and the concept overview can stand alone or serve as the introductory sections of the GDD. The GDD itself contains all the details of the game and can run hundreds of pages long. While it is primarily about gameplay, it can include marketing information, legal agreements, and financial data as well as the detailed technical specifications.

Even the most well-thought-out GDD undergoes numerous changes during game production, where a great idea might not pan out in practice; budget limitations lead to modification or elimination of assets, features, or entire levels; tester feedback points out ways to improve the game experience; or someone on the team has an great and inspirational idea that must be incorporated. The GDD is the tool that will record and communicate these changes to the game development team.

Summary

To get better at making games you need to make more games, and now you know where to begin. You have a grip on the basics of game design and the game development process, and you have some templates to use as a starting point. Keep it simple and start small. Make some games. Play more games. Take note of what you like and don't like about your game experiences. Make more games. Dig deeper into the vast capabilities of Unity and make more varieties of games.

If you are interested in game design, develop your planning and documentation skills in parallel with your coding skills, not instead of. Learning to program is like learning any new language, where regular practice is essential.

Now that you've seen conceptually how to apply game design concepts to the obstacle course example to identify flaws and develop solutions, it's time to get back to scripting.

Putting the Pieces Together and Building Your Game

Now that you've applied some basic game design concepts to the obstacle course concept, you are ready to implement them and create a fully functional prototype (Figure 10-1).

Figure 10-1. Obstacle course prototype with zones of different hazards and enemies

Game development is an iterative process. Even with your grand plan mapped out in your GDD, it will undergo much change and fine-tuning as you implement it. Every time you add a new game object or component you will test it, make sure it behaves properly and meets your quality standards, and fix or adjust what doesn't. You'll test to see how it looks, how it functions, how it interacts, and how it fits into the flow of the game.

With each new addition to the scene, you repeat this process. Sometimes bugs appear that need to get worked out. Sometimes it works as advertised but doesn't fit the flow of the game as originally visualized. Other times you or someone else thinks of a way to make it even better, which requires going back to the drawing board to implement the new changes. With each test comes more feedback, more adjustments, and more refactoring, whether from internal quality control checks or beta tester feedback.

Each cycle of additional refinement is an iteration of the game development process. In this chapter you will implement your game design from Chapter 9, refine it, and get an introduction to how to address snags that might arise along the way.

Implementing the Design

Summing up the design changes from Chapter 9, first you divided the obstacle course into seven zones, in a particular order according to the game design concepts you learned and applied: 1. Land Mine, 2. Moving Platform, 3. Cannon, 4. Pendulum, 5. Laser, 6. Blizzard, 7. Enemy (Figure 10-2).

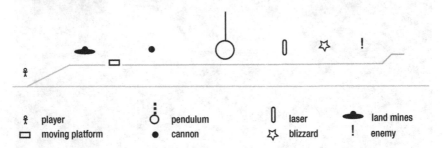

Figure 10-2. Revised obstacle course design

You also determined some additional criteria. The obstacle course should become more difficult the further the player advances. Within each zone, you will populate the hazards in such a way as to make the zone more difficult from start to finish. You will provide a narrow safe area between each zone for the player to catch his breath and regroup before diving into the following zone.

First, divide the empty sections into zones of similar size according to the z coordinate. Find the already defined points, such as where the ramp joins to the elevated track, either side of the moving platform, at the start of the first pendulum and the end of the third, and finally where the elevated track joins with the second ramp. All that remains is to divide the elevated track between the end of the third pendulum and the beginning of the ramp into three parts (Figure 10-3):

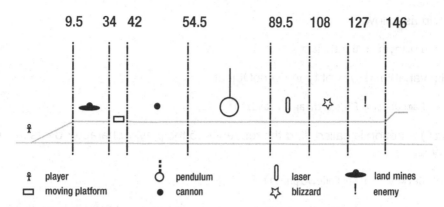

Figure 10-3. Borders of zones identified by z-coordinate position

Any project can be broken down into component parts that make for manageable tasks. In this case, you already have the obstacle course broken down into zones, so the methodical approach is to take them one at a time in order.

Playtesting and Cheat Codes

It can get a little tedious to restart the game and run up the ramp each time the player character gets killed while you are playtesting the obstacle course, but there is a way around this: you can build in shortcuts.

This is the origin of cheat codes—game developers needed a way to quickly playtest a particular behavior or feature of a game, and certain "cheats" such as invulnerability, infinite wealth, or super power facilitated this. Today an entire industry has grown around cheat codes, and game developers often purposefully leave them in the final production version.

Open your Obstacle Course scene if it isn't already. The first cheat code is going to reposition the player character to the top of the ramp. In the Project panel Assets folder, create a new script named Cheats. Open the script in MonoDevelop and edit the code as follows:

```
#pragma strict

public var player : GameObject;

function Start () {
        player = GameObject.FindWithTag("Player");
}

function Update () {
        if(Input.GetKeyDown(KeyCode.Alpha1)) {
                if (player != null) {
                        player.transform.position = Vector3(0, 9, 18);
                        player.gameObject.GetComponent(GoRagdoll).ExitRagdoll();
                }
        }
}
```

This breaks down as follows:

(1)   `public var player : GameObject;`

Declare a public variable player of type GameObject.

(2)   `player = GameObject.FindWithTag("Player");`

When the `Start()` function is called, find the reference to the player character by its Player tag and assign it to player.

(3)   `if(Input.GetKeyDown(KeyCode.Alpha1)) {`

With each frame `Update()` call, check to see if the player has pressed the 1 key on the alphanumeric keyboard. If so, execute the subsequent block of code.

(4)   `if (player != null) {`

Test for the presence of a valid GameObject reference. If not null, execute the block of code.

(5)   `player.transform.position = Vector3(0, 9, 18);`

Move the player to the top of the ramp by resetting its Transform position coordinates.

(6)   `player.gameObject.GetComponent(GoRagdoll).ExitRagdoll();`

If the player character was killed, it needs to be reset out of ragdoll mode for the player to continue. You will create the `ExitRagdoll()` function next.

In the Unity editor top menu, select Game Object ➤ Create Empty. In the Hierarchy select the new game object and rename it Cheats. The sole purpose of this game object is to hold the cheat code scripts. Change its Transform position to (0, 20, 0) just to get it out of the way. Now attach the Cheats script either by dragging the script onto the Cheats game object in the Scene view or in the Inspector with Add Component ➤ Scripts and select the Cheats script from menu.

You still need to create the `ExitRagdoll()` function for the player character. In the Project panel Assets ➤ Scripts folder, select the GoRagdoll script and open it in MonoDevelop. This function simply reverses everything that occurred in the `GotoRagdoll()` function created in Chapter 7. First, select the `GotoRagdoll()` function and copy it. After the close bracket of the `GotoRagdoll()` function, paste the copied code back into the script, then change the copied function name to ExitRagdoll. Change all the boolean flags to their alternate settings and your `ExitRagdoll()` function should now read as follows:

```
function ExitRagdoll () {
        if (childRigidBodies != null) {
                for (var childRigidBody : Rigidbody in childRigidBodies)
                {
                        childRigidBody.isKinematic = true;
                }
        }
        if (childColliders != null) {
                for (var childCollider : Collider in childColliders)
```

```
                {
                        childCollider.enabled = false;
                }
        }

        gameObject.collider.enabled = true;
        gameObject.rigidbody.isKinematic = false;
        gameObject.GetComponent(Animator).enabled = true;
        gameObject.GetComponent(ThirdPersonCharacter).enabled = true;
        gameObject.GetComponent(ThirdPersonUserControl).enabled = true;
        }
```

Save the script, return to the Unity editor, save the scene, then playtest. The player character returns to the top of the ramp anytime you press 1. If the player character was killed, it is reanimated and ready to go. Awesome—this will definitely speed up playtesting!

Land Mine Zone

All we need for a land mine is the land mine itself and a contact-triggered explosion. The resources in the Sample Assets will make constructing a land mine quick and simple by using the Ball prefab for the Land Mines and the Explosion particle effect for the land mine detonation.

In the Project panel, drill down to the Assets ➤ Sample Assets ➤ Vehicles ➤ Rolling Ball ➤ Prefabs folder and open it. In it you will find a Ball prefab. You could have used Unity's primitive sphere, but this black ball looks a little more ominous.

Drag a prefab Ball into the Scene view and set its Transform position to (0, 9, 18). In the Hierarchy, rename it Land Mine. Since the collider is embedded in the track, the physics engine will move the Land Mine according to this apparent "collision," which you don't want. With Land Mine still selected in the Hierarchy, in the Inspector find the Sphere Collider component and check Is Trigger. Next, in the Rigidbody component, uncheck Use Gravity so the Land Mine will stay put on Play. Immediately underneath, check the Is Kinematic box. This will prevent surrounding land mines from being affected by the explosive force of a detonating mine.

Continuing further down in the Inspector, the Ball and the Ball User Control scripts are not needed. Click the cog icon and select Remove Component in the context menu for each of these script components (Figure 10-4).

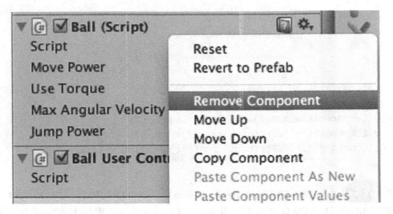

Figure 10-4. Remove the Ball and Ball User Control scripts from the Land Mine game object in the Inspector

Finally, you will need a script that tells the Land Mine to explode if the player character comes in contact with it, destroying the land mine and killing the player character. In the Project panel open Assets ä Script, then create a new script named LandMineExplosion and open it in MonoDevelop. Edit the code as follows:

```
#pragma strict

public var victim : GameObject;
public var explosionPrefab : GameObject;

function Start () {
        victim = GameObject.FindWithTag("Player");
}

function OnTriggerEnter (collider : Collider) {
        if (collider.gameObject == victim) {
                Explosion();
        }
}

function Explosion () {
        victim.GetComponent(GoRagdoll).GotoRagdoll();
        Instantiate (explosionPrefab, transform.position, Quaternion.identity);
        Destroy(gameObject);
}
```

This code breaks down as follows:

     (1)   `private var victim : GameObject;`

1. Declare a private GameObject type reference variable named `victim` for the player character reference.

     (2)   `public var explosionPrefab : GameObject;`

2. Declare a public GameObject type reference variable named explosionPrefab for the explosion particle effect.

```
(3)    victim = GameObject.FindWithTag("Player");
```

3. Find the reference to the player character game object and assign it to victim.

```
(4)    function OnTriggerEnter (collider : Collider) {
              if (collider.gameObject == victim) {
```

4. When the collider detects contact with another game object, check the identity of the other game object to see if it is the player. If it is,

```
(5)    Explosion();
```

5. Call the Explosion() function.

```
(6)    function Explosion () {
              victim.GetComponent(GoRagdoll).GotoRagdoll();
```

6. In the Explosion() function, access the GoRagdoll script of the character player and call the GotoRagdoll() function.

```
(7)    Instantiate (explosionPrefab, transform.position, Quaternion.identity);
```

7. Instantiate (create) an instance of the Explosion particle effect prefab.

```
(8)    Destroy(gameObject);
```

8. Destroy the Land Mine game object.

Save the script and return to the Unity editor. Attach the LandMineExplosion script to the Land Mine game object. With the Land Mine game object selected, take a look at the Land Mine Explosion script component and notice that the PrefabExplosion property is empty. In the Project panel, open the Assets ➤ Sample Assets ➤ Effects ➤ Particle Systems ➤ Prefabs folder and find the Explosion prefab. Drag the Explosion prefab onto the Land Mine game object. Now drag this prefab into the PrefabExplosion property field in the Inspector. Your land mine is complete.

To make it a prefab for the many land mines you need for this zone, open your Assets ➤ Prefabs folder in the Project panel, and drag the Land Mine from the Hierarchy into it.

Before populating the mine field, notice that you can make land mines of differing heights and widths by sinking the land mine further into the elevated track. (Figure 10-5).

Figure 10-5. Placement of the Land Mine game object on the y-axis determines exposed hazard size

You will populate the mine field by dragging and dropping Land Mine prefabs from the Prefab folder in the Project panel. Put yourself back in game design mode and consider how you are going to lay out the minefield. A few possibilities are shown in Figure 10-6, starting with a simple pattern of even size and spacing.

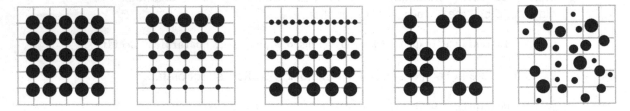

Figure 10-6. Various dispersal patterns for land mines

Keeping in mind that you want to make the zone progressively more difficult from start to finish, you might consider increasing size or density of the mines as the player progresses. Alternatively, you might wish to construct the minefield with only one survivable path, or use a completely random distribution.

Which way to go? That depends on which you think is more fun and in keeping with the theme of your game, but as you place the land mines and playtest, you might shift to a different option depending on how the pattern works out during gameplay.

Keep the player in mind as you contemplate the layout of the land mines. The player has just begun, and so is just beginning to get a feel for the movement and responsiveness of the player character. Try creating a path that begins wide, with easy turns, but becomes more narrow and tortuous, which in turn makes the player use the controls more precisely. You might even require a jump to the final "safe" area at the edge of the gap to the moving platform. Playtest and adjust until you are satisfied with the layout. Save the scene.

As you manually populate the zone, you will have a lot of Land Mine game objects in the Hierarchy view. You can use empty game objects to keep things more organized and manageable. In the Unity editor top menu, select Game Object ➤ Create Empty and name it Land Mines. Set the Transform position to (0, 5, 18) to tuck it in under the elevated track at the beginning of the mine field zone.

In the Hierarchy view, select the first Land Mine game object. Scroll down to the last one, only this time press and hold the Shift key before you click it. This will select everything in between the first and last Land Mine game objects in the list. Drag and drop this collection onto the Land Mines game object. Much better! Save the scene again.

Moving Platform Zone

The moving platform obstacle is good to go as a functional hazard. Just make sure that the player can get to the moving platform from the "safe" area at the border with the mine field zone.

As you test this, you will find that your cheat code takes you back to the beginning of the minefield. Time to add a cheat code for testing the moving platform. In the Project panel, open the Assets ➤ Scripts folder. Double-click the Cheats script to open it in MonoDevelop. In the Update() function, copy the code for the cheat and paste the copy immediately after the closing brace of the conditional statement. Change this conditional to KeyCode.Alpha2 and the new position to (0, 9, 33.5) as follows:

```
function Update () {
        if(Input.GetKeyDown(KeyCode.Alpha1)) {
        ...
        }

        if(Input.GetKeyDown(KeyCode.Alpha2)) {
                if (player != null) {
                        player.transform.position = Vector3(0, 9, 33.5);
                        player.gameObject.GetComponent(GoRagdoll).ExitRagdoll();
                }
        }
}
```

With this addition you can quickly reposition the player on the far side of the minefield by pressing 2 on the keyboard.

With five zones to go, you can imagine how cluttered the Update() function will get. Time for a little refactoring. Edit the Cheats script code to the following:

```
#pragma strict

public var player : GameObject;
private var relocationPoint : Vector3;

function Start () {
        player = GameObject.FindWithTag("Player");
}

function Update () {
        CheckInput();
}

function CheckInput () {
        if(Input.GetKeyDown(KeyCode.Alpha1)) {
```

```
            relocationPoint = Vector3(0, 9, 18);
            RelocatePlayer();
    }
    else if(Input.GetKeyDown(KeyCode.Alpha2)) {
            relocationPoint = Vector3(0, 9, 33.5);
            RelocatePlayer();
    }
}

function RelocatePlayer(){
    if (player != null) {
            player.transform.position = relocationPoint;
            player.gameObject.GetComponent(GoRagdoll).ExitRagdoll();
    }
}
```

This code breaks down as follows:

(1)   **private var relocationPoint : Vector3;**

1. Declare a private variable relocationPoint of type Vector3.

(2)   **CheckInput();**

2. Call the CheckInput() function from the Update() function. Now you can easily see that you are checking for user input each frame.

(3)   function CheckInput () {

3. Create a new CheckInput() function and move the code that checked the player's input from the Update() function here.

(4)   relocationPoint = Vector3(0, 9, 18);

and

relocationPoint = Vector3(0, 9, 33.5);

4. Assign the new position associated with this key to the relocationPoint variable.

(5)   **RelocatePlayer();**

5. Call the RelocatePlayer() function.

(6)   **function RelocatePlayer(){**

6. Create the RelocatePlayer() function . . .

(7)   **player.transform.position = relocationPoint;**

7. which begins with assigning the value of the Vector3 in the relocationPoint variable as the new position of the player character.

Notice the conditionals in the CheckInput() function also changed slightly from two if conditionals to an if - else if sequence. You could have left them as two if conditionals, but else if is more efficient. As an example, assume you have created cheat keys for each of the seven zones. When you use seven if conditionals, each conditional is checked each time the function is called.

Say the user presses the 3 key:

Processor	Code
Evaluates conditional: false	if Alpha1 key pressed
Evaluates conditional: false	if Alpha2 key pressed
Evaluates conditional: true	if Alpha3 key pressed
Processes code block contained in conditional	
Evaluates conditional: false	if Alpha4 key pressed
Evaluates conditional: false	if Alpha5 key pressed
Evaluates conditional: false	if Alpha6 key pressed
Evaluates conditional: false	if Alpha7 key pressed
Evaluates subsequent code . . .	

Using else if in a sequence of conditionals means that each conditional will be evaluated until one is found to be true, and the remaining else if conditionals can be skipped once the true condition has been identified.

Again, assume the user presses the 3 key:

Processor	Code
Evaluates conditional: false	if Alpha1 key pressed
Evaluates conditional: false	else if Alpha2 key pressed
Evaluates conditional: true	else if Alpha3 key pressed
Processes code block contained in conditional	
Not evaluated	else if Alpha4 key pressed
Not evaluated	else if Alpha5 key pressed

| Not evaluated | else if Alpha6 key pressed |
| Not evaluated | else if Alpha7 key pressed |

Evaluates subsequent code . . .

Any efficiencies you can introduce to your code reduces the processing load, improving overall game performance.

Cannon Zone

You created a cannon in Chapter 8, so the next step is to make it a prefab. In the Project panel, open the Assets ➤ Prefab folder. In the Hierarchy, select the Cannon game object. Drag and drop it into the Prefab folder. Delete the Cannon game object from the Hierarchy view.

Just as you did for the Land Mine Zone, think about how you are going to populate this zone with the cannons. This time you have two dimensions to work with in the placement of the cannons: along the z-axis as the player progresses through the zone, and along the y-axis at varying heights relative to the player character. By varying the heights, the player can add utilizing the player character's "crouching" animation to avoid the hazards.

You can manually position the cannons by dragging them from the Prefab folder and dropping them into the Scene view, then setting the Transform position coordinates to your liking. As an alternative, you can also use scripts to populate the scene with game objects such as hazards. For example, create a script that directs a random distribution of cannons throughout the zone.

In the Project panel, open the Assets ➤ Scripts folder and create a new script named RandomCannonPositions. Open it in MonoDevelop and edit the code to the following:

```
#pragma strict

public var prefab : GameObject;
public var amount : int = 10;

function Start () {
        for (var i : int = 0; i < amount; i++)
        {
                var position: Vector3 = Vector3(5, Random.Range(9.0, 11.0),
                Random.Range(44, 53));
                Instantiate(prefab, position, Quaternion.Euler(0, 0, 90));
        }
}
```

This breaks down as follows:

```
(1)     public var prefab : GameObject;
        public var amount : int = 10;
```

1. Declare the prefab reference variable of type GameObject, and the amount variable of type int and assign it a value of 10.

```
(2)     for (var i : int = 0; i < amount; i++)
```

2. The for loop will repeat as many times as the value of amount.

```
(3)     var position: Vector3 = Vector3(5, Random.Range(9.0, 11.0),
Random.Range(44,       53));
```

3. With each loop, create a position Vector3 type variable and assign it an x-coordinate value of 5 to position it to the right of the elevated track, a y-coordinate between 9 and 11 because the surface of the elevated track is at the y-coordinate of 9 and the player character is 2 units tall, and a z-coordinate between 44 and 53, the boundaries of this zone.

```
(4)     Instantiate(prefab, position, Quaternion.Euler(0, 0, 90));
```

4. Create a new instance of the cannon prefab with the previously generated position and a rotation of 90 around the z-axis to aim it across the width of the elevated track.

Save the script. In the Unity editor, create an empty game object from the top menu Game Object ➤ Create Empty. Name the new game object Hazard Setup and attach the RandomCannonPositions script. Drag the Cannon prefab from the Assets ➤ Prefab folder in the Project panel to the Prefab property of the RandomCannonPositions script in the Inspector. Now position the Hazard Setup game object out of the way in the Scene view. Save the scene.

If you playtest now, you'll notice that all the cannons fire at once. To vary the launch frequencies, find the LaunchProjectile script in the Assets ➤ Scripts folder in the Project panel and open it in MonoDevelop. Add a Start() function with code that selects a random value for frequency:

```
#pragma strict

public var projectile : GameObject;
public var force : float = 25;
public var frequency : float = 2.0;
private var nextLaunch : float = 0.0;

function Start () {
        frequency = Random.Range(0.5, 2.5);
}

function Update () {
        if (Time.time > nextLaunch) {
```

```
        nextLaunch = Time.time + frequency;
        var projectileInstance : GameObject = Instantiate(projectile,
                transform.position, transform.rotation);
        projectileInstance.rigidbody.AddForce (projectileInstance.transform.forward
                * force, ForceMode.Impulse);
        Destroy(projectileInstance, 2);
        }
}
```

Save the script and save the scene. Now when you playtest, the cannon zone has a nice distribution of cannons and projectile frequencies (Figure 10-7).

Figure 10-7. The completed Cannon Zone

You can easily add another cheat code to facilitate your testing by adding the following to the RelocatePlayer() function in the Cheats script:

```
else if(Input.GetKeyDown(KeyCode.Alpha3)) {
        relocationPoint = Vector3(0, 9, 43);
        RelocatePlayer();
}
```

Make any adjustments you feel improves the gameplay to your satisfaction. Don't forget to save the scene and save the project. Another zone complete—woo!

Pendulum Zone

In keeping with the game design that has varying levels of intensity with each zone, the cannon zone is of higher intensity than the moving platform zone, while the pendulum zone is of a lower intensity than the cannon zone, which in turn is more challenging than the previous low-intensity moving platform zone. That's a lot of ups and downs!

The pendulums are already built. If you want to add to the difficulty of this zone, you can change their number, size, and properties. If you want to move them around, you can select the pendulum ball with the chain links as a group by holding down the left mouse button while dragging the cursor over them. A transform gizmo appears, which you can use to move them as a collection where they maintain their position relative to one another. Since they are a group, take a moment to create an empty game object to serve as a Pendulum parent game object, then do the same for the other two. This is a simple prototype—imagine how cluttered and unwieldy the Hierarchy could get with a more complex game!

You can also reuse some assets to add to the challenge, such as adding land mines. You can place them manually or create a script that distributes them, much like you did for the cannons.

In the Project panel, open the Assets ➤ Scripts folder and create a new script named RandomLandMinePositions. Open it in MonoDevelop and add the following code:

```
#pragma strict

public var prefab : GameObject;
public var amount : int = 10;

function Start () {
        for (var i : int = 0; i < amount; i++)
        {
                var position: Vector3 = Vector3(Random.Range(-3.5, 3.5),
                        Random.Range(8.5, 9.0), Random.Range(55, 89));
                Instantiate(prefab, position, Quaternion.identity);
        }
}
```

Breaking this down, the only differences here from the RandomCannonPositions script are the following:

```
(1)      var position: Vector3 = Vector3(Random.Range(-3.5, 3.5),
                Random.Range(8.5, 9.0), Random.Range(55, 89));
```

1. The position x- and z-coordinate ranges reflect the width and length of the zone along the elevated track, and the y-coordinate range varies how much the land mine extends above the surface of the elevated track.

```
(2)      Instantiate(prefab, position, Quaternion.identity);
```

2. When the Instantiate() function is called, Quaternion.identity is the equivalent of saying "no rotation."

Save the script, then attach it to the Hazard Setup game object in the Hierarchy. With the script selected, open the Assets ➤ Prefab folder and drag the Land Mine prefab to the Prefab property in the Inspector. Save the scene and playtest. You can change the number of land mines with the amount property in the Inspector, and you can add the following cheat to the RelocatePlayer() function in the Cheats script to get the player character back to this zone quickly:

```
else if(Input.GetKeyDown(KeyCode.Alpha4)) {
        relocationPoint = Vector3(0, 9, 54);
        RelocatePlayer();
}
```

As always, when you've got it tweaked the way you like it, save the scene and save the project.

What if you don't want a random arrangement? Besides manually placing the prefabs, you can also use scripts to place hazards in regular patterns. In the Project panel, open the Assets ➤ Scripts folder and create a new script named RegularLandMinePositions. Open it in MonoDevelop and add the following code:

```
#pragma strict

public var prefab : GameObject;

public var xPos : float = -3.5;
public var yPos : float = 8.5;
public var zPos : float = 55.0;

public var numberWidth : int = 8;
public var numberLength : int = 34;

function Start () {
        for (var i : int = 0; i < numberLength; i++)
        {
                for (var j : int = 0; j < numberWidth; j++)
                {
                        var position: Vector3 = Vector3(xPos, yPos, zPos);
                        Instantiate(prefab, position, Quaternion.identity);
                        xPos++;
                }
        xPos = -3.5;
        yPos = yPos + 0.05;
        zPos = zPos + 1;
        }
}
```

This code breaks down as follows:

     (1)   `public var prefab : GameObject;`

1. Declare the public reference variable prefab of type GameObject to hold the reference to the prefab that will be used in this script.

     (2)   `public var xPos : float = -3.5;`
                  `public var yPos : float = 8.5;`
                  `public var zPos : float = 55.0;`

2. Declare the public variables xPos, yPos, and zPos of type float to hold the x, y, and z coordinates of each instantiated prefab and assign their initial values.

     (3)   `public var numberWidth : int = 8;`
                  `public var numberLength : int = 34;`

3. Declare the public variable numberWidth to hold the number of prefabs to be placed across the width of the elevated track and assign an initial value of 8; similarly, declare the public variable numberLength to hold the number of prefabs to be placed down the length of the elevated track and assign an initial value of 34.

```
(4)    for (var i : int = 0; i < numberLength; i++)
```

4. This for loop iterates through the number of rows to be created.

```
(5)    for (var j : int = 0; j < numberWidth; j++)
```

5. This loop iterates through the number of prefabs to be instantiated for each row.

```
(6)    var position: Vector3 = Vector3(xPos, yPos, zPos);
```

6. The x, y, and z coordinates are assigned to the variable position.

```
(7)    Instantiate(prefab, position, Quaternion.identity);
```

7. The new instance of the prefab is created at the assigned position and with no rotation.

```
(8)    xPos++;
```

8. The x coordinate is incremented by 1 for each prefab created in this row. The loop repeats, placing the next prefab alongside the previous one.

```
(9)    xPos = -3.5;
```

9. When a row of prefabs is complete, the x coordinate is reset to the initial value for the next row.

```
(10)    yPos = yPos + 0.05;
```

10. The y coordinate is incremented by 0.05 for the next row.

```
(11)    zPos = zPos + 1;
```

11. The z coordinate is incremented by 2, placing the next row 2 units further along the elevated track.

Save the script. Attach script to the Hazard Setup game object in the Hierarchy. With the Hazard Setup game object selected in the Hierarchy, you can see in the Inspector that it has both the RandomLandMinePositions script and the RegularLandMinePositions script attached to it. Be sure to uncheck the RandomLandMinePositions script component to deactivate it; the RegularLandMinePositions script should remain checked.

In the Project panel, open the Assets ➤ Prefab folder, then assign the Land Mine prefab to the Prefab property of the RegularLandMinePositions script in the Inspector. Save the scene.

Playtest to see the pattern, in which each successive row the land mine is positioned higher than in the previous one. This zone becomes solid land mines by the end, impossible to cross (Figure 10-8).

Figure 10-8. Prefab land mines distributed in a regular pattern using a script

Change the following line of code:

```
for (var i : int = 0; i < numberLength; i++)
```

to

```
for (var i : int = 0; i < numberLength/2; i++)
```

and the line:

```
zPos = zPos + 1;
```

to

```
zPos = zPos + 2;
```

Save the script and playtest. The first code change means half as many rows were created, while the second places them 2 units apart instead of 1. Experiment with changing the number and spacing of rows, and the number and spacing of prefabs in each row. Arrange it how you like it best, until you have two alternatives of random and regularly spaced for land mine placement in this zone that can easily be alternated by enabling and disabling the respective scripts.

Laser Zone

You can apply many of the previous approaches to populating the Laser Zone with hazards—regular spacing, random spacing, stationary lasers, or changing speeds, for example. In this case you will start with lasers at regular 0.5-unit spacing down the length of the zone, moving across the width of the elevated track at different speeds.

First make the laser hazard prefab by dragging the LaserCube game object from the Hierarchy to the Assets ➤ Prefab folder in the Project panel and name it Laser. Delete the LaserCube game object from the Hierarchy.

In the Project panel, open the Assets ➤ Scripts folder and create a new script named Laser Layout. Edit the code to the following:

```
#pragma strict

public var prefab : GameObject;

public var zPos : float = 91.0;
public var numberLength : int = 16;

function Start () {
        for (var i : int = 0; i < numberLength * 2; i++)
        {
                var position: Vector3 = Vector3(-3.8, 12, zPos);
                Instantiate(prefab, position, Quaternion.identity);
                zPos = zPos + 0.5;
        }
}
```

Breaking this down: ·

> (1)   `public var prefab : GameObject;`

1. The public reference variable of type GameObject to hold the reference to the prefab game object.

> (2)   `public var zPos : float = 91.0;`

2. Declare the public variable zPos of type float and assign it the value of the beginning of the zone.

> (3)   `public var numberLength : int = 16;`

3. Declare the public variable numberLength of type float and assign it the value of the length of the zone.

> (4)   `for (var i : int = 0; i < numberLength * 2; i++)`

4. This for loop will create and position one new prefab with each iteration. Since the lasers are quite narrow, placing them 0.5 units apart means you need twice as many, and so the for loop iterates two times the length of the zone.

    (5)   `var position: Vector3 = Vector3(-3.8, 12, zPos);`

5. Declare a Vector3 type variable named position to assign the initial position of the laser prefab. In this zone, the starting x and y coordinates for the laser prefabs are fixed, so only the z coordinate of each prefab needs to be varied and assigned in order to space them out along the zone.

    (6)   `Instantiate(prefab, position, Quaternion.identity);`

6. Instantiate the laser prefab with the new position and no rotation.

    (7)   `zPos = zPos + 0.5;`

7. Advance to the next position by adding 0.5 units to the newly instantiated prefab's z coordinate.

Save the script and attach it to the Hazard Setup game object in the Hierarchy. Select Hazard Setup in the Hierarchy, then select the Laser prefab in the Prefabs folder in the Project panel and assign it to the Prefab variable in the Laser Layout script component in the Inspector. Playtest, and take note that only one laser emits sparks when it hits the elevated track where it is supposed to (Figure 10-9).

Figure 10-9. All but one of the sparks particle systems appears out of place

This aberration is coming from the Laser prefab's Laser script, which is attached to the child empty Game Object. In the Assets ➤ Prefab folder, expand the Laser prefab and select the LaserBeam child to display its properties in the Inspector (Figure 10-10).

Figure 10-10. The Laser's child LaserBeam in the Project panel and its Laser script component in the Inspector

There is no game object assigned to the Sparks property field, but one laser has sparks in the right place while the rest do not. Open the Laser script in MonoDevelop. In the Start() function you'll find the line of code assigning the Flare particle system to the sparks reference variable:

```
function Start () {
        sparks = GameObject.Find("Flare");
```

The Start() function is called once. It finds the first game object named Flare and assigns it to sparks, then moves on to execute the rest of the code block. This is why you have one laser with sparks in the right place. Delete this line of code and save the script. Assign the Flare particle system to the Sparks property by dragging the Flare child game object of the Laser prefab from the Project panel (Assets/Prefabs/Laser ➤ Flare) and drop it into the Sparks property field in the Inspector. Playtest and now the sparks all appear where the laser hits the elevated track (Figure 10-11).

Figure 10-11. Each of the sparks particle systems appears where its laser hits the surface of the elevated track

The lasers all work properly now, but moving in a synchronized fashion doesn't make for much of a challenge. To address this via code, find the MoveLaser script and open it. To randomize the speed of each laser prefab, add the following line of code to the `Start()` function:

```
function Start () {
        offset = transform.position.x - 0.2;
        speed = Random.Range(1.0, 3.0);
}
```

The `Random.Range()` function should be quite familiar by now. Remember, you can always use ⌘+' to open its script reference documentation. You can see the random distribution of lasers in Figure 10-12.

Figure 10-12. The laser zone after applying random speeds to the laser prefabs

The cheat code for this zone is:

```
else if(Input.GetKeyDown(KeyCode.Alpha5)) {
        relocationPoint = Vector3(0, 9, 90);
        RelocatePlayer();
}
```

Add it to the list of others in the `RelocatePlayer()` function in the Cheats script.

While repositioning and reviving the character player is a handy cheat, it can be difficult to assess everything about the hazard you want to inspect while simultaneously dodging death. Another common and handy cheat is invincibility. To add invincibility, add the following code block to the `if else` sequence in the `CheckInput()` function:

```
else if(Input.GetKeyDown(KeyCode.Alpha0)) {
        player.gameObject.GetComponent(GoRagdoll).Invincibility();
}
```

This breaks down as follows:

```
(1)     else if(Input.GetKeyDown(KeyCode.Alpha0)) {
```

1. As with the other cheats, this checks to see if the player has pressed the 0 (zero) button. If true,

```
(2)     player.gameObject.GetComponent(GoRagdoll).Invincibility();
```

2. Get the GoRagdoll script of the player game object and call the Invincibility() function that you will create next. Save the Cheats script, then open the GoRagdoll script. First add the invincible variable as follows:

```
        #pragma strict

        private var childRigidBodies : Rigidbody[];
        private var childColliders : Collider[];
(1)     public var invincible : boolean = false;
```

1. First, add a public variable of type boolean named invincible and assign it the value of false. This way when the game starts, the player is not invincible.

At the end of the script, add the Invincibility() function:

```
        function Invincibility () {
(2)             invincible = !invincible;
        }
```

2. This is a simple toggle, where the value of invincible is reassigned to its opposing boolean value.

Finally, in the GotoRagdoll() function, add a conditional to test for whether or not the player is invincible before turning him into a ragdoll:

```
        function GotoRagdoll ()
            {
(3)     if (!invincible) {
                if (childRigidBodies != null) {
                    for (var childRigidBody : Rigidbody in childRigidBodies) {
                        childRigidBody.isKinematic = false;
                    }
                }
                if (childColliders != null) {
                    for (var childCollider : Collider in childColliders) {
                        childCollider.enabled = true;
                    }
                }
                gameObject.collider.enabled = false;
                gameObject.rigidbody.isKinematic = true;
                gameObject.GetComponent(Animator).enabled = false;
                gameObject.GetComponent(ThirdPersonCharacter).enabled = false;
                gameObject.GetComponent(ThirdPersonUserControl).enabled = false;
            }
        }
```

3. In this `if` conditional, it tests to see if the contents of the parentheses is true. Using `!invincible` is a shorthand for "the opposite of the value of `invincible`." If `invincible` is true, then `!invincible` is `false`. If the conditional tests false, then the subsequent code block is not executed, which means the player character is not converted to a ragdoll.

Save the script, scene, and project. Playtest your newfound invincibility!

Blizzard Zone

The first thing to address is repositioning and resizing the Blizzard game object containing the killer particle system. Select the Blizzard game object in the Hierarchy, then in the Inspector change the Transform position coordinates to (-10, 11.5, 117) to center it in the zone. Recall that the –10 x-offset is to allow the player time to see and react to the approaching snowflakes (Figure 10-13).

Figure 10-13. Blizzard of deadly snowflakes crossing the elevated track

Still in the Inspector, scroll down to the Shape module of the Particle System component. Change Box X to 17 to expand the particle-emitting surface to the length of the zone. The snowflakes are now less dense, since they are adhering to the Emission module's rate of 10.

Chapter 8 provided an overview of particle systems and their modules and properties. You can go through these properties and reset them in the Inspector to account for the new size and location of the particle emitter. But how would you go about making this zone more difficult as the player proceeds according to your game design? Through scripting, of course.

To make the snowflakes emit with a higher velocity the farther the player proceeds through the zone, open the Project panel, open the Assets ➤ Scripts folder, and create a new script named BlizzardZone. Open it in MonoDevelop and edit the code to the following:

```
#pragma strict

public var playerTransform : Transform;
public var rateIncrease : float = 1;
```

```
private var rate : float;

function Update () {
        if (playerTransform.position.z > 109 && playerTransform.position.z < 126) {
                rate = playerTransform.position.z - 104;
                gameObject.particleSystem.startSpeed = rate * rateIncrease;
                }
}
```

This code breaks down as follows:

```
(1)      public var playerTransform : Transform;
```

1. Declare the public variable playerTransform of type Transform that will hold the reference to the player character's transform.

```
(2)      public var rateIncrease : float = 1;
```

2. Declare the public variable rateIncrease of type float that will allow you to adjust the rate of change of the blizzard property through the Inspector.

```
(3)      private var rate : float;
```

3. Declare the private variable rate of type float that will be used along with the player character's position to calculate a rate that varies in accordance with the player character's progress.

```
(4)      if (playerTransform.position.z > 109 && playerTransform.position.z < 126)
```

4. This if conditional contains two tests. The first is to test if the player character's transform position z coordinate is greater than 109, which means he has entered the blizzard zone. The second is to test if the player character's transform position z coordinate is greater than 126, meaning he has exited the blizzard zone on the far side. The && operator represents the logical AND operator. The first condition AND the second condition must be true for the entire conditional statement to return a true result. This in turn causes the subsequent block of code to be executed.

```
(5)      rate = playerTransform.position.z - 104;
```

5. The rate variable is assigned the value of the player character's transform position z coordinate value minus 104. 104 is an arbitrary amount based on the original value of the Start Speed property being 5, such that when the player first enters the Blizzard Zone that begins at a z coordinate of 109, the Start Speed will still be 5.

```
(6)      gameObject.particleSystem.startSpeed = rate * rateIncrease;
```

6. Multiply the new rate based on the player character's position by the
    rateIncrease value that you can use in the Inspector to adjust how rapidly
    the startSpeed value changes as the player moves within the zone, then
    assign it to the Blizzard game object's particle system Start Speed property.

Save the script and attach to the Blizzard game object. Back in the editor, select the Blizzard game object in the Hierarchy, then drag the Third Person Character Ragdoll from the Hierarchy to the Player Transform field of the Blizzard Zone script in the Inspector. Playtest and note the change in snowflake speeds as the player runs around. In addition to adjusting initial particle system properties in the Inspector, you can easily control them during gameplay. MonoDevelop's autofill function can assist you by displaying the available particle system properties (Figure 10-14);

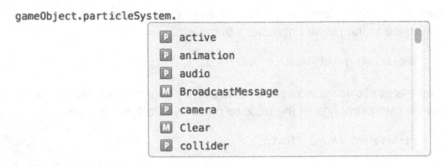

Figure 10-14. Particle system properties displayed in MonoDevelop's autofill pop-up window

Don't forget to add the cheat code for this zone to the RelocatePlayer() function of the Cheats script:

```
else if(Input.GetKey(KeyCode.Alpha6)) {
        relocationPoint = Vector3(0, 9, 108);
        RelocatePlayer();
}
```

Have fun experimenting with altering different particle system properties or even multiple properties based on player progression. When you have the Blizzard zone the way you like it, save the script, the scene, and the project.

Enemy Zone

In this zone you are graduating from hazards to an enemy that has enough intelligence to direct an attack on the player. You will create a simple drone enemy that targets and chases after the player while the player is in its zone.

To create the enemy drone, open the Assets ➤ Prefab folder and drag a land mine prefab onto the Scene view. Rename it Enemy Drone in the Hierarchy, then in the Inspector give it a Transform position of (0, 10, 145). The Land Mine prefab already explodes on contact with the player character, so the only thing to add here is the ability to find the player character and hunt him down.

When the Player exits the Blizzard Zone into the small safe area between zones, he can see the ominous drone at the far end. The player has already learned from the land mines that the black ball is not friendly, but to up the tension he won't know the nature of the attack this time until it is initiated (Figure 10-15).

Figure 10-15. The player character faces the enemy drone

In the Project panel Assets ➤ Prefab ➤ Scripts folder, create a new script named EnemyDroneAI. Open it in MonoDevelop and edit the code as follows:

```
#pragma strict

public var playerTransform : Transform;
public var speed : float = 3.0f;

private var drone : Vector3;
private var target : Vector3;
private var distance : float;

function Update () {
        if (playerTransform.position.z > 128 && playerTransform.position.z < 145) {
                transform.LookAt(playerTransform);
```

```
          drone = transform.position;
          target = playerTransform.position + Vector3(0, 0.6, 0);
          distance = speed * Time.deltaTime;
          transform.position = Vector3.MoveTowards(drone, target, distance);
    }
}
```

This code breaks down as follows:

> (1)   public var playerTransform : Transform;
>   public var speed : float = 3.0f;

1. Declare the `playerTransform` Transform public-type variable to hold the reference to the player character's transform for targeting, and the `speed` float-type variable to make the speed of the drone adjustable from the Inspector during playtesting.

> (2)   private var drone : Vector3;
>   private var target : Vector3;
>   private var distance : float;

2. Declare the private variables that will hold the values required by the `MoveTowards()` function: the position of the drone, the position of the player character, and the distance between the two.

> (3)   if (playerTransform.position.z > 128 && playerTransform.position.z < 145)

3. This conditional checks to see if the player character's z Transform position is greater than 128, in which case the player character has entered the drone's zone. It also checks to see if the player character's z Transform position is less than 145, meaning he hasn't exited the zone on the far side. The `&&` logic operator means that if both of these conditions are true, then the player character has entered the zone and has not exited it, and the player character is within the enemy drone's zone.

> (4)   transform.LookAt(playerTransform);

4. The `transform.LookAt` function rotates the drone's transform so it's forward vector points toward the player character by taking the player character's Transform as its argument.

> (5)   drone = transform.position;
>   target = playerTransform.position + Vector3(0, 0.6, 0);
>   distance = speed * Time.deltaTime;

5. To move the enemy drone toward the player character, you must assign the current position of the drone, the point it is to proceed toward, and the distance to be moved. The player character's Transform position is based on his feet, so Vector3(0, 0.6, 0) is added so the drone will stay above the surface of the elevated track but remain low enough that the player character could still jump over it as an evasion tactic.

(6)   transform.position = Vector3.MoveTowards(drone, target, distance);

6. The drone's new transform.position is calculated by the MoveTowards() function by taking the drone's position, the player character's position, and the distance to be moved as arguments.

Don't forget to add your cheat code to the CheckInput() function of the Cheats script for getting to this zone quickly:

```
else if(Input.GetKey(KeyCode.Alpha7)) {
      relocationPoint = Vector3(0, 9, 127);
      RelocatePlayer();
}
```

Save the script and attach it to the Enemy Drone game object. The playerTransform property needs to be populated in the Inspector, which can be done by dragging the Third Person Character Ragdoll from the Hierarchy and dropping it into the property field. Playtest, adjusting the drone speed in the Inspector until it is sufficiently challenging for you. Save the scene and save the project. Check it out—all the killer zones of the Obstacle Course are complete. Great job!

Debugging

Unexpected behaviors, from catastrophic crashes to anomalies like the sparks not lining up with the lasers you saw earlier in this chapter, are called **bugs**. Finding and fixing these problems is called **debugging**. Unity has a special Debug class for just this purpose. You used the Debug.Log function in Chapter 2 to display messages on the Console, and the Debug.DrawRay function in Chapter 7 to make a raycast visible in the Scene view while testing. As your scenes and scripts become more complex, you are more likely to see bugs, and also to identify and correct them efficiently.

Compiler Errors

When you click the Play button to run the game scene in the Game view, first the compiler translates your script code so the processor can understand it. If the compiler finds errors in your code it will let you know. The Unity compiler gives you a big notification in the Scene view of any such errors it finds when you attempt to playtest (Figure 10-16):

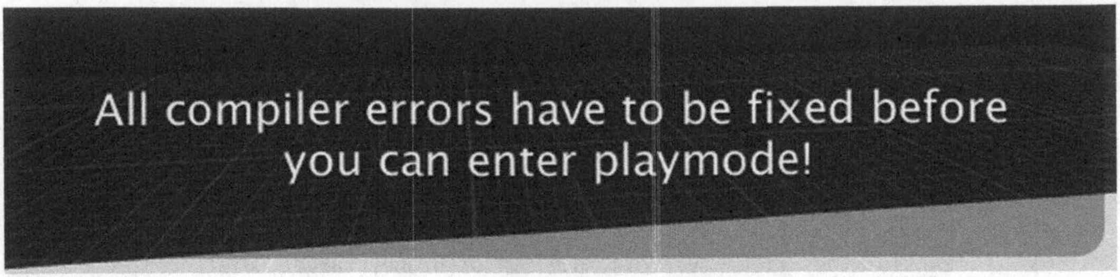

All compiler errors have to be fixed before you can enter playmode!

Figure 10-16. Compiler error message display in the Scene view

Under the Console tab in the Project panel, additional information regarding the error will also appear (Figure 10-17):

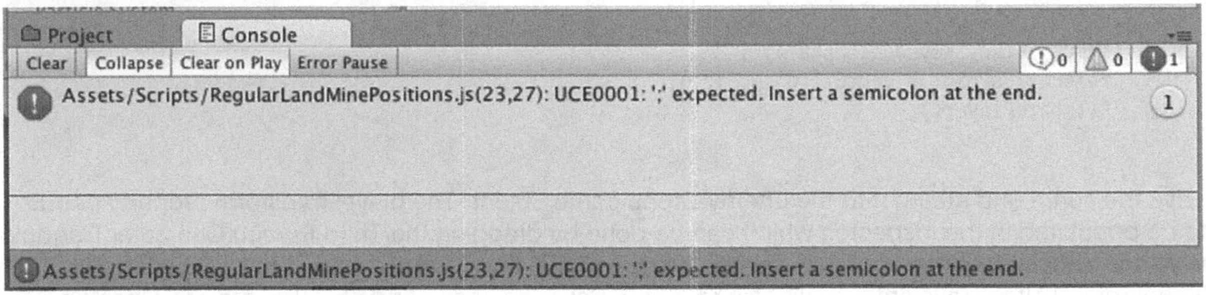

Figure 10-17. Compiler error information displayed in the Console

This error breaks down as follows:

1. `Assets/Scripts/`

In the Assets/Scripts folder,

2. `RegularLandMinePositions.js`

the RegularLandMinePositions.js script

3. `(23,27)`

has an error on line 23 column 27

4. `UCE0001`

with an abbreviated error code identification UCE0001 for User Created Error 0001 missing semicolon,

5. `';' expected.`

with an error description

```
6. Insert a semicolon at the end.
```

and a debugging suggestion to insert a semicolon at the end of this line of code.

If you double-click the error message on the bottom, MonoDevelop will open with the cursor at the location of the error. Test this by opening one of your scripts, deleting a semicolon from a line of code, and saving the script; then close MonoDevelop. Now try to playtest, and watch the compiler error messages appear in the Console tab of the Project panel and in the Scene view. Fix the error by reinserting the semicolon, and save your script.

An error on one line of code can cascade to make subsequent lines of code also appear to have errors. Once the first bug is fixed, these other pseudo-bugs will also disappear now that the compiler can read subsequent lines of code correctly. For this reason, when debugging you want to start with the first error that appears and methodically work your way through resolving the bugs in order.

Warnings

Whereas the compiler error in the previous example had a red stop sign icon to indicate the scene cannot be played until the error is fixed, a warning uses a yellow yield-sign icon to catch your attention regarding a problem, but also indicates the scene will still play (Figure 10-18).

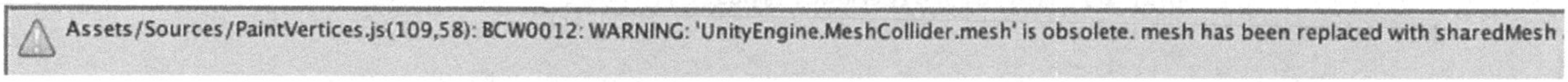

Assets/Sources/PaintVertices.js(109,58): BCW0012: WARNING: 'UnityEngine.MeshCollider.mesh' is obsolete. mesh has been replaced with sharedMesh

***Figure 10-18.** Warning message displayed in the Console*

Examples of warnings include notification of an unused variable, or a Unity function that will be deprecated (obsolete) in upcoming versions.

You can create your own warnings with `Debug.LogWarning`. It works much like `Debug.Log` but displays the warning icon in addition to the message and object context. To try this out, in the Unity editor Project panel, open the Assets ➤ Scripts folder and find the ImpactForce script. Open it in MonoDevelop and add the following line of code to the `Start()` function:

```
Debug.LogWarning("Warning!", this);
```

Save the script, playtest, and see your new warning appear in the Console (Figure 10-19).

Project
Console
Clear
Collapse
Clear on Play
Error Pause
Warning!
UnityEngine.Debug:LogWarning(Object, Object)

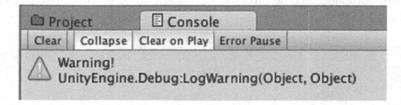

***Figure 10-19.** Debug.LogWarning message displayed in the Console*

Although you can still playtest with warnings present, you definitely want to resolve these prior to publication of your game.

Runtime Errors

Runtime errors are errors that occur after your scripts have been successfully compiled and your game is running. The simplest example of a runtime error is a divide-by-zero error.

With the ImpactForce script still open in MonoDevelop, first delete or disable the warning in the Start() function you created in the previous section. Now introduce a divide-by-zero error by editing the ImpactForce() function to the following:

```
function ImpactForce () {
        var colliders : Collider[] =
                Physics.OverlapSphere(transform.position - Vector3(0, 4, 0), 10);

        for(var cldr : Collider in colliders)
        {
                if(cldr.rigidbody == null) continue;
                var a : int = 0;
                cldr.rigidbody.AddExplosionForce(10, transform.position - Vector3(0,
                        4/a, 0), 10, 0, ForceMode.Impulse);
        }
}
```

This breaks down as follows:

```
(1)     var a : int = 0;
```

1. Declare an int type variable a and assign it the value of zero.

```
(2)     cldr.rigidbody.AddExplosionForce(10, transform.position - Vector3(0,
                4/a, 0), 10, 0, ForceMode.Impulse);
```

2. Divide the y component of the Vector3 calculation by a to create the divide-by-zero error.

Save the script and playtest.

Notice that the script compiled, and no error messages appeared in the Console until after the scene was running (Figure 10-20).

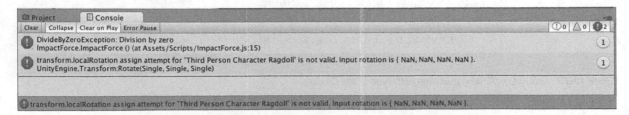

Figure 10-20. Runtime errors displayed in the Console

When an error occurs during runtime, Unity creates an **exception** object, then **throws** the exception. The exception must be **caught** and dealt with for execution of the script to proceed. If your script doesn't provide a means to handle the exception properly, a default handler catches the exception and generates the error message. Depending on the error, it may even **crash**, or terminate the game.

In this example, since the error occurs in the code block for calculating the explosive force on the boxes around the player character when he lands, when this error is thrown the boxes remain stacked neatly because the explosion force could not be properly calculated or applied.

Looking again at Figure 10-20, you can see that two error messages were generated: one for the mathematical error of dividing by zero, followed by the subsequent inability to calculate the Vector3 coordinates of the argument used in AddExplosionForce(). By addressing the first error listed in the Console first, when you fix the divide-by-zero bug, the second related error will also be resolved. Remove the error, save the script, and playtest, and your scene is up and running error-free again.

You can also create your own error messages using Debug.LogError. Add the following line of code as the first line of the ImpactForce() function:

```
Debug.LogError("My test error message", gameObject);
```

Save the script and playtest. The error message complete with red icon appears in the Console as expected. While the error message you created appears to act the same as a LogWarning message other than the icon, Debug.LogError also works in conjunction with the Unity debugger to help you follow the execution of your script step by step at runtime. While using the Unity debugger is a more advanced topic, for future reference be aware that there are more complex uses of the Debug class you will eventually find useful.

Exception Handling

You have already written code that helps to prevent throwing exceptions. Look again at the OnCollisionEnter() function of the KillOnCollision script:

```
function OnCollisionEnter(other : Collision) {
        if (other.gameObject.name == "Third Person Character Ragdoll")
        {
        other.gameObject.GetComponent(GoRagdoll).GotoRagdoll();
        }
}
```

The conditional checks to make sure the game object involved in the collision is the player character before accessing and calling the GotoRagdoll() function on its GoRagdoll script component. Suppose that you didn't check and wrote the function simply as:

```
function OnCollisionEnter(other : Collision) {
        other.gameObject.GetComponent(GoRagdoll).GotoRagdoll();
}
```

This might have made sense when the only moving game object was the player character. But as you continued to build the obstacle course, you added other moving objects—the enemy drones. If the player were to retreat along the obstacle course to escape the drone, and the following drone impacts with a hazard with a KillOnCollision script component, the script would try to access and call the GotoRagdoll() function of the GoRagdoll script component, but the enemy drone doesn't have one and so an error would occur. With the conditional in place, if the collision involves the enemy drone, the conditional tests false and does not execute the code block calling GotoRagdoll(), so no error occurs.

There is an almost infinite number of combinations of error types and scenarios within which they might occur. The best way to learn how to address errors is in practice by finding and solving them as they appear, and by learning more respective exception-handling code as you go. You'll come across many examples within the sample projects and tutorials that Unity has made available in the Asset Store. If you are presented with an error you can't resolve, the best next step is to do a quick search on the Unity3D Community page, under Answers and/or Forums. Most likely you'll find someone has run into the same problem and the answer is readily available.

Summary

This chapter has been fairly intensive, as you pulled together the player character and hazard prototypes to implement the game design you put together in the previous chapter. You experienced the iterative process of game design and created cheat codes to facilitate testing the obstacle course prototype. You learned how to revive the player character and make him invincible.

As you progressed through each hazard zone, you learned more ways to utilize scripts and prefabs to quickly populate the scene with hazards in regular patterns or with unpredictable randomization. Through the use of scripts you learned to adjust hazard game object properties in real time in response to player movement. You also created your first enemy and animated it with a simple AI script.

You repurposed assets to conserve time and resources for prototype development. You also refactored code to make it more efficient and you learned the basics of debugging. Whew—you covered a lot of ground and got a lot of good practice in design implementation as you fleshed out the obstacle course prototype. Great job!

Chapter **11**

Enhancing The User Experience: GUI and Sound

The term *video game* is used to describe games that are played via a video monitor or screen of some sort. Early video games were limited to text and keyboard characters on monochrome displays, but they have since evolved into complex game experiences that use 3D imagery, stereo sound, and—depending on the platform—motion detection and sensory feedback capabilities.

The Graphical User Interface or GUI is a visual overlay that assists the player by communicating information including score, inventory items, and maps, and also can provide additional means for the player to interact with the game.

Sound is also crucial to a robust and rich game experience. Music is used to set the mood of the game; to communicate hints and information regarding gameplay to the user using (anything from simple sounds to narrative dialog); or, as sound effects, to augment the corresponding visual action ensuing on the monitor.

Creating GUI Controls

Creating and using GUI controls is accomplished through scripting and the OnGUI() function. While you can add GUI scripts to any game object or GUI code to any script, keeping them organized makes it easier to edit, update, and troubleshoot your project. In the Unity editor top menu, select GameObject ➤ Create Empty and name it GUI. Like the Directional Light and Audio game objects, the precise Transform position is not important. The GUI controls you create will be displayed based on the screen coordinates you designate for them rather than the game world coordinates of the GUI game object.

Display Text

The most fundamental manner in which the GUI communicates with the user is by displaying text. The label and box are very simple controls that do just this. In fact, the only difference between a label and a box is that a label displays only the text, while a box is a label with a dark background around it.

Label

To create a label, first you will need a script. In the Project panel, open the Assets ➤ Scripts folder, then create a new script and name it GUIScript. Open GUIScript in MonoDevelop and edit the code to the following:

```
#pragma strict

function OnGUI() {
        GUI.Label(Rect(0, 0, 125, 25), "A label displays text");
}
```

This code breaks down as follows:

> (1)   function OnGUI()

1. The OnGUI() function used for creating GUI controls is called every frame.

> (2)   GUI.Label(Rect(0, 0, 125, 25), "A label displays text");

2. Call the Label() function of the GUI class and pass it the x and y screen coordinates, the width and height of the label followed by the text to be displayed in the label.

Save the script, attach it to the GUI game object, save the scene, and run. You will see the label text displayed in the upper left corner of the Game view (Figure 11-1).

Figure 11-1. The new label text displayed in the upper left corner of the Game view

Rect

The Rect variable deserves a little more explanation. It represents a 2D rectangle where the (x, y) coordinates represent where the upper left corner of the rectangle will be positioned according to the screen coordinates. The screen coordinates are based on the height and width of the target platform display and are independent of the (x, y, z) coordinates of the game world (Figure 11-2).

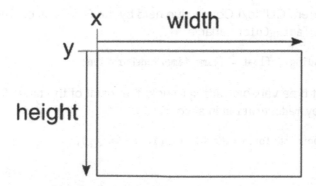

Figure 11-2. Rect variable properties defining the size and position of a 2D rectangle depicted in the Unity Scripting Reference

In the GUIScript, experiment with changing the (x, y) values to relocate the label. When you also experiment with the Rect size properties, you will find that when you make the label smaller, the text is cut off and does not reduce in size along with the rectangle's dimensions.

Fading Out

Suppose at the start of the game you would like to inform the player how to make the player character crouch and jump with a message that fades away after 3 seconds. Edit the GUIScript to the following:

```
#pragma strict

public var fadeDuration : float = 3;

function OnGUI() {
        var fadingColor : Color;
        fadingColor = GUI.contentColor;
        var fading : float = (Time.time/fadeDuration);
        GUI.contentColor.a = Mathf.Lerp(1, 0, fading);

        GUI.Label(Rect(0, 0, 250, 25), "Press C to crouch or Space to jump");
}
```

Breaking this down:

>   (1)   `public var fadeDuration : float = 3;`

1. Declare a float type variable fadeDuration and assign it a value of 3.

>   (2)   `var fadingColor : Color;`

2. Declare a reference variable fadingColor of type Color. Recall that Color is made up of r, g, b, a values where a, the alpha value, represents the transparency such that 1 is fully opaque and 0 is fully transparent.

>   (3)   `fadingColor = GUI.contentColor;`

3. Assign the current GUI text Color value held by the GUI class contentColor variable to the fadingColor variable.

>   (4)   `var fading : float = (Time.time/fadeDuration);`

4. Declare a float type variable fading to hold the result of the time since game start divided by fadeDuration in seconds.

>   (5)   `GUI.contentColor.a = Mathf.Lerp(1, 0, fading);`

5. Use the `Mathf.Lerp()` function to smooth the transition of the alpha value, then assign the new value to `GUI.contentColor.a`, which holds the reference color for the GUI text to be rendered.

```
(6)    GUI.Label(Rect(0, 0, 250, 25), "Press C to crouch or Space to jump");
```

6. Create a label whose upper left corner will be positioned in the upper left corner of the platform screen, with the text instructions that will be displayed using the newly calculated and assigned alpha value.

Save the script, save the scene, and playtest. You will see the message appear in the upper left corner, then fade away over 3 seconds. You can change the length of time it stays visible by adjusting `fadeDuration` in the Inspector.

Box

Add the following line of code to the end of the `OnGUI()` function to see the difference between a Label and a Box:

```
GUI.Box(Rect (0, 75, 100, 50), "This is a box");
```

This works exactly like `GUI.Label`. Save the script and play. The dark background of the box is a little difficult to see against the dark skybox of the Obstacle Course scene, so you may have to pan the camera around a little to see it (Figure 11-3).

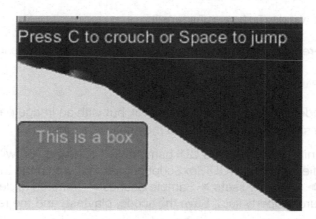

Figure 11-3. A GUI.Label and GUI.Box displayed in the Game view

Notice that the text for the label and the box both fade away. This is because `GUI.contentColor` in the code you wrote for the fading message applies to all of the content in this `OnGUI()` function. One way to address this is to use different scripts for the various GUI controls.

Remove the `GUI.Box(Rect (0, 75, 100, 50), "This is a box");` line of code and save the script.

In the Project panel Assets ➤ Script folder, select Create and make a new script named GUIBoxScript. Edit the code as follows:

```
#pragma strict

function OnGUI() {
        GUI.Box(Rect (0, 75, 100, 50), "This is a box");
}
```

Save the script, attach it to the GUI game object, save the scene, and playtest. This time the text in the box remains visible while that of the label fades away.

Image

You can display images instead of text. Edit GUIBoxScript to the following:

```
#pragma strict

public var boxTexture : Texture2D;

function OnGUI() {
        GUI.Box(Rect (0, 75, 100, 50), boxTexture);
}
```

This breaks down as follows:

> (1)   `public var boxTexture : Texture2D;`

1. Declare a reference variable boxTexture of type Texture2D for the image file.

> (2)   `GUI.Box(Rect (0, 75, 100, 50), boxTexture);`

2. This line of code creates the GUI box control, but with an image parameter instead of the string parameter used in the previous example.

Save the script. In the Unity editor, with the GUI game object selected you will see the Box Texture property with an empty field appear in GUIBoxScript component within the Inspector. In the Project panel, open the Assets ➤ Sample Assets ➤ Sample Scenes ➤ Textures folder. Drag the gui_reticle image into the Box Texture property field. Save the scene, playtest, and the reticle image appears in the box. Outstanding!

Remember, you can use ⌘+' with the cursor on GUI to open the Unity Scripting Reference and find the various options available for customizing the contents of GUI.Box or any of the GUI controllers.

Text Input

At times you may want input from the player. The TextField and TextArea GUI controls serve this purpose, where the only difference between them is that TextField holds one line of text and TextArea can hold many.

TextField

In the Project panel Assets ➤ Scripts folder, create a new script named GUITextInputScript. Open it in MonoDevelop and edit the code to the following:

```
#pragma strict

var textFieldString : String = "A one-line text field";

function OnGUI () {
        textFieldString = GUI.TextField (Rect (0, 130, 120, 30), textFieldString);
}
```

This code breaks down as follows:

> (1)   public var textFieldString : String = "A one-line text field";

1. Declare the String type textFieldString variable and assign it an initial message string "A one-line text field".

> (2)   textFieldString = GUI.TextField (Rect (0, 130, 120, 30), textFieldString);

2. Remember that OnGUI () is called every frame. The String variable textFieldString will reflect the contents of the GUI.TextField as the player edits it.

Save the script, attach it to the GUI game object, and see it appear as a script component in the Inspector. You can edit the initial message directly in the Text Field String property within the Inspector, or watch it change during playtesting to reflect any changes made to the GUI.TextField during gameplay.

TextArea

A TextArea works just like a TextField. In MonoDevelop, edit the GUITextInputScript to the following:

```
#pragma strict

var textFieldString : String = "A one-line text field";
var textAreaString  : String = "A multi-line text field";

function OnGUI () {
        textFieldString = GUI.TextField (Rect (0, 130, 120, 30), textFieldString);
        textAreaString = GUI.TextArea (Rect (0, 175, 75, 75), textAreaString);
}
```

Save the script and playtest. Now the TextArea will wrap around the new lines of text that occupy its space when you add more.

More Controls

Many of the common interactive elements are available as GUI controls, including buttons, toggles, and sliders. When creating any of the GUI controls you will notice they all follow the pattern of position–size–content.

Button

The basic button responds once when clicked, at the release of the mouse button. It returns `true` when clicked and otherwise `false`. In your script, you use a conditional to test for the true state; it then executes its block of code when the button is clicked.

In the Project panel Assets ➤ Scripts folder, create a new script named GUIButtons. Open it in MonoDevelop and edit the code to the following:

```
#pragma strict

function OnGUI () {
        if (GUI.Button (Rect (25, 260, 100, 30), "Click Me")) {
                Debug.Log("Button has been clicked");
        }
}
```

This code breaks down as follows:

> (1)   if (GUI.Button (Rect (25, 260, 100, 30), "Click Me"))

1. This efficient line of code creates the GUI button and tests its state at the same time.

> (2)   Debug.Log("Button has been clicked");

2. If the button state returns `true`, meaning it has been clicked, the `Debug.Log` statement will appear in the Console.

Save the script, attach it to the GUI game object, and playtest. Click the button to confirm "Button has been clicked" appears in the Console.

You could put any kind of code into this conditional statement. Since you already know how to write code that affects the game object to which the script is attached and any other game object in the scene, your code here can affect any game object behavior. Save the scene and the project.

Repeat Button

The repeat button differs from the button in that it returns `true` every frame as long as the repeat button is pressed.

In MonoDevelop, edit the GUIButtons script code to the following:

```
function OnGUI () {
        if (GUI.Button (Rect (25, 260, 100, 30), "Click Me")) {
                Debug.Log("Button has been clicked");
        }

        if (GUI.RepeatButton (Rect (25, 300, 100, 30), "Click and Hold")) {
                Debug.Log("The repeat button is being pressed");
        }
}
```

Save the script and playtest. Compare the action of the two buttons and notice that the repeat button's Debug.Log statement is printed to the Console every frame as long as the repeat button is held.

Screen

The left side of the Game view is getting crowded with controls, so before adding more controls, you will move the buttons to the right side. Unity provides you with a handy Screen class that can provide you with information such as screen resolution and size, or whether the mouse cursor is shown or hidden. In this example you will use the Screen.width and Screen.height variables to help with GUI control placement.

To move the button to the upper right corner, edit its position in the GUIButtons script to the following:

```
if (GUI.Button (Rect (Screen.width - 100, 0, 100, 30), "Click Me")) {
```

Since the button position coordinates coincide with its upper left corner, you have to subtract the width of the button. Otherwise, its left side would begin on the last pixel of the right side of the screen.

Move the repeat button beneath it by editing its position in the GUIButtons script to the following:

```
if (GUI.RepeatButton (Rect (Screen.width - 100, 50, 100, 30), "Click and Hold")) {
```

Save the scene and playtest to see the new button positions.

Likewise you can reposition the player instructions in the label to the center of the screen by editing its code in the GUIScript script as follows:

```
GUI.Label(Rect(Screen.width/2, Screen.height/2, 250, 25), "Press C to crouch or Space to jump");
```

If you save and playtest now, the label will appear too low and too far to the right. This is again because the upper left corner of the label is what is positioned at the (Screen.width/2, Screen.height/2) coordinates. You can manage this as you did the buttons, but to maintain centering this time, subtract half the respective width and height of the label. The line of code should now look like this:

```
GUI.Label(Rect(Screen.width/2 - 125, Screen.height/2 - 12.5, 250, 25), "Press C to crouch or Space to jump");
```

Save the script, save the scene, and playtest to see the fading message appear in the center of the screen.

Toolbar

A toolbar is a collective row of buttons, where only one of the buttons can be selected at a time.

In the GUIButtons script, edit the code to the following:

```
#pragma strict

private var toolbarSelectedButton = 0;
private var toolbarButtonNames : String[] = ["TB Button 1", "TB Button 2", "TB Button 3"];

function OnGUI () {
            if (GUI.Button (Rect (Screen.width - 100, 0, 100, 30), "Click Me")) {
            Debug.Log("Button has been clicked");
    }

    if (GUI.RepeatButton (Rect (Screen.width - 100, 50, 100, 30), "Click and Hold")) {
            Debug.Log("The repeat button is being pressed");
    }
    toolbarSelectedButton = GUI.Toolbar (Rect (25, 25, 250, 30), toolbarSelectedButton,
toolbarButtonNames);
}
```

Breaking this down:

> (1)   `private var toolbarSelectedButton = 0;`

1. Declare a private variable `toolbarSelectedButton` to designate which button will be in the selected state when the toolbar is created. As before, computers start counting at 0 instead of one, so this line of code designates that the first button will be selected.

> (2)   `private var toolbarButtonNames : String[] = ["TB Button 1", "TB Button 2",`
> `"TB Button 3"];`

2. Declare a reference variable `toolbarButtonNames` that will hold a String type array, followed by the assignment of the actual name strings in quotations. The square brackets "[]" represent an array. The number of name strings simultaneously designates the number of buttons to be created within the toolbar.

> (3)   `toolbarSelectedButton = GUI.Toolbar (Rect (25, 25, 250, 30),`
> `toolbarSelectedButton, toolbarButtonNames);`

3. The `toolbarSelectedButton` variable holds the state of the currently selected button along with the toolbar initiation code. For a toolbar, the pattern here is: position, toolbar size, the selected button, then the button names.

Save the script, save the scene, and playtest. Notice that the first button is initially in a selected state, and that you cannot select more than one button at a time.

Toggle

The toggle switch takes a slightly different pattern in its initiation because it always holds a boolean value representing whether it is "on" or "off." In the Project panel Assets ➤ Scripts folder create a new script named GUIToggleAndSliders. Open it in MonoDevelop and edit the code to the following:

```
#pragma strict

var toggle : boolean = false;

function OnGUI () {
        toggle = GUI.Toggle (Rect (Screen.width - 100, Screen.height - 100, 100, 30), toggle,
"Toggle switch");
        Debug.Log(toggle);
}
```

This breaks down as follows:

> (1)   var toggle : boolean = false;

1. Declare a private boolean variable toggle to hold the current state of the toggle switch.

> (2)   toggle = GUI.Toggle (Rect (Screen.width - 100, Screen.height - 100, 100, 30), toggle, "Toggle switch");

2. You've seen this code configuration earlier with TextField and TextArea, where the variable is assigned the value of the control that is created all in one line. The pattern for a toggle is: position, size, toggle state, and the string of text to appear next to the toggle switch.

> (3)   Debug.Log(toggle);

3. Display the current state of the toggle switch in the Console.

Save the script, attach it to the GUI game object and playtest. As you select and deselect the toggle, the corresponding state of the toggle switch is printed to the Console with each frame.

Sliders

Sliders have a sliding knob that can be moved from one end of the slider to the other along the scale you assign it, where the ends of the slider represent the minimum and maximum values of the scale. Sliders can be oriented horizontally or vertically.

To create sample horizontal and vertical sliders, in MonoDevelop edit the GUIToggleAndSliders script's code as follows:

```
#pragma strict

var toggle : boolean = false;
var horizSlider : float = 0.0;
var vertSlider : float = 0.0;

function OnGUI () {
        toggle = GUI.Toggle (Rect (Screen.width - 100, Screen.height - 100, 100, 30), toggle,
"Toggle switch");
        Debug.Log(toggle);
        horizSlider = GUI.HorizontalSlider (Rect (Screen.width/2, 25, 100, 30), horizSlider, 0.0, 10.0);
        Debug.Log(horizSlider);
        vertSlider = GUI.VerticalSlider (Rect (Screen.width/2, 50, 100, 30), vertSlider, 0.0, 10.0);
        Debug.Log(vertSlider);
}
```

This breaks down as follows:

```
(1)     var horizSlider : float = 0.0;
        var vertSlider : float = 0.0;
```

1. Declare a float type variable to hold the position of the horizontal and vertical slider knobs.

```
(2)     horizSlider = GUI.HorizontalSlider (Rect (Screen.width/2, 25, 100, 30),
horizSlider, 0.0, 10.0);
```

2. The float horizSlider will be assigned the new position of the slider and redraw the slider accordingly with each frame. The pattern here is: position, size, current value of the slider, minimum value, and maximum value.

```
(3)     Debug.Log(horizSlider);
```

3. Log the horizontal slider value to the Console.

```
(4)     vertSlider = GUI.VerticalSlider (Rect (Screen.width/2, 50, 100, 30),
vertSlider, 0.0, 10.0);
```

4. The vertical slider takes the same parameters as the horizontal slider, following the pattern of: position, size, current value of the slider, minimum value, and maximum value.

```
(5)     Debug.Log(vertSlider);
```

5. Log the vertical slider value to the Console.

Save the script, save the scene, and playtest to watch the horizontal and vertical slider values change when you move their respective knobs.

At this point the Game view is getting pretty crowded (Figure 11-4).

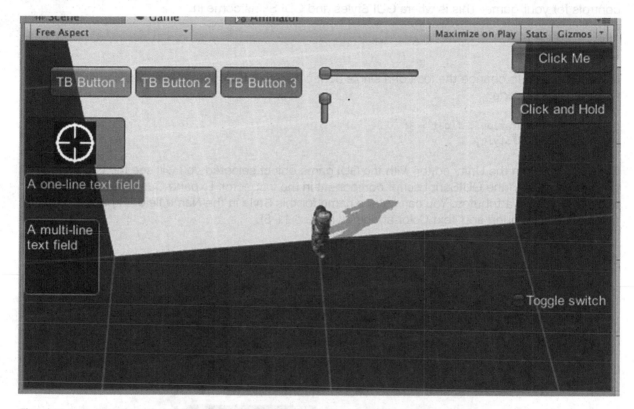

Figure 11-4. *Assorted sample controls in the Game view*

This is a great example of what not to do—too many controllers reduce the player's ability to see the game, and can detract from the gameplay experience when not implemented properly. The use of game controls should be determined in the game design phase, long before you sit down to the computer. Whether you use controls for maps, inventories, scores, ammo, health, or whatever information you would like to impart to the player, be as efficient as possible.

In this example, the only control that is pertinent to the Obstacle Course prototype is the fading label. You could have put the code for all of the sample controllers into one script, but creating a few helps keep your sample code organized and now allows you to select the GUI game object and disable all of the scripts except the GUIScript. Save the scene and playtest, and only the fading label remains.

Unity provides a broad range of GUI methods from GUI.SelectionGrid, which functions as a multirow toolbar for GUI.changed to quickly test if the reader has interacted with any of the controls. Unity also has more advanced controls such as compound controls, scroll views, and windows. If your GUI requires something more complex, you can always dig into the documentation and see what more Unity has to assist you.

Customizing Controls

Game design addresses both the function and look of your game. So far you've dealt with the function and placement of GUI controls, but you will also want to customize the appearance of the controls for your game. This is where GUI Styles and GUI Skins come in.

GUI Styles

Use a GUI Style to change the look of a single control. Open GUIScript in Monodevelop and add the following line of code:

```
public var fadeDuration : float = 3;
var guiStyle : GUIStyle;
```

Save the script. In the Unity editor, with the GUI game object selected you will see the Gui Style property appear in the GUIScript script component in the Inspector. Expand Custom Gui Style to show the custom attributes. You can enter a name for this Style in the Name field. Expand Normal to show the Background and Text Color attributes (Figure 11-5).

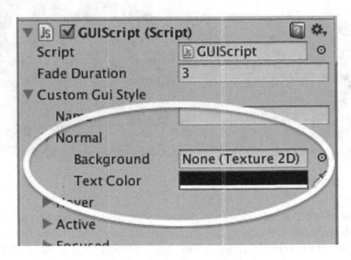

Figure 11-5. Custom Gui Style property in the GUIScript script component in the Inspector

Choose a new Text Color. For the Style to be applied to the fading label, you will have to edit GUIScript and pass in the guiStyle argument to GUI.Label as follows:

```
GUI.Label(Rect(Screen.width/2 - 125, Screen.height/2 - 12.5, 250, 25), "Press C to crouch or Space to jump", guiStyle);
```

Save the script and play. This time the instructions for the player in the GUI label will appear in the new text color.

GUI Skins

You could create a GUI Style for each control in your game. If you have a more complex game with many controls, using a GUI Skin may be a more efficient method for customization. A GUI Skin is a set of styles that will be applied to all of the controls.

Since a skin is an asset, you'll create it from the Project panel by selecting Create ➤ GUISkin and naming it myGUISkin. In the Inspector you'll find a list of GUI controls (Figure 11-6), each of which can be expanded to reveal its customizable attributes. Remember to keep your project organized, so take a moment to create a new folder named MyGUISkins, then drag and drop the myGUISkin asset into it.

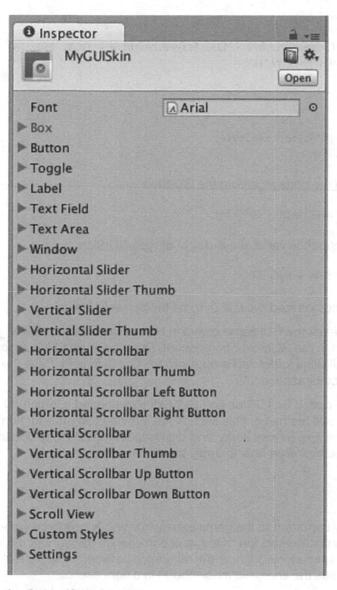

Figure 11-6. GUI Skin properties displayed in the Inspector

In the Inspector, expand the Label ➤ Normal property and change the text color to a different color than what you used with the GUI Style in the previous example. In MonoDevelop, edit GUIScript as follows:

```
#pragma strict

public var fadeDuration : float = 3;
var guiStyle : GUIStyle;
var myGuiSkin : GUISkin;

function OnGUI() {
        GUI.skin = myGuiSkin;
        ...
        GUI.Label(Rect(Screen.width/2 - 125, Screen.height/2 - 12.5, 250, 25), "Press C to
crouch or Space to jump", guiStyle);
}
```

Breaking this down:

> (1)   var guiStyle : GUIStyle;
> guiStyle

1. First, delete the code regarding the GUIStyle.

> (2)   var myGuiSkin : GUISkin;

2. Declare a reference variable myGuiSkin of type GUISkin.

> (3)   GUI.skin = myGuiSkin;

3. Assign the customized myGuiSkin to be the active GUI.skin.

Save the script then select the GUI game object in Hierarchy. In the Inspector, you will see a Gui Skin property has appeared in the GUIScript component. Drag the myGUISkin asset from the Project panel Assets ➤ MyGUISkins folder and drop it into the Gui Skin field. Save the scene and playtest to see the new text font color applied.

You can even mix and match GUI Styles and GUI Skins as needed. Getting the details just right is important to the quality of the game. This section has provided an introduction to GUI controls and how to customize them. Experiment away, and dig deeper into the Unity documentation for more advanced tools and examples on how to apply them. Have fun!

Audio

Audio is tremendously important to the game experience and is used in a variety of ways to great effect. The background music sets the mood, and can change throughout a game to reflect various situations the player experiences, such as the difference between suspenseful music to indicate impending danger versus the energetic music found in a fight scene.

It can also give the player cues, such as imparting a rising sense of urgency by increasing the tempo of the music. Character and NPC dialog gives hints and directives to the player in keeping with the storyline of the game. Even in simple arcade-like games, small bits of sound that end in a rising pitch provide positive reinforcement to the player, while a lowering of pitch reinforces a negative event or action.

The absence of sound is also effectively used at times. For example, it is used in shooter games to maintain a sense of realism when a nearby flash-bang detonation is followed by silence, then a realistic ear-ringing whine that fades away as the normal game sounds fade in while the player character recovers.

Sound effects are used in conjunction with the environment and action of the game. In realistic-themed games you will find ambient background noise, whether from crickets at night, background traffic, nearby running machinery, or passing NPCs. More specific sound effects to the game action would be the engine of the vehicle being driven revving, the crunch and splat of impacts in a fight scene, or the sound of footsteps while the player character is in motion.

Some games are based on sound as primary gameplay, as in such popular games as *Simon* and *Guitar Hero*. The game *Lurking* utilizes a novel and creepy application of sound where the sound waves from the player's actions (in white) and the enemies (in red) illuminate the game world (Figure 11-7). Take a moment to check out the trailer at www.lurking-game.com for an excellent example of sound used both to set the mood of the game and to drive the actual gameplay.

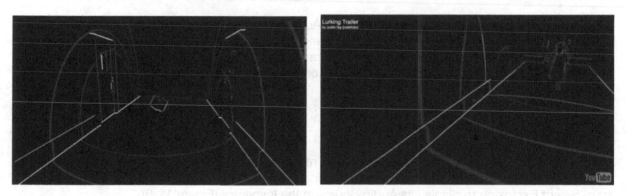

Figure 11-7. Images from the Lurking trailer, *www.lurking-game.com*

Audio Listener

Just as the Main Camera is the eyes of the game, the Audio Listener component is the ears. When you create a new scene, the Audio Listener is added to the Main Camera by default. In the Hierarchy, select Free Look Camera Rig ➤ Pivot ➤ Main Camera. In the Inspector you will find the Audio Listener Component. If you try to expand the Audio Listener, nothing happens because it has no properties (Figure 11-8).

Figure 11-8. The Audio Listener component has no properties to display in the Inspector

It works as-is to receive or "hear" input from any Audio Sources in the game scene, then play the sound through the game platform speakers. Depending on the game needs, the Audio Listener might instead be attached to the main player character or some other game object, but then it must be removed from the Main Camera because only one Audio Listener component can be present in each scene.

Audio Source

The Audio Source is the game object component responsible for playing the sound. In the Project panel open the Assets ➤ Prefabs folder and expand the Land Mine prefab to reveal the Explosion icon. Select Explosion to display its Audio Source in the Inspector (Figure 11-9).

Figure 11-9. Explosion Audio Source component in the Inspector

Unlike the Audio Listener, you can have any number of Audio Sources in your game. Sound performance, like game performance, is limited by the processing power of the target platform. as well as its specific sound processing and speaker capabilities.

The Audio Source functions like a speaker in the game where the **Audio Clip** is the actual sound file the Audio Source plays. Scripting can be used to adjust any properties in the Audio Source component, including changing the audio clips to be played.

Mute is a simple enabled/disabled toggle for muting the sound. The various **Bypass** effects are Pro-version only. Audio Sources with **Play On Wake** enabled will begin playing when the game object with audio source component is created. Audio can be **looped** just like animation clips, where the audio clip restarts each time it finishes playing all the way through.

Assigning a **priority** allows Unity to adjust to the audio capability of the platform. Lower-priority sounds will be swapped out for higher-priority sounds if the performance limitations are exceeded. In Unity, 0 is the most important.

The relative loudness of the sound clip is controlled with the **volume** property that uses a 0 to 1 scale indicating 0% to 100% of volume, while **pitch** controls the frequency of the sound waveform, where a higher pitch corresponds to a higher key on the musical scale.

You can choose between **2D** and **3D** sound, which in turn have various adjustable properties. 2D sound is best for audio such as background music that plays uniformly regardless of where the player is in the game world. 3D sounds vary in relation to the player's position.

3D vs. 2D Sound Properties

Whether or not an audio clip is 2D or 3D depends upon its import settings. 3D audio refers to sound in the 3D game world. Audio Sources can be attached to game objects throughout the game scene. The volume of 3D sound varies with the distance and movement of the Audio Listener.

2D sound plays at the same volume regardless of the position of the Audio Listener. Its only property, **Pan**, controls the volume between two speakers, where the default 0 means the two speakers play the sound at equal volumes. Moving the slider left increases the volume out of the left speaker, while moving the slider to the right increases the volume out of the right speaker (Figure 11-10).

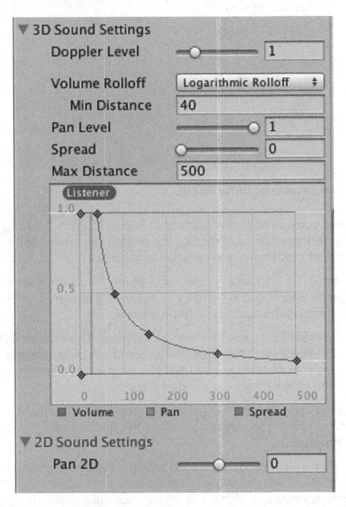

Figure 11-10. 3D and 2D Sound Setting properties in the Inspector

3D sound can be fine-tuned via the 3D Sound Settings properties. The **Doppler Level** distorts the sound based on movement to create a Doppler-like effect where the sound is of a higher pitch when moving towards the sound source and lower when moving away from the sound source.

3D sound acts as if it is emitted from a specific location in the game world, such that the volume is loudest at the source and diminishes as one moves away. The **Volume Rolloff** property determines the rate at which the sound diminishes with distance. The default is Logarithmic, as it is in the real world. You also have a Linear option and a Custom option.

Min Distance is the minimum distance from the audio source where the volume reaches 100%. 3D sound is managed by the Unity game engine according to the **Pan Level**, where 0 is essentially 2D sound and 1 is fully 3D. **Spread** is a more advanced audio setting that has to do with speaker systems. **Max Distance** is the maximum distance at which the change in sound due to volume rolloff ends. Typically this is also the farthest point at which you can still pick up any sound from the source.

Audio Clip

The source audio files are the audio clips, regardless of file type. Unity supports `.aif`, `.wav`, `.mp3`, and `.ogg` formats. You already have one in your project within the Land Mine prefab (Figure 11-11).

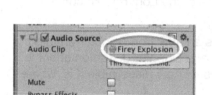

Figure 11-11. Firey Explosion audio clip in the Land Mine prefab Audio Source component and its properties

Audio Settings

There are audio settings that affect sound for the entire project. You can access these settings in the Audio Manager from the Unity Editor top menu by selecting Edit ➤ Project Settings ➤ Audio, and the Audio Manager appears in the Inspector (Figure 11-12).

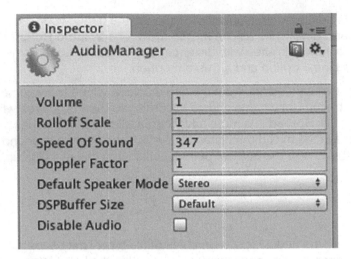

Figure 11-12. Project-wide audio settings handled by the AudioManager

The volume setting of the Audio Source component allows you to set its relative volume. The AudioManager **Volume** property controls the overall volume of all sounds that are playing.

For 3D audio, the Volume Rolloff allows you to choose between Linear, Logarithmic, and Custom. **Rolloff Scale** in the AudioManager is where you can adjust the shape of the Logarithmic curve to affect the rate of rolloff.

Speed of Sound defaults to the speed of sound at sea level and has an affect on Doppler-enabled sounds. The Audio Source's Doppler Level property sets how much of a Doppler distortion effect is applied to an audio clip, while the AudioManager's **Doppler Factor** sets how discernible it is, where 0 is completely turned off and 1 is the most audible.

Default Speaker Mode sets the number of channels available and defaults to 2 for stereo speakers.

The **DSPBuffer Size** is best left alone, as it has to do with how the CPU processes the aggregate sound files, and is an advanced topic beyond the scope of this book.

Audio Testing

At the top of the Scene view, you'll find a button with a speaker on it that represents the Audio Preview mode (Figure 11-13). Rather than having to playtest the game in order to test the game audio, you can simply toggle on the Audio Preview mode and move the scene camera around the game world.

Figure 11-13. Audio Preview toggle in the Scene view

Adding Audio to the Obstacle Course

Before you can add audio to the Obstacle Course prototype, you'll need to download a few more free assets from the Asset Store. In the Unity editor top menu select Window ➤ Asset Store. Search for "Free music pack" to find the sample audio pack by Alchemy Studio (Figure 11-14). Click the blue Download button, then click Import when prompted.

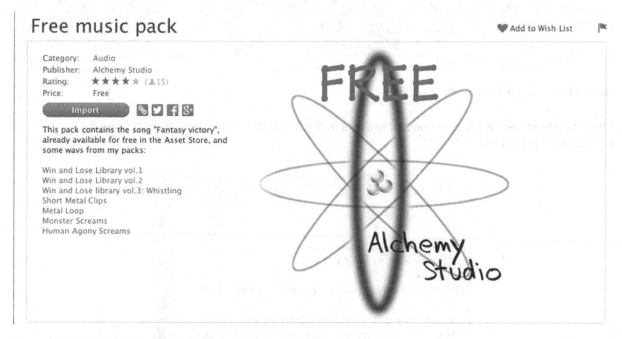

Figure 11-14. Free music pack in the Unity Asset Store

First, keep your project organized. In the Project panel select the Assets folder, then Create ➤ Folder, and name it Audio. Move the Free Pack folder that you just imported into the Audio folder then select it to see its contents.

Permission and Credits

When using assets from the Asset Store in your game, always take a look at any Readme files to see if there are any requirements or limitations (Figure 11-15). A requirement might be to list the asset creator in the credits, while a limitation would be something like you cannot sell or resell an asset that you download whether it is free or purchased.

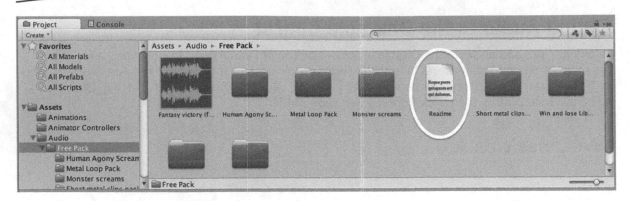

Figure 11-15. Readme file in the Free Pack folder

Click the Readme file once to see its contents in the Inspector, or double-click to open it in MonoDevelop (Figure 11-16).

Figure 11-16. Contents of the Readme file displayed in the Inspector

First is a thank-you, along with an invitation to rate and comment on this asset in the Asset Store. Feedback is important for knowing what people want and especially for helping anyone with any problems they might have with the asset, including identifying new bugs. You'll want feedback on your games, too, so take the time to provide the same.

Next is a request for an email regarding how you are using the asset, and the information to be included in the credits. It is fun to know how your work is being used, and personally fulfilling to know that people like the product that you put so much effort into.

Consider the contributors to the Asset Store as your extended team. Matteo Bosi of Alchemy Studio graciously gave permission for us to use this pack for this project. Drop a quick email to Matteo, introduce yourself, and let him know you are using his free pack for your prototype. Make this a habit, and in no time you'll have new friends from all over the world that love making games, too. The game development community is very supportive and understanding of the trials and tribulations of the game development process. They will help you out, cheer you on, and celebrate along with you when you publish your game. Be sure to share the love by reciprocating.

Keep reading the Readme file, and you'll find a link for more sound assets by Alchemy Studio and where you can listen to a sample before importing to your project. This is common practice, as you will recall from the sample videos of the Alien and Spartan King animation clips, and saves you from having to import everything just to test it out.

Music

Music is used in a variety of ways, including in the background and in response to game play. You will use scripts to guide the behavior of the audio effect for just about everything that will have more complex behavior than Play On Awake.

Background Music

First, start with the most simple example. In the Unity editor top menu, select GameObject ➤ Create Empty, name it Audio, and set its Transform position to (0, 0, 0). With the Audio game object selected in the Hierarchy, in the Inspector select Add Component ➤ Audio ➤ Audio Source.

In the Project panel where you have the Free Pack folder open, you'll see the Metal Loop folder. Open the folder to see four audio clips and another Readme file. You'll learn from the Readme file that the first clip is a complete music track, and the other three are the same track broken down into its intro, a middle section designed to be looped, and the end. Select the "Loop 16 - 145 bpm - complete" file to display its properties in the Inspector (Figure 11-17).

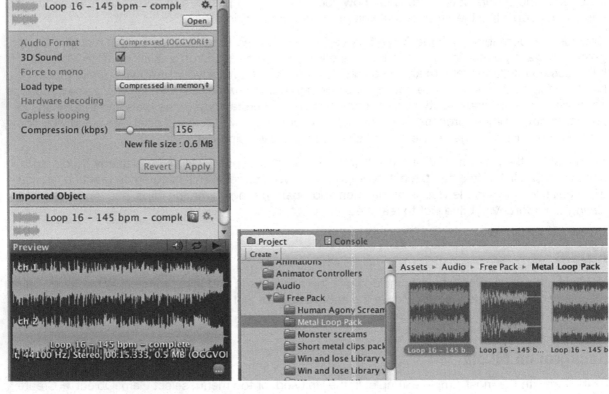

Figure 11-17. "Loop 16 - 145 bpm - complete" in the Project panel and the Inspector

Uncheck 3D sound so the volume will be uniform regardless of the player character's position or movement. Select the Audio game object in the Hierarchy, select "Apply" if prompted by an Unapplied import settings dialog, and drag the "Loop 16 - 145 bpm - complete" audio clip into the Audio Source component's Audio Clip property field. Play On Awake should be checked by default. If not, go ahead and check it. Since this is background music that you want to have play uniformly the entire time the game is being played, give it the highest priority of 0. Save the scene and play.

The audio clip plays from start to finish, then stops. Try checking the Loop property of the Audio Source and play again. Now the audio clip repeats, but not very smoothly between loops, which is where the partial audio clips come into play.

To have continuous background music, you want the intro to play once at the beginning followed by the loop section that will keep on looping, and for this behavior you'll need a script.

In the Project panel, select the Assets ➤ Scripts folder, then create a new script named BackgroundMusic. Open it in MonoDevelop and edit the code to the following:

```
#pragma strict

function Start () {
        PlayBackgroundMusic();
}
```

```
function PlayBackgroundMusic () {
        if(audio.isPlaying == true) {
                audio.Stop();
        }
                audio.Play();
}
```

This breaks down as follows:

```
        (1)     PlayBackgroundMusic();
```

1. Keep the `Start()` function uncluttered by putting the code block for playing the background music in its own function, `PlayBackgroundMusic()`, which is called from the `Start()` function.

```
        (2)     if(audio.isPlaying == true)
```

2. Check to see if the audio clip is already playing. It's good practice to add this test rather than simply using `audio.Play()` by itself, to avoid strange audio behavior.

```
        (3)     audio.Stop();
```

3. If the audio clip is already playing, stop it.

```
        (4)     audio.Play();
```

4. Start playing the audio clip from the beginning.

In the Inspector, uncheck Play On Awake and Loop in the Audio Source component. Attach the BackgroundMusic script to the Audio game object. Save the scene and playtest. At this point you have the script equivalent of Play On Awake.

Next change the audio clip by dragging the "Loop 16 - 145 bpm - intro" intro clip from the Project panel into the Audio Clip property field of the Audio Source component in the Inspector. Save and playtest, and now the intro clip plays immediately and only once.

In MonoDevelop, edit the BackgroundMusic script to:

```
#pragma strict

public var musicLoop : AudioClip;
private var introMusicIsPlaying : boolean = true;
private var looping : boolean = false;

function Start () {
        PlayBackgroundMusic();
}
```

```
function Update() {
        if (!audio.isPlaying) {
                introMusicIsPlaying = false;
        }
        if (!introMusicIsPlaying && !looping) {
                looping = true;
                LoopBackgroundMusic();
        }
}

function PlayBackgroundMusic () {
        if(audio.isPlaying == true) {
                audio.Stop();
        }

                audio.Play();
}

function LoopBackgroundMusic () {
                if(audio.isPlaying == true) {
                audio.Stop();
                }
                audio.clip = musicLoop;
                audio.loop = enabled;
                audio.Play();
}
```

Breaking this down:

```
(1)     public var musicLoop : AudioClip;
```

1. Declare a reference variable of type AudioClip to hold the second audio clip to be played, and name it musicLoop.

```
(2)     private var introMusicIsPlaying : boolean = true;
```

2. Declare a private boolean variable named introMusicIsPlaying and set it to true, since PlayBackgroundMusic() is called from the Start() function and will immediately begin playing the intro clip.

```
(3)     private var looping : boolean = false;
```

3. Declare a private boolean variable named looping and set it to false.

```
(4)     if (!audio.isPlaying)
```

4. In the Update() function, check to see when the intro clip is finished playing. Remember that ! means NOT, so this line of code can be read as "If the audio clip is not playing," which will be true when the intro clip is over.

```
(5)     introMusicIsPlaying = false;
```

5. Once the intro clip is through playing, toggle the `introMusicIsPlaying` boolean variable to `false`.

```
(6)      if (!introMusicIsPlaying && !looping)
```

6. If the intro music is not playing, and `looping` is still set to `false`, then it's time to switch audio clips.

```
(7)      LoopBackgroundMusic();
```

7. Call the `LoopBackgroundMusic()` function, which you will write next.

```
(8)      if(audio.isPlaying == true) {
                 audio.Stop();
         }
```

8. It is a good practice when changing audio clips to call the `audio.Stop()` function before changing out the audio clip.

```
(9)      audio.clip = musicLoop;
```

9. Switch the current audio clip to the audio clip referenced by `musicLoop`.

```
(10)     audio.loop = enabled;
```

10. Enable the Loop property of the Audio Source.

```
(11)     audio.Play();
```

11. Play the new audio clip.

In the Unity editor, assign the "Loop 16 - 145 bpm - loop" audio clip by dragging and dropping it into the Music Loop property field of the BackgroundMusic script component of the Audio game object. Save and playtest. Now the intro audio clip rolls seamlessly into the loop audio clip, which in turn loops for the duration.

Something isn't right here, however: as the player character progresses farther along the obstacle course, the music fades. This is because the audio clips' initial import settings are for 3D. In the Project panel, open the Assets ➤ Free Pack ➤ Metal Loop Pack, and select each audio clip to uncheck the 3D Sound property in the Inspector. If an Unapplied Import Settings dialog box appears, choose Apply. Save the scene, playtest, and now the background music plays continuously and uniformly, regardless of the player character's position along the obstacle course.

Event-Triggered Sound

One method to play a short clip in response to gameplay is with a trigger.

The Free Pack folder has a Fantasy Victory (free) audio clip. The player's successfully dodging the enemy drone and making it to the final platform of the elevated track marks successful completion of the obstacle course, so you'll play this audio clip when the player character makes it this far.

If you're thinking ahead to beginning with an empty game object, adding an Audio Source component, then dragging the Fantasy Victory (free) audio clip into the Audio Clip property, you would be right. Even better, Unity has a few handy shortcuts to save you those steps.

Drag and drop the Fantasy Victory (free) audio clip into the Hierarchy. Be sure to drop it between game objects, not on a game object (that would appear highlighted). The Fantasy Victory (free) game object will appear in the Hierarchy, with an Audio Source attached and the Fantasy Victory (free) audio clip already assigned to the Audio Clip property.

Drag the clip again into the Scene view, and notice that a green circle with a + symbol appears as you drag it over other game objects in the scene. If you drop the audio clip onto a game object, Unity will create an Audio Source component and attach it to the game object automatically. Be careful—if the game object already has an Audio Source with an assigned clip and you drop this one onto it, the new audio clip will replace the previously assigned audio clip. Don't actually drop Fantasy Victory (free) into the Scene view right now. If you already did, use the Remove Component option to delete it so you have only the first one, made up of a Fantasy Victory (free) game object with only Transform and Audio Source components.

Move this game object to a Transform position of (0, 11.5, 150), putting it centered at the top of the final ramp. If you were to playtest now, the clip will play immediately since Play On Awake is checked by default. Uncheck it in the Inspector. While still in the Inspector, select Add Component ➤ Physics ➤ Box Collider. Check IsTrigger, and change the values of Center to (0, 1, 0) and Size to (8, 2, 0.2).

You'll need a script to play the audio when the player comes into contact with this trigger collider, so in the Inspector select Add Component ➤ New Script and name it VictoryMusic, then click Create and Add. Recall that this method of creating a new script creates it in the Assets root folder. Keep your project organized by moving it to the Assets ➤ Scripts folder, then open it in MonoDevelop. Edit the code to the following:

```
#pragma strict

public var backgroundMusic : GameObject;

function OnTriggerEnter () {
        backgroundMusic.GetComponent(BackgroundMusic).PlayVictoryMusic();
}
```

You've seen this kind of code before. It breaks down as follows:

> (1)   `public var backgroundMusic : GameObject;`

1.   Declare a public reference variable backgroundMusic of type GameObject that will be used to hold a reference to the Audio game object.

> (2)   `function OnTriggerEnter ()`

2.   When the player character enters the collider volume, OnTriggerEnter() is called since the collider is set to IsTrigger.

> (3)   `backgroundMusic.GetComponent(BackgroundMusic).PlayVictoryMusic();`

3. Get a reference to the BackgroundMusic script component attached to the Audio game object and call the PlayVictoryMusic() function, which you will write next. Another approach would have been to stop the background music, then play the victory music audio clip using this game object and script, but since it is background music, for the sake of keeping your project organized it is a better practice to keep it contained by a single dedicated game object.

Save the script, then attach it to the Fantasy Victory (free) game object. Select the Fantasy Victory (free) game object in the Hierarchy, then drag the Audio game object from the Hierarchy into the Background Music field of the Victory Music script component.

In MonoDevelop, return to the BackgroundMusic script and add the following lines of code:

```
#pragma strict

public var musicLoop : AudioClip;
private var introMusicIsPlaying : boolean = true;
private var looping : boolean = false;
public var victoryMusic : AudioClip;

function Start () {
        PlayBackgroundMusic();
}

function Update() {

}

function PlayBackgroundMusic () {

}

function LoopBackgroundMusic () {

}

function PlayVictoryMusic () {
        if(audio.isPlaying == true) {
                audio.Stop();
        }
                audio.clip = victoryMusic;
                audio.Play();
}
```

Breaking this down:

```
(1)    public var victoryMusic : AudioClip;
```

1. Create a reference variable `victoryMusic` of type AudioClip. As a public variable, you can easily test different audio clips by dragging and dropping them into the Victory Music field in the Inspector.

```
(2)    function PlayVictoryMusic () {
```

2. Create a new `PlayVictoryMusic()` function.

```
(3)    if(audio.isPlaying == true) {
             audio.Stop();
       }
             audio.clip = victoryMusic;
             audio.Play();
```

3. These are the same steps you performed earlier for swapping out audio clips, only this time the new audio clip is the Fantasy Victory (free) audio clip.

Save the script. With the Audio game object selected in the Hierarchy, drag the Fantasy Victory (free) audio clip from the Assets ➤ Free Pack folder in the Project panel into the Victory Music field of the Background Music script component. Save the scene and save the project.

Run the player character around and you'll notice that when the player character enters the trigger volume, the audio clip plays, which is what you want, but you'll also notice if the player character runs away from the vicinity of the Fantasy Victory (free) game object, the music fades away. The audio clip is set to 3D sound, with the Volume Rolloff set to Logarithmic Rolloff.

Select the Fantasy Victory (free) clip in the Project panel, then in the Inspector uncheck 3D Sound, then Apply if prompted. Save the scene, playtest again, and now with 2D sound the music stays at the same volume regardless of the player character's movement. Sweet victory!

Sound Effects

The term *sound effect* generally applies to audio clips that are not music or spoken dialogue. Sound effects more commonly use 3D sound as they often correlate to specific game objects in the scene.

Open the Assets ➤ Sample Assets ➤ Vehicles ➤ Car ➤ Audio folder and find the Low Acceleration audio clip. Select it and confirm that the 3D Sound box is checked in the Inspector. Select the Enemy Drone game object in the Hierarchy, then move the cursor over to the Scene view and press F to bring the Enemy Drone game object into view.

Drag the Low Acceleration audio clip from the Project panel and drop it onto the Drone. An Audio Source component will be automatically created with the Low Acceleration file already assigned to the Audio Clip property when it appears in the Inspector. In the Scene view, the audio source gizmo consisting of a speaker symbol will also appear (Figure 11-18).

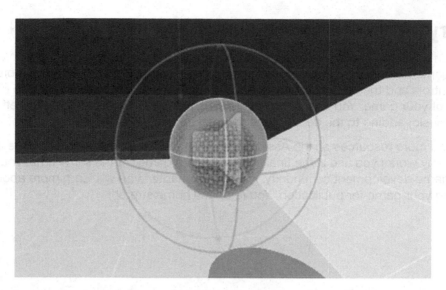

Figure 11-18. *The Drone game object's audio source gizmo in the Scene view*

In the Inspector, check Play On Awake and Loop. Set the Min Distance to 2 and the Max Distance to 20 in the 3D Sound Settings section.

For now, disable the background music by unchecking its Audio Source component on the Audio game object. Save the scene and playtest.

As the player approaches the final zone, you begin to hear the drone's audio. When the player enters the zone and the enemy drone begins moving, the volume increases as the drone gets closer. Since the Volume Rolloff property is set to its default of Logarithmic Rolloff, the volume increases at an accelerating rate the closer the drone gets. The enemy drone is definitely more intimidating with sound effects.

Right now, the Audio Listener is attached to the Main Camera child object of the Free Look Camera Rig - Pivot. Remember that you can only have one Audio Listener per scene, so find the Main Camera in the Hierarchy, then in the Inspector disable the Audio Listener component by unchecking the box near its name.

Back in the Hierarchy, find the Third Person Character Ragdoll and select it. In the Inspector, select Add Component ➤ Audio ➤ Audio Listener. Playtest again and you'll find that the sound of the drone is even better when it approaches because the player character gets much closer to the drone than the camera does.

Find the Audio game object in the Hierarchy and re-enable the Audio Source for the background music. Use the Volume setting in the Audio Source components to find the right balance between the background music and the special effects.

Each and every detail matters and makes the difference between a good game and a great game. The crackly audio for the laser sparks should emit from the same location as the sparks, not the laser source above the player. Adding a Doppler effect to the projectiles adds to the impression of their speed, and a "whoosh" heavy with bass tones lends the pendulums an impression of their heaviness.

Summary

Pat yourself on the back—you have covered the basics of UnityScript and are well on your way to becoming a game developer. You are able to communicate with the player and add more interactivity using GUI controls and the OnGUI() function, and you can customize these controls to conform with the look of your game. You also added audio in its many forms, including sound effects and background music, adding to the depth of the game experience.

You have found more resources on the Asset Store and have remembered to credit the asset creators with any works you use in the final version of your game. At the same time, you met new peers in the game development community. In the next chapter, you will learn more about testing and optimizing your game for publication. You're on the home stretch!

Chapter 12

Optimizing Your Game

Optimization is a broad subcategory of game development that can be its own career field, much like animation. In simple terms it is the process of improving the efficiency of game performance. It sounds simple, anyway.

Each target platform has limitations in terms of the processing power of its CPU (central processing unit) and GPU (graphics processing unit). The more detailed a scene, whether with a few highly detailed models or a great many less detailed moving parts, the higher the demand on the processors.

When the demand gets to be too much, game performance suffers: the player experiences long load times, lags and other glitchy gameplay, or worst of all, the game crashes. The **optimization** process is the series of decisions or tradeoffs made between maintaining game performance and the quality of the graphics.

Target Performance

Target performance is typically stated in terms of a desired frame rate or frames per second (fps). As discussed in Chapter 4, too low a frame rate and you lose the illusion of animated movement. While in general higher frame rates should result in a better-quality visual experience, more complex games requiring more processing per frame might run more smoothly at the lower end of the acceptable fps target range.

Consoles and PCs have much more powerful processors than mobile platforms, so let's examine games for mobile devices since they have the most limitations. Different mobile platforms have distinct capabilities, and different versions of mobile devices will vary as well, with older units generally having less memory and slower processors. You must decide early in the design phase what your target market within the platform will be, which will in turn guide the target frame rate you select.

The two most popular mobile platforms, Apple and Android, take different approaches. Apple is a closed-source operating system engineered by Apple that works on devices manufactured by Apple. Android is an open-source operating system engineered by Google and used by a number of different device manufacturers. When a newer version of an operating system is released, depending on its processing capability older devices may or may not be capable of supporting the newer operating system's features.

Apple generally has only a few iPhone or iPad devices on the market at any given time, and its users adopt operating system upgrades at a greater than 90% rate within a few months. Android users own devices from a number of different manufacturers that have different capabilities at any given time. With manufacturers adding new devices over time, while some users hold on to their older devices, you have a much broader range of capability within the Android mobile device category, especially when you consider that Android users have a less consistent adoption rate of newer versions of Android (Figure 12-1), older versions of which may or may not support certain features you would like in your game.

Version	Codename	API	Distribution
2.2	Froyo	8	0.8%
2.3.3 - 2.3.7	Gingerbread	10	14.9%
4.0.3 - 4.0.4	Ice Cream Sandwich	15	12.3%
4.1.x	Jelly Bean	16	29.0%
4.2.x		17	19.1%
4.3		18	10.3%
4.4	KitKat	19	13.6%

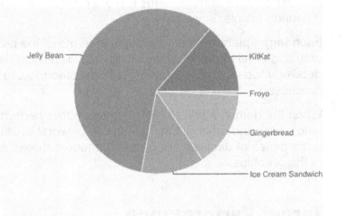

Data collected during a 7-day period ending on June 4, 2014.
Any versions with less than 0.1% distribution are not shown.

Figure 12-1. *Relative number of devices running on a given version of the Android platform*

You must take this information into consideration depending upon how much of the Android mobile device market you wish to target, which in turn guides where you will set your target performance frame rate. All of this decision making takes place early on in the game design phase.

Tracking Your Target

In the Unity editor, run the Obstacle Course scene. In the Game View top menu, you will find a Stats button. Click this and an overlay of various performance statistics will appear, including the FPS (Figure 12-2).

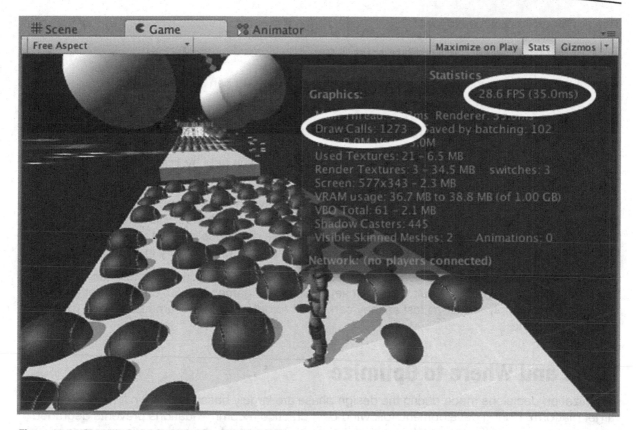

Figure 12-2. Stats displayed in the Unity editor Game View

The **Draw Calls** stat goes into even more detail, indicating the number of things that the CPU needs to render. It is important to understand that one game object may be rendered multiple times per frame for each of the effects applied to it, such as pixel lights, shadows, and reflections. Using less of these things by applying them only where they make a significant contribution to the look of the game reduces draw calls, which means less work for the CPU.

You can set the target frame rate using a simple script. In the Project panel, open the Assets ➤ Scripts folder and create a new script named SetTargetFrameRate. Open it in MonoDevelop and edit the code to the following:

```
#pragma strict

public var frameRate : int = 50;

function Awake () {
      Application.targetFrameRate = frameRate;
}
```

This code breaks down as follows:

```
(1)     public var frameRate : int = 50;
```

1. Declare a public variable frameRate of type int so you can adjust it from the Inspector.

```
(2)     Application.targetFrameRate = frameRate;
```

2. Set the Application class targetFrameRate to the value held by frameRate.

Save the script. In the Unity Editor top menu, select Game Object ➤ Create Empty and name it TargetFrameRate. Attach the SetTargetFrameRate script, save the scene, and play. Notice that the FPS doesn't hold at precisely 50 and might even appear to have no effect. This is because the target frame rate is not an absolute limit. To see a more noticeable difference in the stats, change the Frame Rate to 25, play again, and you'll see the FPS in the stats window vary in a range closer to 25.

As you review the Application.targetFrameRate documentation in the Scripting reference, you'll see that setting it to –1 is a default value that sets web player games to a 50–60 fps target and tells standalones to simply render as fast as they can. Don't forget to change Frame Rate back to 50 when you're done.

When and Where to Optimize

Optimization decisions made during the design phase are largely based on known limitations of the target platform. During development, following best practice recommendations prevents degraded performance from inefficient development techniques. Beyond that, the optimization process becomes very dynamic in response to the unique characteristics of the game as the myriad details that can affect performance come together.

Design Phase

More decisions than just choosing the target frame rate occur in the design phase. When considering the game art, the target platform's capabilities come into play. A general practice is not to use any more vertices for a model than is necessary, but the CPU rendering limitation is based on everything within the scene, including other factors such as the use of color, light, and shadows, not just one model or another. Refer to the documentation of the target platform for specifics.

Mobile devices generally can't handle more than 100,000 vertices, while PCs are more on the order of several million. You might choose a much lower level of background detail for a mobile game than you would for a PC-based game to preserve the detail of your primary game object models.

Another mobile device limitation is in file size for downloading. Incorporating the reuse of models, textures, and materials into the game design helps to keep the overall file size down.

Development Phase

Observing the time-honored maxim "If it ain't broke, don't fix it," remember that the purpose of optimization is to maintain the level of game performance you are targeting. When your game performs at this level from start to finish, you are done!

The visual impact on the player is a significant contributor to the game experience, which is why the tools for game graphics get down to the per-pixel level and require multiple renders to incorporate every last detail of light, reflections, shadows, and so forth. Visual graphics aren't the only factors that can impede game performance. Physics, animation, audio, and more can cause performance bottlenecks, too.

As you construct the game and conduct iterative testing, bottlenecks may occur under noticeable conditions of gameplay, such as when a complex model comes into view, during a particular animation sequence, or with a high-emission-rate particle system, and they are best addressed directly.

If the cause of a bottleneck isn't so obvious, Unity has a variety of tools to help you identify it. The Editor Profiler is a fantastic tool for evaluating your game both in the Editor or on a test device, but it is only available in the Pro version. Built-in profilers are available for iOS and Android. Nevertheless, you can still obtain helpful information about your game from the Build Log.

Creating a Build Log

In the Unity editor top menu, select File ➤ Build Settings (Figure 12-3). Drag the Obstacle Course scene from Project panel and drop it into the Scenes in Build window. Make sure PC, Mac & Linux Standalone is selected in the Platform window for Unity to build the correct file type for the platform you are targeting. Click Build, then choose where you would like the file saved when prompted and click Save.

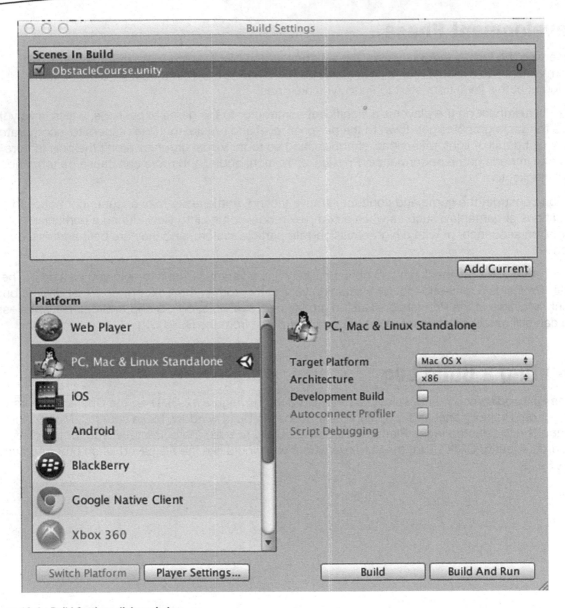

Figure 12-3. Build Settings dialog window

When Unity is finished building the game, you can access the Build Log by selecting the Console tab in the Project panel. Find the icon for the drop-down menu in the upper right corner, then select Open Editor Log (Figure 12-4).

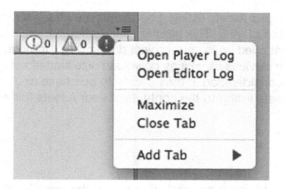

Figure 12-4. Console drop-down menu

The Build Log will appear in the Console app window. Among other information, you can find a listing of asset types that make up your game along with their relative size (Figure 12-5).

```
Textures      12.1 mb        42.5%
Meshes        1.6 mb         5.7%
Animations    1.6 mb         5.7%
Sounds        5.1 mb         18.1%
Shaders       381.4 kb       1.3%
Other Assets  412.6 kb       1.4%
Levels        2.5 mb         8.9%
Scripts       447.4 kb       1.5%
Included DLLs 4.1 mb         14.3%
File headers  166.1 kb       0.6%
Complete size 28.5 mb        100.0%

Used Assets, sorted by uncompressed size:
 4.0 mb          14.0% Assets/Sample Assets/Sample Scenes/Textures/
gui_touchZone_background.png
 2.2 mb          7.8% Assets/Audio/Free Pack/Metal Loop Pack/Loop 16 - 145 bpm - intro.wav
 2.2 mb          7.8% Assets/Audio/Free Pack/Metal Loop Pack/Loop 16 - 145 bpm - loop.wav
 1.3 mb          4.7% Assets/Standard Assets/Third Person Character/Textures/ethan_nrm.psd
 1.3 mb          4.7% Assets/Standard Assets/Third Person Character/Textures/ethan_dff.png
 881.0 kb        3.0% Assets/Standard Assets/Third Person Character/Models/Ethan.fbx
 682.8 kb        2.3% Assets/zombie_lowres.fbm/ZombieLowRes_Texture_2k.jpg
 682.8 kb        2.3% Assets/Sample Assets/Prototyping/Textures/prototype_white_dff.png
 682.8 kb        2.3% Assets/Sample Assets/Prototyping/Textures/prototype_green_dff.png
 682.8 kb        2.3% Assets/Sample Assets/Prototyping/Textures/prototype_blue_dff.png
 682.8 kb        2.3% Assets/Sample Assets/Prototyping/Textures/prototype_black_dff.png
 498.4 kb        1.7% Assets/Sample Assets/Prototyping/Models/prototype_floor.fbx
 398.4 kb        1.4% Assets/Sample Assets/Audio/Explosions/Firey Explosion.wav
 365.3 kb        1.3% Assets/Standard Assets/Third Person Character/Animation/Stand Turn.fbx
 341.4 kb        1.2% Assets/Sample Assets/Environment/Skyboxes/Textures/MoonShine/
```

Figure 12-5. Information displayed in the Build Log

Underneath you will find a Used Assets listing. Load times are affected by the size, and game players want to get straight to playing. This means optimization can be implemented here by removing unused assets that piled up in your project during development. Mobile users have greater memory constraints on their devices as well as download size limitations designated by their service providers, so app size is a consideration in their choice to purchase or download your game. By comparing the Used Assets listing to the contents of your Assets folder, you can safely remove any unused assets.

Scripts

Script optimization has been touched on lightly throughout the book in references to good coding practices, efficient code, and refactoring. There are a variety of techniques you can implement to optimize your code. You can incorporate some of these into your standard coding practices, while other examples demonstrate different approaches you might take while optimizing until you achieve target performance.

Static Typing and #pragma strict

One such practice you have been following consistently but it bears more explanation now.

MonoDevelop created every script for you beginning with the line #pragma strict. This line tells the compiler to interpret the following code "strictly," which in turn forces you to use static typing or else a compiler error is thrown.

Static typing refers to the typing of variables when you declare them. In the following line of code, you explicitly declared myVariable to be of type int:

```
var myVariable : int = 2;
```

You could alternatively declare the variable as follows:

```
var myVariable = 2;
```

Unity automatically converts this to statically typed code using a method called **type inference**. While this capability allows for the writing of simpler code, if the variable cannot be type-inferred Unity will rely on dynamic typing.

In **dynamic typing**, Unity has to figure out what the variable type is based on the value assigned to it. "Figuring out" takes time, and taking time affects game performance. Sticking with static typing helps performance, while #pragma strict helps to make sure that you do.

Caching Component Lookups

This scripting technique is particularly effective for scripts that are used frequently, but the tradeoff is that it takes a little more code. The GetComponent() function is an example of a **lookup**. Finding the component in the game object takes time and affects performance. The idea here is to look up a reference once, then **cache** or store the reference in a private variable to be available for use in the script later. In other words, avoid using GetComponent() in the Update() or FixedUpdate() functions where possible. You have used this technique in your GoRagdoll script:

```
#pragma strict

private var childRigidBodies : Rigidbody[];
private var childColliders : Collider[];
public var invincible : boolean = false;

function Start ()
     {
             childRigidBodies = gameObject.GetComponentsInChildren.<Rigidbody>();
             childColliders = gameObject.GetComponentsInChildren.<Collider>();
     }
...
```

The ragdoll rigidbodies and colliders were found with the GetComponentsInChildren() function lookup, then assigned to their respective arrays in the Start() function.

More Scripting Optimization Alternatives

Anywhere you can reduce or avoid frame-by-frame computations improves performance. Some of these are more advanced methods not covered in detail here, but you can explore them in more depth when pertinent to a particular project.

Use Triggers

In the LaunchProjectile script, you reduced the number of projectile game objects that Unity has to track on by using the Destroy() function to remove each projectile 2 seconds after it was instantiated:

```
Destroy(projectileInstance, 2);
```

While this is definitely an improvement from letting the projectile clones pile up, Unity still has to track each object and check its lifespan until it reaches 2 seconds. One alternative solution to the Destroy() function would be to use a trigger instead. First, comment out this line of code.

In your Obstacle Course scene, create a Cube game object and name it DestroyProjectileTrigger. Set its Transform position to (−12, 10.5, 47) and its scale to (1, 3, 10). Remove the Mesh Filter and Mesh Renderer components so you have a simple Box Collider. Check Is Trigger in the Box Collider component.

In the Project panel Assets ➤ Scripts folder, create a new script named DestroyProjectile and open it in MonoDevelop. Edit the code as follows:

```
#pragma strict

function OnTriggerEnter(other : Collider) {
        Destroy(other.gameObject);
}
```

Attach the script to the DestroyProjectileTrigger game object and save the scene. Play and watch the projectiles disappear as they enter the trigger volume. Behind the scenes, Unity instantiates the game object and the physics engine handles the movement as before, but now Unity has no more calculations to do with the game object until it enters the trigger volume.

Placing the trigger volume right next to the elevated track will minimize the life span of the projectile, gaining more efficiency in game performance. Change the Transform position to (–4, 10.5, 47) and play.

The projectiles are disappearing at the far edge of the track, but the tracer trail that is still over the track blinks out instantly, which doesn't look as good as it did when flowing all the way across. This is an example of the tradeoffs involved in optimization. Which is more important, the visual effect of the tracer or the efficiency gained by having the trigger volume so close to the elevated track? You decide.

Also, from a gameplay point of view, what happens if the player character were to run or jump into it? Uh oh—not good. You know from the KillOnTrigger script how to check the identity of other, so you can implement a solution if you choose to keep the trigger volume within reach of the player character:

```
#pragma strict

function OnTriggerEnter(other : Collider) {
        if (other.gameObject.name == "Projectile")
        {
                Destroy(other.gameObject);;
        }
}
```

You might wonder why the player would jump off the side in the first place. It might be accidental, it might be they are exploring, or it might be just for the heck of it. As you develop your games, you must consider what they can do in addition to what they are "supposed" to do and take appropriate steps to eliminate bugs as you just did here.

Object Pooling

You will learn more advanced solutions as you continue to build your programming skills. **Object pooling** takes optimizing the projectile prefabs a step further. Instantiating and destroying objects also has a notable computational overhead. Instead of instantiating and destroying game objects over and over, an array of the game object prefabs is created as a "pool" to be drawn from as needed, then returned to when no longer in use.

Coroutines

A **coroutine** can suspend its execution in one frame, then pick up and continue executing the next frame, over any length of frames. When you call another function from within Update() or FixedUpdate() functions, the function you call is run from start to finish each frame. At a 60fps frame rate, this means the function is also called and executed 60 times per second. Often you don't need a function called *every* frame, though you would like it run periodically. In comparison, a function called every tenth of a second, which is still plenty fast for many game tasks, is called six times less at 10 calls per second. This significant increase in efficiency can be achieved using coroutines.

Mecanim Optimization Tips

As with scripts, Unity's Scripting Reference provides general guidelines for making your Mecanim animations more efficient (Table 12-1). Most of these go beyond the degree of difficulty covered in this book, but having this information available can help you with character design whether you are creating them yourself or working with an artist.

- Use hashes instead of strings to query the Animator.

- Implement a small AI Layer to control the Animator. You can make it provide simple callbacks for OnStateChange, onTransitionBegin, and so forth.

- Use State tags to easily match your AI state machine to the Mecanim state machine.

- Use additional curves to simulate Events.

- Use additional curves to mark up your animations (e.g., in conjunction with target matching).

- Runtime optimizations:

    - Always optimize animations by setting the animator's Culling Mode to Based on Renderers, and disable the skinned mesh renderer's Update When Offscreen property. This way animations won't be updated when the character is not visible.

    - An additional good practice in animation is using hash IDs. When working with the animator, the use of **hash identifiers** is an optimizing method whereby names of states and parameters are assigned to integers. The use of integers instead of strings in turn reduces processing overhead.

If you are interested in digging deeper into Mecanim optimization, you can find more information in the Unity Manual, http://docs.unity3d.com/Manual/MecanimPeformanceandOptimization.html.

Project Settings

Once you have minimized the performance impact of individual bottlenecks, if you haven't yet achieved your target game performance goal you can address more generalized optimization decision points from a project-wide point of view.

Unity's Project Settings used in optimization are global settings, meaning they apply to the entire project (Figure 12-6). Whether or not you want or need to adjust any particular category of settings depends on anything from the target performance, the game, or the target platform to the types of performance issues that crop up during development. Take a logical approach and adjust those settings that will make the biggest difference first.

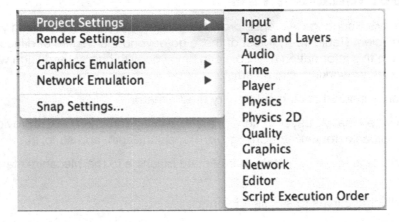

Figure 12-6. Project Settings in the Unity Editor Edit ➤ Project Settings menu

Quality Settings Manager

Quality of graphics and rendering speeds are tradeoffs: the higher the quality you select, the more complex the rendering, and thus a lower frame rate. The Quality Settings manager allows you to select different levels of graphic quality for each of the various target platforms: web player, standalone, iPhone, Android, Blackberry, and Google Native Client (Figure 12-7).

Figure 12-7. Project Settings Quality Settings Manager

The green checks indicate the default setting, which you can change by clicking the arrow in the Default row in the column for the target you are addressing via its Default menu (Figure 12-8).

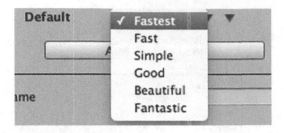

Figure 12-8. Default menu in the Quality Settings Manager

The **Name** property is for your convenience so you can easily refer to a particular combination of quality settings that you have designated. You can add a new quality level by using the Add Quality Level button or delete it by clicking the trashcan icon.

Pixel lighting is a rendering method that calculates the effect of your lights for every screen pixel. The **vertex lighting** method is more efficient, in that only the effect of light on model vertices is calculated and the remainder of the model surface lighting is interpolated from these values.

Dynamic lighting means that the effect of a light on a game object is calculated every frame, whether it be pixel or vertex lighting. If you have more than one pixel light illuminating a mesh, the mesh is rendered once for each light, which adds up quickly in terms of processing overhead.

The **Pixel Light Count** property in the Quality Settings Manager is for setting the number of pixel lights used in Forward Rendering, the standard rendering process. It is recommended that you not let any one game object be illuminated by more than one pixel light, especially on mobile devices.

Alternatives include **Lightmapping** for static game objects, where the brightness of the surface of the game object is precalculated. You can find the step-by-step procedure for lightmapping in the Unity Manual. The end result is that game will run up to three times faster than it would with only dynamic lighting.

Moving right along with the Quality Manager settings, **Texture Quality** sets the resolution globally, meaning for the entire project. Higher resolutions take more processing. For a more customized approach, you can use the Texture Import settings to assign the resolution for each texture.

Anisotropic textures are when a filtering process is applied to a texture to change its appearance. This is commonly used on flat surfaces like the ground to make it look better at shallow angles.

The remainder of the settings delve into more technical aspects of lighting and shadows, some of which require Unity Pro to use. Lighting and shadows are the keys to excellent visual effects, but they can be very expensive in terms of performance. For now, here are the sufficient takeaway points:

1. The Quality Settings can be used to optimize graphic quality by target platform and texture resolution, along with lighting and shadows.

2. Use lightmapping to bake static lighting.

3. Limit game objects to illumination by one Pixel Light, especially for mobile devices.

Physics Manager

The physics engine has some built-in performance optimization functions, such as "sleeping." When a rigidbody's movement and rotation go below a certain limit, the physics engine considers it stopped. Until the rigidbody is put in motion again, say by another force acting on it or a game object colliding with it, the physics engine does not burn processing capacity updating it.

The Sleep Velocity and Sleep Angular Velocity property values in the Physics Settings Manager designate the "sleep" threshold (Figure 12-9). If necessary, you can always access a rigidbody to wake it up by using the rigidbody.WakeUp() function in a script.

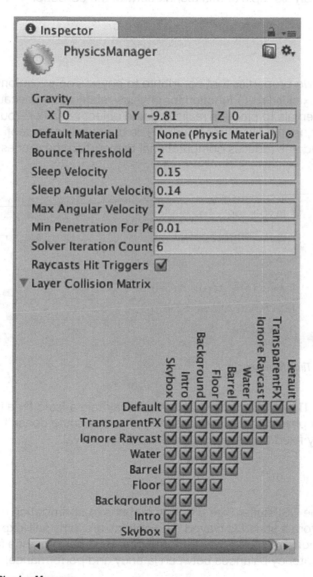

Figure 12-9. Project Settings Physics Manager

Another method for increasing efficiency of physics calculations is through the use of **layers**. Layer is one of the properties found in the Inspector that is used to categorize a game object by group. Just as game objects can have the same tag, game objects can also share the same layer. The Collision Matrix at the bottom of the Physics Manager is used to select which layers will interact with which other layers in the scene. Only game objects in layers that interact can collide, reducing the processing load.

A standard practice when working with complex game objects that require colliders is to use a collection of child primitive colliders rather than a mesh collider where possible. Mesh colliders take up a lot of processing power, and have limitations such as not registering collisions with other mesh colliders. You have seen an example of this technique with the collection of primitive colliders used for the ragdoll effect.

Time Manager

The Time Manager has two properties that contribute to physics optimizations (Figure 12-10). You know that you use the FixedUpdate() function for physics-related code because physics calculations depend on fixed time intervals to produce realistic game object behavior. You can use the **Fixed Timestep** property to adjust the fixed time interval. The optimization tradeoff here is that the higher time interval between updates reduces computational demand on the processor, but the physics will be less accurate.

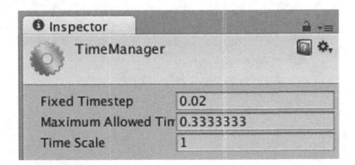

Figure 12-10. Project Settings Time Manager

The **Maximum Allowed Timestep** property also helps maintain a fixed time interval by capping the amount of time spent on physics calculations, so the physics engine doesn't bog down the frame rate if there are too many fixed updates during a fixed time interval.

Audio Manager

In the Audio Manager, the DSPBuffer Size property pertains to optimization (Figure 12-11). Latency refers to the lag time before a sound is played. The options are fairly self-explanatory, where Best latency favors more responsive sound over performance, Best performance favors sound quality over latency, and Good latency balances between latency and performance.

Figure 12-11. *Project Settings Audio Manager*

Good practices in using audio includes using native WAV or AIFF audio for smaller sound effects. These files are already decompressed so they won't need to be decoded at runtime. As with any unused assets, unused audio files remaining from the project development phase should be deleted.

Player Settings Manager

The more immediately useful cross-platform settings are in the first section (Figure 12-12). The other sections vary by target platform and require an understanding of the platform's particulars before you venture into making adjustments there.

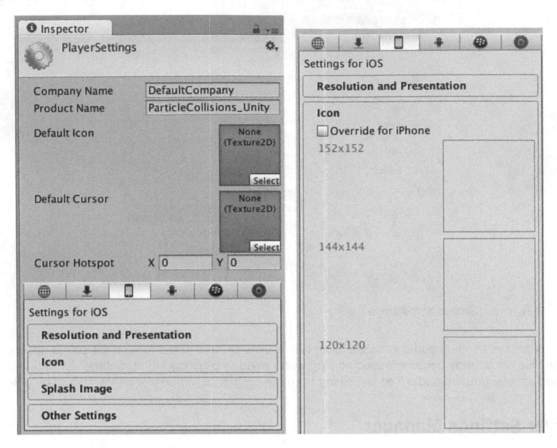

Figure 12-12. Project Settings Player Settings Manager and expanded icon fields

This contains the product name for your game title and the fields for the game icon and splash image textures. Be sure you have the right target platform selected before adding your icon textures—each one has its own size requirements. If you don't use the correct size, at best it will look odd and at worst it can lead to a rejection from the supporting application store.

Tags and Layers Manager

The Tags and Layers Manager is where you create and edit the tags and layers (Figure 12-13). Working with game objects in groups, especially by restricting operations in groups that don't require them, reduces processing overhead.

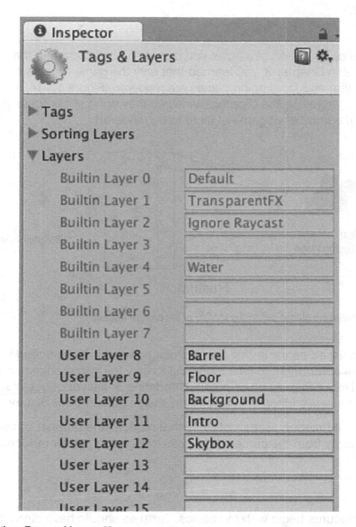

Figure 12-13. Project Settings Tags and Layers Manager

Project Settings Classes

The Project Settings managers are accessible through scripting to alter any of their properties by using their respective classes such as Physics, AudioSettings, and PlayerSettings. All the details including sample code can be found in the Unity Scripting Reference. Although they are global settings, you may come across situations where you would like to change these global settings between one scene and the next.

More Graphics Optimizations

Lighting optimizations were discussed previously in the Quality Settings Manager section. Cameras, textures, shaders, meshes and more that all fall under the general category of graphics can also be fine-tuned for better game performance.

Cameras

There are a number of optimization strategies you can apply to cameras. In the introduction to the camera component in Chapter 3, you learned that only the game objects in the frustum of the camera between the near and far clipping planes are rendered (Figure 12-14), a built-in operation called Frustum Culling. Adjusting the clipping planes so they don't encompass a larger area than necessary minimizes the number of game objects to be rendered.

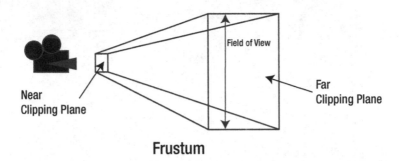

Figure 12-14. *Near and far clipping planes define the volume of the camera frustum*

The use of layers, discussed earlier in this chapter, can be used in conjunction with the Culling Mask property of the camera component to limit rendering to only the game objects only in designated layers. Or, if you need more than an all-or-nothing rendering of a layer of objects, you can use the Camera.layerCullDistances() function in a script to assign different cull distances to each layer.

Level of Detail (LOD) is a Pro-only feature of Unity that reduces the number of triangles rendered for an object the further away from the camera it is. Less triangles to render reduces the processor load.

Textures

Good practices with textures begin with the basics. Textures should have dimensions based on powers of 2, as in 2, 4, 8, 16 and so on. The width and height don't have to be identical values. More memory is used for non–power-of-2 dimensions, which in turn slows down the GPU. Another optimization approach is to use a compressed texture file format to reduce memory usage.

More optimization can be achieved with the adjustment of texture import settings properties. Search for Textures in the Project panel, and select one (if necessary, temporarily change the Texture Type to Advanced) to view these properties in the Inspector (Figure 12-15).

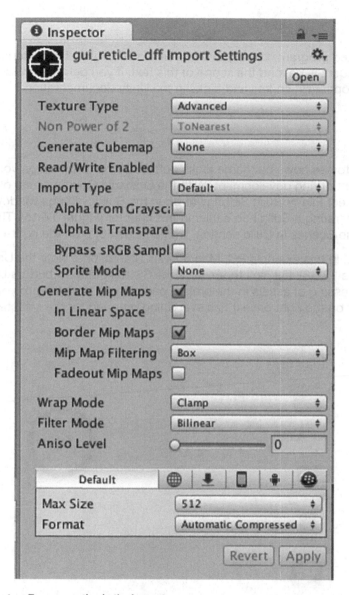

Figure 12-15. Advanced Texture Type properties in the Inspector

With the texture selected in the Project panel, use the **Max Size** property in the Inspector by reducing to the smallest value that still maintains the desired degree of quality in detail.

Unity can produce smaller versions of power-of-2–sized textures and use them for the smaller triangles when the game object is further from the camera. This process is called **mip mapping,** and is enabled by checking the Generate Mip Maps box. Mip maps do cost more in terms of memory but is usually a worthwhile exchange for better performance. An exception to this guideline is with UI elements or 2D games where these textures remain a fixed distance from the camera.

Shaders

Shaders are customized programs usually directed at the GPU used for customized visual effects. While the topic of shaders is beyond the scope of this text, if you delve into this area of graphics you can find a number of optimization tips and tricks in the Unity documentation.

Publishing

When you would like to see how your game looks outside of the Unity editor, you can play it as a standalone at any point during development. With the Obstacle Course scene open in the editor, from the top menu select File ➤ Build Settings to open the Build Settings window just like you did in the process for generating a Build Log earlier in this chapter (Figure 12-15). The Obstacle Course scene will still be in the Scenes In Build section, with an index of 0 on the right-hand side.

First select a platform, in this example PC, Mac & Linux Standalone. Note the Unity logo on the right-hand side (Figure 12-16). If it isn't there, click the Switch Platform button. Unity will do some assessment and processing of assets in the project particular to the platform you choose, and the Unity logo will appear on the right once it has everything prepped for the selected platform.

Figure 12-16. The Unity logo appears to the right of the selected target platform

Now you can click the Build button, choose the name and location for saving the standalone version of the game, then click Save for Unity to build the game. The resultant game files depend on the build target. On a Mac you will get an app bundle, and for Windows you'll get a folder of resources along with the .exe file. You can go ahead and play it yourself, or distribute these files to share your game. Go ahead and give your new standalone a whirl.

The first thing you will see is a black screen with Unity logo (Figure 12-17). While all games will have this as the default introductory screen, only Pro users can change it.

Figure 12-17. The Unity logo appears first as the standalone game is loading

Changing Scenes

Even the simplest of games have a splash screen, so you need to know how to switch from one scene to another with the `Application.LoadLevel()` function.

Back in the Unity Editor, save the Obstacle Course scene and save the project. Then select File ➤ New Scene from the top menu to create a new scene. Again in the top menu, select GameObject ➤ Create Empty, then name it GUI.

In the Project panel Assets ➤ Scripts folder, create a new script named SplashGUI, open it in MonoDevelop, and edit the code to the following:

```
#pragma strict

function OnGUI() {
        GUI.Label(Rect(0, 0, 125, 25), "Splash screen");
        if (GUI.Button (Rect (Screen.width/2 - 50, Screen.height/2 - 15, 100, 30), "Start")) {
                Application.LoadLevel(1);
        }
}
```

Save the script, attach it to the SplashGUI game object, and save the scene as SplashScene. You used the OnGUI() function and created GUI labels and buttons in Chapter 11. In this line of code, the number 1 corresponds to the index assigned in the Build Settings screen:

```
Application.LoadLevel(1);
```

You want the splash screen to be first, so it should have an index of 0 followed by the Obstacle Course scene with an index of 1.

To accomplish this, in the Unity editor top menu once again select File ➤ Build Settings to open the Build Settings window. From the Project panel Assets ➤ Scenes folder, drag SplashScene into the Scenes In Build section. When you do, it will be added to the bottom after the Obstacle Course scene and assigned an index of 1. All you have to do to rearrange them is to click and drag any item in the list to where you want it (Figure 12-18).

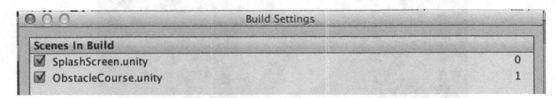

Figure 12-18. Scenes reordered to put the splash screen first in the Build Settings window

Click Build and, when prompted, save and replace the old Obstacle Course build with this newer one. Now when you play the standalone, when the Unity logo fades away the SplashScreen scene appears (Figure 12-19).

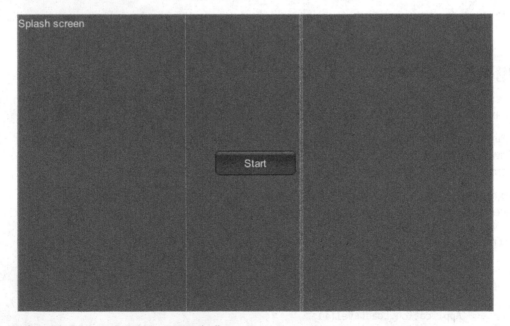

Figure 12-19. SplashScreen scene appears automatically

Click the Start button and there you have it—the Obstacle Course scene appears.

Summary

Great job—you have made it to the finish line! You can fine-tune your game's performance, you have been introduced to the `Application.LoadLevel()` function for switching between scenes, and you have published a standalone version.

Don't be daunted by the volume of details involved in optimization; just know that there are many tools at your disposal to address game performance issues. For now, a good start is to commit yourself to following best practices in coding your scripts and following some basic precepts collected in a handy checklist provided in the Unity documentation (Table 12-1):

Table 12-1. *Simple Checklist to Make Your Game Faster, Found in Unity's Scripting Reference*

Keep vertex count below 200K–3M per frame when targeting PC, depending on the target GPU.

If you're using built-in shaders, pick ones from the Mobile or Unlit categories. They work on nonmobile platforms as well, but are simplified and approximated versions of the more complex shaders.

Keep the number of different materials per scene low—share as many materials between different objects as possible.

Set Static property on all nonmoving objects to allow internal optimizations like static batching.

Do not use Pixel Light when it is not necessary—choose to have only a single (preferably directional) pixel light affecting your geometry.

Do not use dynamic lights when it is not necessary—choose to bake lighting instead.

Use compressed texture formats when possible, otherwise prefer 16-bit textures over 32-bit.

Do not use fog when it is not necessary.

Learn benefits of Occlusion Culling and use it to reduce the amount of visible geometry and draw-calls in cases of complex static scenes with lots of occlusion. Plan your levels to benefit from occlusion culling.

Use skyboxes to "fake" distant geometry.

Use pixel shaders or texture combiners to mix several textures instead of a multi-pass approach.

If writing custom shaders, always use smalls possible floating-point format:

- fixed/lowp—for colors, lighting information, and normals.

- half/mediump—for texture UV coordinates.

- float/highp—avoid in pixel shaders, fine to use in vertex shader for position calculations.

Minimize use of complex mathematical operations such as `pow`, `sin`, `cos`, etc. in pixel shaders.

Choose to use less textures per fragment.

Except for hardware and compiler limitations, a good many of these suggestions are more guideline than rule. You may choose not to follow some of the recommendations from this chapter, but that's okay. When you are satisfied with the performance of your game, you can decide whether or not spending more time working on further optimizations is an exercise in diminishing returns.

The important thing is that you know good practices that enhance performance and where to find help with optimization in the documentation when addressing performance issues that may crop up during development.

You now have a foundation in basic programming using UnityScript and in the use of the Unity editor. This is only the beginning of more fun and excitement. In the next chapter are a number of resources to continue your journey into the field of game development, meet your peers, and—most importantly—have fun making games.

Where to Go from Here

Congratulations—you've now got the fundamentals of UnityScript under your belt. When learning any new language, becoming truly proficient takes time and practice, practice, practice. Like any technical field, game development is continually and rapidly advancing, which means spending a portion of your programming time for learning should become a standard component of your game development routine. What does this mean for a game developer? Make more games!

This chapter contains an abundance of resources, including where to get specific answers to highly technical questions, how to connect with the game development community, how to keep up with the latest news, and how to build your professional portfolio. If you haven't joined in yet, this book's companion web site is www.learn-unityscript.com, where you can introduce yourself, get involved, meet like-minded game developers, get words of encouragement, and share your games—don't hold back on bragging rights!

It's easy to get inundated with information, so keep building your skills as your top priority. This means dedicating hands-on time *using* Unity. Don't have an idea for a game? Then read on to learn more about game jams and contests. Explore specific platforms or focus on learning more about a particular area of game development that may have grabbed your attention, such as animation or AI.

Scripting and Other Technical Resources

It is no surprise that online forums serve as the prevalent gathering places for game developers all across the globe. There are two types of forums available: purely technical forums and discussion forums.

The purely technical forums are geared toward problem solving for practical projects and have a specific format, while the discussion forums can include just about anything developer related including best practices, news, announcements, jobs, or simply casual conversation.

Technical Forums

The Unity web site is the first and foremost resource for Unity developers. **Unity Answers** is the technical forum found at http://answers.unity3d.com. Figure 13-1 shows the layout, with questions as thread titles along with correlating topic tags, indicators for how many times the question has been viewed, whether or not any answers have been posted, whether any answer has been accepted by the original poster, and votes from the developer community (usually based on the quality and usefulness of the question).

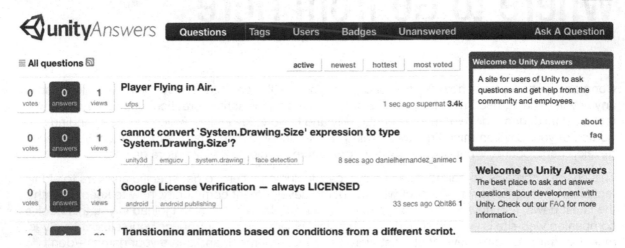

Figure 13-1. Questions posted on Unity Answers

While no question is a dumb question, there is an etiquette for using the forum. The developer community is generally friendly and willing to help, but the emphasis is on helping you learn, not writing your scripts for you. The stance of the technical forum members is that you should have made every effort to come up with a solution on your own before posing a question. Most importantly, it means you have written some code for your script and performed some initial research such as searching the Unity documentation for a solution on your own. If you've done what you can and you are still stuck, it is time to turn to Unity Answers.

Before asking a question, search for it first. Keep an eye on the tags of similar questions that come up in the search results that might help you refine your search. Odds are that the same question has been asked before and an answer is already available.

If you can't find a solution for your particular issue, then it is time to pose a question of your own. A good question is very specific, has a detailed description of what you've attempted and the result of those attempts, and includes a snippet of the actual code. Use hyperlinks to reference the documentation that you've reviewed and describe your interpretation of it, as well as to any questions on the forum with solutions that you used and your results. Oftentimes the process of posing a good question can lead you to the answer on your own. Support for adding hyperlinks, code formatting, file attachment, and more can be found in the toolbar of the question form (Figure 13-2).

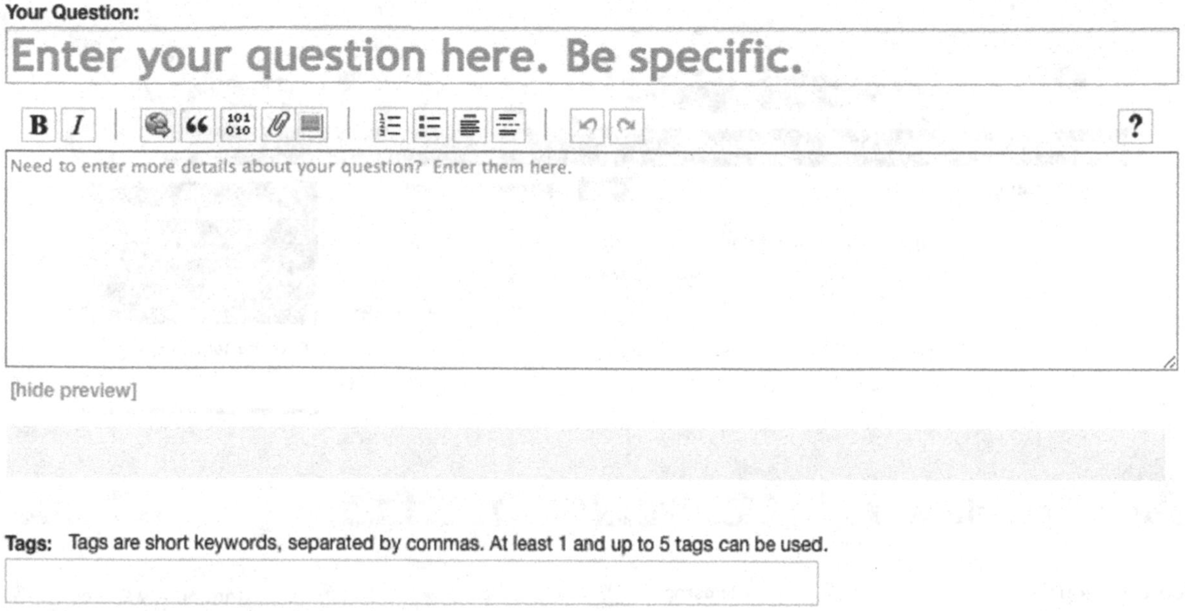

Your Question:

Figure 13-2. *Question form for Unity Answers*

Most of the forums provide for accumulating reputation or karma points, as well as fun badges for different forms of participation. You can earn points for both good questions and good answers. Answer questions when you can, even if you don't feel like an expert. Being able to communicate a solution in an understandable fashion not only gives you warm fuzzies for helping someone else, but also solidifies the concept in your mind and serves as a confidence builder.

Stack Exchange is a huge developer resource that contains a number of categories of forums. **GameDev**, found at `http://gamedev.stackexchange.com`, is, as you might guess, for game developers. **StackOverflow**, at `http://stackoverflow.com`, is geared more toward pure programming questions that might be helpful for questions regarding coding for the target platform of your game.

The GameDev Stack and Stack Overflow sites also have a direct question-and-answer community-rated format (Figure 13-3).

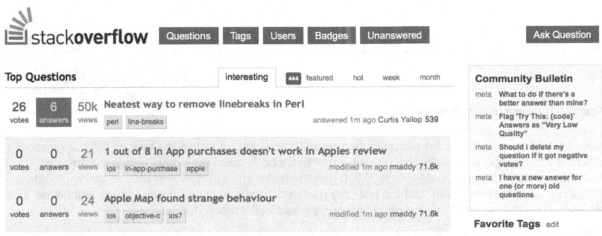

Figure 13-3. Stack Exchange forums with the community rated question-and-answer format

Other Developer Forums

Another popular game developer resource is **Gamasutra**. Programming-related topics can be found at www.gamasutra.com/category/programming. It contains subcategories of Programming Features, Programming Updates, Programming Blogs, and Programming Jobs (Figure 13-4). Gamasutra has more of a blog format and is better suited for helping you keep up with the latest goings-on in the game developer community than for specific technical answers.

Figure 13-4. Gamasutra has a less formal structure than a purely technical forum, with broader topics

While Unity has crossed the threshold of being the majority choice among game developers, you'll also see references to other game engines here. The "post mortems" developers contribute after game publication as they analyze what went right and wrong in the development and publication processes provide excellent practical learning points straight from the trenches.

Platform-Specific Developer Resources

Manufacturers of the various target platforms want developers to create games for their respective systems and so provide significant developer support. At the very least they will provide documentation, but most have similar forums of their own. Usually they have some combination of technical documentation, tutorials, a technical forum, and a developer community forum.

While most of these forums require you to create a user account, the requirements can vary widely. Some require legal business-entity information such as a tax ID to register, while others don't require this until you are ready to publish. Some charge fees, though again this might not be required until you are ready to publish. None require that you purchase the hardware, but it is a best practice and strongly recommended to test your game on the target platform hardware and not just the virtual simulator before publishing.

The following are a few of the more common sites:

Sony: http://us.playstation.com/develop (Figure 13-5). If you aren't in the United States, Sony has additional forums for other regions, so take a moment to do a quick search for yours.

Figure 13-5. Sony PlayStation developer registration

Microsoft: www.xbox.com/en-US/developers (Figure 13-6). This is the Xbox developer site, but it also addresses developing for the Web, Kinect, and Windows PCs, tablets, and phones.

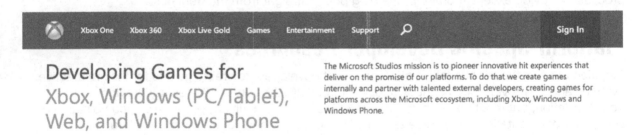

Figure 13-6. Microsoft Xbox developer registration, with more information for their other devices

Nintendo: http://wiiu-developers.nintendo.com (Figure 13-7). Console compatibility with Unity is prominently featured on the Nintendo developer site.

Unity for Wii U

Unity is an integrated development environment spanning multiple platforms and used by over 1 million developers worldwide. Highlights include fast and powerful 3D graphic functionality, animation, AI, scripts, and SFX — all helping enable expressive and fast game development. With Unity for Wii U, of course all the various Wii U features are supported, such as the Wii U GamePad and Wii Remote controllers, and it provides strong support for developing games that make great use of these Wii U features.

Nintendo pays for the Unity License on Wii U for all licensed Nintendo Developers.

Figure 13-7. Unity support featured on the Nintendo developer site

Apple: `http://developer.apple.com` (Figure 13-8). Within its developer site Apple has separate forums for its iOS and OSX developers, but a common forum for its software development tool Xcode.

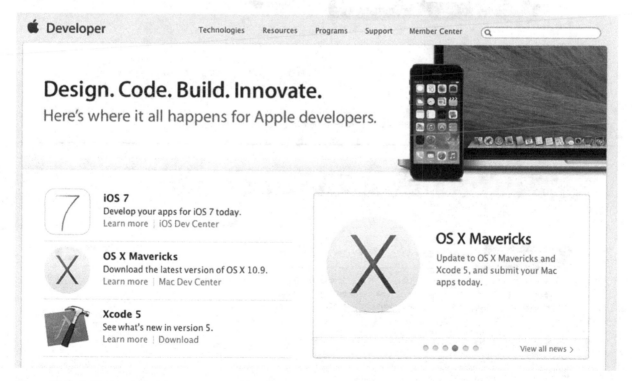

Figure 13-8. Apple's central site for Xcode developers

Android: `http://developer.android.com` (Figure 13-9). Android differs from Apple and Microsoft regarding mobile devices because it is an operating system released by Google and used by a number of different manufacturers resulting in a variety of Android-based developer forums. **Samsung** is the dominant hardware manufacturer internationally and provides additional support for its Android developers at `http://developer.samsung.com/forum/en` to capitalize on the capabilities of Samsung devices in particular, beyond mobile phones to its televisions and wearable technology.

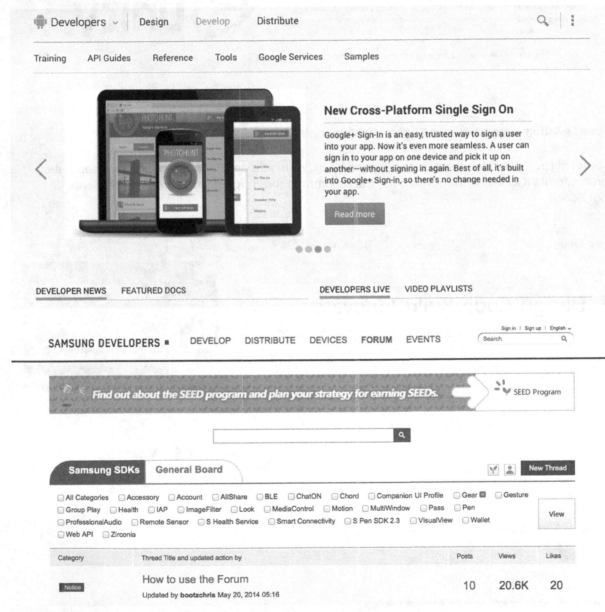

Figure 13-9. Android and Android-based Samsung product developer web sites

You definitely get the most bang for your buck from a marketing perspective by creating games for the well-established, popular game platforms. If you have an interest in up-and-coming technologies or just want to try something different, there are other lesser-known game venues that also support Unity:

Sphero: http://developer.gosphero.com. Sphero is a robot ball game platform that is controlled by Android or iOS devices, which integrate its real-world robotic antics with the device camera input and GUI display into a hybrid remote control/augmented-reality game environment—or, in a reverse fashion, it can be used via its sensors as a game controller itself.

A **plug-in** is a software component that extends an already existing software application with a new feature or features. The Sphero plug-in for Unity is available directly through the Unity Asset Store (Figure 13-10).

Figure 13-10. The Sphero plug-in in the Unity Asset Store

The two leading augmented-reality software development kits, **Vuforia** at http://developer.vuforia.com/resource/skd/unity and **Metaio** at http://dev.metaio.com/sdk/getting-started/unity3d also support Unity, though you have to go directly to their respective sites rather than through the Unity Asset Store (Figure 13-11).

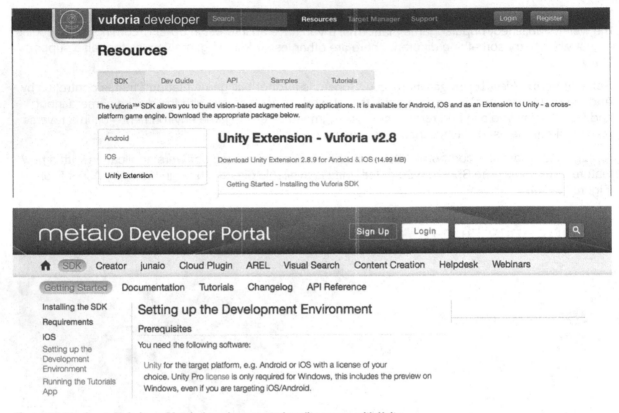

Figure 13-11. Create Vuforia- or Metaio-based augmented-reality games with Unity

Leap Motion: `http://developer.leapmotion.com`. Leap Motion is a motion-detecting controller. Developer support is provided directly on their site. The number of proprietary and independently created Leap Motion assets available on the Unity Asset Store continues to grow (Figure 13-12).

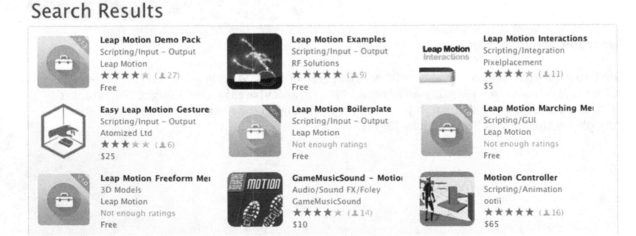

Figure 13-12. Assets for the Leap Motion controller available on the Unity Asset Store

Oculus Rift: `http://developer/oculusvr.com/forums`. This virtual reality headset adds to Windows-, Mac OS- or Linux-based systems' game experience with an immersive visual display that is responsive to the player's head movement (Figure 13-13) .

Figure 13-13. The Oculus Rift headset and motion detector

Even with this multitude of game developer support forums, Unity Answers is your best first stop for technical help with Unity game development. You can broaden your search to general game development and programming forums, or reach out to focused platform-specific developer groups, depending on your need. You are certain to find friendly assistance anywhere within the game developer community as you narrow down your area of interest and settle on a few favorite forums.

Casual Groups, Organizations, and Gatherings

Unity developers are everywhere, and there are many venues to choose from for getting together with your new peers. The not-so-technical **Unity Forums** can be found just next to the Answers tab in the Unity Community menu (Figure 13-14).

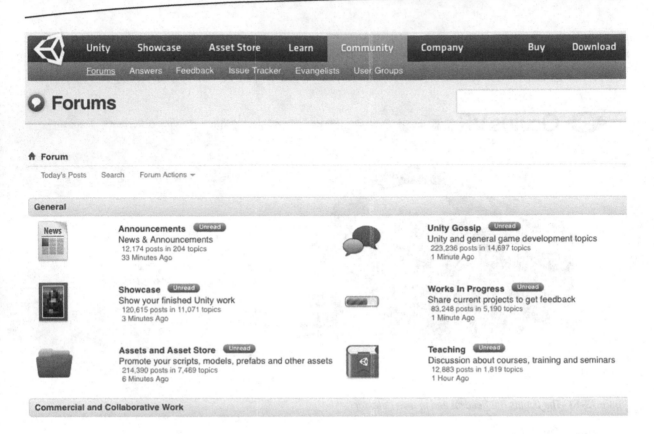

Figure 13-14. The Unity Community Forums

Here you can hang out with the online Unity developer community. If you'd like to get together in person, choose the **User Groups** tab to find a local group. You will find that many of these groups are listed on **Meetup**, a web site that serves as a central repository for finding local groups for people with shared interests of any kind.

If you don't see a group in your area in the Unity User Groups listing, try searching www.meetup.com directly. You can find newer, smaller local Unity groups here; if there are none, you can list Unity game development as an area of interest so you can be notified when a group in your area is established. You might even consider starting one yourself. Local group events vary and can be purely social get-togethers, technical presentations, feedback sessions on group members' projects, hands-on tutorial sessions, or anything the members are interested in.

The **GDC** (Game Developers Conference) is THE annual event in the game development industry, where tens of thousands of game development industry members gather. Lectures and tutorials, contests and awards, workshops, networking functions, parties, and more occur over the days of this huge gathering. All the particulars can be found at www.gdconf.com.

Unity has its own annual conference, called **Unite**. Unite is held in a different city in North America each year, with additional regional venues around the world (Figure 13-15). You will find all things Unity here: technical, artistic, as well as business. There are hands-on training workshops, talks from industry veterans, and sneak peeks of new features and products. You don't have to attain a certain level of experience or publish a game to attend. In fact, there is an additional Unity Training Day just prior to Unite for the completely inexperienced to get an introduction to Unity before the main conference begins. More information about Unite and the Unity Training Day is on the Unity3D web site at http://unity3D.com/unite.

Unite 2014 in Seattle
Seattle, August 20-22, 2014 - Learn more »

Unite Brazil
São Paulo, TBA

Unite Mexico
TBA

Unite Australia
Melbourne, October 27, 2014

Unite Japan
Tokyo, April 07-08, 2014
Learn more »

Unite Korea
Seoul, April 09-10, 2014
Learn more »

Unite China
Bejing, April 13-14, 2014
Learn more »

Unite Taiwan
Taipei, April 17-18, 2014
Learn more »

Figure 13-15. Primary and regional locations for Unite in 2014

The **IGDA** (International Game Developers Association) is a large nonprofit professional organization that advocates for the industry and provides member benefits including year-round sponsored events, discounts, educational webinars, and more. It can be found at www.igda.org.

Game Jams

Game Jams are great way to improve your skills in a super-fun high-intensity setting. Game jams are essentially organized group challenges, where individuals or teams must create a game from scratch within a short period of time, usually 24 to 48 hours.

Teams are formed from the participants at the start of the game jam. Their goal is to produce a functioning game prototype. This prototype must conform to the game jam's guidelines, which might designate such things as a theme or feature that must be used.

Participants might be anyone involved in game development including programmers, artists, and game designers, but levels of proficiency vary. No matter how new you are or how many hours you can participate, there will be something you can do to contribute. Simple things such as searching for assets or recording sound effects are valuable contributions. Some jams allow for participation via Internet, but the real point of the jam is to get together to make friends and have some fun.

Global Game Jam: http://globalgamejam.org. The big annual game jam event held every January. This is a coordinated event held simultaneously at hundreds of locations around the world.

Ludum Dare: http://ludumdare.com. Online game jam held every four months consisting of two concurrent events (the Competition and the Jam). The Competition is the more intense of the two, where you must work alone, creating all game code and assets according to the theme within 48 hours. The Jam is more relaxed, allows for teams and reuse of existing assets, and gives you 72 hours to finish.

Nordic Game Jam: http://nordicgamejam.org. One of the largest game jams in the world, held in Denmark.

If a big event seems daunting or inconvenient, or is simply too far away, try starting with **One Game a Month**: http://onegameamonth.com (Figure 13-16). It is open to all but is probably the friendliest, least intimidating, and most encouraging game jam site. The events are online, with a new challenge every month.

Figure 13-16. One Game a Month: a congenial, low-key online game jam site

If you are interested in a jam, you should be able to find one that suits you on sites like `http://gamejamcentral.com` or with a simple online search.

A word about sponsored events: Always read the fine print. Typically the prizes are simply bragging rights with a bonus of game promotion from the game jam organizers. Some game jams rules can include transferring some or all rights to the games produced during an event, so be sure you are aware of the requirements.

Contests and Awards

In general, contests are a competition that offer a reward for winners and sometimes runners-up, while awards and award ceremonies offer recognition for significant achievements of some kind. You might find contests where the only prize is bragging rights, and award ceremonies that offer a nice prize package in addition to the award itself.

Contests

Contests are usually sponsored and offer a prize to the winner. Like jams, these competitions can take place locally or online, with prize packages large and small, but they usually have a deadline on the order of months because they are looking for a polished end product rather than a whipped-together prototype. Large cash prizes are often sponsored by companies as an incentive for developers to focus on producing games that utilize their software or hardware products. Packages can include free licenses, additional promotion, and other valuable goodies.

As an example, at the time of this writing Unity and Microsoft have a contest for Unity games that targets the Windows and Windows Phone platforms (Figure 13-17).

Figure 13-17. Example contest and prize offerings

Keep an eye on Unity, game platform manufacturers, and industry organizations event web sites for contest announcements. Broaden your search to include "app developer" in addition to "game developer," as many app contests have game categories. If you live in a metropolitan area, check the calendar for your local conference center for video game, electronics, and app-related events. Usually the results of the contest are announced at the event, so bear in mind that contest rule publication dates and submission deadlines will occur much sooner than the actual event.

Read the fine print. Know the deadlines, know the rules, and know the ramifications of the participation agreement. If you miss the deadline, you can't win. If you don't follow the rules, you might be disqualified. If you don't read the fine print, you just don't know what might happen. I've seen people taken by surprise that they lost ownership rights to their game by entering it in a contest.

Using the Windows Store example, to be eligible for the contest your game had to be published on the Windows Store between May 1, 2014 and July 20, 2014, so there is no question that the game still would have belonged to you. On the other hand, this means that your game had to go through the submission process for the Windows Store, which means you probably should have had your business entity set up. If you are accustomed to submitting that just-finished assignment to your boss or professor minutes before the deadline, your game probably won't make it to the judges in time.

Awards

Awards are typically tied to a certain event, though they might be the reason for the ceremony itself.

The annual Unite conference mentioned previously has awards for recognizing achievements and advancements in Unity-based games. A variety of award categories and descriptions are listed in Table 13-1.

Table 13-1. Award Categories and Descriptions for the 2014 Unite Event

Category	Description
Best 3D Visual Experience	Submissions for this category will be judged based on artistic merit including thematic and stylistic cohesion, creativity, and/or technical skill.
Best 2D Visual Experience	Submissions for this category will be judged based on artistic merit including thematic and stylistic cohesion, creativity, and/or technical skill.
Best Gameplay	Intuitive control, innovation, creativity, complexity, and fun are what make games enjoyable and entertaining—we're looking for games that excel in one or all of these areas.
Best VizSim Project	Unity projects come in all shapes and sizes; this year we're looking for projects that have some real world grounded applications for visualization, simulation, and training.
Best Non-game Project	Unity-authored products that fall outside of games or VizSim including projects such as art, advertisement, interactive books and comics, digital toys, interactive physical installations, and informational programs will want to submit for this award.
Best Student Project	This award is for projects worked on by students currently being completed as part of the curriculum of an educational institution. Projects will be judged based on creativity, technical merit, and overall artistic cohesion among graphics, sound, and presentation.
Technical Achievement	Any project that provides an excellent example of technical excellence in Unity including but not limited to graphics, scripting, UI, and/or sound.
Community Choice	This category will be voted on by the community of game developers and represents the favorites of the community across the board.
Golden Cube (best overall)	This award is for the best overall project made with Unity in the last year. Everything from technical achievement and visual styling to sound production and level of fun will be taken into account to choose an overall winner.

E3, the Electronic Entertainment Expo put on by the **Entertainment Software Association**, is held every year at the Los Angeles Convention Center. It is followed later in the year by the **Game Critics Awards**, which are chosen from the best of E3 by an independent media group that covers the video game industry.

Specialized industries with a role in video games are also beginning to recognize the significance of the game development industry in their field. The **Annie Awards**, the animation industry's version of the Academy Awards that historically recognized animation in television and movies, has more recently added the "Best Animated Video Game" category.

When you consider results such as four of the six games winning the 2014 Apple Design Awards having been made with Unity, you can see how following these conferences and award ceremonies can give you an idea of latest trends as well as what level of quality to strive for in your games.

Code Sources

You don't read a dictionary to learn a foreign language, and you don't read the Unity documentation from front to back in one sitting to expand your scripting skills. Instead, you write more scripts as you make more games.

There is a vast array of Unity scripting classes to add to your knowledge base, but don't worry—you'll pick it up as you go. You now have a solid foundation in how to program in UnityScript, and you know to reference the documentation for further explanation and sample code snippets. Referencing these as you go solidifies the basic concept, while the context of a game makes it easier to remember both how and why you used that class or approach.

At the same time, you don't have to do everything from scratch, nor do you want to. More often than not, another programmer has attempted a solution to a similar problem you are facing in some facet of your own game, and these solutions are available to you. Utilizing these scripts will rapidly advance your game development, while learning any new UnityScript classes or a different approach to solving a practical problem will rapidly advance your skill set.

One source of scripts is the Unity Asset Store. Scripts are assets, too, so you will find a wide variety of scripts in a number of subcategories here (Figure 13-18).

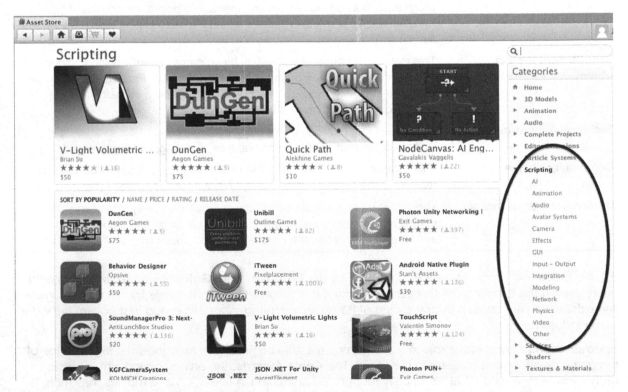

Figure 13-18. Scripting asset categories available on the Asset Store

GitHub, an online code repository collection where developers share and collaborate, is another great archive of open source code. The various developer forums are also a resource of focused code solutions to specific problems and a platform for lively debate about alternative approaches to problem solving.

More Than a Hobby

If your goal is to find employment as a game developer, it's never too soon to think about portfolio and résumé building. Whether you have a formal education or not, potential employers will want to see what kind of skills you have. Even if you aren't aware of employer expectations, learning them will give you a guide for refining your developing skills to meet industry standards.

Portfolio

The difference between a résumé and a portfolio is that a résumé is a written summary of your professional skills and educational background, and a **portfolio** is a collection of examples of your work such as code, demos, and even completed games.

A portfolio is a necessity for getting into the game industry, whether you are a self-taught programmer or have a degree. In fact, one of the most common requirements you will see for an entry-level position is "Bachelor's degree in Computer Science or equivalent work experience." A formal education isn't required if you can demonstrate through your portfolio that you have what they are looking for. In either case, the contents of the portfolio are the same, the only difference being that for students, projects from coursework should be identified separately from independent projects.

The portfolio is a collection of the best samples of your game development work. Let's face it, your first couple of games probably won't be award winners, but they are significant for other reasons. They show your skills, and they show your ability to learn and to stick with a project to the end.

I landed my first paying game developer gig through an individual I met at a Meetup event for developers. I didn't have much of a portfolio at the time, but I had developed a few small productivity mobile apps for a local startup company. His comment, "This tells me you can finish and publish a project," surprised me because I just hadn't thought of it that way.

In fact, at the time we were chatting and I showed him the apps on my phone, I had no idea he had come to that meeting looking for someone to hire. I didn't think I had enough skills or knowledge yet because I was painfully aware of how much I had yet to learn. That project turned into a second one, both of which I successfully completed, and I learned a great deal in the process. As I mentioned, given how rapidly the field of video game development is advancing, there will always be much to learn.

You should have a few **complete games** in your portfolio. Complete means splash screens; menus that include the basics of starting, pausing, and exiting the game; player options; essentially all of the ancillary interaction of the game with the player, in addition to the gameplay itself. Games in more than one genre, 2D and 3D, show depth and versatility.

You can also have **feature demos**: fragments of games that focus on specific features in which you are demonstrating a skill, such as AI or special effects. Programmers aren't expected to have professional-grade art skills; hence the term **programmer art** for placeholder, often lesser-quality art assets used to demonstrate the functionality of a game. That being said, do the best you can to make a good first impression better. It's okay to use assets from the Asset Store or collaborate with an artist to up the quality of your demos, just be sure to give credit for items that you did not create yourself.

Since you are now a game developer, your portfolio must include **source code**. When you take a look at entry-level job openings, you will see desired skills such as these:

- "Design, implement, test, debug, and maintain code to required coding standards."
- "Test, debug, and extend other Software Engineers' code."
- "Port existing technologies to new platforms."

Game development is a team sport where you will be working with other developers, you may be picking up where a previous developer left off, and others will be building on your code. Organized, efficient, easy-to-read code is vital to a professional developer. A potential employer will not take the time to decipher your brilliant solution to a game development problem if it is buried in sloppy, hard-to-read code. Remember, they receive many inquiries from applicants and only the best are going to get a closer look.

Web Site

A web site is simply a means to provide public access to your portfolio. While emailing a `.zip` file of your portfolio tends to lead to a host of trouble, including files that may never be received or cannot be opened by the intended recipient, emailing a link is simple and straightforward.

If your intent is to get noticed professionally, either as a potential employee or freelancer, your web site must be professional, too. Don't mix in personal blogs or private information, but do always make your contact information easy to find.

The web site design should be streamlined, so your demos are easy to access with minimal clicks, and the layout and background art should not distract from the demos themselves.

Tailor Your Presentation

Tailor your portfolio to feature the demonstrations that are most relevant to the job description. Your portfolio should emphasize the primary skill set required for the position. As you can imagine, there is a difference between various entry-level positions beyond general Gameplay Programmer such as Multiplayer Gameplay Programmer, Graphics Programmer, or Tools Programmer.

Research the company and its products. Research the developer who will be interviewing you and familiarize yourself with their work. Game developers are super-enthusiasts. so you should be familiar with their games and be prepared to discuss what games you like to play, too.

Get Honest Feedback

The game developer community can be a great source for feedback to polish your games and can give you guidance on good coding practices. Unity provides professional support services at `https://store.unity3d.com/products/support` (Figure 13-19).

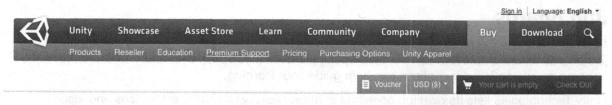

Professional Unity assistance with your project

- Reduce time to market by getting timely advice on best practices and approaches
- Make your title stand out in the market with an impressive frame rate and visual appeal
- Get ahead of the curve by using inside knowledge from support engineers
- Offload complex engineering tasks to the team who provide the engine

Figure 13-19. Unity offers professional support for art, scripting, debugging, and more

The first projects I worked on in a startup collaboration were a learning experience for the whole team, all beginners. When we thought we were ready to publish, we hired a professional developer to review our work. It was a fun exercise that gave us confidence in what we had done well, and provided fast-tracked, focused learning for the areas where we needed improvement while also significantly shortening approval times for publication.

Remember to share the love as you see your fellow developers soliciting feedback for their projects by giving them thoughtful, detailed comments that outline what you think is done well and suggesting improvements where you can.

Murphy Is Everywhere

Murphy's Law states that anything that can go wrong, will go wrong. Really, really wrong. I was extremely nervous for my first important interview—rehearsing my brilliantly prepared responses and clutching my lucky penny in my pocket while I waited my turn. Right in the middle of the interview, a button popped off my shirt and landed square on the interviewer's desk. There was a moment of stunned silence as we both stared at the button in surprise and horror, then I grabbed my blouse and he grabbed his phone. Fortunately his secretary had a safety pin, and once I pulled myself together we proceeded with the interview. I didn't dissolve into a puddle of mortification and I went on to make the short list, though I wasn't the final choice. After that experience, subsequent interviews were a breeze.

Whether for a job inquiry or an interview, always have backup screenshots and videos that you can use in the event the demo fails, which happens more often than you might think for a variety of reasons. Remember: They are busy, your inquiry is one of many, and you want to make it easy for them to see what you can do. Demo failures do occur, but good screenshots and video along with your source code will support your job inquiry or prevent an interview from coming to an immediate awkward halt.

This applies to a web site portfolio as well; have screenshots and gameplay video alternatives available along with the playable demo just in case.

Job Boards

Most of the online developer hangouts already mentioned include career guidance, and many have job boards where employers can post job openings. Even if you aren't yet ready to search for a job, keeping an eye on job descriptions can help guide your learning.

Unity Technologies lists its own job openings at `http://unity3d.com/company/jobs` and also provides a place for job seekers and job offerings to be posted within its Community forum at `http://forum.unity3d.com`. This includes an area for those looking for team members for noncommercial projects (Figure 13-20).

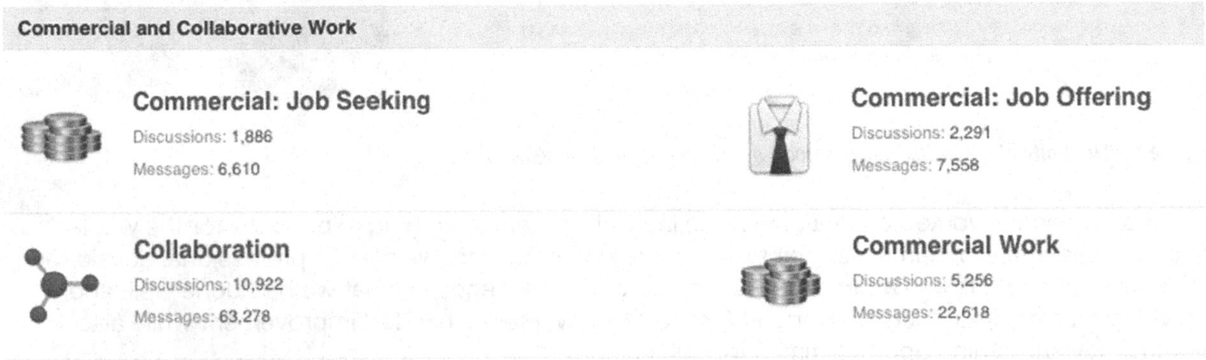

Commercial and Collaborative Work

Commercial: Job Seeking
Discussions: 1,886
Messages: 6,610

Commercial: Job Offering
Discussions: 2,291
Messages: 7,558

Collaboration
Discussions: 10,922
Messages: 63,278

Commercial Work
Discussions: 5,256
Messages: 22,618

Figure 13-20. Unity Forum Commercial and Collaborative Work board

Stackoverflow has `http://careers.stackoverflow.com`, GitHub has `http://jobs.github.com`, and Gamasutra has `http://jobs.gamasutra.com`. Each of the console manufacturers have job listings on their respective sites or their subsidiary video game software companies, such as *The Last of Us* creator Naughty Dog, a Sony subsidiary, or Blizzard, an Activision subsidiary. There are also the independent video game studios, from the AAA giants like EA Games on down to local startups.

There are also career sites with job openings for developers, from general sites like CareerBuilder. com or some more tech- or online-specific sites for job seekers and freelancers such as Startupers, Authentic Jobs, and We Work Remotely.

For freelancers, `www.freelancer.com` has a dedicated Unity3D category. Other freelancing sites such as Elance and oDesk provide a platform for freelancers beyond bidding on work that includes support for managing project flow and processing payments.

The Asset Store is a great sources of scripts, and is also a venue where you can share your own scripting solutions. If you feel you've written a particularly handy script that may have broader application, you can consider submitting it to the Asset Store. This also serves the same purpose as publishing a game for your portfolio—an original, published product.

Summary

This is it, your commencement into the world as a budding game developer. Start small and build on what you've learned so far. Don't discourage yourself by starting with that dream project that would take a AAA studio dozens of developers, many years, and millions of dollars to produce. Whatever your goal in game development, enjoy every step of the journey and each small accomplishment as a victory.

Get involved in the community, especially the Unity Forum, Answers, and wiki. Whatever your favorite flavor, whether it's Facebook or some other venue, you are likely find Unity and game developers are well represented. Twitter is a way developers commonly communicate as well as a great way to get the word out about your games. Keep up with Unity by following @unity3d. You can find me at @j9suvak and many more developers on my Twitter follow list. Don't be shy, come on and jump right in.

Welcome to the fun!

Index

V, W, X, Y, Z

Get the eBook for only $10!

Now you can take the weightless companion with you anywhere, anytime. Your purchase of this book entitles you to 3 electronic versions for only $10.

This Apress title will prove so indispensible that you'll want to carry it with you everywhere, which is why we are offering the eBook in **3 formats** for only $10 if you have already purchased the print book.

Convenient and fully searchable, the PDF version enables you to easily find and copy code—or perform examples by quickly toggling between instructions and applications. The MOBI format is ideal for your Kindle, while the ePUB can be utilized on a variety of mobile devices.

Go to www.apress.com/promo/tendollars to purchase your companion eBook.